CARLYLE, EMERSON AND THE TRANSATLANTIC USES OF AUTHORITY

Interventions in Nineteenth-Century American Literature and Culture
Series Editors: Christopher Hanlon, Sarah R. Robbins, Andrew Taylor

Available

Liminal Whiteness in Early US Fiction
Hannah Lauren Murray

Carlyle, Emerson and the Transatlantic Uses of Authority: Literature, Print, Performance
Tim Sommer

Forthcoming

Melville's Americas: Hemispheric Sympathies, Transatlantic Contagion
Nicholas Spengler

Crossings: Nineteenth-Century American Literature and Culture at a Juncture
Edward Sugden

The Aesthetics of History and Slave Revolution in Antebellum America
Kevin Modestino

www.edinburghuniversitypress.com/series/incal

CARLYLE, EMERSON AND THE TRANSATLANTIC USES OF AUTHORITY

Literature, Print, Performance

Tim Sommer

EDINBURGH
University Press

Edinburgh University Press is one of the leading university presses in the UK. We publish academic books and journals in our selected subject areas across the humanities and social sciences, combining cutting-edge scholarship with high editorial and production values to produce academic works of lasting importance. For more information visit our website: edinburghuniversitypress.com

© Tim Sommer, 2021, 2023

Edinburgh University Press Ltd
The Tun – Holyrood Road, 12(2f) Jackson's Entry, Edinburgh EH8 8PJ

First published in hardback by Edinburgh University Press 2021

Typeset in 10/12.5 Adobe Sabon by
IDSUK (DataConnection) Ltd

A CIP record for this book is available from the British Library

ISBN 978 1 4744 9194 5 (hardback)
ISBN 978 1 4744 9195 2 (paperback)
ISBN 978 1 4744 9196 9 (webready PDF)
ISBN 978 1 4744 9197 6 (epub)

The right of Tim Sommer to be identified as the author of this work has been asserted in accordance with the Copyright, Designs and Patents Act 1988, and the Copyright and Related Rights Regulations 2003 (SI No. 2498).

CONTENTS

Acknowledgements vi
Abbreviations ix

Introduction: Transatlantic Literary Culture and the Uses of Authority 1

Part I: Anglo-American Literary and Cultural Identities
1 Race and Nationhood in the Mid-Nineteenth-Century Transatlantic Field 39
2 Usable Pasts: Anglo-American Literature and the Authority of Tradition 69

Part II: Authority and Authorisation in the Anglo-American Print Market
3 'Transatlantic Bibliopoly': Carlyle's Early American Print Career 103
4 'A Yankee Pocket Edition of Carlyle'? Emerson on the British Market 132

Part III: Performing Nationhood on the Transatlantic Lecture Circuit
5 Touring Anglo-America: Emerson as Transatlantic Lecturer 163
6 (De-)Authorising Eloquence: Carlyle and Transatlantic Public Speech 194

Epilogue: From Sectional Conflict to Posthumous Consecration 223

Bibliography 236
Index 261

ACKNOWLEDGEMENTS

An effort at mapping historical networks of transatlantic contact and exchange, what follows has its own history of indebtedness – both intellectual and material, both trans- and cisatlantic. This book is a revised version of my doctoral dissertation, 'Transatlantic Authority: Carlyle, Emerson, and Nineteenth-Century Anglo-American Literary Space', which I submitted at the University of Heidelberg in 2019. My single largest debt is to my supervisor, Günter Leypoldt, whose influence – a term I challenge throughout the book but am using here in an unreservedly affirmative sense – is everywhere apparent in these pages and whose support has been of tremendous importance to me. My work on this book also significantly benefited from conversations with interlocutors from beyond Heidelberg. Conference papers and seminar presentations drawn from earlier versions of individual chapters received generous feedback from audiences at Boston University, University College Cork, the University of Dundee, the University of Edinburgh, Justus-Liebig-Universität Gießen, Harvard University, the University of London and the University of Oxford. In the summer of 2019, an international symposium on 'Transatlantic Literary Authority' at the University of Heidelberg allowed me to present my research as work on the dissertation was drawing to a close. I would like to thank Annika Bautz, Katie McGettigan, Meredith McGill, Joe Rezek, Gisèle Sapiro, Julia Straub and Tom Wright, in particular, for stimulating discussions on that occasion and beyond. I am grateful to Günter Leypoldt for co-organising this conference with me, and to the German Research Foundation for funding the event.

ACKNOWLEDGEMENTS

Over the years that I have been working on this book, many individuals in many different contexts helped with queries, shared knowledge and ideas and/or commented on drafts. My thanks go to Kasia Boddy, Thomas Constantinesco, David Damrosch, Leslie Eckel, Kai Gräf, Kevin Hilliard, Stefan Höppner, Claudia Jetter, Ewan Jones, Paul Kerry, Philipp Löffler, Dan Malachuk, Michèle Mendelssohn, Barry Murnane, Joel Myerson, Margit Peterfy, Dietmar Schloss, Clemens Spahr, Jan Stievermann, Marcus Waithe and David Winters.

Much in the chapters that follow draws attention not only to intellectual exchanges, but also to the importance of material and economic manifestations of patronage and endorsement. This book itself could not have been written without such forms of encouragement. I am grateful, in particular, to the German Academic Scholarship Foundation for generously supporting my academic career both before and during my time as a doctoral candidate. Through its funding of the research group 'Authority and Trust', based at the Heidelberg Center for American Studies, the German Research Foundation enabled me to benefit from an extended period of undistracted work on the project. The members of the collective – both senior faculty and my fellow doctoral researchers – provided a vibrant atmosphere that facilitated the speedy completion of the manuscript. Travel grants from the German Academic Scholarship Foundation, the German Research Foundation, the Transatlantic Studies Association and the Ralph Waldo Emerson Society allowed me to present earlier versions of parts of this book at international conferences on both sides of the Atlantic.

An important part of the archival depth of my account of nineteenth-century transatlantic authority derives from research conducted at Harvard University's Houghton Library in 2017 – a stay that was made possible through a Visiting Fellowship the library kindly awarded me. The first draft of the manuscript was completed at the University of Cambridge, where, during the 2019 Lent Term, I was an Academic Visitor at the Faculty of English. I would like to thank librarians and archivists at the following institutions: Boston Public Library; University Library, English Faculty Library and Trinity College Library, Cambridge; Houghton Library, Widener Library and Child Memorial Library, Harvard University, Cambridge, Massachusetts; National Library of Scotland, Edinburgh; University Library and English Department Library, Heidelberg; National Archives of the United Kingdom, Kew; British Library and National Art Library, London; Bodleian Library, University of Oxford. I am grateful to Houghton Library (specifically the Ralph Waldo Emerson Memorial Association deposit) and the National Library of Scotland for permission to quote from unpublished manuscript material.

At Edinburgh University Press, I am indebted to series editors Chris Hanlon, Sarah Robbins and Andrew Taylor, who have been unfailingly enthusiastic about this book from the start and who have provided vital support. My thanks also go to the anonymous readers of the manuscript, whose stimulating comments allowed me to clarify key points. I am grateful to Susannah Butler, James Dale, Ersev Ersoy, Michelle Houston and Wendy Lee for steering the manuscript through the production process.

A substantial part of *Carlyle, Emerson and the Transatlantic Uses of Authority* is concerned with nineteenth-century reprinting and the legal frameworks in which it was taking place. In the twenty-first century, texts continue to travel through various material incarnations, and this book is hardly an exception. Fragments from Chapter 4 were originally published in *Harvard Library Bulletin* as part of an article entitled '"If It Were in My Power to Help You": Victorian Literary Patronage in Four Unpublished Thomas Carlyle Letters' (*Harvard Library Bulletin* 27.3 [2016], pp. 120–40). Sections from an essay on 'Shakespearean Negotiations: Carlyle, Emerson, and the Ambiguities of Transatlantic Influence', first published as a chapter in *Thomas Carlyle and the Idea of Influence*, edited by Paul E. Kerry, Albert D. Pionke and Megan Dent (Madison, NJ: Fairleigh Dickinson University Press, 2018), pp. 129–43, reappear in substantially revised form in the Introduction and are reprinted by permission of Rowman & Littlefield (all rights reserved). Earlier versions of Goethe-related material from Chapter 2 and two paragraphs from Chapter 4 were originally published as 'Material Exchange, Symbolic Recognition: *Weltliteratur* as Discourse and Practice in Goethe, Carlyle, and Emerson', *Publications of the English Goethe Society* 90.1 (2021), pp. 53–71 (copyright English Goethe Society, reprinted courtesy of Taylor & Francis). Portions of Chapter 3 and of Chapter 4, as well as a paragraph in the Introduction, include revised material that first appeared as 'Embedded Authorship: Thomas Carlyle, Ralph Waldo Emerson, and Nineteenth-Century "Transatlantic Bibliopoly"', *Book History* 24.2 (2021) (published by The Johns Hopkins University Press, copyright 2021 SHARP). In all of the above cases, I am grateful to the editors and reviewers involved for their helpful comments and feedback, and to the respective journals and publishers for granting permission to reprint the material in question.

Last – but certainly not least – I wish to thank my family and friends for their vital help (not only) during the time I was writing this book. I owe my biggest debt of gratitude to Adriana Lopez, whose support and encouragement defy words.

ABBREVIATIONS

AW	*Emerson's Antislavery Writings*. Ed. Len Gougeon and Joel Myerson. New Haven: Yale University Press, 1995.
CE	*The Works of Thomas Carlyle*. Ed. Henry Duff Traill. 30 vols. London: Chapman and Hall, 1896–9 (= *Centenary Edition*).
CEC	*The Correspondence of Emerson and Carlyle*. Ed. Joseph Slater. New York: Columbia University Press, 1964.
CL	*The Collected Letters of Thomas and Jane Welsh Carlyle*. Ed. Charles Richard Sanders et al. 47 vols to date. Durham, NC: Duke University Press, 1970–.
CW	*The Collected Works of Ralph Waldo Emerson*. Ed. Alfred R. Ferguson et al. 10 vols. Cambridge, MA: Belknap Press of Harvard University Press, 1971–2013.
EL	*The Early Lectures of Ralph Waldo Emerson*. Ed. Stephen E. Whicher, Robert E. Spiller and Wallace E. Williams. 3 vols. Cambridge, MA: Belknap Press of Harvard University Press, 1959–72.
HGL	*Carlyle's Unfinished History of German Literature*. Ed. Hill Shine. Lexington: University of Kentucky Press, 1951.
Houghton	Houghton Library, Harvard University, Cambridge, MA.

JMN	*The Journals and Miscellaneous Notebooks of Ralph Waldo Emerson*. Ed. William H. Gilman et al. 16 vols. Cambridge, MA: Belknap Press of Harvard University Press, 1960–82.
L	*The Letters of Ralph Waldo Emerson*. Ed. Ralph L. Rusk and Eleanor M. Tilton. 10 vols. New York: Columbia University Press, 1939, 1990–5.
LHL	*Lectures on the History of Literature, Delivered by Thomas Carlyle, April to July 1838*. Ed. J. Reay Greene. London: Ellis and Elvey, 1892.
LL	*The Later Lectures of Ralph Waldo Emerson: 1843–1871*. Ed. Ronald A. Bosco and Joel Myerson. 2 vols. Athens: University of Georgia Press, 2001.
NTC	*Two Note Books of Thomas Carlyle*. Ed. Charles Eliot Norton. New York: Grolier Club, 1898.
Rem	Thomas Carlyle. *Reminiscences*. Ed. Kenneth J. Fielding and Ian Campbell. Oxford: Oxford University Press, 1997.
TN	*The Topical Notebooks of Ralph Waldo Emerson*. Ed. Ralph H. Orth et al. 3 vols. Columbia: University of Missouri Press, 1990–4.
WTC	*The Norman and Charlotte Strouse Edition of the Writings of Thomas Carlyle*. Ed. Mark Engel et al. 5 vols to date. Berkeley: University of California Press, 1993–.

Short forms are used parenthetically and are followed by the respective volume, page and/or archival call number(s). Unless explicitly noted otherwise, all emphases in quotations are those in the original.

INTRODUCTION: TRANSATLANTIC LITERARY CULTURE AND THE USES OF AUTHORITY

Surveying a selection of Ralph Waldo Emerson's writings for the *London and Westminster Review* in March 1840, English poet and politician Richard Monckton Milnes discovered in them a familiar 'voice' speaking to British readers from across 'the broad Atlantic' (1840: 186). Understanding his task to be one of explicating contemporary American literature to his English periodical audience, Milnes simultaneously thinks of himself as merely retranslating transatlantic artefacts that themselves were adaptations of English sources – a corpus from which he singles out the books of his own literary mentor, Thomas Carlyle. Just like the fictional editorial figure of Carlyle's novel *Sartor Resartus* (1833–4), Milnes faced the problem of how a foreign cultural artefact might 'be brought home ... to the business and bosoms' of the 'English nation' (*WTC* 2: 8). Where *Sartor Resartus* posits an unbridgeable gap between interpretive communities in England and Germany, Milnes's strategy becomes one of establishing common ground, of reading Emerson's transatlantic texts against the background of their cisatlantic origins. Carlylean transplantations, Emerson's distinctly American variations on British themes demonstrate that 'the plant is assimilated to the climate and the soil, although the seed may have been brought from elsewhere' (1840: 186). Beneath superficial differences of nationality, however, Emerson's and Carlyle's writings to Milnes are merely 'the opposite colours' of essentially 'the same shield' (ibid., 198). Reconfiguring cross-cultural exchange as an intra-cultural event, he describes Carlyle and Emerson as authors moving within a shared Anglo-American literary space marked by a common linguistic and cultural identity.

Milnes was not alone among his contemporaries to register an affinity between the two writers; the connection between Carlyle and Emerson was perceived by commentators on the other side of the Atlantic as well. In a diatribe against the 'New School in Literature and Religion', published two years before Milnes's review, Unitarian theologian and Harvard professor Andrews Norton had similarly highlighted the importance of Carlyle's writing for contemporary New England authors. Although less interested than Milnes in the benefits of transnational exchange, Norton's account of the birth of the American Romantic 'new school' out of the combined spirits of 'German speculatists' and 'that hyper-Germanized Englishman, Carlyle' nevertheless ends up retracing a transatlantic intellectual genealogy (1992: 33). If, in de-Anglicising Carlyle and Emerson, Norton ultimately follows a different path from Milnes (who reads a common Anglo-Saxonism as their shared defining trait), both agree that contemporary Anglophone literary culture was irreducible to a single individual national context.

Carlyle and Emerson became involved in this transatlantic field to an extent that Milnes and Norton could hardly have foreseen. Following an initial encounter during Emerson's first European tour in 1833, the two took up an intense literary correspondence that would end up chronicling their engagement with the Anglo-American public sphere over a period of almost four decades. They helped each other to find a transatlantic audience and shaped the way in which contemporary readers in Britain and the United States approached books such as *Sartor Resartus*, *Nature* (1836), *On Heroes, Hero-Worship, and the Heroic in History* (1841) or *Representative Men* (1850). Through their literary friendship and their sustained professional collaboration, Carlyle and Emerson consolidated their status as transatlantic intellectual authorities and mutually reinforced their reputations as two of the century's foremost essayists and cultural critics.

Placing Milnes and Norton at the beginning of a discussion of Carlyle and Emerson is a way of acknowledging that thinking about the two writers in tandem goes back to their own contemporaries. It is also to suggest, however, that the manner in which Milnes and Norton reflect on the relationship between Carlyle and Emerson is mirrored both terminologically and conceptually in many later critical accounts. Like nineteenth-century commentators, subsequent generations of scholars have often tended to view Anglo-American literary and cultural contact through the lens of intellectual indebtedness. Milnes and Norton are just two early examples of this sustained discourse of transatlantic influence. It was common among contemporaries on both sides of the Atlantic to think of Emerson as something of a disciple of Carlyle. Edgar Allan Poe saw in him 'little more than a respectful imitation of Carlyle' (1846: 313), Carlyle's wife thought of his essays as a 'bad imitation of Carlyle's most Carlylish *translations* of Goethes [sic] most Goetheish passages' (*CL* 13: 122) and diarist Henry Crabb Robinson extended this diagnosis of second-degree epigonality to implicate Carlyle himself in the charge when he described Emerson's writings as 'a bad imitation of Carlyle who himself imitates Coleridge ill' (qtd in Ashton 2006: 42).[1]

Although most later critical accounts of the relationship between the two figures abandon the normative implications behind these diagnoses of deficient originality, the idea of Emerson's intellectual dependence on Carlyle (and, in turn, that of Carlyle's own reliance on the literature and philosophy of German Romanticism) has proved remarkably persistent in transatlantic comparative criticism from its beginnings in the first half of the twentieth century to some of its most recent incarnations.[2] My point here is not to deny that Carlyle's writing had an impact on Emerson but rather to suggest, with Susan Manning and Andrew Taylor, that 'transatlantic literary studies . . . are sadly impoverished when formulated in terms of one-way influence' (2007: 7). There are many ways of thinking about reception, of course, but the traditional approach to influence has tended to privilege the textual and the conceptual at the expense of the symbolic and the material.[3] Asking how American Transcendentalism derived its idealist tenets from Carlyle's and Coleridge's readings of Kant and Schelling has often entailed neglecting why American writers of Emerson's generation assigned greater cultural authority to British Romantic discourse than to homegrown writing or how the print products in which this discourse was first articulated found their way to New England readers. Combining intellectual history with cultural sociology and book history, *Carlyle, Emerson and the Transatlantic Uses of Authority* argues for a transatlantic comparativism that – while retaining an interest in the mechanics of textual transfer and adaptation – aims at providing a thicker description of the discursive and institutional dimensions of nineteenth-century transnational exchange.

Rather than suggesting a general comparative reading, this book presents an account that puts the transatlantic itself centre stage. Using Carlyle and Emerson as extended case studies, I am concerned with how nineteenth-century British and American authors conceptualised the nation and the authority of transatlantic culture, and with how these conceptualisations were in turn conditioned by concrete cultural formations such as the Anglo-American print market and the transatlantic lecture system and tied to specific themes and narratives such as Anglo-Saxonist racialism or Romantic literary historiography. In order to retrace these structures and the complex relationships that existed between them, this book builds on recent work in transatlantic literary and cultural studies that has extended the archive of transatlantic comparativism beyond the textual and the ideational, and that, in so doing, has begun to shed light on larger social, cultural and racial discourses, on material forms of textual circulation and on patterns of oral performance and audience response. Paul Giles (2001; 2006), Amanda Claybaugh (2007), Elisa Tamarkin (2008) and Christopher Hanlon

(2013) have provided important insights into the cultural and political contexts of nineteenth-century transatlantic writing. Exploring transatlantic print culture, Meredith L. McGill (2003), Jessica DeSpain (2014) and Joseph Rezek (2015) have reconstructed how practices of printing and reprinting shaped the writing and the dissemination of British and American authors over the course of the century. The professional environment of the transatlantic lecture tour has been covered in recent studies by Amanda Adams (2014) and Tom F. Wright (2017). I contribute to the critical conversation initiated by this scholarship through developing the idea of transatlantic authority into an analytical framework that enables us to pay simultaneous attention to a range of historical and institutional contexts that have so far mostly been studied in isolation.

The new transatlantic criticism that has emerged over the past two decades has significantly broadened our understanding of Anglo-American literary exchange and interaction, and it has often done so through turning from canonical writers to previously neglected figures or to larger formations that transcend the individual author as a unit of analysis. Reorienting itself away from the classic reference points of the comparativist tradition, none of this newer work has concerned itself with revisiting the nexus between Carlyle and Emerson – writers whom their contemporaries recognised as quintessential representatives of cultural contact between Victorian Britain and the antebellum United States. This book explores the rich historical archive that transatlantic scholarship has been opening up since the turn of the millennium and brings this analysis to bear upon two key authors whose extended relationship was last covered in greater detail more than four decades ago. Mainly interested in biography and authorial psychology, Kenneth Marc Harris's *Carlyle and Emerson: Their Long Debate* (1978) stopped short of taking into account what transcends its two subjects, both in terms of the larger transatlantic sphere in which they were situated and in terms of the material contexts that determined their exchanges.[4] When it comes to print culture, for example, Harris notes that Carlyle's and Emerson's extensive exchange of letters during the 1830s and 1840s implies 'a growing concern with business, trade, [and] publishing', but he quickly turns away from the larger implications of this observation when he suggests that 'the main function of the correspondence' was to provide a forum for 'the meeting of two powerful minds' (1978: 130–1). This book, by contrast, reads Carlyle and Emerson not as isolated individuals engaged in an abstract intellectual debate, but as historical figures embedded in a transatlantic network of people, discourses, objects and institutions. It thus seeks to shed new light on canonical figures through directing attention to contexts and issues against the background of which they have not commonly been discussed.

Seen in such a larger perspective, statements of the kind formulated by Milnes and Norton not only reflect on intellectual indebtedness but also testify to the existence of a closely interrelated Anglo-American cultural sphere.

Where twentieth-century criticism often imagined nineteenth-century Anglophone literary exchange as dominated by national animosities between Britain and the United States,[5] many of Carlyle's and Emerson's contemporaries instead acknowledged the unity – if not the unanimity – of transatlantic culture in the century following American independence. 'Whatever may be the character of the political relations between Great Britain and the United States', American diplomat and man of letters Alexander Everett, the first transatlantic reviewer of *Sartor Resartus*, noted, 'the two countries must always, in a literary view, be regarded as one great community' (1834: 6–7). When Carlyle wrote to Emerson that Milnes's essay in the *Westminster Review* would 'la[y] the first plank of a kind of pulpit for you here and throughout all Saxondom' (*CEC* 264), he was similarly taking for granted the existence of a shared transatlantic public sphere – a formation sustained through publishing, periodical criticism and the medium of the literary lecture.

Milnes's endorsement of Emerson and Norton's hostile reaction to Carlyle's New England impact thus raise a set of questions that go well beyond matters of influence. In which material forms did Carlyle's writings reach his original American readers, for example, and how did the London editions of Emerson's books shape his mid-century British reception? What is the larger cultural rationale behind Norton's characterisation of Carlyle as 'hyper-Germanized' instead of English? Is Milnes's depiction of Carlyle and Emerson as quintessentially Anglo-Saxon indicative of a larger British tendency to reclaim the cultural production of what he calls 'that other and greater England' across the Atlantic (1840: 201)? Who is endowed with the necessary degree of intellectual and critical authority to pronounce such verdicts, and by which audiences are these in turn acknowledged as relevant and authoritative? This book suggests that such questions come into clearer focus if we think of figures such as Carlyle, Emerson, Milnes and Norton as agents in a transatlantic cultural formation in which invocations and denials of the transatlantic – channelled through concrete material objects and practices – work as strategies for cultural authorisation.

Treating Victorian and antebellum literature and culture as entangled rather than as separate entities, *Carlyle, Emerson and the Transatlantic Uses of Authority* offers a contribution to an ongoing critical debate about the relationship between culture and nationhood. Questioning the heuristic primacy of the nation as a cultural signifier, paradigms such as postcolonial studies, transnationalism or world literature have all endeavoured to shift the focus of critical attention from more traditional comparative narratives towards tracing hybrid literary and cultural formations. As a self-described 'liberating transdisciplinary framework' (Kaufman and Macpherson 2000: xix), transatlantic literary studies has likewise often sought to interrogate the physical and the symbolic boundaries of the nation-state. This theoretical premise has manifested itself in a gradual reorientation of critical projects away from the

Anglo-American focus at the heart of classic studies such as Robert Weisbuch's *Atlantic Double-Cross: American Literature and British Influence in the Age of Emerson* (1986) or Leon Chai's *The Romantic Foundations of the American Renaissance* (1987) and towards broader cultural and geographical frames of reference that include the 'transamerican' (Brickhouse 2004), the 'pan-Atlantic' (Almeida 2011: 1–18) or the 'transoceanic' (Burnham 2019).[6] While much recent transatlantic work has usefully troubled earlier literary historical genealogies and helped to expand traditional canons of texts and contexts, the field's 'soaring rhetoric of transgression' (Rezek 2014: 795) has, at the same time, tended to obscure the many ways in which the nation and the idea of national culture historically informed transnational cultural contact. To nineteenth-century writers like Carlyle and Emerson, the nation was a reality precisely because they conceived of themselves as members of a literary sphere that was international in reach. Making sense of this seeming paradox requires an approach that, in Caroline Levine's words, 'continues to work with the borders of the nation, but . . . also recognizes the networks that carry all kinds of transnational objects across and around the nation' (2013: 664) – networks that operate on a scale at once smaller and larger than that of the nation-state.

Focusing on Anglo-American literary culture rather than on the Atlantic at large, this book reads the national against the background of the transatlantic instead of deconstructing it entirely.[7] As I will be arguing throughout what follows, the transatlantic mindset that manifests itself in nineteenth-century British and American writing was shaped by a complex combination of the national, the subnational and the supranational. One of my key claims will be that, in their engagement with the idea of authority, Carlyle and Emerson fused nationalist and cosmopolitan vocabularies and that it was their transatlanticism that allowed them to navigate between and across the various 'scales of aggregation' (Dimock 2006) that these rhetorics implied. Their writings are marked by what Christopher Hanlon has recently described as 'a pendular experience of Atlantic awareness' in which 'the global and the local' coexist (2016: 59). In Carlyle's and Emerson's reflections about Britain and the United States, the transatlantic features both as a contact zone and as a scene of cultural conflict. '[W]e and you are *not* two countries', Carlyle insisted in his first letter to Emerson in August 1834, 'but only two *parishes* of one country' – a transatlantic community that he nevertheless saw as periodically disrupted by 'dirty temporary parish feuds' (*CEC* 102). At different points in their extended careers as writers, lecturers and cultural critics, Carlyle and Emerson chose either to conjure up the idea of transatlantic kinship or to highlight the importance of sectional difference. Providing a firmer grasp of the concrete historical contexts in which such decisions took place is one of the central aims of my enquiry.

DIMENSIONS OF TRANSATLANTIC AUTHORITY

This book suggests that paying attention to questions of literary and cultural authority allows us to understand these contexts and their impact on nineteenth-century Anglo-American writers and texts better, thus opening up a new avenue for research into a field that by now is well established. Authority is a multifaceted phenomenon that surfaces on a number of different levels. Milnes's and Norton's diagnoses of Carlyle's sway over his American contemporaries attest to the presence of a type of authority that is tied to a specific individual. That this can be highly volatile becomes evident in the subsequent trajectory of Carlyle's reputation, which, from the late nineteenth century onwards, steadily declined. Despite his considerable cachet as a cultural icon during his own lifetime, the 'strange contracting influence' that Carlyle himself recognised the passage of time invariably had 'on many a wide-spread fame' ultimately also came to affect his own status (*CE* 26: 24). Emerson, on the other hand, gradually turned from the image of the imitative Carlylean acolyte to that of a national icon. His and Carlyle's shifting commands of cultural authority have translated into markedly different degrees of institutional relevance. Thanks to an idiosyncratic style that, at times, goes to the extreme of self-contradiction, Emerson has appealed to academic readers from across a broad range of critical persuasions – lending himself to be celebrated as an intellectual founding father, critiqued as a champion of American exceptionalism and rediscovered as a pioneer of literary cosmopolitanism.[8]

Carlyle's conversion in the 1840s and 1850s to a racially inflected politics of power, on the other hand, has resulted in him becoming 'a casualty of his own excesses', 'dismissed as a mystical reactionary' (Small 2017: 536; Mendilow 1993: 603). Asking how contemporaries came to terms with the pro-slavery and anti-democracy attitudes that manifested themselves in texts such as the 'Occasional Discourse on the Negro Question' (1849) or the late essay 'Shooting Niagara: And After?' (1867), Elisa Tamarkin (2016) has suggested that most of Carlyle's nineteenth-century readers recognised in him a kind of authority that cancelled out both rational objections and emotional responses, neutralising at once an argumentative opposition to his claims and the ethical repulsion they provoked. Even someone like Frederick Douglass, who, in an 1869 speech, characterised Carlyle as '[a] man to whom despotism is the savior and liberty the destroyer of society', counted him among the 'most potent European prophets', an 'eminent' writer whose 'advice' was not easily rejected (2018: 283). To his contemporaries on both sides of the Atlantic, Carlyle's appeal as a writer and lecturer was such that his authority compensated for the rhetorical 'excesses' of his writings. With this charm gradually wearing off once he had fallen silent, subsequent generations of readers became increasingly disenchanted with him, seeing in him an intransigent writer whose topics and style, in contrast to Emerson's, quickly grew outdated. From the sage to whom most contemporaries could show deference, Carlyle's image turned into that of a different kind of visionary – a 'prophet with a sinister message' (Schapiro 1945: 97), whose own authority in the twentieth century diminished to the degree to which he retrospectively appeared as an advocate of extreme forms of political power. What continues to make Carlyle's case intriguing from a historical point of view is the challenge of comprehending the fluctuations of his appeal for his original British and American audiences – the members of a mass readership as much as fellow author professionals such as Dickens, Mill, Arnold, Emerson, Douglass and Whitman.

For someone concerned as much as Carlyle was with the vicissitudes of contemporary fame and posthumous consecration, such a boom-and-bust career comes with an added sense of irony. He routinely distinguished between transitory popularity and more lasting forms of recognition and did so especially when writing about literary figures – in essays such as 'Burns' (1828), 'Boswell's Life of Johnson' (1832) or 'Sir Walter Scott' (1838). As Chris R. Vanden Bossche has shown, Carlyle was preoccupied throughout his career with his own status as an authority and with the authority of literary authorship, more generally.[9] He was concerned just as well with larger transformations of authority in the religious, political and social fields. Confronted with the erosion of traditional structures of power, he began his career seeking refuge in an 'aesthetic transcendentalism' and ended up, in his later writings, finding salvation only in 'political authoritarianism' (Vanden Bossche 1991: viii). David G. Riede has similarly described a shift in Carlyle's intellectual biography from a belief in the 'literary authority' of authors as 'inspired seers' to increasingly violent 'assertions of the authority of great visionaries' in fields other than the literary (1991: 269). While I tend to agree with these readings, in what follows I am interested more specifically in the Anglo-American dimensions of Carlyle's – and his contemporary readers' – struggle to come to terms with the problem of authority. Both his notion of the literary profession and his idea of social order – key themes in Vanden Bossche's and Riede's narratives – remain insufficiently understood without a sense of his engagement with phenomena such as the transatlantic print market or American popular democracy.[10]

Carlyle's and Emerson's trajectories of recognition illustrate that authority can be understood as a property ascribed or denied to individual figures. It also operates on another scale, however – as an index to concentrations of symbolic power in the larger cultural sphere. That Emerson wrote about English subjects considerably more often than Carlyle did about American ones, for example, was the result not simply of personal preferences but of an unevenly distributed degree of authority granted to British and American culture by the inhabitants of the nineteenth-century transatlantic world. Where Carlyle's explicitly American-themed writerly output is comparatively small,

Emerson engaged with English literature in a full-scale lecture series, dedicated one of his commercially most successful books – the 1856 *English Traits* – to the contemplation of British culture, history and manners, and commented on these themes extensively throughout his life as a published essayist and public performer.[11] He experienced Britain first-hand during three extensive European trips in 1832–3, 1847–8 and 1872–3, but never managed to convince Carlyle to reciprocate these visits. Although Carlyle liked to emphasise transatlantic proximity and imagine Britain and the United States as 'two parishes of one country', he had a clear sense of the power dynamics underlying that special relationship. Suggesting that paying a visit was a form of paying respect, he explained to Emerson that it was the Americans who should travel to London rather than he to them. '[A]ll Englishmen from all zones and hemispheres', he believed, 'will, for a good while yet, resort occasionally to the Mother-Babel' (*CEC* 205). The 'head-quarters' of the transatlantic 'community', the American Everett conceded at around the same time, were located 'in the parent country' (1834: 8). Remarks such as these testify to the hegemony of English culture in the United States even after political autonomy had turned into a fact – and during a period in Anglo-American relations marked by transatlantic competition between British imperialism and American expansionism. As Tamarkin and others have demonstrated, the crisis of British political power in the long aftermath of the Revolution and the War of 1812 was, to some extent paradoxically, accompanied by an enduring American subscription to the authority of British culture and manners that was all the more pervasive because it rested not on force or coercion but on voluntary submission and identification.[12] Statements like Everett's and Carlyle's illustrate Hannah Arendt's larger argument that authority stems not so much from 'the power of the one who commands' as it does from a specific type of relationship 'whose rightness and legitimacy' is acknowledged by 'the one who obeys' (1961: 93). The cultural authority of the British centre, in other words, depended on its recognition in the American periphery. It remained operative for as long as writers of Everett and Emerson's generation were prepared to accept that standards of literary and cultural excellence were defined 'in the parent country'.

To make sense of how individual and collective forms of transatlantic cultural centrality of the kind I have just discussed came into being, it is helpful to turn to sociologist Max Weber's classic definition of authority as 'legitimate domination', a framework that has been among the most influential modern theorisations of the term (1978, 1: 215). A social phenomenon that differs from mere power or force, authority to Weber derives its influence from a recognition of its validity through those who instinctively respond to its call. In his taxonomy of three 'pure types' of authority, Weber distinguishes between different mechanisms of appeal capable of providing legitimacy to domination: (1) *rational–legal* forms of authority, which ground themselves in established rules and structures of command; (2) *traditional* forms of authority, which draw their force from inherited convictions and customary behaviour; and (3) *charismatic* forms of authority, which originate with the 'extraordinariness' of an individual (see ibid., 212–45). Authority to Weber is something virtual rather than empirically quantifiable – 'not a thing', as Richard Sennett explains, but 'an act of imagination' (1993: 197). Its effects are real, nonetheless.

Occupied with the political dimension of domination, Weber leaves the cultural work of authority largely unaddressed. Even where he writes about religious communities, for example, he is thinking about questions of leadership and social hierarchy rather than about the far-reaching effects that authority exerts on cultural dispositions. As sociologist Frank Furedi has pointed out more recently, authority can alternatively be conceptualised as a force that extends beyond the political realm and comes with a larger 'cultural, social and symbolic significance' (2013: 7). This more capacious definition of the term offers greater analytical potential for a discussion of the nineteenth-century transatlantic context. To be sure, Weber's framing of authority as political legitimacy seems pertinent to a discussion of the American Revolution and its questioning of the rightfulness of British colonial power. But the more the Revolution receded into the historical background, the more a concern with political authority became superseded by deference to – or attempts at an appropriation of – British cultural authority. Although Emerson, for example, is still often reduced to his famous dismissal of 'the courtly muses of Europe' (*CW* 1: 69), he did not shy away from paying homage to English achievement. Where contemporaries like his one-time Transcendentalist ally Orestes Brownson complained that the United States was suffering from a crisis of cultural identity which saw domestic authors continuing to 'write as Englishmen, not as Americans' (1838: 436), Emerson called the existence of such simple national binaries into question and instead explored a more complex transatlantic identity marked by its composite nature.

That nineteenth-century American responses to British culture were ultimately not uniformly affirmative points towards a second blind spot in Weber's theory. By presenting authority in terms of legitimate power and voluntary submission, Weber does not account for what happens if domination and its recognition fail to come together. Sennett in this context speaks of a 'split between authority and legitimacy' that exists in situations in which hierarchies remain in place while their validity becomes disputed (1993: 45). Though primarily derived from the observation of political and psychological phenomena, Sennett's reflections on the different forms the contestation of authority can assume – from 'disobedient dependence' to 'fantas[ies] of the disappearance of authority' (ibid., 28) – also shed light on mechanisms of literary and cultural domination. The idea of 'disobedient dependence', for example, captures well the double bind in which readers of the late Carlyle were torn, like Emerson, between a condemnation of his 'errors of opinion' and a celebration of his literary 'merit' (*JMN* 15: 367), or in which American writers turned against a British cultural authority whose legitimacy they questioned at the same time that they acknowledged its rational–legal, traditional or charismatic appeal.

My use of the term *authority* in the chapters that follow builds both on Weber and on the richer culturalist notions of the concept that I draw from Sennett and Furedi. As a heuristic category, the idea allows for the productive discussion of two sets of binaries in which authority figures as (1) *collective* or *individual* (the authority of a national culture as it operates both within and beyond the boundaries of the nation, or the authority of a writer as it is recognised or called into question by a given audience) and as (2) *discursive* or *embodied* (authority as an abstract rhetoric and a virtual force, or authority as something that manifests itself in a specific cultural practice or the materiality and legal–economic status of a textual artefact). Collective authority, for example, describes the ability of English culture and its literary heritage to haunt nineteenth-century American (but also British) readers and writers (a subject covered in greater detail in Chapter 2). Closing in on individual authority allows us to look, for instance, at Emerson's emergence as an authoritative figure among mid-century British and American audiences or, more generally, at how his and Carlyle's status as Victorian sages developed from the 1830s onwards. The discursive aspect of authority calls for an account of general patterns in the rhetorical construction of its collective or individual forms (the transatlantic appeal of British literary institutions or Carlyle's role as transcendental visionary in 1830s New England, which I retrace in Chapter 1). Making sense of how authority becomes embodied requires paying attention to environments such as the print market (see Chapters 3 and 4) and the lecture circuit (see Chapters 5 and 6) – transatlantic cultural spheres in which authors were validated through the circulation of texts as well as through public performances and their subsequent media coverage.

Accounting for how such different dimensions of authority operate and change over time requires a larger perspective on the overall system in which people, objects and discourses are located. Pierre Bourdieu's idea of the literary field – a model of literary production and reception that maps internal power hierarchies at the same time that it charts the relationship between literary culture and adjacent fields such as the political and the economic – offers a helpful analytical vocabulary for conceptualising such a framework. The main concern of Bourdieu's literary sociological work has been to explain how divisions have historically emerged and to account for the strategies that agents in a given field follow as they seek to preserve or transform the system of rules that governs it. Concentrating on writers and their role in this overall structure, Bourdieu understands authority to be synonymous with 'literary legitimacy' (1996: 224). His theory of the field accordingly aims at accounting for 'what creates the authority with which authors authorize' both themselves and the positions they occupy (1993: 76).

Although Bourdieu 'often speaks of the literary field in the singular, as a global phenomenon' (Leypoldt 2009: 37), his work has largely focused on the French literary sphere and its historical and structural idiosyncrasies. Over the past two decades, the challenge of transnationally expanding his approach has been taken up in a number of critical projects, the most ambitious of which has been Pascale Casanova's *The World Republic of Letters* (2004). Like Bourdieu's literary field, Casanova's 'world republic' is marked by 'incessant . . . challenges to authority and legitimacy' (2004: 175). The authors located in this global formation constantly compete with one another in their attempts to acquire 'literary capital' (ibid., 13), a resource that can assume a range of different forms (from the universally recognised cultural prestige of a nation's time-honoured literary tradition to the institutional consecration of an individual writer). Analysing the strategies at the disposal of actors moving within this configuration, Casanova identifies two different authorial types: 'national' writers (who, usually conservative, emphasise the regional specificity of the space from which they speak) and 'international' writers (who, usually avant-garde, subscribe to notions of literary autonomy and aesthetic universality) (see ibid., 108–15).

While the global scale of Casanova's approach allows her to internationalise Bourdieu's framework, her discussion of concrete examples of the workings of the 'international field' can at times be rather sweeping (ibid., 109). Where she writes about the nineteenth-century emergence of American literature on the global scene, for example, she simply counts figures such as Emerson and Whitman as national writers motivated by a logic of differentiation that categorically rejects prior forms of authority and tradition (see ibid., 222, 243–4). Yet Emerson, a transatlantically published writer firmly situated in an international public sphere, throughout his career sought to mediate between a nativist vocabulary of American self-authorisation – his dismissal of 'the courtly muses of Europe' – and a more open language of global connection that emphasised Anglo-American genealogical and cultural proximity. The population of the United States, he never tired of pointing out, was one 'of English descent and language' and English literature accordingly represented a shared 'splendid inheritance' on which American writers and readers could draw (*CW* 5: 24; *EL* 1: 75). This sense of cultural continuity informs many of Emerson's transatlantically themed writings, perhaps most notably the essays that make up *English Traits* (which I discuss in greater detail in Chapter 5). Like Cooper's earlier *Notions of the Americans* (1828) and Hawthorne's later *Our Old Home* (1863), the book is foreign ethnography as much as self-portraiture, built around a strategic mixture of praise and censure designed to appeal to audiences in both Britain and the United States. Diplomatic negotiations such as these suggest that nineteenth-century transatlantic literary culture comprised a multiplicity of overlapping positions which – rather than neatly conforming to the terms of Casanova's 'great dichotomy . . . between national and international writers' (2005: 81) – allowed authors to probe the wide spectrum between these two identities and experiment with a range of different uses of transatlantic authority.

A more nuanced picture than the one provided by Casanova has emerged from studies that adapt Bourdieusian methodology to the scale of the transatlantic rather than the global. Amanda Claybaugh, for example, uses the framework of the 'Anglo-American literary field' (2007: 6) to show how British and American realist fiction responded to contemporary discourses of social reform. Joseph Rezek has more recently drawn on both Bourdieu and Casanova to retrace the symbolic dynamics and book historical realities of the nineteenth-century 'Anglophone literary field' in which Scottish, Irish and American writers were working with and against their relational 'provinciality' vis-à-vis London – rather than Casanova's Paris – as a cultural centre (2015: 8, 4).[13] Both Claybaugh and Rezek are concerned with writing and print rather than with orality and performance, however, and both focus on fiction rather than on the essayistic prose characteristic of the discourse of Victorian sage figures. This book suggests that print and performance need to be considered side by side as interconnected arenas for the production of transatlantic authority and that closer attention needs to be paid to the non-fictional prose of essays, reviews and lecture texts – genres in which claims to authority were often formulated most explicitly.

Boundary Making: Literature, Gender, Race

The ways in which mid-century writers such as Carlyle and Emerson sought to describe themselves as cultural authorities and in which they conceived of culture itself as a source of authority were closely bound up with different forms of demarcation and self-positioning. As Bourdieu suggests, making distinctions is a characteristic manifestation of the 'struggles' between the members of a given field, with these distinctions themselves reflecting the complex distribution of power within that space (1993: 42). Where each agent 'is trying to impose the *boundaries* of the field most favourable to [his or her] interests', authority is both the condition for and the effect of such moments of demarcation (Bourdieu 1996: 223). In the case of Carlyle and Emerson, one of these boundaries related to the definition of the literary. The majority of Carlyle's and Emerson's work consists of non-fictional prose – cultural history, literary criticism, social analysis, philosophical reflection – rather than literature in today's more narrow sense, and in their own texts the two display a catholic understanding of the term *literature* that encompasses writing of a wide range of different types, contents and styles (from religious texts, philosophical treatises and historiography to poetry and fiction). Broadly speaking, what counts as 'literary' during the eighteenth and nineteenth centuries gradually becomes transformed and narrowed down in the context of a shift that Raymond

Williams has characterised as revolving around 'an increasing specialization of literature to "creative" or "imaginative" works' and the related 'development of a concept of "tradition" within national terms' (1977: 48). While Carlyle's and Emerson's writings clearly illustrate the latter tendency towards a particularist notion of literary history (as I show in Chapter 2), they were less inclined to let go of a more capacious residual notion of literature that provided for the role of the man of letters and the cultural authority attached to it.[14] When Carlyle spoke on 'The History of Literature' in a series of lectures he gave in London in the late 1830s, he thus discussed Shakespeare along with Luther and John Knox, and Laurence Sterne along with George Whitefield and Edward Gibbon. In a lecture course of his own delivered at around the same time, Emerson similarly considered figures such as Francis Bacon or Scottish Enlightenment writers Dugald Stewart and James Mackintosh as belonging to the tradition of English 'literature'. This inclusion of religious, philosophical and critical writing in Carlyle's and Emerson's accounts of literary history on the one hand conveniently mirrored the nature of their own work, but it also at the same time indicated their scepticism about the increasing centrality of fiction – a scepticism that found expression in Emerson's anxiety about contemporary novels and 'the immense extension of their circulation through the new cheap press' (*CW* 10: 251) or in Carlyle's disdain for the 'street-fiddling' debasement of the art of writing in the nineteenth-century age of literature as 'trade' (*CE* 30: 26).

Such attempts at distancing themselves and the avowed seriousness of their own purpose from the tastes of the mass reading public were aimed at salvaging their authority as cultural producers from what Carlyle and Emerson consistently described as the social and economic threat of the erosion of that same authority. But this strategy was, of course, at the same time indicative of a specific gendering of the idea of authority that was deeply ingrained in Victorian and antebellum culture. To the extent that novel writing and reading in the nineteenth century became thought of as a domestic affair, the discrediting of fiction provided a way of excluding female authorship from influence in the public sphere. To use Mary Poovey's Bourdieusian turn of phrase, gender and gender representations in this context formed 'the sites at which struggles for authority occurred, as well as the locus of assumptions used to underwrite the very authority that authorized these struggles' (1988: 2). This larger gendered dimension of mid-century conceptualisations of authority manifests itself, for example, in Carlyle's notion that 'true' writing was a heroic form of intellectual labour distinctly marked as masculine or in Emerson's conviction that world history's most important individuals were all representative *men* rather than women.[15] The result of the 'struggles for authority' that Poovey and others have retraced, the large-scale rise of the female author as a publicly as well as critically acclaimed figure is a phenomenon that gains full traction only after the period on which this book focuses. I analyse transatlantic authority through closing in on Carlyle and Emerson because both occupied key positions in the mid-century literary field and were recognised as such by many of their contemporaries, male and female alike (Harriet Martineau, Margaret Fuller and George Eliot among the latter). If gender as such does not lie at the centre of the chapters that follow, it is because the subject does not surface in mid-century discussions of transatlantic literary culture as explicitly and as extensively as do other issues. The way in which I theorise and historicise authority can, I hope, nevertheless provide a starting point for future enquiries into female dimensions of transatlantic authority and thus address a complex set of questions that lie beyond the thematic scope of this book.[16]

What Carlyle, Emerson and their contemporaries certainly did think about when contemplating Anglo-American authority was racial and national identity. In addition to contested definitions of the literary and to gendered models of authorship, this was another key area in which the inclusion and exclusion mechanisms of the literary field were powerfully at work. Seen from this perspective, the later Carlyle's white supremacist harangues, for instance, were a way of asserting a racial hierarchy that allowed him to fashion himself as a member of a privileged in-group. For much of their lives as literary intellectuals, the Scottish Carlyle and the American Emerson were striving hard to self-describe as Anglo-Saxon and as characterised – in spirit, if not in fact – by a metropolitan English identity. As I argue in Chapter 1, they did so at least in part because, especially during the early years of their careers, they were almost unanimously attacked as 'un-English' or 'hyper-Germanized' (Sewell 1840: 455; Norton 1992: 33). For writers such as Carlyle and Emerson, an affirmative use of the racial language of Anglo-Saxon identity – and a problematic distinction between those that belonged to it and those that did not – offered a way of working against such nationally inflected charges and of laying claim to a kind of intellectual and linguistic authority that was fundamentally coded in ethnic or racial terms (and that tended to marginalise black writers and lecturers such as Douglass, who, at mid-century, were becoming increasingly visible in the spheres of print and performance). Carlyle and Emerson, as much as their contemporary critics, were thus working in a framework that sociologist Andreas Wimmer has theorised as a culture of 'ethnic boundary making' marked by a range of different 'classificatory practices and networking strategies' (2013: 206). Throughout what follows, I am interested in how such practices and strategies manifested themselves, both in the more abstract terms retraced in Chapters 1 and 2 and in the concrete institutional contexts that I single out for treatment in the rest of the book.

Print Culture: Authority, Authorship, Authorisation

If authority was shaped through such different forms of boundary drawing and definitional discrimination, a space in which its effects surfaced most immediately in the context of nineteenth-century transatlantic exchange was the domain of print. Authorial acts of self-positioning were ultimately inseparable from more concrete material forms of transnational circulation, and it is to this key connection that important book historical research has drawn attention since the turn of the millennium. McGill's pioneering *American Literature and the Culture of Reprinting, 1834–1853* (2003) emphasised the importance of reprinting and helped to establish a field of enquiry that has more recently been enriched by Rezek's work on the orientation of peripheral Anglophone writers towards metropolitan commercial and critical power (see 2015), by DeSpain's account of the transatlantic migration of bodies, books and texts (see 2014) and by Katie McGettigan's discussion of the nineteenth-century British reprinting of American literature (see 2017a, 2017b). The importance that such scholarship assigns to books and their dissemination derives from the fact that the nineteenth century witnessed a drastic expansion of the print market, a development that was coupled to larger trends such as mass literacy and its concomitant democratisation of reading, the intensification of industrialisation and the increasing dominance of market capitalism. In his 1829 essay 'Signs of the Times', Carlyle gestured towards these connections when he described the contemporary mechanisation of literary production – the fact that 'books are not only printed, but, in a great measure, written and sold, by machinery' (CE 27: 62) – as part of a larger set of socio-economic phenomena.

Such developments affected local markets and domestic economies, but their cultural effects also made themselves felt on a larger international scale, as can be seen in the fact that American responses to British cultural authority were crucially conditioned by the large-scale transatlantic availability of English texts and books. The power imbalance between Britain and the United States thus manifested itself not merely in terms of cultural prestige but also in terms of the empirics of the transatlantic print market. That in the first half of the nineteenth century more readers on both sides of the Atlantic read books by Scott or Dickens than by Cooper or Irving was, to an important extent, the result of the fact that British writers were closer to the consecrating centre of the Anglophone literary world. Yet their greater stock of 'literary capital' was ultimately as much the cause as it was the result of the strong presence of their books in the transatlantic marketplace.

Symbolic power and market penetration were hence factors that mutually reinforced one another. Contemporary commentators – from centre as well as periphery – largely agreed that culturally, as well as economically, the antebellum United States was (still) a 'developing country' (McVey 1975: 80). Emerson himself gave voice to such a sense of belatedness when, comparing an English with an American edition of Carlyle's *Critical and Miscellaneous Essays* (1838–9), he noted that the 'beauty' of the English volumes made him 'despair of our American arts' ('Our types, paper, and ink', he admitted to Carlyle, 'are all much inferior to yours'). Emerson could 'wish the disparity might end with the book, & did not extend to the contents', but ultimately felt compelled to acknowledge that transatlantic differences in quality were of a material as well as of an intellectual kind.[17] The statement in which, for writers of Emerson's generation, such feelings about the marginality of American literature crystallised was a question Sydney Smith had asked in the *Edinburgh Review* in 1820 ('In the four quarters of the globe, who reads an American book?') (1820: 79). Smith's taunt formed part of a larger argument that pitted American economic success against a perceived lack of civilisational achievement, but transatlantic cultural inequality was, in fact, closely bound up with trade imbalances. Throughout the second third of the nineteenth century, British books represented a considerably larger trade volume than American ones in the transatlantic literary marketplace (see Winship 1999).

Import and export statistics provide evidence for just one part of the overall market, however, to the extent that they describe only a trade in books as physical objects. In the nineteenth-century United States, British texts were mainly circulating in the form of domestic reprints – not as British but as American books. Many American publishers judged British titles a safer bet than domestic literary productions – not necessarily because they felt an innate cultural superiority of the former over the latter, but because, in the absence of American copyright protection for foreign writers, British books could be cheaply reprinted and sold. Although this threatened their own success with domestic audiences, not all American authors resented this practice. In an early address entitled 'On the Best Mode of Inspiring a Correct Taste in English Literature', Emerson, for instance, was openly calling for the dissemination of 'cheap editions . . . of the best authors: Bacon, Milton, [and] Shakspeare [*sic*]', confessing that he would be 'glad to see cargoes of these books sailing up the Missouri and Red river and the bales unloaded by the half Indian hunter of the west prairie' (*EL* 1: 215). Instinctively identifying literary history's 'best authors' with the pinnacles of a more specifically English canon, the young Emerson was fully prepared to subscribe to contemporary British standards of taste. As McGill (2003: 43) has pointed out, however, the American reprinting of British texts was also understood by many of Emerson's compatriots as an insurrectionary act of defiance that promised to topple transatlantic power structures – as a practice that, along with creating a democratically and ethnically diversified access to highbrow literature (the 'cheap editions' of the English hyper-canon at the disposal of 'the half Indian hunter'), attacked the market monopoly of British publishing houses abroad at the same time that it radically envisioned what Sennett calls the 'disappearance of authority'. The large-scale reprinting of English literature in the nineteenth-century United States was thus not simply a symptom of cultural subordination but also a cultural practice that contemporaries understood as an affirmation of transatlantic autonomy.

Such antagonistic interpretations of Anglo-American print culture notwithstanding, there was much reciprocal commercial and symbolic exchange in terms of both production and reception. American writing was not, after all, faring as badly as Smith had claimed. Widely disseminated in nineteenth-century Britain, it formed a market segment that, like its transatlantic counterpart, was dominated not by imported books but by English reprints. American literature was gradually enhancing its position in the domestic print market as well, in what John Tebbel has described as a 'steady swing away from British to American authors' (1972: 221). Commentators of the generation following Smith's offered much of the same diagnosis. In an 1845 book entitled *American Facts*, US publisher George Palmer Putnam was drawing on a statistical synopsis of how many American publications of the 1830s and early 1840s were 'Original American' and how many 'Reprinted' to show that 'the United States do not entirely rely upon foreign sources for their intellectual sustenance' (1845: 82–3). Residing in London at the time of issuing the book – a title that, aimed at British readers, appeared under the imprint of his firm's London branch office –, Putnam was also taking the local market into account, contending that the British were avid readers of American literature, the 'number of American books reprinted in England' being 'much greater than is usually supposed' (ibid., 86).[18] The rise of American literature continued throughout the second half of the century – a period that, Amanda Claybaugh has argued, saw a gradual equalisation of power structures in the literary field, over the course of which British symbolic dominance became balanced by economic and numerical factors (the growing influence of American publishing houses as well as the rapidly increasing size of the American reading public) (2007: 16). Yet a residual sense of the unequal distribution of transatlantic literary authority continued to shape contemporary sensibilities. Putnam's ultimate case for the importance of American literature, for example, rested not on sales figures and market penetration but on the opinion of the British critical elite. The highest praise he could imagine for the most accomplished among his compatriots' books was not their wide transatlantic circulation, but the fact that they had been 'pronounced by English critics as superior to any others', including contemporary British publications (1845: 83).

The simultaneity of an increasing availability of American literature in nineteenth-century Britain and the continued orientation of American readers, writers and publishers towards English critical authority suggests that the two nations were linked through a shared print market as much as through a common discursive culture. As Claybaugh has pointed out, 'the transatlantic circulation of texts' established an 'Anglo-American public sphere' (2007: 3) – a space in which political persuasions, economic interests and cultural authority were closely intertwined with one another. The dissemination of British texts across the nineteenth-century United States and the reprinting of American books in Victorian England were linked to shifting configurations of cultural centrality at the same time that they resulted from a legal framework that rendered transatlantic reprinting an attractive business model. In the United States, the Copyright Act of 1790 protected books published domestically, but only those written by 'citizens or permanent residents' (Winship 1999: 101). It was not until the passage of the International Copyright Act of 1891 (the so-called Chace Act) that the copyright of foreign authors was secured under US law, but even then only under specific preconditions (one of which was that books had to be manufactured in the United States to qualify for protection). The situation in Britain was more complicated and the legal framework – as well as its interpretation by authors and law professionals – more fluid. Unlike in the United States, the main criterion for copyright eligibility was not an author's citizenship but – at least during certain periods – the first publication of a title in Britain. The International Copyright Act passed in the House of Commons in 1838 in principle granted international copyright protection, but with the United States unwilling to enter a bilateral agreement, it failed to limit the unauthorised reprinting of American texts in Britain. The 1842 Copyright Amendment Act – for which Carlyle had campaigned together with a host of other eminent Victorians – established a domestic system that was more beneficial to British authors than previous legislation, but it protected neither British copyright holders in foreign markets nor foreign writers in Britain. The passage of international copyright acts in 1838 and again in 1844 was of use only to those foreign authors whose countries had entered a reciprocity agreement that guaranteed the protection of British copyright abroad.[19]

During much of the nineteenth century, the legal status of foreign intellectual property thus remained profoundly ambiguous on both sides of the Atlantic. Even where no compulsion was involved, however, American firms were often prepared to pay British authors in exchange for printing their books. There were several rationales behind such payments. They usually allowed printing from advance sheets and with explicit authorial sanction, which in turn rendered it likely that a publisher's *de facto* – if not *de jure* – property in a book would be recognised by domestic competitors. In the United States, a network of publishers complied with a system known as 'trade courtesy', a set of conventions that ensured that they acknowledged each other's privilege to print and sell works exclusively to which they could establish a recognisable claim.[20] But relying as it did on the shaky foundations of unwritten ethical codes, the American courtesy system was beginning to disintegrate in the late 1830s, just as the failed British International Copyright Act of 1838 led to a surge in unauthorised reprints of American books in Britain – at the precise point at which Carlyle and Emerson were entering the transatlantic marketplace. In this increasingly competitive climate, securing manuscript copies or advance sheets of a new work through flat payments or royalty arrangements became all the more relevant, giving publishers a temporal advantage over rivalling reprinters and thus helping them to secure a profit.

The volatile mid-century status of the foreign intellectual property claims of British and American writers gave crucial importance to the support of friends and patrons abroad. A British writer's American contact, for instance, could negotiate a courtesy arrangement with a local publisher, who would then bring out a book over whose textual and editorial decisions at least a moderate degree of authorial control could be exerted and whose publication could be expected to yield at least some form of payment. A British friend could do the same for an American author, endorse a text as worthy of the reader's attention or alternatively certify the fact that the edition in question was an authorised one. As I show in greater detail in Chapters 3 and 4, Carlyle and Emerson extensively engaged in such kinds of activity on each other's behalf. What began on a relatively modest scale soon developed into a complex set of endeavours that came to involve accounts with various publishers and that entailed developing innovative strategies for warding off unauthorised reprinters. Emerson provided vital help with the publication of Carlyle's works in the United States at a time when Carlyle himself was struggling to find publishing opportunities in England (for years he had failed to convince a British publisher to take on *Sartor Resartus* and it would be a Boston firm that first collected his early periodical essays in book form). As his Unitarian critic Andrews Norton had noted, Carlyle in the late 1830s could boast of 'a degree of fame' in the United States 'disproportioned to what he enjoy[ed] at home' (1992: 34). His initial failure in the English market made him turn towards alternative audiences and contemplate seeking his own sphere of influence elsewhere, on the provincial outskirts of Anglo-American literary space. As I show in Chapter 6, Carlyle habitually contrasted his American 'fame' with a misrecognition 'at home' and drew much of his claim to the authority of an avant-garde prophet from this 'disproportioned' reception abroad. Moving in a range of 'authorial economies' (Jackson 2008) that, in addition to sales figures, revolved around social capital and critical recognition, Emerson negotiated agreements with publishers in New York, Boston and Philadelphia that guaranteed Carlyle a share of the profits generated by the sales of American editions of his writings. Emerson advanced publication costs, wrote advertising statements and even reviewed some of the editions he himself had seen through the press. By the early 1840s, Carlyle had become indebted to him in financial terms as much as in other currencies (not least the symbolic value of getting his name and reputation spread abroad, which eventually made British publishers pay attention to his potential success with readers). Carlyle responded to Emerson's support through helping to circulate his writings in England and through supporting the London publication of his two volumes of *Essays* in the early 1840s. He supplied prefaces in which he offered his own critical authority to market Emerson's books and he collaborated with his friend's English publisher to determine the transatlantic reach of Victorian copyright law.

To retrace these complex textual, economic and legal interactions, Chapters 3 and 4 of this book employ what McGettigan has described as 'a layered book history' that 'integrat[es] attention to publishing archives, material texts, and literary language' (2017b: 730). Nineteenth-century transatlantic reprinting and textual dissemination generated a cultural disposition that found expression in the physical appearance and paratextual framing of editions as much as in the rhetoric that authors, publishers and reviewers employed to imagine the cultural geography in which they were moving. When Carlyle, for instance, was speaking of 'the republication of books in that Transoceanic England, New and improved Edition of England' (*CEC* 180), he used the marketing language of the book trade to comment on transatlantic relations more generally, acknowledging American claims to cultural novelty while at the same time highlighting their British origins through an image of textual genealogy and bibliographical dependence. Carlyle's and Emerson's transatlantic publishing illustrates the subtle ways in which the material aspects of the Anglo-American marketplace and the content of the texts circulated in it speak to one another. Emerson's prefatory remarks to the first American edition of *Sartor Resartus*, for example, mirror the rhetoric of the book's fictional editorial persona, and his complaint, in the essay 'The Young American' (1844), that the United States was inundated with English books was ironically undercut when the text itself was beginning to flood the British market in the form of a cheap unauthorised pamphlet reprint.

Where the experience of seeing their work pirated abroad signalled a loss of authorial control, British and American writers such as Carlyle and Emerson were seeking to regain authority over their texts and the modalities of their material circulation. As market participants they partly had to relinquish authority to other actors in the field (publishers, fellow authors, reviewers) when it came to printing and selling their books in an international context. Contributing to the making of their reputations, transatlantic publishing was, at the same time, constantly accompanied by struggles to assert their legal authority as literary creators. To ask how nineteenth-century writers navigated the Anglo-American literary marketplace is to suggest that we need to think of them not merely as authors, but as assuming a number of additional roles – that of the literary agent negotiating business agreements, that of the marketing expert whetting an appetite for new literary products, that of the editor proofreading galleys and that of the critic reviewing recent publications. Reprinting, in other words, did not so much do away with authorial agency as it reconfigured and diversified the contours of literary authorship. Looking at how the transatlantic market turned writers into professionally embedded authors thus goes beyond simply thinking of them as the disenfranchised casualties of the reprint trade. Commonly described as subject to decontextualisation, reformatting and decentralised dissemination, writing in much recent scholarship on reprinting has tended to take precedence over authors, who often figure as the hapless victims of impersonal market structures that extend far beyond single individuals. Where reprinting is read as a practice that 'disrupted the connections of books as human transmissions', publication almost inevitably emerges 'as an independently signifying act' – independent, that is, from authors as historical agents and active participants in the publishing process (DeSpain 2014: 10; McGill 2003: 5). This book argues instead that we need to think more systematically about the strategies that authors developed to respond to an environment that threatened to render their authority as cultural producers obsolete. Paying attention to a broad range of print cultural discourses and practices – from the literary to the economic and the legal – reframes the figure of the mid-nineteenth-century Anglo-American author at the same time that it reorients questions of transatlantic authority away from an exclusively textual framework and towards a richer form of historical contextualisation.

Anglo-American Lecturing and Performative Charisma

If publishing was one way of acquiring and defending one's transatlantic cultural authority, another means for self-authorisation offered itself in the form of public lecturing, which by the 1830s had become a major new cultural arena on both sides of the Atlantic. Plans for organising educational events to provide popular instruction outside of the institutional confines of the academy had emerged in Britain towards the end of the eighteenth century. What was a well-established movement by the beginning of the second third of the following century had originally grown out of an effort to offer education to those without access to formal university training. The first so-called 'Mechanics' Institutes' opened in Glasgow and London in the early 1820s and contributed to an already existing metropolitan market for public lecturing that, in addition to natural science events, also provided a platform for the literary lectures of figures such as Coleridge and Hazlitt at venues like the Royal and the Surrey Institutions (which had been founded in 1799 and 1808, respectively). The campaigning that had led to the establishment of such institutions in Britain soon resulted in the emergence of similar structures in the United States, where the culture of public lecturing thrived in the context of what became known as the 'lyceum' movement.[21] Like the respective national book markets, the British and American lecture systems were structurally intertwined. Speakers from both countries frequently crossed the ocean and their topics of choice often had a transatlantic touch. Figures as diverse as Dickens, Douglass, Stowe and Oscar Wilde could count on their lectures and readings being reported by both the British and the American press, which often engaged in a practice of mutual reprinting that circulated performances among a geographically dispersed set of readers, whose numbers often far exceeded the size of live audiences.

In addition to paying attention to print culture, this book sheds light on such transatlantic dimensions of lecturing as well as on specifically Anglo-American manifestations of oratorical authority. Over the past ten years, scholarship has begun to take into account the fact that many nineteenth-century authors were part of a culture of public performance that brought them into contact with the different sections of a larger transatlantic audience. Amanda Adams, for example, has argued that authorship and authority had to be increasingly embodied on the lecture stage where a rapidly expanding print industry was physically and symbolically distancing authors from their readers. The public appearances of British and American lecturers, she emphasises, 'depended on a culture . . . that saw the popular lecture as a central part of the international literary world' (2014: 9). To lecturers themselves this wider sense of belonging came alive through the very logistics of the system in which they were moving. With travel to different parts of one's own country or across the Atlantic as a key element of the profession, lecturing could create a feeling of geographical dislocation that allowed touring intellectuals to adopt a defamiliarised perspective on the social and cultural phenomena around them. Emerson's activity as a lecturer, for example, led him to travel widely across both the United States and Great Britain, and Carlyle's plans to lecture in New England – though never realised – at least suggested to him the possibility of a change of place. Encouraging him to make good on his promise of an American tour, Emerson assured Carlyle that 'the view of Britain' was 'excellent from New England' (*CEC* 283).

The transatlantic lecture circuit invited speakers to imagine a range of different audiences and thus to detach themselves, if only temporarily, from their own national point of view. Historians of nineteenth-century lecture culture have often tended to emphasise the opposite, however. Angela Ray, for instance, describes the American lyceum as an institutional space 'in which people explicitly called selfhood or nationhood into being' rather than into question (2005: 7). Public lecturing, in her analysis, enabled a discursive creation of national identity that in turn allowed audiences to experience the nation collectively. Adams and others have more recently challenged such accounts. Tom F. Wright, for example, contends that lecturing was not only, as Ray had argued, 'a medium that was helping to unify an emerging national public', but just as importantly 'a common discursive space in which speakers and audiences could contemplate the ambivalent relationship' between their own nation and 'the world beyond its borders' (2013: 2). The lyceum, Wright points out, 'was as much about looking outward as inward' (ibid.).[22]

If transatlantic lecturing invited national self-assertion and cosmopolitan detachment at the same time, the special relationship between Britain and the United States rendered the seemingly self-evident distinction between nation and globe – and between nationalism and cosmopolitanism as forms of attachment to either the one or the other – difficult to maintain. Widening one's perspective to take into view what lay across the Atlantic certainly was a form of 'looking outward', but it was at the same time a way of looking 'inward' not only in a nationally self-affirmative sense but also insofar as nineteenth-century lecturers often imagined Britain and the United States as two halves of the same unified transatlantic 'nation' – a space that, while extending across the globe, had its own sense of inwardness and cultural coherence. In the nineteenth-century lecture hall, the adoption of an Anglo-American perspective was thus a cosmopolitan enterprise as much as it was a transatlantic extension of the logic of nationhood. Hence Carlyle, for example, could be a faithful disciple of Goethe in subscribing to the idea of a world literary universalism and at the same time suggest that Britain and the United States formed a single 'Transatlantic Saxon Nation' marked by a specific set of shared ethnic and cultural characteristics (*CE* 29: 179). The mindset to which transatlantic lecturing gave rise thus occupies an intermediary position between the national and the cosmopolitan conceptualisations of culture that Ray and Wright see as clashing on the lecture platform (just as the complex reality of transatlantic reprinting destabilised the distinction between what Casanova calls 'national' and 'international' writers). Relying for its success on the shared symbolic repertoires of a unified public sphere, the transatlantic lecture circuit provided an important institutional framework for the rhetorical affirmation of the kind of Anglo-American identity that lecturers such as Carlyle and Emerson were routinely invoking in print and on stage.

As many writers quickly realised once they had entered the arena of public speaking, lecturing granted them access to audiences on both sides of the Atlantic. It provided a way of bolstering their domestic reputation through demonstrating the extent of foreign demand for their work and thus often formed a crucial component of claims to transatlantic cultural authority. Performances on the lecture stage contributed to the production of this kind of legitimacy in a number of different ways. Historian Donald Scott has pointed towards key factors through which the institution of the lyceum itself managed to establish its status as a culturally relevant site of public debate – a status from which lecturers could draw a corresponding degree of authority. The secret, Scott observes, lay in a composite strategy that combined a recourse to 'traditional sources of intellectual authority' – those of more well-established forms of public speech such as political and religious oratory – with the mobilisation of 'new styles of democratic legitimacy' which manifested themselves in attempts at securing positive newspaper coverage or championing the ideal of the participatory character of the public lecture (1983: 298–9). What Scott and others have explored to a lesser extent is the role the physical dimension of lecturing played in the institution's claim to relevance – something that comes into clearer focus, for example, with the help of sociologist Jeffrey Alexander's (2011) analysis of the relationship between performance and power. Authority, from this point of view, is something that has to be continuously reaffirmed in order to create a sense of its own legitimacy. Alexander's communicative approach to public speaking invites us to think about the institutional and geographical settings in which transatlantic lecture performances took place, but also to consider the broader cultural–symbolic backgrounds out of which their linguistic and semiotic repertoires emerged.

In contrast to the often well-documented modern examples of social performance that Alexander uses as case studies, an analysis of nineteenth-century lecturing has to rely on a more limited amount and a smaller variety of historical sources. In many cases the original lecture texts themselves do not survive and contemporary newspaper coverage often forms the main source for the reconstruction of the content of a lecture, the speaker's performance and the reaction of the audience. Disseminating summaries of lectures at the same time that they were commenting on their content and delivery, lecture reports are situated at the intersection of what Alexander terms 'distributive' and 'hermeneutical' forms of 'social power' (2011: 67–8): firmly enmeshed in the cultural dynamics of the contemporary lecture system, they have to be carefully contextualised to determine what was said where, to whom and with what effect.[23] What the mixed mediality of the genre demonstrates is that print and performance were mutually interdependent. To Carlyle and Emerson, as for many of their writer–lecturer contemporaries, the boundaries between oral performance and printed text were often permeable. Transcriptions of their lectures were frequently printed in contemporary newspapers and the argument of major books such as *On Heroes* and *Representative Men* had first been aired on the lecture platform. The transatlantic lecture circuit in more than one way intersected with transatlantic print culture, as did the respective authorising mechanisms to which both media gave rise. This contiguity of speech and print allowed not only mainstream writers to build their authority as public figures; as Wright (2017: 49–80) and Hannah-Rose Murray (2020) have recently demonstrated, it was also a crucial component in the Victorian reception of African American abolitionist orators such as Douglass, Moses Roper and William Wells Brown, whose forays into the arena of public speech coincided with those of many of their white contemporaries (some of whom resented such competition, as I demonstrate in Chapter 6).

In terms of the depth and extent of his own involvement, Carlyle was more persistently concerned with the book market. He delivered lectures in his early forties but effectively abandoned the profession once his financial situation was beginning to improve, thanks in large part to the success of his books in the United States.[24] Emerson, by contrast, pursued a lecturing career that, launched upon his farewell to the ministry in the early 1830s, lasted for nearly half a century. He delivered an estimated 1,500 lectures between 1833 and his death, and in the 1850s, at the climax of his career and popularity as a public speaker, read about seventy of them each year all across the United States (Wilson 1999: 78). A genuine transatlantic lecturing persona, Emerson spoke widely on English and American subjects and was one among many mid- and late-nineteenth-century American writers and intellectuals who crossed the ocean to lecture in Britain. A considerable part of his second stay in Europe in 1847–8 was dedicated to appearances on the lecture stage, first in northern England and Scotland, and later in London. Consolidating his reputation both at home and abroad, the British tour secured a wide transatlantic coverage of his lectures in the years to come. Although Carlyle's experience as a performer on stage was more limited, public speaking had transatlantic implications for him as well. Even if, unlike Emerson, he never made the transatlantic passage, the prospect of American lecturing was almost constantly on his mind during the 1830s, when the promise of a successful tour abroad served as a welcome antidote to what he perceived to be the unjust neglect of his writings at home.[25]

Through performances before packed auditoriums and the subsequent dissemination of printed lecture reports, Carlyle and Emerson reached large audiences and amplified the reputations they had begun to build with books like *Sartor Resartus* or *Nature* (whose initial print runs guaranteed only a limited circulation). For both of them, lecturing before crowds of eager listeners offered a way of satisfying 'a profound desire for relevance' (Field 2001: 485) – and it illustrated such public recognition with a somatic immediacy that the medium of print lacked. The lecture experience, to Carlyle and Emerson, was a means of reassuring themselves that they were in command of an audience that acknowledged their authority as public intellectuals. While the main allure of lecturing, at least initially, was its ability to secure a reliable income at a time when their books still largely failed to do so, it was of equal importance in that it created a sense of rhetorical empowerment – the 'feeling of superiority over [an] audience' that Carlyle described as among the main incentives for taking to the stage (*CEC* 274).

Both urged by their families to enter the ministry, Carlyle and Emerson were quick to realise that the secular pulpit they chose instead constituted an alternative source of legitimacy. Lecturing, Thomas Augst has pointed out, was a practice that betokened 'not the debasement of intellectual authority but rather its popularization for a mass audience' (2003: 129). It formed an institutional space that, despite its commercial and secular character, was pervaded by a residual imagery of oracular wisdom, prophetic insight and charismatic power. 'I preach in the Lecture-Room', Emerson wrote to Carlyle in 1837, referring to the lecture auditorium elsewhere as 'the true church of today' (*CEC* 171; *JMN* 7: 277). When Carlyle was contemplating his potential lecture tour of the United States, he similarly imagined himself as speaking from a 'Pulpit', 'preaching far and wide' to the American public (*CEC* 134, 275) – cultivating in his lecturing style a prophetic 'fire of zeal and conviction' that contemporary commentators described as a key component of his rhetorical success (Anon. 1838b: 4).[26] What such remarks about the 'translated religiosity' (Wright 2020: 215) of nineteenth-century lecturing illustrate is that the credibility of professional lecturers depended on demonstrating the proximity between themselves and the power of their religious precursors, the authority of the prophet (in its 'intense' charismatic form) or that of the preacher (in its 'attenuated' institutionalised form).[27]

Nineteenth-century commentators largely agreed that this quasi-religious form of literary authority could more easily be created in the context of an oral performance culture than through the mediation of print, a technique of communication that imposed a temporal and geographical distance between speakers and their audiences. Summarising 'The American Lecture-System' for the British *Macmillan's Magazine* in 1868, Thomas Wentworth Higginson, for example, contrasted oratory and print by emphasising that, while lacking sufficient literariness, 'speech sometimes yields such moments of inspiration as make all writing seem cold' (1868: 56). Nevertheless, what appears to be more significant than such diagnoses of an inherent difference between speaking and writing is the extent to which nineteenth-century author–lecturers attempted to bridge the gap between the two media forms in order to translate into print the ecstasy of extemporaneous 'inspiration' and the oratorical authority which it generated. Acutely aware of their own dependence on publication and material dissemination, Carlyle and Emerson sought stylistically to replicate the rhythms and inflections of natural speech in order to carry over the immediacy of the oral statement into the medium of print. In their published writings, they were striving hard to preserve the rhetorical flexibility and somatic presence they had experienced in the transatlantic lecture hall.

Scope and Structure

Prolific authors popular with contemporary readers and real or virtual lecture audiences on both sides of the Atlantic, Carlyle and Emerson provide a glimpse into a cultural formation that transcends both themselves and their writings. This book uses their relationship to reflect on broader questions in the history of transatlantic intellectual contact and to think more generally about nineteenth-century notions of cultural authority. My approach in the following six chapters and the Epilogue is marked by a thematic and methodological pluralism. Neither purely philological nor purely sociological nor purely book historical, *Carlyle, Emerson and the Transatlantic Uses of Authority* seeks to illuminate nineteenth-century transatlantic literary culture through attending to a range of different media environments (from texts to print to performance) and through employing a synthesis of different methodologies (including archival reconstruction and critical close reading). Drawing on recent work in transatlantic literary and cultural history to locate textual production at the intersection of institutional spheres and professional networks, this book argues for a new understanding of nineteenth-century Anglo-American writing and public speaking as cultural practices shaped by a complex combination of literary, political, legal and economic conceptualisations of authority. What follows not only contributes to the fields of Carlyle and Emerson scholarship, but also intervenes in larger debates about race and national identity, print culture and the public sphere as well as the histories of transatlantic authorship and transnational literary exchange.

My argument falls into three parts, each of which comprises two chapters. Part I, 'Anglo-American Literary and Cultural Identities', provides a starting point for my subsequent readings by situating transatlantic writing in a broader historical context. It covers British and American debates about identity and history that in turn form the background for my discussion of print and performance in Chapters 3 to 6. Chapter 1 opens with an analysis of the function of ascriptions of racial and national identity in Carlyle's and Emerson's early transatlantic reception before turning to an investigation of nineteenth-century racialist rhetoric more generally. Carlyle's and Emerson's critics – New England Unitarians and New York Young Americans as much as Tory intellectuals and Victorian novelists – tended to exclude them from membership of the Anglo-American literary sphere while their supporters resorted to the rhetoric of race to make a case for their reintegration. Carlyle and Emerson themselves reflected extensively on the question of racial identity and the chapter reads the texts in which they did so – from Carlyle's early *Lectures on the History of Literature* to Emerson's later *English Traits* – against the backdrop of a larger mid-century Anglo-American discourse of Anglo-Saxon history and culture. My argument throughout the chapter – and throughout the book as a whole – is that assertions and denials of biological kinship and cultural belonging played a crucial role in the complex contemporary debate about transatlantic authority.

This debate surfaced in contemporary writing about race and national identity, but it also appeared prominently in literary criticism and literary historiography. Chapter 2 surveys Carlyle's and Emerson's lectures, essays and occasional writings concerned with the relationship between literature and nationality to demonstrate that – drawing on a handful of (near-)contemporary German and French authors such as Johann Gottfried Herder, Friedrich Schlegel, Germaine de Staël and Victor Cousin – the two positioned themselves at the crossroads of cultural nationalism and literary cosmopolitanism. They read English literature as an index to national and racial identity and argued that its history could illuminate the past, present and future of the Anglo-American relationship. Conceptualising continuity and change in literary history in different terms, however, they ended up developing conflicting interpretations of what Weber describes as the authority of tradition. Where Carlyle's narrative emphasised the past achievement and future global dominance of metropolitan writing, Emerson tended to invest in the authority of the English canon to locate the future of a specifically Anglo-American tradition in the cultural periphery.

Such self-authorisation was informed by the larger concepts of identity and heritage analysed in Chapter 1, but it emerged in the concrete historical settings at the centre of the four chapters that form Parts II and III of the book – chapters which move from my previous discussion of the guiding discourses of transatlantic literary culture to the institutional environments in which these manifested themselves. Part II, 'Authority and Authorisation in the Anglo-American Print Market', retraces the contemporary printing, dissemination and reception of Carlyle's writings in the United States and of Emerson's writings in Britain, drawing extensively on original archival research and using a large variety of sources that include correspondence, publishers' accounts and legal documents. Chapter 3 focuses on the American publication of Carlyle's books from *Sartor Resartus* to *Oliver Cromwell's Letters and Speeches* (1845) and draws attention to the economic and symbolic contexts of these editions. Emerson was heavily involved in these print transactions as a literary agent, bookseller, editor and critic. Increasingly confronted with the negative effects of a thriving trade in unauthorised reprints, he and Carlyle set out to protect the latter's overseas income through experimenting with economic strategies that ranged from the circulation of manuscript copies to the transatlantic import and export of whole print runs. The chapter highlights Carlyle's efforts to achieve American recognition of British writers' copyright claims and demonstrates how in the 1840s he and Emerson succeeded in securing agreements with American publishers despite the absence of such transatlantic legal authority.

Although he was aware of the economic and reputational potential that the Anglo-American print world offered, it took Emerson until the early 1840s to develop an interest in the transatlantic publication of his own works. Chapter 4 provides an account of British editions of his writings published during that decade. Carlyle's presence in these books – through his prefaces as well as through the ubiquity of his name on title pages and in contemporary reviews – was a crucial factor in the image that publishing gave Emerson among his contemporary British readers. The chapter demonstrates that this exemplifies a larger tendency in mid-century British and American criticism to think of reprinting as an index to the distribution of transatlantic cultural authority. Where English commentators found that Emerson was little more than a 'Yankee pocket edition of Carlyle' (Gilfillan 1848: 22), their American colleagues discovered in his success abroad evidence of a shifting balance of power. Emerson's books had been pirated in England since the late 1830s, but he began to benefit financially from this interest in his writing only when Carlyle's London publisher James Fraser issued an authorised edition of *Essays: First Series* in 1841. Emerson sought to emancipate himself from Carlyle when he decided to sell his subsequent books through the firm of John Chapman, but he enlisted Carlyle in his attempt to use international copyright legislation to rebuild the cultural and economic authority of literary authorship.

The two chapters that comprise Part III of the book ('Performing Nationhood on the Transatlantic Lecture Circuit') proceed from print to public speech and move from Carlyle's and Emerson's experience with the transatlantic book market to their careers as lecturers. Highlighting the close material links between lecturing and publishing (from journalistic coverage of individual events to book versions of lecture courses), I illustrate that nineteenth-century British and American writers tended to think of oral performance as offering a more direct form of access to cultural authority. My interest here is in how Carlyle and Emerson experimented with the opportunities that the institutional framework of the public lecture provided, in how it established their authority as key players in the Anglo-American literary sphere and in how they themselves reflected on public speech as a transatlantic cultural phenomenon. Chapter 5 focuses on Emerson and opens with a discussion of his early lectures on English and American topics. In his courses on 'English Literature' (1835–6) and 'New England' (1843–4), he developed a distinctive rhetoric for addressing questions of transatlantic authority that were raised by a discussion of British tradition and American identity (topics discussed at greater length in Chapters 1 and 2). This early experience served him well during his British lecture tour of 1847–8, when he confronted transatlantic audiences whom newspaper coverage had primed to see in him 'the philosopher of America' (Anon. 1847h: 5). Upon his return to the United States, Emerson lectured extensively on transatlantic topics and eventually developed his travel notes into the 1856 *English Traits*, a book whose cultural and intermedial complexities I dissect in the final section of the chapter. My key contention here is that, across his career-long engagement with Anglo-American topics on the lecture stage, Emerson capitalised on the inherent characteristics of performance (the fugitive nature of live deliveries and the changing composition of audiences) to experiment with a diplomatic voice that allowed him to cater to British and American sentiments at the same time.

Like Emerson, Carlyle was interested in the medium of the public lecture and in the opportunities it promised for reaching out to a transatlantic audience. Building on the previous chapter's discussion of transatlantic speaking and performative authority, Chapter 6 concentrates on Carlyle's early activity as a lecturer, as well as on his later commentary on the relationship between intellectual labour and the public sphere. Carlyle consistently associated the lecturing profession with the charismatic authority of the religious prophet and it was this imagery that informed his plans for a lecture tour of the United States in the 1830s. When he eventually assumed the secular 'pulpit' of the lecture platform in London towards the end of the decade, his performances not only featured substantial transatlantic commentary but also became objects of scrutiny for American newspapers, which either reprinted British reports of the lectures or featured material from their own correspondents. Where Emerson steadily intensified his commitment to the professional identity of the transatlantic lecturer, Carlyle gradually turned away from his earlier enthusiasm about the charismatic authority public speaking afforded the contemporary author. Reading some of his most controversial writings, including the 'Occasional Discourse on the Negro Question' and *Latter-Day Pamphlets* (1850), I argue that Carlyle's critique of eloquence ultimately derived from his growing concern about the waning authority of the writer as a public intellectual – a concern that grew out of his diagnosis of the political and cultural impact of American democracy, which in turn sparked off an extended debate among his transatlantic readers.

Most of my discussion in these chapters focuses on the period between the early 1830s and the late 1850s, the climactic years both of Carlyle and Emerson's friendship and of their correspondence. It was this quarter-century that witnessed their most extended engagement with literary subjects and the busiest years of their careers as transatlantically published writers and lecturers. Returning to this period at several points, the Epilogue brings together the key themes of the book and shows how discourses of racial identity and cultural history, as well as the institutional spaces of print and lecturing, developed in the final decades of the nineteenth century. The American Civil War and its aftermath had a lasting effect on the transatlantic special relationship, not least because the conflict called previous ideas of Anglo-American authority into question and forced writers to re-evaluate their roles and responsibilities as intellectuals addressing broader political concerns. Such transformations can be gauged from Carlyle's and Emerson's divergent responses to the war as well as from the ways in which these resonated with contemporary audiences on both sides of the Atlantic. That the war ultimately strengthened rather than severed literary and cultural ties between Britain and the United States becomes evident in the publication of a diverse range of print products – posthumous editions, biographical accounts and literary histories – that authorised the two writers as icons of transatlantic contact and exchange.

Notes

1. By the time such diagnoses of transatlantic influence became mainstream, Coleridge's writings had, of course, themselves been identified as heavily intertextual, with critics such as Thomas De Quincey and James Frederick Ferrier accusing him of plagiarising the work of the German idealist Schelling, among others (see Mazzeo 2007: 17–48 and Vardy 2010: 26–44, 64–80 on this debate and its repercussions). The charge of plagiarism and the stigma of imitation formed part of the same late-Romantic distinction between originality and epigonality, a complex binary that, conceptually and semantically, was even more highly charged when it involved writers of different national and linguistic backgrounds.

2. In the 1920s, Frank T. Thompson, for instance, set out 'to determine ... the net result of Carlyle's influence upon Emerson' (1927: 438). Criticising such financial rhetoric as 'a credit and debit calculus in matters of the mind' indicative of a shallow comparativism, René Wellek a generation later nevertheless similarly traced how German idealist terminology 'came to Emerson through ... Carlyle' (1970: 35; 1943: 49). David Greenham is among those who have more recently been speaking systematically of 'Carlyle's influence on Emerson' again (2012: 46). Investigating Emerson's debts to Coleridge, Samantha Harvey has proposed 'assimilative' borrowing as 'a new category of influence' to advance beyond prior narratives (2013: 9); yet her insistence that ideas become the subject of 'warping, reinterpreting, and renewing ... in new climates' (ibid., 2) ultimately remains tied to the organicist imagery of influence that surfaces in nineteenth-century writers like Milnes (who imagined Emerson as an American 'plant' sprung from Carlyle's English 'seed') or George Eliot (who described Carlyle in similar terms as 'an oak' whose 'acorns have sown a forest' [1992: 187]).
3. The often normative (post-)Romantic language of influence obviously needs to be distinguished from more descriptively oriented (post-)structuralist models of intertextuality (as developed by Julia Kristeva, Gérard Genette and others), which are concerned with determining the nature of the relationship between different texts (from citation and allusion to pastiche and parody) (see Clayton and Rothstein 1991 and Orr 2003). While the latter approach has been productively applied to the poetics and compositional practices of nineteenth-century writers (see, for example, Stievermann 2007) or become expanded into larger reflections about language, genre and style (a perspective whose analytical potential Manning's own work eloquently illustrates [see Manning 2005 and 2013]), my point here is that textualist methodologies are often not fully attuned to the historical realities and authorial motivations that lie behind textual exchanges – aspects that come into clearer focus in historicist or cultural–sociological readings.
4. No substantial analysis of the Carlyle–Emerson relationship has appeared since Benjamin Lease's Emerson-centred account in his *Anglo-American Encounters: England and the Rise of American Literature* (1981: 178–207), a discussion that provides little more than a summary of biographical facts. In her wide-ranging history of the Transcendentalist movement, Barbara Packer reconstructs Carlyle's impact on Emerson and his circle, but – much like Harris's and Lease's – her narrative largely concentrates on the history of ideas rather than on how those ideas were travelling (see her chapter on 'Carlyle and the Beginnings of American Transcendentalism' in 1995: 362–75).
5. For classic versions of this narrative, see Spencer 1957, Bloom 1973 and Weisbuch 1986.
6. There has also, of course, been a renewed interest in the Anglophone Atlantic (see Rezek 2015 and Shields 2016). For surveys of subfields and tendencies in transatlantic studies, see Armitage 2002, Rezek 2014 and Giles 2016.
7. My argument to that extent represents what Armitage describes as a 'trans-Atlantic' approach, a perspective that 'assumes the existence of nations' but operates with an analytical framework that 'joins states, nations, and regions within an oceanic

system' (2002: 20). Rezek, who calls this paradigm 'literature in English', speaks of a method of 'cross-cultural comparison' that seeks to shed light on an Anglophone cultural sphere which it sees as united by 'shared aesthetic qualities, common ideological investments, and transatlantic reading practices' (2014: 793).

8. For these three types of response, see, respectively: Miller 1964 and Bloom 1973; Dallal 2001 and Rowe 2003; Dimock 2001 and Buell 2003. See also Voelz 2010: 175–204 for a perceptive account of the disagreements between representatives of these different positions and Wider 2000 on Emerson's critical reception, more generally.
9. See Vanden Bossche 1991. The etymological and conceptual relationship between authority and authorship is retraced in more general terms in Pease 1995 and Donovan, Fjellestad and Lundén 2008. For a historically more specific argument about how Romantic writers such as Blake, Wordsworth and Coleridge legitimised themselves as literary authorities, see Riede 1991.
10. More recent research on aspects of nineteenth-century literary and cultural authority has begun to acknowledge the importance of a transatlantic analytical framework (see, for example, Williams 2006 and Leypoldt 2009 – studies that focus on figures such as Arnold and Whitman).
11. The discrepancy between Carlyle's limited interest in things American and Emerson's lifelong orientation towards European culture is a characteristic manifestation of nineteenth-century economies of transatlantic authority. As late as the 1880s, Henry James noted that the American writer '*must* deal, more or less, even if only by implication, with Europe: whereas no European is obliged to deal in the least with America' (1987: 214).
12. It was a 'profound reinvestment in the symbolic authority of England', Tamarkin argues, that indicated 'the loss of real authority for an empire . . . that could at best influence the imagination of the colonies it no longer ruled' (2008: xxiv). Writing about the aftermath of the Revolution, historian Peter J. Marshall likewise finds that 'transatlantic values survived the sundering of imperial links' (2012: 314). Earlier critical accounts had tended to stress that 'postcolonial' American writers (Buell 1992) were motivated by a desire to see the transatlantic authority of English culture 'erased' (Weisbuch 1999: 197). See Hanlon 2013 for a more recent argument about the coexistence of Anglophilia and Anglophobia in the antebellum United States.
13. In addition to these more specific applications, there has been an extended discussion about the general comparative implications of Bourdieu's work. For the outlines of an 'intercultural theory of the literary field', see Espagne and Werner 1994; for reflections on the location of the literary field 'between the national and the transnational', see Jurt 2009.
14. On the more general Romantic shift from 'letters' to 'literature', see Guillory 1993: 121–4 and Klancher 2000.
15. For discussions of Carlyle and Emerson against the background of nineteenth-century discourses of masculinity, see Sussman 1995: 16–72 and Leverenz 1989: 42–71, respectively.
16. This is of course not to suggest that nineteenth-century gender and authorship has been a neglected subject. For a classic discussion of conflicting images of 'female authority' in the eighteenth- and nineteenth-century novel, see Armstrong 1987:

28–58. The rise of the 'woman of letters' during the Victorian period is covered in Peterson 2009, and the gendered nature of literary celebrity during the latter half of the century in Easley 2011. DeSpain's (2014) and Rezek's (2015) studies of transatlantic reprinting and Adams's (2014) and Wright's (2017) work on nineteenth-century performance culture also feature important recent discussions of female figures.

17. Unpublished letter to Carlyle of 31 January 1841 (National Library of Scotland, Acc.7988).
18. A fervent advocate of international copyright, Putnam was deflecting British complaints of American literary piracy by arguing that the British themselves were engaged in transatlantic reprinting on a significant scale. Putnam was advancing his argument before the spectacular transatlantic success of Harriet Beecher Stowe's *Uncle Tom's Cabin* (1852), which sold an estimated one and a half million copies in Britain and its colonies within the first year of its original publication (see Altick 1998: 384 and St Clair 2004: 522). The reception of Stowe's book led contemporary commentators on both sides of the Atlantic to acknowledge that Smith's claim that American books were not read was not, or at least no longer, accurate (see Winship 2007: 367–8).
19. On nineteenth-century Anglo-American copyright regulations and the legal and political debates by which they were accompanied, see Barnes 1974, Seville 2006: 146–252, McGill 2003: 45–108 and Baldwin 2014.
20. On trade courtesy, see Tebbel 1972: 208–14, McVey 1975: 73–4 and Winship 1999: 101–2; see Spoo 2013: 13–64 for a comprehensive discussion of the practice as 'a coherent and elaborate system of informal property norms' (38).
21. In Britain, lecturing soon branched out from the Mechanics' Institutes to more clearly market-oriented forms of public speaking aimed at a socially more widely stratified audience. The American 'lyceum' underwent a similar transformation from a civic and educational enterprise into a more extensive commercial system. For histories of nineteenth-century American lecturing, see Bode 1968, Scott 1980 and Ray 2005; on British institutions and practices, see Hewitt 2002, Klancher 2013: 51–84 and Zimmerman 2019.
22. See Ray 2013 for a critical rejoinder to Wright's argument, which he develops in greater detail in his *Lecturing the Atlantic: Speech, Print and an Anglo-American Commons 1830–1870* (2017).
23. On the methodological challenges of reconstructing nineteenth-century lectures as historical performances, see Zimmerman 2019: 16–23; on lecture reports as sources, see Wright 2017: 6–7.
24. Carlyle gave seven lectures on 'German Literature' in 1837, followed by twelve more general sessions on the 'History of Literature' the year after, then six lectures on 'Revolutions of Modern Europe' in 1839 and, finally, in 1840, the series of six lectures that a year later were published as *On Heroes, Hero-Worship, and the Heroic in History*. Carlyle spoke mostly extemporaneously and no manuscripts for any of the first three cycles survive. There is newspaper coverage of the first and the third series and a comprehensive contemporary transcript of the 'History of Literature' course, published posthumously in 1892 (see *LHL*).

25. The relatively short period of time that Carlyle devoted to his engagement with the lecturing profession has led to a critical neglect of this aspect of his career. Among the handful of brief discussions of the contents and contexts of his lecturing, see Cumming 2004, Edwards 2013 and Wright 2020. There is abundant scholarship on Emerson as a lecturer. The more recent criticism has mainly focused on his lecturing persona and style, the reception of his lectures and his position in the context of mid-nineteenth-century lecture culture (see, for example, Augst 2003: 114–57, O'Neill 2008, Koch 2012 and Arbour 2013).
26. On the relation between religious and secular oratory in Emerson's lecturing, see Robinson 1982, Railton 1991: 23–49 and Warren 1999: 29–51, as well as my discussion of this aspect in Chapter 5 below. Ten years before Emerson's letter, Carlyle had used a similar type of imagery to identify 'the true Church' with 'the Guild of Authors' (*NTC* 263). When he declares that '[t]he grand Pulpit is now the Press' (ibid.), he authorises himself as speaking from that new print platform and, like Emerson, he conceptually conflates the media spheres of print and lecturing.
27. On the distinction between 'intense and concentrated' as opposed to 'attenuated and dispersed' types of charisma, see Shils 1972: 110–18. In drawing attention to the institutional background of nineteenth-century lecture culture and its valorisation of religiously inflected oratorical performance, my argument departs from the more traditional view of 'Victorian' figures such as Carlyle and Emerson as secularised writers that illustrate a 'shift of literary authority . . . from the romantic prophet-bard to the . . . man of letters' (Riede 1989: 88) or that point towards a connection between 'the disenchantment of inherited forms of vocational prestige (the mysteries of the priesthood or medicine) and the consecration of a new form of cultural authority' (Salmon 2013: 13). An environment in which print professionalism met pulpit prophecy, mid-century lecturing complicates such straightforward narratives of secularisation because it bolstered a type of authority that effectively combined emergent and residual elements.

Part I

Anglo-American Literary and Cultural Identities

I

RACE AND NATIONHOOD IN THE MID-NINETEENTH-CENTURY TRANSATLANTIC FIELD

In a disparaging review essay he contributed to his own *Select Journal of Foreign Periodical Literature* in 1833, Harvard theologian Andrews Norton turned against Carlyle and his purportedly harmful New England influence in terms that foreshadowed those of his later critique of Emerson and the American Transcendentalists. The occasion for the piece was a group of texts commemorating the recently deceased Johann Wolfgang Goethe, whose literary achievements Norton considered questionable at best (*Elective Affinities* to him was 'a cold, disgusting story of complicated adultery', *The Sorrows of Young Werther* 'a book too silly to cry over' [1833: 253]). Among the eulogies Norton was reviewing for the *Select Journal* were two unsigned essays Carlyle had written in the summer of 1832. Norton summarises one of these as 'an apotheosis . . . of the German poet and novelist' and suggests – on the sole basis of stylistic evidence – that it could only have been written 'by a countryman of his [Goethe's] own' (ibid., 250). The premise behind this assumption was that writing alone could be a sufficient indicator of a writer's nationality. Preferring the virtues of 'English taste' over the excesses of continental poetics, Norton forges a distinctly Anglo-American alliance against the supposed failings of the Goethean 'art of the new school' when he contends that '[t]he writer of the two articles belongs to a school of which we have few examples in England or our own country, but the disciples of which are numerous on the continent of Europe and especially in Germany' (ibid., 260–1). Positing two separate transnational cultural spheres, each internally unified while at the same time sharply demarcated from the other, Norton locates himself safely within the borders of the Anglo-American republic of letters that his transatlantically inclusive 'we' invokes.[1] 'The New School in Literature and Religion', Norton's 1838 refutation of Emerson's Harvard Divinity School Address, maps much of the same literary territory. With Carlyle at this point no longer anonymous in the United States, Norton mentions his name explicitly and qualifies it with the epithet 'hyper-Germanized Englishman' (1992: 33). That a British writer was, after all, capable of reproducing 'the crabbed and disgusting obscurity' (ibid.) of the continental school – as Norton was suggesting in the 1838 text – hardly affected his Anglo-American worldview, however. Carlyle, to him, had simply de-Anglicised himself: while still nominally an 'Englishman', his adoption of a 'hyper-Germanized' style and diction had denaturalised and thus expelled him from the Anglo-American literary sphere.

This chapter explores such ascriptions or denials of nationality and reconstructs how they served nineteenth-century commentators to characterise British and American writers. I am equally concerned with how authors such as Carlyle and Emerson themselves employed the language of ethnic identity to make sense of Anglo-American culture and their place in it. The first and second sections of the chapter centre on the role of style, nationality and ethnicity in the history of Carlyle's and Emerson's early transatlantic reception. My focus here is on how references to the national identity of authors operated to locate them either within the purview or beyond the fringes of the Anglo-American literary field. Though disagreeing in their verdicts, both detractors and supporters of Carlyle and Emerson were moving within a standard nineteenth-century framework that linked literary authorship to questions of racial, cultural or national identity. Individual aspects of this framework are highlighted in greater detail in the chapter's third and fourth sections – the rhetoric of race, in particular, which supplied a pervasive language for signalling belonging or exclusion. I here proceed from an analysis of racialist discourse in the first half of the nineteenth century more generally, drawing attention to a widespread contemporary terminological conflation of race and nation, and focusing more specifically on what racially inflected writing at mid-century had to say about the relationship between Britain and the United States. I then turn to the ways in which Carlyle and Emerson themselves were writing from within this framework, arguing that their positions as peripheral figures (Carlyle as Anglicised Scot, Emerson as self-fashioned North American Anglo-Saxon) shaped their contributions to the overall debate, but also that these contributions can be read as attempts at self-inscription into the Anglo-American public sphere. The moments of ethnolinguistic and ethnonational boundary drawing that we witness in Carlyle's and Emerson's transatlantic reception show how 'individual and collective actors behave strategically' to consolidate their own position and define identity to their own advantage (Wimmer 2013: 205). The samples of nineteenth-century

British and American racialist writing analysed in this chapter illustrate how fundamentally cultural authority in the transatlantic context was related to categories of national and racial difference, and how profoundly membership in a biologically, linguistically and culturally defined community mattered to those moving within – as well as to those seeking admission to – the Anglophone literary field during the second third of the century.

CRITICAL STEREOTYPES: NATIONALITY AND STYLE

Like many of his contemporaries, Norton linked national identity to questions of style and expression. Hence the suggestion, in 'The New School', that Carlyle's denaturalisation was evidenced by 'an over-excited and *convulsionary* style' whose 'anomalous combinations' 'abus[e]' what Norton described as a transatlantically shared 'common language' (1992: 34). What Norton implied was that Carlyle's injection of Germanic expressions into the English language had resulted in a hybridised dialect that unhealthily destabilised the difference between the two. This kind of argument illustrates what Eric Hobsbawm has described as 'philological nationalism', an 'insistence on the linguistic purity of the national vocabulary' that serves to maintain precisely those boundaries that Carlyle's 'anomalous' style, from Norton's point of view, had rendered dangerously permeable (1990: 56). Languages, Hobsbawm writes, work 'as criteria of in-group membership' (ibid., 51), and they do so here as well, insofar as Carlyle's style leads Norton to exclude him from the Anglo-American literary field.[2] Where Hobsbawm thinks of language as a tool used to define the borders that differentiate national communities from one another, what turned the English language into a special case was that it extended beyond a single nation-state. The forms of inclusion and exclusion that the discourse of philological nationalism entailed with nineteenth-century British and American writers was thus one that identified the United States as part of a transatlantic national formation (an Anglo-American community that existed across the boundaries of two separate modern nation-states).

The type of criticism that Norton advanced against Carlyle in 1830s New England was analogous to that voiced by commentators on the other side of the Atlantic. Aesthetic and critical vocabularies were transatlantically synchronising not only, as Norton was suggesting, between the continental 'new school' and its American followers, but also between the self-appointed guardians of 'English taste' in London, Edinburgh and Boston. Reviewing Carlyle's *The French Revolution* (1837) for the London *Athenæum*, Sydney Owenson, Lady Morgan, a successful novelist of Irish descent, set out 'to protest against all and sundry attempts to engraft the idiom of Germany into the king's English' (1971: 47). Mixing the botanical imagery of hybridisation with a sartorial image that could have come straight from Carlyle himself, she implicitly agreed with Norton that, '[w]ith respect to language', 'every nation must be permitted to "speak for itself"' since 'foreign grammatical idioms are ever ill-assorted patches, which disfigure, and cannot adorn, the cloth to which they are appended' (ibid., 48). In a largely positive assessment of *The French Revolution* for the London *Times*, William Makepeace Thackeray complained of its 'Germanisms and Latinisms', advising 'the admirers of simple Addisonian English' to steer clear of Carlyle's book (1971: 69). The *Edinburgh Review* – once a forum for Carlyle's essays on German literature and culture – employed a rhetoric of denaturalisation that closely matched Norton's. Its reviewer's strong 'dislike' for Carlyle's 'bastard English' (Merivale 1840: 412) brought the racialist undercurrent of Owenson's imagery of botanical cross-breeding (her attack on 'the pedantry of engrafting on any language foreign modes of expression' [1971: 48]) even closer to the surface. Though located at the opposite end of the political spectrum, the Tory *Quarterly Review* displayed a similar distaste for Carlyle's style, voicing its anxieties about the potentially harmful effects of his writing on the nature and integrity of English national character. Revisiting almost the entirety of his literary output of the 1820s and 1830s, William Henry Sewell, an Anglican clergyman with Tractarian sympathies, concluded that Carlyle's tendency to 'import . . . from Germany' revealed his fundamentally 'un-English' character (1840: 455). '[W]hat will become of our "pure well of English undefiled"', Sewell wondered, 'if our graver literature is infected with German' (ibid.)? Where Thackeray had invoked the Augustan Addison as the tutelary saint of a quintessentially English linguistic identity, Sewell resorted to Spenserian language to express his concerns about the wider national and 'moral significancy' of style (ibid.).[3]

If language and national identity were closely intertwined in contemporary British commentary on Carlyle, the same pattern appears across a range of mid-century American responses that extend well beyond Norton and Unitarian New England. A review of *The French Revolution* in the Richmond-based *Southern Literary Messenger*, for example, noted that Carlyle's liberal use of the English language endangered the racial essence, the 'Anglo-Saxon' 'body and heart of our language' (Anon. 1838a: 323). Lacking 'the raciness and pungent force possessed by the Anglo-Saxon', Carlyle's Germanic neologisms equalled 'foreign intruders' that threatened 'to overcrow the natives' (ibid.). Resembling British remarks on Carlyle's 'bastard English', this anthropomorphisation of language forms the backbone of a racially essentialist idiom of literary identity. If such rhetoric could almost be expected from a Southern source, it surfaced just as well in Northern criticism of Carlyle's books. Young American Lewis Gaylord Clark, for instance, disapproved of Carlyle's 'Germanized intellect' in an 1840 editorial for *The Knickerbocker* (1840: 525), and the New York religious press likewise complained of his 'attempt to sew his German patch-work on his English style' (a metaphor that, like Owenson's, subconsciously references the cloth imagery of *Sartor Resartus*) (Anon. 1849b: 238).

Calling into question Carlyle's nationality by referring either to him or to his writing as 'hyper-Germanized' or 'un-English' entailed locating him outside the boundaries of the Anglo-American literary field at the same time that it allowed those who passed this kind of judgement to place themselves safely on the inside and to self-authorise as gatekeepers. As Pierre Bourdieu has pointed out, such practices of inclusion and exclusion are the rule rather than the exception. Boundary demarcations, he explains, almost always represent a way of monitoring the ostensible 'purity' of a social group. They depend on a clearly circumscribed 'definition of belonging' that not only excludes those beyond the fringes of the definition from membership but that goes so far as to categorically 'deny them existence' (1996: 223). If Bourdieu mainly takes into view criteria of group membership specific to the cultural sphere (the conditions that need to be in place for someone to pass muster as an artist or be recognised as a writer), in the nineteenth-century Anglo-American context the same dynamics also applied to more general cultural–geographical acts of boundary drawing – discursive struggles in which the possession of a certain kind of ethnic capital counted as the prime condition for inclusion and in which authorship was tied up with notions of linguistic and national identity.

That a large number of not just British but also American reviewers assigned such importance to the purity of 'Anglo-Saxon' English suggests that the antebellum United States was indeed less Anglophobic than had often been assumed prior to the recovery of the period's pervasive orientation towards Britain in more recent scholarship (see Tennenhouse 2007 and Tamarkin 2008). The examples cited above register a voluntary affiliation with British taste and English expression across a wide spectrum of geographical location and ideological persuasion, from New England Unitarians to New York Young Americans and Southern racialists. Denying Carlyle the legitimacy of the bona fide Englishman – and thus adopting a British critical consensus – enabled American commentators to affirm their status as equal members of a transatlantic public sphere and to appropriate the cultural authority of metropolitan discourse. This larger transatlantic debate about language, style and national identity took on additional meaning in the context of contemporary discussions of Emerson. Known as the American editor of Carlyle's books, and more generally as a partisan of the continental 'new school', Emerson quickly began to be lambasted on both sides of the Atlantic as 'un-English' in terms that often closely resembled those employed in indictments of Carlyle.

A New England example of this is a review of *Nature* (1836) in the January 1837 *Christian Examiner*, written by Francis Bowen, then a young Unitarian, later the editor of the *North American Review* and the successor of James Walker, the *Examiner*'s editor, as Alford Professor at Harvard. Much like Norton on Carlyle, Bowen complained that Emerson's writing featured extravagant Germanisms foreign to the English language, which had to be artificially altered through 'copious importations from the German and Greek, before it can answer the ends of the modern school' (1837: 377). This practice of enrichment had been followed 'to such an extent', however, 'that could one of the worthies of old English literature rise from his grave, he would hardly be able to recognise his native tongue' (ibid.). If the spirits of Chaucer, Spenser and Addison that haunt contemporary criticisms of Carlyle are thus tangible also in Bowen's account of *Nature*, they surface even more prominently in an October 1841 review of the first series of Emerson's *Essays* in the London *Athenæum* – the same venue that four years before had featured Owenson's musings on the harmful effects of linguistic hybridisation. Leafing through Emerson's book, the anonymous reviewer wondered 'whether we are not labouring at low Saxon or high Dutch' (Anon. 1841e: 803). With his eccentricities of style and expression forming 'unnatural innovations in the tongue of Milton and of Shakspeare [sic]', Emerson had to be counted among the 'defilers of the pure "well of English"' (ibid.) – a verdict with which the reviewer was following Sewell's opinion on Carlyle, published the year before. The fact that Emerson's was an 'un-English English' excluded him from membership of the transatlantic community of Anglophone writers (ibid., 804). Like Carlyle, Emerson also came under attack from Southern reviewers at home. Admonishing him to 'use his mother tongue without affectation and speak in pure Addisonian English', the *Southern Quarterly Review* was even more explicit than other contemporary print organs about its exclusionary agenda (Anon. 1846: 539). Although he might 'call himself an American', Emerson, in the eyes of the Southern reviewer, 'belongs to no nation or tribe or kindred of scholars who deserve the name' (ibid.). Counting neither as an Englishman nor as an American, he is so thoroughly denationalised through his style that he ends up as a stateless subject, an outlaw deprived of any meaningful identity within the exclusionist logic of the nineteenth-century transatlantic republic of letters.[4]

What such ubiquitous commentary on Carlyle's and Emerson's status as non-English or ultra-German authors illustrates is that by the second third of the century the Anglo-American literary field had become thoroughly nationalised. As familiar as the idea of national writers or nationally marked writing may sound today, it would have been considerably less self-evident before the end of the eighteenth century. This transition period witnessed what Pascale Casanova has called the 'Herderian Revolution', a 'process of literary nationalization' that established 'the belief that national traditions are fundamentally different' from one another (2004: 107, 105). The charge of Carlyle's and Emerson's supposed Germanness would have been much less powerful before then, both because there was not yet a firmly established vocabulary to link style to national character and because what mattered in the literary sphere was to aspire to standards of excellence that were understood to be of a transhistorical as well as a transnational nature. It was only in the wake of the late-eighteenth-century flowering of cultural nationalism that the language of national distinctiveness and its concomitant rhetoric of inclusion and exclusion became fully naturalised (a development that was, ironically enough, mainly shaped by German writers). What the new paradigm suggested was, in Anthony Smith's words, that 'to each nation there corresponds a distinct historical culture, a singular way of thinking, acting and communicating, which all the members share (at least potentially) and which non-members do not and, as non-members, cannot share' (2001: 27). As several of the texts covered in this section demonstrate, however, literary discourse became not simply nationalised. The rhetoric of nationality was accompanied by an equally pervasive discourse of race that only partially overlapped the concerns of nationalism. I address this interplay between the logics of nation and race in what remains of this chapter, before turning to the more specifically literary and literary historical repercussions of Herderianism in Chapter 2.

RACE AND RACIAL IDENTITY: USES AND ABUSES

Contestations of Carlyle's national identity did not long remain unanswered, but the defences with which his American supporters responded formed part of the same overall logic of the charge. Rather than countering his image as a 'hyper-Germanized Englishman' through downplaying the importance of literary nationality, they in fact reaffirmed it. Englishness was a desirable quality to both groups of commentators, whose disagreement merely arose over the question of whether Carlyle was a genuine representative of it or not. What appears more prominently in the defences than in the attacks, however, is a shift from the national to the racial. Carlyle's allies – Emerson and Henry David Thoreau chief among them – routinely vindicated him through arguing not for his Englishness but his more elemental Saxonness. Such a more flexible rhetoric of race allowed for a transatlantic appropriation of Carlyle that was situated within a Herderian framework at the same time that it transcended the restrictive logic of literary nationality. For Emerson and other Transcendentalists, depicting Carlyle as a genuinely 'Saxon' writer was not least an act of self-defence, an authorisation strategy aimed at dispelling doubts about their own precariously hybrid status. As in the case of critics who excluded Carlyle and Emerson from the Anglo-American field, such defences were acts of self-inclusion. Emerson's description of *Sartor Resartus* is a case in point. Already upon reading the serialised version of the book in 1834, he remarked in private that its author was 'perhaps now the best Thinker of the Saxon race' (*CEC* 100). When he prepared a preface for the American edition of the book two years later, one of the main aims of the text was to demonstrate that, in spite of 'the German idioms' 'sportively sprinkled' across his pages, Carlyle nonetheless counted as a 'sincere' English writer (*CW* 10: 56). Like several later British and American critics drawing on the book's own metaphorics of cloth, Emerson's conclusion revolved around the claim that 'the foreign dress and aspect of the work' were ultimately 'quite superficial', merely 'cover[ing] a genuine Saxon heart' (ibid.). Reviewing Emerson's edition for the *Christian Examiner*, Nathaniel Langdon Frothingham, a Unitarian minister and member of the Transcendental Club, defended Carlyle as well, though in terms slightly less emphatic. There could 'be no reasonable objection to the roughest Germanisms' of the book's 'highly characteristic' manner of expression, Frothingham suggested, simply because Carlyle was 'a writer, whose English' was 'sterling and deep' (1836: 77–8). Perhaps the most radical of the defences was put forward in James Freeman Clarke's essay 'Thomas Carlyle: The German Scholar', published in the Transcendentalist *Western Messenger* in February 1838. Not only did Clarke deride the inability of the British aesthetic elite to recognise Carlyle's literary merit (what Norton read as a sign of English intellectual health); he also, at a more fundamental level, questioned the very existence of the boundaries that cut different nations and literatures off from one another. Carlyle's major achievement as a translator and periodical writer, to Clarke, was to have 'broken down the wall of division which rose between the two great and kindred literatures of England and Germany' and thus to have demonstrated the artificiality of national distinctions in the literary sphere (1838: 422).

Carlyle himself was arguing along similar lines when he reflected on his own style. In response to his friend John Sterling's critique of the linguistic eccentricities of *Sartor Resartus*, he sketched the outlines of a polyglot poetics tailored to the contemporary cultural moment. The nineteenth century, he contended, was everything but 'a time for Purism of Style': 'with whole ragged battalions [*sic*] of Scott's-Novel Scotch, with Irish, German, French and even Newspaper Cockney ... storming in on us', 'the whole structure of our Johnsonian English' was effectively 'breaking up from its foundations', thus making the idea of a single descriptive standard of stylistic purity look increasingly out of touch with linguistic reality (*CL* 8: 135). By the end of the 1830s, Carlyle was nevertheless trying to revise his image – championed by admirers like Clarke – as a mediator between English and German literature and to fight against his reputation – created by Norton and others – as the high-priest of Teutonic obscurantism. Even in his early essays, he had openly confronted what English critics liked to dismiss as German 'mysticism'.[5] Written after Carlyle had published his most important work on German literature, *Sartor Resartus* to some extent represented a turn away from his previous subjects. Emerson's and Frothingham's praise of the book as one written in 'sterling' English by an author of 'genuine Saxon' character was foreshadowed in the text itself – which, given the role of its philistine fictional English editor, reads in part like an ironic commentary on German idealism. Carlyle's irony, to be sure, works both ways, applying in equal measure to the stereotype of the cloudy German philosopher (embodied by his protagonist Diogenes Teufelsdröckh) as well as to that of the helplessly blinkered English critic. In *Sartor Resartus*, Carlyle created a satirical target for a range of readers and critics rather than simply defending his 'Germanism'. With *Chartism* (1840), *Past and Present* (1843) and *Oliver Cromwell's Letters and Speeches* (1845), he was turning not only from literature to politics but also from German to English topics, thus paving the way for his own reintegration into the Anglo-American literary sphere.

This thematic reorientation was a key reason why later critics on both sides of the Atlantic were increasingly ready to concede that Carlyle might be genuinely 'English' or 'Saxon' after all. An August 1841 summary account of 'Traits and Tendencies of German Literature' in *Blackwood's Edinburgh Magazine*, for example, concluded with a vignette of Carlyle as a prime specimen of 'the modern Teutonic spirit', but the piece also departed from such conventional wisdom in declaring that he was 'at the same time something better than German' because 'his raciness, his dramatic breadth of brush, seem thoroughly English' (Anon. 1841a: 160). Like the earlier scathing criticism of Carlyle's corruption of the English language, this type of British opinion reached the United States in the form of transatlantic reprints.[6] Together with domestic revaluations of Carlyle's literary nationality by writers such as Emerson, Frothingham and Clarke, it occasioned a recalibration of American critical vocabularies across a range of different ideological convictions. The New York-based *Democratic Review*, usually reserved about all things English, found in Carlyle's writing on the anti-monarchical Cromwell 'a vigorous Anglo-Saxon manliness' capable of retroactively assimilating the foreign anomalies it had previously absorbed (Anon. 1850b: 36). Much of the same verdict came from the other end of the political spectrum. The *Southern Quarterly Review*, which in 1846 had violently excluded Emerson – and by implication Carlyle – from membership of any national literary community whatsoever, came to a different conclusion two years later. Seizing on the authoritarian tendency of his more recent writing, the journal now rejoiced over the fact that Carlyle was 'making an impress wherever the Saxon tongue and Saxon blood prevail' (Anon. 1848f: 77). In so doing, the *Southern Quarterly* spelled out the biological determinism that informed the racially inflected stylistics of mid-century criticism at large. Taking up the Spenser reference popular with many contemporary commentators, the anonymous Southern reviewer even went so far as to argue that Carlyle was an exemplary reformer of the English language:

> That he has corrupted the 'pure well of English undefiled,' we think . . . without foundation. On the contrary, it may be safely contended, that by resuscitating the Saxon branch of our language, and by the formation of words and sentences in accordance with its genius and analogies, he has discovered a new vein of beauty, and has largely contributed to show the capacity and richness of the English tongue. (ibid., 83)

If, from a sufficiently abstract point of view, English and German were not different but related – a shared 'Saxon' or 'Teuton' identity of the languages that the early Carlyle had himself emphasised, arguing that 'the character and spirit of the two are Kindred' (*HGL* 30) and that the Germans' 'Saxon speech' was also the modern Englishman's 'mother-tongue' (*CE* 26: 85) – Carlyle's cross-fertilisation of contemporary English with the residual 'Saxon' energy of modern German appeared less like an act of deracination than one of re-racination. The language of race (of 'Saxon tongue and Saxon blood') now works as a unifying discourse that conjures away national difference. To the extent that the Anglo-Saxonism of the kind employed in the pages of the *Southern Quarterly* in the late 1840s destabilised the boundaries between German, English and, ultimately, American language and nationality, it functioned as an inclusionary strategy that guaranteed Carlyle's presence in the transatlantic canon. However seemingly inclusive, this type of reasoning ultimately came at the price of a racial essentialism whose supremacist flipside Carlyle's own writing would soon come to reflect.

One of the most extended arguments for Carlyle's rightful place in Anglo-American literary culture came from the pen of Emerson's friend Thoreau. In an essay on 'Thomas Carlyle and His Works', first published in *Graham's American Monthly Magazine* in the spring of 1847 and based on a lecture delivered before the Concord Lyceum in February of the previous year, Thoreau employed the same racial vocabulary as the *Southern Quarterly* and the *Democratic Review* and anticipated the revisionist essence of their verdicts. Rehearsing Carlyle's conventional image as a continental character, Thoreau declares at the beginning of the essay that 'we need not dwell on this charge of a German extraction, it being generally admitted, by this time, that Carlyle is English' (1975: 225–6). Thoreau does end up dwelling on the issue, however – certainly in part because the question of Carlyle's intellectual location on the global literary map had not yet been resolved to the degree that the essay's opening gambit implied. One strand of the exculpatory strategy that follows in the text forms part of a transatlantic debate over the nature of Romantic and Transcendentalist writing. As we have seen, Carlyle in his early essays had himself defended German idealist philosophy and its literary counterpart from conservative charges of mysticism and infidelity. Thoreau now exonerated Carlyle on essentially the same grounds, responding both to British criticism of him and to domestic attacks on the transatlantic 'new school', more generally. Thoreau's defence of Carlyle as profoundly rational – '[h]e is no mystic', '[h]is books are solid and workmanlike, as all that England does' (ibid., 226, 228) – resembles Carlyle's defence of Kant and Novalis, but it also works to recalibrate the image of his American followers. Writing about Carlyle allows Thoreau to present a robust Transcendentalism marked by common sense rather than mistiness and to advance this argument in a domestic debate, initiated by Norton, about the character of the 'new school'. In addition to this depiction of Carlyle and Transcendentalism at large as 'solid' and 'practical', the essay also comments on the relationship between style and ethnic identity, deriving the assertion that 'Carlyle is English' from the corresponding claim that '[h]e utters substantial English thoughts in plainest English dialects' (ibid., 226). Thoreau comes closest to the racialist rhetoric of the *Southern Quarterly* when he suggests that

> no writer is more thoroughly Saxon [than Carlyle]. In the translation of . . . fragments of Saxon poetry, we have met with the same rhythm that occurs so often in his poem on the French Revolution. And if you would know where many of those obnoxious Carlyleisms and Germanisms came from, read the best of Milton's prose, read those speeches of Cromwell which he has brought to light, or go and listen once more to your mother's tongue. (ibid., 227)

In contrast to the trope of the 'pure well of English' and its recourse to a courtly–bourgeois line of tradition that extends from Chaucer via Spenser to Addison, Thoreau constructs an alternative literary historical genealogy that locates Carlyle in the context of a more radically demotic and liberal–republican canon of English writing. Adopting a *longue durée* perspective that looks back even beyond Chaucer to the mystically 'fragment[ary]' past and idiomatic 'rhythm' of an ethnically purified 'Saxon poetry', Thoreau emphasises that the 'thorough[ness]' of Carlyle's 'English' literary identity is ultimately a question of race rather than nationality. Calling attention more to Carlyle's – and Emerson's – genuine 'Saxonness' than to their 'Englishness' created a more capacious transatlantic framework that downplayed the importance of national difference. As 'Saxon', Emerson could be counted as part of an Anglocentric literary sphere without having to discount his Americanness, and Carlyle could be seen as quintessentially English without jettisoning his appeal for a less affirmatively Anglophile readership.

Anglo-American Anglo-Saxonism

The fact that defences of Carlyle and Emerson as 'thoroughly Saxon' understood themselves as rebuttals of the charge of the two writers' purportedly 'un-English' character demonstrates that there was a fair amount of conceptual overlap between the mid-nineteenth-century vocabularies of nation and race. As the century progressed, however, authorship tended to be increasingly perceived in relation to racial rather than purely national markers of similarity and difference. Writing about the development of eighteenth-century ethnographic and historical discourse, Nicholas Hudson has noted a gradual 'shift from a fascination with national difference to a preoccupation with "race"' (1996: 251). Charting the transatlantic genealogy of racial Anglo-Saxonism, Reginald

Horsman has pointed to a 'continuing confusion over race, language, culture, and nationality' that persisted throughout the nineteenth century (1981: 302). 'When people used the term "race"', historian Robert Young writes, 'occasionally they meant something close to what we now think of as ethnicity, occasionally they meant something more like biological race, but most usually they used the term without it being anchored in any precise meaning at all' (2008: 43). Such terminological imprecision was useful for writers who, as part of a transatlantic literary sphere, had an interest in determining the nature of national characteristics as they related to forms of identity that transcended the nation-state. This became especially pertinent against the backdrop of the emergence of global empires such as the British – political and cultural processes in which national and ethnic identity needed to be simultaneously maintained and conceptually expanded.[7] The same ambiguity that Young describes with regard to nineteenth-century writing about race can also be detected in the use of national signifiers. This, too, Eric Hobsbawm has noted, was marked by 'a surprising degree of intellectual vagueness' (1990: 24). Modern scholarly accounts of what distinguishes nation from race (or 'ethnic group') are thus of limited use in making sense of the historical semantics of the two concepts.[8] Hobsbawm's own definition of the nation as 'a social entity' that 'relates to a certain kind of modern territorial state', for instance, hardly reflects – as he himself concedes – a nineteenth-century understanding of the term in which the nation is imagined not primarily as a political unit but as an ethnic as well as a cultural community (ibid., 9).[9]

Although the conceptual repertoires of race and nationhood tended to overlap, however, the two nevertheless operated on different scales, with race functioning as a more extensive rhetoric that allowed for a suspension of regional and national difference. If with nineteenth-century writers the term *nation* could assume some of these transnational qualities as well, it was often through the admixture of a racial semantics. The simultaneity of these two discourses of identity enabled English and American authors to imagine themselves as part of both a particularised and a universalised community, both as British or American citizens *and* as (Anglo-)Saxons. Depending on context, either national difference or racial identity could be highlighted. Paying attention to the rhetoric of race and its complex links to that of the nation can thus lead to an alternative assessment of nineteenth-century Anglo-American literary relations that differs from more conventional narratives that put the nation and nationalism (in the 'modernist' sense of the terms) centre stage. Where the latter is a story of national antagonism and transatlantic division, the former reveals how the vocabulary of race not only supplemented but also challenged and in part undercut the claims of cisatlantic nationalisms.

If nationalism has traditionally occupied a more prominent role than race in discussions of transatlantic literary culture, this is of course not to suggest that race as such has been a neglected subject. Much indeed has been written about nineteenth-century British and American varieties of racialist thought, especially its exclusionary dimension.[10] My more specific focus here is on the transatlantic arguments that the logic of race allowed writers on both sides of the Atlantic to make about heritage, identity and authority. Eighteenth- and nineteenth-century racialist thinking consisted of an ensemble of classificatory systems and narratives devised to chart, as well as compare and contrast, different characteristics. These included the racial typologies developed by Carl Linnaeus and Johann Friedrich Blumenbach, as well as fields such as physiognomy, phrenology or craniometry (championed by Franz Joseph Gall, Johann Kaspar Lavater and others). Mostly of continental European origin, these often pseudo-scientific discourses also proved influential in the English-speaking world. What was most immediately important from a transatlantic point of view, however, was a more specific set of beliefs that, developing in tandem with such larger debates, related more narrowly to Anglo-Saxon identity. Horsman has shown in detail how sixteenth- and seventeenth-century British writers associated the Anglo-Saxon past with liberty and free government and how an Enlightenment racialism then differentiated more systematically between the Anglo-Saxon and other races. It was only in the early decades of the nineteenth century that Anglo-Saxonism became a fully fledged essentialist ideology of blood. 'Of central importance' in this shift of focus, Horsman points out, 'was the Romantic emphasis on the uniqueness, the peculiar qualities, of individuals and peoples' (1981: 25). The Anglo-Saxonism fuelled by such complementary desires for singularity and community was equally popular in Britain and the United States.

Before the mid-nineteenth-century turn to racial essentialism, one form that Anglo-Saxonism took was historical and philological research. Never clearly distinct from contemporary 'scientific' racialism, such culturalist writing was informed by a similar interest in developmental trajectories (the organicist vocabulary of roots and branches, after all, translated well from botany into racial anatomy, history and linguistics). Historiographic accounts of the Anglo-Saxon settlement and grammars of Old English abounded in the first half of the nineteenth century, with British books often reprinted across the Atlantic: Sharon Turner's *History of the Anglo-Saxons* (1799–1805) retold early English history up to the Norman conquest, Benjamin Thorpe's *Analecta Anglo-Saxonica* (1834) offered a combination of grammar and anthology, John Petheram's *Historical Sketch of the Progress and Present State of Anglo-Saxon Literature in England* (1840) provided an institutional history of Anglo-Saxonist scholarship and John Mitchell Kemble's *The Saxons in England* (1849) presented a more strongly racialised version of Turner's history.[11] From Thomas Jefferson onwards, there was a keen American interest in the subjects covered by these books. Writing about Thorpe, Kemble and others for the

North American Review in 1838, Henry Wadsworth Longfellow justified this transatlantic fascination through arguing that the Anglo-Saxon language was not an exclusively English concern. Acquiring a taste for Old English to Longfellow was the constitutional duty of 'the Anglo-Saxon student on this side of the Atlantic' as well, for the simple reason that '[t]he Anglo-Saxon language was the language of our Saxon forefathers in England' (1838: 93).

The transatlantic logic behind Longfellow's essay is characteristic of its time. It was by around 1840 that a site-specific Saxonism had morphed into a global Anglo-Saxonism, 'a form of soft racialism' that, as Young has pointed out, identified 'cultural and linguistic' features as key markers of an 'international English character' which could be seen as extending across the Atlantic (2008: xii). 'Anglo-Saxon' now no longer denoted only a language but also signified a specific kind of racial identity (see ibid., 180–1). Young suggests that Anglo-Saxonism was a firmly hegemonic discourse that predominantly served the colonial centre to maintain and expand its authority in the peripheries. But there was, in fact, a variety of uses to which Anglo-Saxonism was put by writers on both sides of the Atlantic. It could be employed affirmatively either by English commentators intent on resurrecting a transatlantic colonial relationship as part of a global British empire or by Americans keen on having a share in English history and culture. But it could just as well serve a divisive use in the context of declensionist or ameliorationist narratives (for instance, with British racial theorists who depicted Americans as degenerate Saxons or with Americans using it to describe themselves as more advanced than the British).

It was in the late 1840s and early 1850s that such conflicting uses of transatlantic Anglo-Saxonism peaked. Young's idea of the discourse as a British-centred attempt at ethnic unification manifests itself perhaps most distinctly in the pages of *The Anglo-Saxon*, a short-lived magazine published in London in 1849 and 1850. The inaugural issue opened with an 'Address to Anglo-Saxons' that charts the global reach of the race and invokes its purportedly divine mission ('the native of every clime', the Saxon was 'a messenger of heaven to every corner of this Planet') (Anon. 1849a: 4). An editorial in the third issue of the periodical answers its titular question 'Who Are the Anglo-Saxons?' through a similar gesture of global expansiveness. That the main purpose of the text was to incorporate Americans into the far-flung family of Englishmen becomes evident when the author considers terminological alternatives to the signifier 'Anglo-Saxon':

> Perhaps in the points of priority and locality, Briton or British would be the more correct and original family designation. But this title has been so long appropriated by the inhabitants of the British Islands, that if used as a family name, it would virtually exclude the millions of Americans who will soon form the larger half of our family circle. (Anon. 1849c: 5–6)

If the already composite political semantics of 'British' was not capacious enough to cover the United States as well, a new term was needed to enable the remote 'millions of Americans' to feel part of an Anglocentric cultural identity.

A more self-confidently cisatlantic position was formulated in Louis Klipstein's *Analecta Anglo-Saxonica* (1849), a massive anthology of Old English writing modelled on Thorpe's London *Analecta*, first published fifteen years before. In his 'Introductory Ethnological Essay', Klipstein advances a supremacist argument whose racial dimension is politically wide-ranging:

> The progress of the Saxons, or Anglo-Saxons, ... is one of wonderful interest. ... In Britain, indeed, we behold them now arrived at a degree of eminence that Rome in her proudest days would have envied, – an eminence that we would pronounce unsurpassable, did not the future, faintly foreshadowed by the past and the present, open a vista for their colonies transplanted to the shores of this continent, in which visions of still brighter glory arise. A giant in youth – in infancy, shall we say? – what will not the American branch be in the vigor of manhood, unfettered as it is, in the career which its inherent destiny has assigned it ... ? (1849: 96)

The Southerner Klipstein thus agrees with the racialist views propounded in the London *Anglo-Saxon*, but he gives their shared racial narrative a distinctively American twist. Where the British periodical was prepared to grant that the population of the United States would 'soon form the larger half of our family circle', Klipstein expands on this anticipation of numerical dominance to come up with a vision of universal American supremacy already on the horizon. His phrasing is diplomatic (as in the favourable comparison between modern-day Britain and ancient Rome), but the main objective of his argument is to present the United States as a future power that will relativise the achievements of the Roman as well as the British empires. The language of race here allows Klipstein to envisage a transfer of power from Europe to North America. Such *translatio imperii* rhetoric is authorised by the idea of an unlimited 'progress of the ... Anglo-Saxons'.[12] At the same time that Klipstein contemplates a bright future for the American nation, however, his imagery remains solidly transatlantic: the United States, to him, are still British 'colonies' and their future success will be but that of 'the American branch' of the Anglo-Saxon family tree.

While championing a similar Anglo-Saxonist transnationalism, British writers such as the contributors to *The Anglo-Saxon* could not easily subscribe to Klipstein's prophecy, which, after all, threatened to turn the tables on the traditional definition of centre and periphery. A less conciliatory version of transatlantic Anglo-Saxonism than that of either *The Anglo-Saxon* or Klipstein came from Scottish anatomist Robert Knox, whose narrative of Anglo-Saxonism's global dispersal in *The Races of Men: A Fragment* (1850) followed a declensionist plot. To Knox, the 'history of the Anglo-Saxon colonies' was not one of collective fraternal dominance, as *The Anglo-Saxon* implied, but rather one of cultural amnesia and political secession:

> [O]n quitting his native soil the Saxon loses all respect for it. He is totally devoid of the weakness called patriotism. His adopted land becomes his fatherland. With the first opportunity he shakes off the despotism of England and sets up for himself: hence, in time, England must lose all her colonies. (1850: 250)

Empires based on the principle of race, to Knox, were thus destined to fail. The main reason for this was not a lack of patriotism, however, but physical and mental deterioration ('Under the influence of climate, the Saxon decays in northern America and in Australia, and he rears his offspring with difficulty' [ibid., 44]). Tapping into an established European discourse about American degeneration, Knox presented the mirror image to Klipstein's ameliorationist vision of the United States as the predestined setting for the future 'vigor' of Anglo-Saxon 'manhood'. Marked by a similar racial essentialism, their different arguments demonstrate that Anglo-Saxonist rhetoric could be employed to pursue a variety of conflicting goals.

Such disagreements were internal as well. Not all US writers, for instance, were willing to concede like Klipstein that Americans were more or less identical with Anglo-Saxons or that they could take pride in this perceived heritage. A review of Klipstein's *Analecta* and his earlier *Grammar of the Anglo-Saxon Language* (1848) in the *North American Review* openly dismissed self-congratulatory American Anglo-Saxonism, pointing to the irony that '[t]he American, however democratic he may be, however slow to admit the claim of any thing hereditary, is yet proud to assert that he too is the free-born child of the same stock' (Anon. 1851: 35). A more radical challenge to mid-century Anglo-Saxonism came from Charles Anderson, an Ohio Republican with black rights sympathies. His 1849 *Address on Anglo Saxon Destiny* begins with an attack on champions of Anglo-Saxonism on both sides of the Atlantic in which Anderson notes

> how decided and how universal is the belief amongst the North Americans and Englishmen of this age, that there is, in what they choose to call (for what reasons I know not,) the *'Anglo Saxon'* Race, some extraordinary power, or capability of accomplishing greater things, than in any other family of men. (1850: 4)

The remainder of the address explores the argumentative inconsistencies of racial Anglo-Saxonism. Anderson starts by questioning the racial terminology employed by its proponents. He wonders 'what present population is generally meant by this phrase of "Anglo Saxon"': 'Are the English people proper and their descendants over the world alone included in it? or are the Scotch and Irish people (who have neither Anglish, nor Saxon relationships,) also embraced within the magic circle of this name?' (ibid., 23). Anderson finds strong terms to censure a racially inflected exceptionalism, the belief 'that the English, or the British, or any other race of men are, in blood or bone, primitively better than, or different from, the rest of mankind' (ibid., 37). But while he departs from the premises of much of the transatlantic Anglo-Saxonist rhetoric covered here, on another level he does little more than rephrase them. Although he replaces 'British' for 'Anglo-Saxon', he still speaks of 'British race' rather than British nation and where he deconstructs the notion of a predominantly English American pedigree, he easily proceeds to 'consider the two nations' – Great Britain and the United States – 'as composed of the same race' (ibid., 27, 25, 25). With Anderson as much as with his contemporaries, racialism was a convoluted affair in which complex combinations of cisatlantic sectionalism and transatlantic commonality resulted in accounts that were more often marked by contradiction than by coherence.

Transatlantic Racialism in Carlyle and Emerson

Like Klipstein, Knox and Anderson, Carlyle and Emerson employed terms such as *Anglo-Saxon* or *race* inconsistently. They used the language of race to define Anglo-American relations, but this strategy derived at least in part from their own contested status in the Anglo-American literary sphere. Both of them – Carlyle as Scot, Emerson as American – were outsiders excluded by birth from a more narrow definition of Englishness. That they championed a comprehensive Anglo-Saxonism points to an underlying desire to locate themselves within a more expansive type of Englishness that allowed for an affiliation from beyond the fringes of the English nation-state. To that extent, Carlyle and Emerson were 'provincial authors' in the sense suggested by Joseph Rezek, who understands provinciality as 'a relational status acquired through engaging with metropolitan culture' (2015: 3, 4). It was this provincial location on the margins of Englishness that, in the 1830s and 1840s, pushed Carlyle's and Emerson's defenders into adopting an inclusive racialist vocabulary and into suggesting that if they were not 'pure' Englishmen, at least they could be described as authentically 'Saxon'.

When French critic Philarète Chasles wrote of Carlyle as 'un *borderer*, ou homme des limites de l'Écosse et de l'Angleterre', he captured his liminal status well (1844: 499). A child of the Lowland peasantry, Carlyle preserved traits of his Scottish provinciality while at the same time trying to gain admission to the English intellectual elite after permanently relocating to London in 1834. Putting himself close to the centre of early- to mid-nineteenth-century

Anglophone literary culture, he became 'an amalgam of metropolitan and Scot' (Campbell 1997: 75). Emerson himself described this hybrid nature of Carlyle's identity when he noted in his English travel journal of 1848 that he 'has the *kleinstadtlich* traits of an islander & a Scotchman, and believes more deeply in London than if he had been born under Bow-bells' (*JMN* 10: 552). Insularly provincial and excessively metropolitan at the same time, Carlyle wrote from the inside while 'stubbornly evincing an outsider's view of "England"' (Lee 2004: 32). It was precisely an inclusive Saxonism that allowed him to conjure away regional difference and to present himself as, after all, part of an in-group.[13] If Emerson did not perhaps orbit around London as closely as Carlyle – or as Irving and Cooper, the two earlier American writers on whom Rezek focuses – he was nevertheless consistently concerned with determining his own place in an Anglophone cultural world in which his inherited location still happened to be provincial rather than metropolitan. Like Carlyle's, Emerson's relationship to Englishness and English literary culture was that of an outsider rather than that of a native. What Lawrence Buell has called his 'residual Anglocentrism' (2003: 371) manifested itself in his use of Anglo-Saxonist rhetoric as a means of highlighting links between Britain and the United States and thus of bringing himself into closer contact with the kind of authority that emanated from the centre.

Carlyle and Emerson had been exposed to mainstream Anglo-Saxonist writing early on.[14] When Carlyle began thinking about the influence of race on literature and culture in the early 1830s, he focused on 'Teutons' rather than Saxons. In his *History of German Literature* (1830), for example, he speaks admiringly of the 'unmixed descent' of 'the German people' and relates this to German literary achievement (*HGL* 14). Lecturing on German literature in London seven years later, he rendered two arguments of the earlier *History* more explicit. The first was that the history of the German people was intimately tied up with that of the contemporary 'Saxons' living around the globe.[15] The second argument related to the idea – merely implied in the *History* – that racial 'intermixtures' (ibid.) could be seen as more advanced than pure types, that the English and American Saxon heirs of Teuton traits represented an improvement. The same ameliorationist line of thinking appears again a year later in another series of lectures – this time on the 'History of Literature' – in which Carlyle presents the Saxons as the most advanced members of the Teuton racial family. 'The English', he explains, are 'one particular tribe of the Teutonic race', 'indisputably the most interesting to us, for it is our own nation, the Saxon or English' (*LHL* 139). Carlyle's collective possessive pronoun ('*our* own nation') includes himself within the perimeters of both the Saxon race and the English nation. But the Teutonism that marks his thinking of the 1830s was also a convenient strategy that allowed him to deflect the type of criticism commonly levelled against his writings during that period. If the English or the Saxons had Germanic roots – if, as Thomas Arnold would similarly claim in his inaugural lecture at Oxford in 1841, 'half of Europe, and all America and Australia, are German more or less completely, in race, in language, or in institutions' (1843: 28) – reproaching Carlyle for infiltrating the English language with Germanisms, and thus for not being genuinely English, had to seem absurdly tautological.

Where, as proponents of racial Teutonism, Carlyle and Arnold occupied a minority position, Emerson's Saxonist interests were more safely mainstream by mid-century standards. In contrast to the early Carlyle, '[b]y "Saxon"', Buell explains, 'Emerson almost always means Anglo-Saxon English, rather than the broader German diaspora' (2003: 371). What his use of Saxonist rhetoric entailed in a specifically transatlantic context has so far been explored only tentatively. The nature of Emerson's more general racialist thinking has been at the centre of an extended critical debate, with commentators such as Nell Irvin Painter (2010: 151–89) seeing him as a white-supremacy figure or Christopher Newfield (1996: 174–208) detecting in his writings a 'corporate' or 'liberal' form of racism. Reginald Horsman (1981: 177–8), Laura Dassow Walls (2003: 166–87) and others, however, acknowledge his indebtedness to contemporary racialist discourse while at the same time emphasising the importance of his sceptical distancing from racial categorisation (the latter kind of reading usually tends to point towards his idealist metaphysics of oneness, in which ethnic or national difference is merely accidental and phenomenal in light of a larger underlying universal humanity). Philip L. Nicoloff (1961), Cornel West (1989: 28–35) and Buell (2003: 258–77) have offered accounts that locate Emerson half-way between hard-boiled supremacism and Transcendentalist universalism.

These differing critical assessments partly derive from the fact that Emerson, much like Carlyle, went through different phases of experimenting with Saxonist ideology. He first expanded on the idea of a racial and spatio-temporal continuity between Britain and the United States in a series of lectures on 'English Literature', read in Boston in the winter of 1835–6. In the second instalment of the course, he draws attention to the 'permanent traits of English national genius', a topic that he introduces in a distinctly transatlantic manner:

> The inhabitants of the United States especially of the Northern portion are descended from the people of England and have inherited the traits of their national character. It has been thought by some observers acquainted with the character of both nations that the American character is only the English character exaggerated . . . (*EL* 1: 233)

Although the lecture as a whole is ostensibly a survey of Old English verse, Emerson here uses literary texts merely as a background for his more general remarks about Anglo-Saxon characteristics, justifying himself by insisting that 'we must read this poetry in the light of the national mind' (ibid., 251). He suggests that the traits of any given race are distinct from those of other ethnic groups and that they are in themselves 'unchangable [sic] features . . . almost as permanent as the grander natural forms of a country, the mountains, rivers and plains' (ibid., 234). Emerson's emphasis on the quasi-geological stability of Saxon attributes sustains his larger argument that the racial continuity between transatlantic Saxons trumps national differences between England and America. As Johannes Voelz has demonstrated, the 'nationalism' of the 'English Literature' series as a whole 'is so focused on the idea of Anglo-Saxonism that its object of boosterism rarely coincides with the American nation-state' (2010: 209). In its deep-historical contours, Emerson's racially inflected idea of the nation is thus transatlantically comprehensive rather than narrowly chauvinist.

While Emerson was retracing the Saxon elements of the American national character, Carlyle gradually abandoned his Teutonism to concentrate on Saxonism and its global expansion, topics that had already surfaced in his London lectures of the late 1830s. In *Chartism* (1840), he presents a sweeping historical panorama that extends from the Anglo-Saxon invasion of Britain to the nineteenth-century neo-Saxonist colonisation of the globe in order to celebrate a quasi-planetary racial mythology:

> [W]hosoever had, with the bodily eye, seen Hengst and Horsa mooring on the mud-beach of Thanet, on that spring morning of the Year 449; and then, with the spiritual eye, looked forward to New York, Calcutta, Sidney Cove, across the ages and the oceans; and thought what Wellingtons, Washingtons, Shakspeares [sic], Miltons, Watts, Arkwrights, William Pitts and Davie Crocketts had to issue from that business, and do their several taskworks so, – *he* would have said, those leatherboats of Hengst's had a kind of cargo in them! A genealogic Mythus superior to any in the old Greek, to almost any in the old Hebrew itself; and not a Mythus either, but every fibre of it fact. (*CE* 29: 172)

Whether 'in the cane-brake of Arkansas' or 'in the Ghauts of the Himalaya', Carlyle's Saxons remain the same everywhere, unaffected by their transplantation into foreign climates (ibid., 175). Although his vision is, by and large, indiscriminately global, he reserves special praise for the Anglo-American Saxon connection. Reflecting on the Puritan exodus to the New World, for example, he suggests that the 'poor little ship Mayflower' contained 'a veritable Promethean spark; the life-spark of the largest Nation on our Earth' (ibid., 179). Carlyle in this context uses the phrase 'Transatlantic Saxon Nation', without fully clarifying whether by this he means the United States or rather a transatlantic community of Saxons that includes the English (ibid.).

Championing the idea of diasporic Saxonness in a range of texts from the late 1830s onwards, Carlyle routinely considered the United States as part of a global imperial formation. In the 1838 *Lectures on the History of Literature*, he speaks of 'our present dominion extending from the Gulf of California, from the mouth of the Gulf of Mexico, away up to the Ganges and Burrampootra, descending even to our antipodes', and in the lectures published as *On Heroes, Hero-Worship, and the Heroic in History* in 1841 he similarly states that 'England, before long, this Island of ours, will hold but a small fraction of the English: in America, in New Holland, east and west to the very Antipodes, there will be a Saxondom covering great spaces of the Globe' (*LHL* 142; *WTC* 1: 96). This pan-Saxonist vision corresponds well with Young's account of a shift from British Saxonism to an imperialist Anglo-Saxonism in the 1840s, a development over the course of which the term *Anglo-Saxon* came to describe 'a global racial and cultural identity' (2008: xi). Where Carlyle differed from the contemporary discourse summarised by Young was in that he continued to speak of Saxons rather than *Anglo*-Saxons, a terminological choice that expressed his belief that a specifically English type of Saxonness would survive intact across the globe. If Anglo-Saxonism enabled what Elisa Tamarkin has described as 'the extension of the romance of a site-specific national identity across the terrain of global empire' (2008: xxxiii), Carlyle's unhyphenated brand of Saxonism remained firmly predicated on a metropolitan type of Englishness.

An image that resurfaces time and again in Carlyle's writings of the late 1830s and early 1840s is that of London as a 'Saxon *Panionium*, a yearly meeting-place of "All the Saxons"' (*CEC* 239). He spelled out the Hellenic referent of the image in an August 1841 letter to Emerson:

> By and by we shall visibly be, what I always say we virtually are, members of neighbouring Parishes; paying continual visits to one another. What is to hinder huge London from being to universal Saxondom what small Mycale was to the tribes of Greece, – a place to hold your Παν-Ιωνιον in? A meeting of *All the English* ought to be as good as one of All the Ionians; and as Homeric 'equal ships' are to Bristol Steamers, so, or somewhat so, may New York and New Holland be to Ephesus and Crete, with their distances, relations, and etceteras! (ibid., 305)

Carlyle once more switches between national and racial vocabularies, but the passage clearly implies that London forms the undisputed colonial centre of the Saxon world. Where, as a result of imperial expansion, England itself threatened to become an elusive signifier, the English 'localist ideology' that manifested itself in such London-centric visions of Victorian Britain as a modern Greece served rhetorically to 'secure England's continuous national identity' (Baucom 1999: 7, 16).

At least in its transatlantic outlines, Carlyle's idea proved compatible with Emerson's emphasis on a predominantly English racial pedigree for Americans. The notion of an Anglo-American connection resurfaces strongly in 'New England', one of Emerson's lecture series of the early 1840s. But although the overall historical narrative behind the course revolves around transatlantic racial continuity, Emerson here introduces a new argument aimed at authorising American aspirations for future centrality. Raising the question of racial purity, Emerson contends that New England was more authentically English than England itself. The seventeenth-century Puritan exodus, he suggests, had turned America into the preserver of Saxon virtues that were disappearing in England itself. The 'New England' lectures thus formulate an American claim to cultural leadership much more explicitly than the 'English Literature' series. In the fourth of the later lectures, for instance, Emerson foretells the imminent transatlantic relocation of the traditionally Eurocentric 'Greenwich meridian of literature' (Casanova 2004: 88):

> it is easy to see that soon the centre of gravity, which long ago begun its travels and which now is still on the eastern shore, will shortly hover midway over the Atlantic main and then, as certainly, fall within the American shore, so that the writers of the English tongue shall write to the American and not to the island public . . . (*LL* 1: 58)

Emerson here predicts a reversal of hierarchies similar to the one Carlyle had grudgingly conceded in hypothetical terms a few years before. His vision is derived from the same *translatio* imagery that also informs Carlyle's idea of nineteenth-century Saxons as latter-day Greeks, only that he gives the idea of a westward transfer of power another turn of the screw.

As Emerson was adapting Anglo-Saxonist rhetoric into a tool for American self-empowerment, Carlyle's writing on race in the course of the 1840s took on an increasingly exclusionist character. There is a clear shift from the universalist rhetoric of global Saxondom in the London lectures and *Chartism* to the violent supremacism of the notorious 'Occasional Discourse on the Negro Question' (1849) and other later texts. Exclusion had, of course, been part of the racial dialectics of some of his earlier comments as well (the apotheosis of Saxon virtues in *Chartism*, for example, relies on a corresponding vilification of the Irish, an element that resurfaces in the later 'Discourse'). But from the mid-1840s onwards, Carlyle increasingly tended to juxtapose Anglo-Saxon whiteness with non-European blackness. Racial identity in his texts was now beginning to be negotiated through a recourse to ethnic alterity, a development towards a racist vision of white supremacy that was rooted in the logic of British imperialism. Carlyle thought of the Empire as a political structure coupled to the idea of an authority grounded in a relational hierarchy of domination and submission, and firmly located in metropolitan Englishness. With an increasingly self-confident mid-century United States no longer uniformly prepared to embrace this basic premise (a shift illustrated by Emerson's writings of the 1840s), Carlyle was beginning to target the ethnic other in an attempt to rediscipline white diasporic 'Saxons' into allegiance.

Carlyle's mounting concern with racial difference illustrates Douglas Lorimer's argument that the 'stereotype of blacks' served the Victorians as a 'photographic negative of the Anglo-Saxon' (1978: 11). But for Carlyle, this also involved an additional form of self-affirmation. His exclusion of black people and the Saxonist supremacism that emerged out of this position reflect what Simon Gikandi has called his 'attempt to disavow . . . his native Scotland in his frustrated quest for the authority of Englishness' (1996: 58). With his own ethnic status profoundly ambiguous, Carlyle positioned himself closer to the core of Anglo-Saxon identity through volunteering to police its boundaries. If the vehemence of his racial rhetoric was growing increasingly pronounced, Carlyle was not alone among his contemporaries in shifting towards a more outspoken language of race. His trajectory illustrates what Reginald Horsman has described as a larger general development in Anglo-American Anglo-Saxonism over the course of the first half of the nineteenth century, one in which an Enlightenment interest in racial difference gradually turned into an emphasis on racial inequality (see 1981: 44).

The form that this new racialist emphasis assumed in Carlyle's 'Occasional Discourse' was controversial even by such contemporary standards, however. First published in *Fraser's Magazine* in December 1849, the text was subsequently enlarged and reprinted in pamphlet form as *Occasional Discourse on the Nigger Question* in 1853.[16] The later title is indicative of the derogatory language that the text displays in both of its versions. Carlyle chooses as his main theme the emancipation of slaves in the British West Indies, complaining that abolition had led both to economic chaos and to a profound crisis of white authority. The racial dualism between black and white individuals that emerges in the text draws on Carlyle's earlier emphasis on Saxon excellence, which resurfaces here in even stronger form when he defends colonialist claims to land ownership through celebrating 'the Saxon British' for having turned the West Indies arable (1849: 674). Commenting on the racialist language of the text, Edward Said has noted that Carlyle's 'writing on the subject' is 'not obscure, or occult, or esoteric', but indeed outspoken about its premises (1993: 123). On closer inspection, however, the 'Occasional Discourse' appears less transparently legible than this would seem to suggest. In an obvious sense, Carlyle does, of course, stand behind the opinions voiced in the text. As Helen Small points out, '[t]he indisputable racism of much of [its] rhetoric . . . is of a piece with much of Carlyle's private writing about race' (2017: 538). But Said's analysis overlooks the extent to which the editorial framing of the text complicates whether Carlyle actually endorses what he is saying. His racialist rhetoric comes packaged in the form of a fictional 'discourse' delivered by an anonymous speaker to an unknown audience and transmitted to the reader through a fictitious 'reporter' (1849: 670). Carlyle often resorted to editorial fiction and fictional speakers and the 'Occasional Discourse' is no exception, imitating as it does the multiply mediated genre of the mid-century lecture report and pointing towards questions of journalistic representation and reliability. Carol Collins, who provides the fullest exploration of the text's play with voices and frames, observes that Carlyle 'removes himself several times from advocating the sentiments of the essay' (1997: 26). Where Said finds Carlyle's prose blindingly obvious, Collins contends that it is 'impossible to pin [him] down to any one stance' (ibid., 30). But this ultimately tends to over-relativise the text. After all, Carlyle wrote and spoke in similar terms in a number of other contexts that came without the camouflage of editorial fiction. Nevertheless, what his use of the distancing device of the frame narrative suggests is that Carlyle was aware of the controversial nature of the racist sentiments to which his text was giving voice and visibility.

Contemporary readers on both sides of the Atlantic in any case did not have much trouble identifying Carlyle as the author of the 'Occasional Discourse'. Quaker poet and abolitionist John Greenleaf Whittier, for example, was convinced that the text had 'the unmistakable impress' of his 'Anglo-German peculiarities' (1854: 34). Linking Carlyle's commentary on the West Indies to the slave system more immediately on his own mind, Whittier found little to distinguish Carlyle's 'coarse brutality' from that of 'a Mississippi slave driver' (ibid., 36). Boston abolitionist Elizur Wright went even further than Whittier when he suggested that Carlyle's 'contempt for the negro ... would be considered a little extravagant' even 'in the patriarchal kingdom of South Carolina' (1850: 34). Closer to home, John Stuart Mill, who like Whittier was in no doubt about the authorship of the 'Discourse', published a strident response to the essay in *Fraser's Magazine* in early 1850. A refutation of Carlyle's claims, his rejoinder concludes with a transatlantic remark on the 'crisis of American slavery' (1850: 31). Whether intentionally or not, Carlyle had acted irresponsibly, Mill suggested, because as a British author he had a large influence on American readers ('The words of English writers of celebrity are words of power on the other side of the ocean' [ibid.]). Concerned about Carlyle's print-propelled authority in the United States, Mill worried that the 'Discourse' might be '[c]irculated ... by those whose interests profit by it, from one end of the American Union to the other' (ibid.). This prediction soon proved correct, as – like much of Carlyle's other writing – the 'Discourse' was being widely reprinted in the United States. Featuring the text in its June 1850 issue, the pro-slavery *DeBow's Review* introduced it with an editorial note that not only identified Carlyle as the author but also expressed strong sympathies with his views. Like Carlyle's 'Discourse' turning against abolitionism, the New Orleans periodical considered the text 'a piece of pungent satire, upon the whole body of pseudo philanthropists, who, within the last few years, have been a curse to our own country, as well as to England' (Carlyle 1850b: 527). As Mill had feared, Carlyle was lending the authority of his name to the racial politics of the South. The 'Discourse' featured in Northern periodicals as well, however. *Littell's Living Age* reprinted the text a few weeks after its original appearance in London, introducing it with a parenthetical caveat: '[We find the following pages in Fraser's Magazine. Are they by Mr. Carlyle? They will be a grief to many of his admirers in this region, and yet they, and others, (if others indeed there be!) will think it desirable to read whatever the sage may write.]' (Carlyle 1850a: 248). This was less determined on the authorship question than Whittier, Mill and *DeBow's*, but obviously because the Boston editors were still hoping that the text would, after all, turn out not to be by Carlyle. Yet even if it should, the paragraph implied, it would still be a rewarding read for an audience inclined to regard it as the latest oracular wisdom from 'the sage' of Chelsea (the vast majority of Carlyle's American readers, according to *Littell's*).

The fictional framing of the 'Occasional Discourse' not only afforded Carlyle and his New England 'admirers' the option of denying responsibility for the text's radical propositions, it also, at another level, presented a critique of a specific kind of Victorian anti-racism. The unnamed speaker addresses his listeners as 'My Philanthropic Friends' and the fictional audience response included in the text (in a manner modelled on the generic conventions of contemporary newspaper reportage) records outrage at the views expressed in the speech (1849: 670). Carlyle used this framework to write against a mid-century evangelical reformism of which Emerson, in texts such as the 1841 'Self-Reliance', had been similarly critical, complaining of the 'miscellaneous popular charities' of 'foolish philanthropist[s]' (*CW* 2: 31, 30). By the mid-1840s, however, Emerson had himself come to champion the abolitionist cause. A new commitment that put him at odds with Carlyle, this manifested itself in texts such as the address on the 'Anniversary of the Emancipation of the Negroes in the British West Indies' that he delivered in Concord in August 1844. That Carlyle was well aware of that shift makes it tempting to read the 'Occasional Discourse' and its depiction of emancipation as economically, politically and morally unsound as a direct response to Emerson's celebration of it as ushering in an era of black self-reliance.[17] Either implicitly or explicitly, Carlyle and Emerson thus participated in a transatlantic debate about abolition.

Yet even Emerson could not entirely leave his earlier racialist convictions behind, to the extent that he was now attempting to square abolitionism and Anglo-Saxonism. With its strong emphasis on notions of freedom and individuality, Anglo-Saxonist ideology itself was to some degree compatible with an anti-slavery attitude – not just for British philanthropists or white American abolitionists, but also for African Americans drawn to England in general (see Dickerson 2008) or to Anglo-Saxonism in particular (see Tamarkin 2008: 231–46). With the Slavery Abolition Act of 1833, Britain had become a reformist model from which antebellum Americans on both sides of the colour line drew inspiration (recourse to the language of Anglo-Saxon identity and the strategic deployment of Anglophilia were key, for example, to the success of African American abolitionist lecturers in mid-century Britain [see Wright 2017: 72–6 and Murray 2020: 90–4]). In his 1844 Concord address, Emerson was trying to marry abolitionist and Saxonist discourse through measuring the civilisational potential of emancipated slaves against a Saxonist rhetoric of strength:

> If the black man is feeble, and not important to the existing races not on a parity with the best race, the black man must serve, and be exterminated. But if the black man carries in his bosom an indispensable element of a new and coming civilization, for the sake of that element, no wrong, nor strength, nor circumstance, can hurt him: he will survive and play his part. (*AW* 31)

As Laura Dassow Walls observes, 'there is an oddly "Darwinian" flavor . . . to the developmental unfolding' Emerson here imagines, one 'wherein only the strongest, most fleet, most prolific, or smartest survive' (2003: 167). Coming close to these virtues is the best evidence for the dignity of formerly enslaved people that Emerson apparently can think of. At the very end of the address, he links Anglo-Saxonism and abolition even more explicitly when he postulates that, 'friendly to liberty', '[t]he genius of the Saxon race' is 'inconsistent with slavery' (*AW* 33). Being Saxon to Emerson requires reaffirming core liberal values in the face of a contemporary moral challenge (the abolition of slavery in the United States) rather than itself being part of the underlying problem of supremacy and exploitation.

As the debate about slavery was bringing questions of race newly to the fore over the decade that followed, Emerson's affirmative Anglo-Saxonism began to falter. Focusing on the shifts and turns in his thought on race between his second trip to England in 1847–8 and the publication of *English Traits* in 1856, Daniel Koch has argued that Emerson's experience of the European revolutions of 1848 and his increasing commitment to the abolitionist cause led to a conversion from his one-time celebration of racial Saxonism to a position that 'ridicule[d] the vanity and self-deceit of racial doctrinism' (2012: 178). Such shifts with Emerson are not usually straightforward, however. He seems truly to advance beyond his earlier beliefs only in *English Traits*, his most extensive statement on England and English character. A whole chapter of the book is dedicated to the question of race, and it presents a more conflicted view of the subject than the 1844 address.[18] The book section opens with an outright rejection of Emerson's prior assumptions about the distinctness of races. What he points out now is that, ultimately, 'each variety shades down imperceptibly into the next, and you cannot draw the line where a race begins or ends' (*CW* 5: 24). If race thus has no concrete material existence outside of the realm of abstract categorisation, racial theory loses its value as a hermeneutics of culture. Emerson explores the 'limitations of the formidable doctrine of race' at greater length as the chapter develops:

> The fixity or inconvertibleness of races as we see them, is a weak argument for the eternity of these frail boundaries, since all our historical period is a point to the duration in which nature has wrought. . . . [T]hough we flatter the self-love of men and nations by the legend of pure races, all our experience is of the gradation and resolution of races, and strange resemblances meet us everywhere. (ibid., 27)

The idea that the 'frail boundaries' of race are nothing more than constructs and that behind a variety of racial appearances lies a unity of deep-structural 'resemblances' is a sign of Emerson's reawakening idealism. Equally important about the passage is its shift from a critique of racial singularity or 'fixity' to one of racial purity. Although Emerson has come to regard the doctrine of 'pure races' as no longer tenable, he seems unwilling to let go of the idea of the superior quality of English racial traits. Devising a new way of arguing for Anglo-Saxon excellence, in a sudden argumentative move he concludes that, if claiming the purity of races is empirically unsound, '[t]he best nations are those most widely related' – an assertion that conveniently squares with his subsequent observation that '[t]he English composite character betrays a mixed origin', that '[e]very thing English is a fusion of distant and antagonistic elements' (ibid.).[19]

Yet in turning to the celebration of an English 'anthology of temperaments' and in thus imagining English traits once again as distinctive and permanent, Emerson has manoeuvred himself into a position that jars with his initial concern about the fleeting nature of racial characteristics (ibid., 28). The 'conceptual mess' (Voelz 2010: 224) that emerges from the chapter is thus the result of a clash between two conflicting tendencies, a transcendence of racial categories and a belief in their hierarchical organisation. Emerson's justification for continuing to rely on the rhetoric of race hence sounds awkwardly provisional: 'we must use the popular category', he writes, 'for convenience, and not as exact and final' (*CW* 5: 29). As a solution to the larger problem this is all the more unsatisfying because it underwrites the rationale for *English Traits* as a whole, a book which rests on the ontological and epistemological premise that something like distinctive 'English traits' – and hence distinctly English 'Ability', 'Manners' and 'Character', to use some of the book's chapter headings – does, in fact, exist in an ethnologically verifiable and analytically productive sense.

While there is thus a considerable fluidity in Emerson's writing on race, especially in his growing awareness of the incompatibility of racial theory with an idealist rejection of determinism, what remains consistent despite these shifts of emphasis is his desire to construct an American racial pedigree. Neal Dolan has argued that *English Traits* retains a strong attachment to Anglo-Saxonism because Emerson seeks 'to secure the deep roots, however mythical, of an Anglo-American commitment to freedom that he worries may be wavering' in the politically charged atmosphere of the 1850s (2009: 267). Yet the liberalist motivation behind Emerson's adherence to Anglo-Saxonism ultimately seems a negligible factor. The book retains the idea of superior Saxon traits, but – like many of Emerson's earlier texts on the subject – it does so primarily in order to argue that these traits have been inherited by Americans. If, in the 'Race' chapter of *English Traits*, Emerson 'waffles on purity and permanence, though in almost everything else he favors continuity' (Painter 2010: 181), this was because such ambiguity suited him best to argue for both transatlantic similarity and American difference. While Emerson and Carlyle thus both tapped into a widely available repertoire of Anglo-Saxonist imagery to describe the transatlantic relationship, the nature of their visions ultimately differed. To Carlyle, the idea of a globally expansive Saxon population allowed for a notion of imperial culture that rallied members of other nations under the banner of Englishness at the same time that it subjected them to the authority of metropolitan culture. For Emerson, by contrast, a similar emphasis on racial community – which remained constant across his many comments on ethnic identity – served to justify an American share in English power while simultaneously opening up the prospect of future dominance.

Notes

1. Inclined to pay homage to 'English taste' and style, the Unitarians were traditionally drawn to viewing themselves, in Daniel Walker Howe's words, as 'belonging to a trans-Atlantic civilization' (1970: 183). Although Howe goes on to qualify this assessment when he writes that Unitarian aesthetics consisted of 'more . . . than mere Anglophilia' (ibid., 185), texts like Norton's demonstrate that, when it came to declaring one's aesthetic allegiances, an affirmative identification with English models won the day.
2. On the relationship between language, group membership and the rise of nationalism, see also Anderson 2006: 67–82.
3. Sewell's quotation is a reference to *The Faerie Queene* (1590/6) and its characterisation of Chaucer as 'well of English vndefyled' (IV.ii.32.8; Spenser 2007: 423).
4. See Guinn 1999 for a more detailed account of Southern responses to Emerson between the 1830s and the 1860s. As Guinn demonstrates, reviewers in the South consistently disapproved of Emerson's style, his theology and his politics (and they stuck with the idea that he was merely parroting Carlyle for much longer than Northern critics).

5. In 'State of German Literature' (1827), for example, Carlyle admitted that 'there is in the German mind a tendency to mysticism' while at the same suggesting that the term was simply a smokescreen for English reviewers to mask their failure to grasp what German writing was actually about (*'mystical*, in most cases, will turn out to be merely synonymous with *not understood*') (CE 26: 72, 70).
6. The passage of the *Blackwood's* essay from which the above quotations are taken was widely reprinted in the United States (see Anon. 1841b and Anon. 1843d for two examples).
7. On these developments, see, in particular, Baucom 1999. As Laura Doyle writes, race 'has sustained the imperial reach of the nation, providing both temporal continuity and socio-spatial integrity – in the face of rupture in both dimensions' (2008: 15). Anglo-Saxonist imagery thus catered both to visions of transatlantic unity and to individual imperial projects predicated on the more narrow logic of the nation.
8. Anthony Smith speaks of 'nation' and '*ethnie*' as 'different concepts and historical formations' (1991: 40): where a nation 'must occupy a homeland of its own' and 'aspire to nationhood and [to] be recognized as a nation', 'ethnic communities generally lack public cultures' as well as a 'political referent' (2001: 12–13). Walker Connor, a proponent of 'ethnic' or 'ethno-nationalism', defines the nation as 'a group of people characterized by a myth of common descent' and thus destabilises the boundary between nation and *ethnie* through likening nation to ethnic group rather than political formation (1994: 75). Connor has himself reflected on the 'terminological chaos' in the use of words such as *nation, state* or *ethnic group* not only in the nineteenth century but also among twentieth-century theorists of nationalism (see ibid., 93–4).
9. For Hobsbawm and other 'modernist' theorists of the nation (such as Ernest Gellner or Benedict Anderson) the phenomenon is a distinctly modern one. 'Primordialists' such as Smith and Connor instead emphasise a historical continuum in the emergence of modern nations. On the difference between these two camps, see Smith 1986: 7–13 and Kumar 2003: 28–30.
10. In addition to Horsman and Young, see, for example, Bolt 1971 on British racialist discourse in the second half of the nineteenth century and MacDougall 1982: 90–103 for a more concise overview of the development of nineteenth-century Anglo-Saxonism and its relation to racial Teutonism.
11. On the history of this type of interest in Old English and Anglo-Saxon language, literature and culture from the mid-eighteenth to the mid-nineteenth centuries, see Niles 2015: 186–264.
12. The medieval *translatio imperii et studii* trope of a westward transition of power and knowledge was a frequent image in nineteenth-century debates about (Anglo-) American culture. See Freese 1996 on the origins of the idea and its manifestations in the period's writing and painting; Weisbuch 1986: 70–5 discusses the same trope as the 'myth of the west'.
13. Young has pointed out that in the aftermath of the Act of Union of 1707 – which turned England and Scotland into Great Britain – 'many North British (that is, Scottish) intellectuals argued that Lowland Scots . . . were Saxons, and that only the Highlanders . . . were Celts' (2008: 30). Horsman paraphrases Carlyle's inclusionary Saxonism when he writes that, as a 'lowland Scot', he 'had little sympathy for the Celts' and instead 'stressed the Norse origins of Scotland's population' (1981: 63).

14. Both of them, for example, had Sharon Turner's *History of the Anglo-Saxons* on their reading lists in the 1820s (see NTC 127 and *JMN* 2: 77).
15. Reporting on one of Carlyle's lectures, the London *Times* noted that he had 'put forth views upon the origin of the early history, the growth, and characteristics of the German people, following them downwards, and involving in them those of the Saxon race – the English, the North Americans, the white rulers of India, and new colonial proprietors of the vast Eastern Archipelago' (Anon. 1837b: 5). On the transatlantic repercussions of such statements, see also Chapter 6.
16. Traditional readings of the 'Occasional Discourse' have tended to relativise either the vehemence of Carlyle's racialist rhetoric or the seriousness with which he engaged it. Gillian Workman, for example, has argued that 'Carlyle's language' in the text 'was surely more a rhetorical device than an expression of racial disgust' (1974: 85), while Ian Campbell (1971) has sought to mitigate the offensive nature of Carlyle's commentary through describing it as founded in his Calvinist upbringing. Among more recent commentators, Jude Nixon (1996) has explored the links between Carlyle's racial rhetoric and the larger imperialist argument of the essay; Helen Small (2017) considers the text as probing the limits of a Victorian culture of free speech.
17. The emancipation address was published in London by Emerson's English publisher John Chapman, and Carlyle, in his capacity as Emerson's English representative, was among its first readers abroad (see Chapter 4).
18. The best critical assessments of Emerson's chapter put an equal emphasis on the affirmative and destabilising dimensions of its appropriation of racial discourse (see Hanlon 2013: 36–9 and Voelz 2010: 224–5 for two such nuanced readings).
19. This notion of mixture also allows Emerson to adopt a diplomatic stance in judging the English and their manners. When he argues that 'nothing can be praised' in the English character 'without damning exceptions, and nothing denounced without salvos of cordial praise' (*CW* 5: 28), this provides a structural template for the constant back and forth between commendation and condemnation that is characteristic of the book as a whole.

2

USABLE PASTS: ANGLO-AMERICAN LITERATURE AND THE AUTHORITY OF TRADITION

Romantic and post-Romantic writers are commonly seen as committed to the project of nation-building – an impression that derives from phenomena such as Johann Gottfried Herder's 'discovery' of distinct national cultures, Walter Scott's literary 'invention' of Scottishness, the dominance of national templates for historiography or the period's quasi-ethnographic interest in regionally specific oral literatures. This chapter revisits some of the more specifically literary arguments that accompanied nineteenth-century Anglo-American political developments and the discourses to which they were coupled (the rise of the British Empire and the rhetoric of global Englishness or westward expansion and Manifest Destiny ideology). I am concerned here with how literary texts were seen as giving expression to national character and with how national character was, in turn, understood as being shaped through literary texts, but I am equally interested in the ways in which writers theorised the emergence of distinct cultural nationalities. From the late eighteenth century onwards, nationality increasingly becomes a literary asset, something to strive for as well as to reflect upon. If such a valuation of national difference on its own specific terms can, to some extent, be seen as a late-Enlightenment manifestation of transcultural tolerance, its nineteenth-century reception was, more often than not, marked by a ready espousal of the notion of cultural idiosyncrasy and by the elevation of individual national qualities over those of other nations. There is also, of course, an alternative tendency to highlight forms of transnational contact and cast literature as the instrument for such cultural exchange. What

I suggest in this chapter is that nationalist and cosmopolitanist frames of reference were not necessarily mutually exclusive argumentative positions and that, to British and American writers alike, the idea of the transatlantic provided a way of negotiating between these two perspectives.

Where the previous chapter has mainly discussed transatlantic conceptualisations of racial identity, I here concentrate on how these debates found expression in writing about literature. Drawing attention to 'the dual connection . . . between, on the one hand, race and nationality, and, on the other, nationality and literature', Kwame Anthony Appiah has noted how closely these three elements were historically linked in the eighteenth and nineteenth centuries (1995: 282). It is with this kind of interconnection in mind that the present chapter builds on questions already in part addressed above. My interest in the following is in the belief that racial or national traits manifest themselves through specific literary forms, in the role assigned to literature as illustrating such traits and in the idea of literary history as an index of racial continuity or change. By way of introduction, the first section of the chapter revisits two basic (late-)Romantic scripts at the disposal of mid-nineteenth-century British and American writers to imagine the relationship between literature and cultural specificity. I begin by drawing attention to the cultural relativism pioneered by Herder – and subsequently popularised through other continental authors such as Germaine de Staël, Friedrich Schlegel and Victor Cousin – before I retrace how this form of thinking about literary nationality surfaced in Carlyle's and Emerson's writing on the literary and the national. I then go on to consider a second important contemporary set of ideas that concerns the relationship between the local and the global, my case study here being Goethe's concept of world literature and its Anglophone origins and impact. When nineteenth-century authors tried to make sense of literature, they resorted to ethnic, political and spatial markers of difference, but they also drew heavily on temporal modes of categorisation, navigating their contemporary field through acts of reading, interpreting and appropriating its past. Looking at English literary history allowed British and American writers to draw inferences about the structure of the contemporary Anglophone literary sphere and its potential future configurations. Sections three, four and five of this chapter analyse concrete examples of such historical narratives and demonstrate more specifically how Carlyle and Emerson deployed the authority of the English tradition as a benchmark for present and future literary production.

Cultural Nationalism From Herder to Emerson

Where modern theories of nationalism often proceed from a constructivist point of view, there is a tendency in Romantic writing – and in the 'organismic conceptions of collectivity' that it often formulates (Cheah 2003: 25) – to think of the nation as a self-evident, quasi-natural entity. Within such a framework, cultural factors are assigned a crucial role in creating an awareness of national identity. Literature is here seen as enunciating nationality and hence emerges as 'the expression of a national spirit' (Wellek 1970: 151), its importance chiefly deriving from this indexical relationship to the national. To Anglophone writers, German impulses proved the richest source for such a conception of literature as a form of national expression. It is difficult to overestimate the importance for Romantic poetics of the pluralist relativism that emerged in late-eighteenth-century thought about culture and nationhood. This surfaces perhaps most prominently in the writings of Herder, who, departing from universalist theories of culture, advanced a comparative model of national characteristics that read culture as an agent differentiating humanity into nationally specific subgroups. Herder thought of national culture as the organic expression of inherent national traits to be judged by their own individual standards (Shakespearean drama could not be fairly measured by Aristotelian criteria, French neoclassical norms did not apply to German *Sturm und Drang* writing and so on). This argument features most extensively in the monumental *Ideen zur Philosophie der Geschichte der Menschheit* (1784–91), which celebrates linguistic and national difference through its core idea that 'every nation is one people, having it's [sic] own national form, as well as it's [sic] own language' (1800: 166). Although to commentators such as Isaiah Berlin 'Herder's nationalism was never political' (1976: 181), he established a logic that had far-reaching repercussions in later cultural as well as political forms of nationalism.¹

Herder's idea of cultural nationality was popularised in the early nineteenth century by a number of writers who fleshed out its more specifically literary implications. Friedrich Schlegel, for instance, spoke more explicitly than Herder about the relationship between national character and literary expression, and more emphatically about the importance of literature in verbalising the cultural essence of nationhood. In his *Geschichte der alten und neuen Literatur* (1815) – a book based on a series of lectures read in Vienna in 1812 and translated into English by John Gibson Lockhart in 1818 (a version printed and sold on both sides of the Atlantic) – Schlegel highlights these elements in particular:

> If we consider literature in its widest sense, as the voice which gives expression to human intellect – as the aggregate mass of symbols in which the spirit of an age or the character of a nation is shadowed forth; then indeed a great and accomplished literature is, without all doubt, the most valuable possession of which any nation can boast. (1818, 1: 274)

Herder's *Ideen* itself reached Anglophone readers in the form of Thomas Churchill's translation of the book as *Outlines of a Philosophy of the History of Man* (1800), but Herderian thought – and contemporary German writing, more generally – was also frequently triangulated through French sources. Eclecticist philosopher Victor Cousin's *Introduction à l'histoire de la philosophie* (1828), for example, provided a detailed summary of Herder's writing that put special emphasis on the doctrine of national specificity.² In the ninth of his introductory lectures, he argues that '[e]very people represents one idea, and not any other' (1832: 271). Like Herder, however, Cousin ultimately concludes that 'there must exist resemblances between [nations], still greater than their differences' (ibid., 267). An important mediator who had popularised cultural relativism outside of Germany before Cousin was Germaine de Staël. Her *De la littérature considérée dans ses rapports avec les institutions sociales* (1800), first translated into English in 1812, offered a general discussion of European national literatures as illustrative of specific national characteristics (which, unlike Herder, de Staël thought of as deriving not so much from natural factors as from differences in political and sectarian dispositions).³ For de Staël – as for Herder, Schlegel and Cousin – literature was a field of key importance because it 'revealed national character' (Manning 2013: 17). More widely read than *De la littérature*, de Staël's *De l'Allemagne* (1810/13) not only provided an extensive account of German national traits but also featured introductions to writers such as Herder and the Schlegel brothers (see 1813, 2: 364–9, 370–88).

Carlyle knew de Staël's writing, but he was also well acquainted with the German sources she was summarising, drawing from them the basic coordinates of his thought about literature and nationality. He read Churchill's translation of Herder in the 1820s (see *NTC* 33–6, 72–7), frequently referred to Schlegel in his early essays and spoke about both authors in his 1837 lectures on German literature.⁴ The idea that literary writing showcases specific national characters surfaces in the introduction to his 1830 *History of German Literature*, in which he explains how literature embodies 'the essential life of the nation':

> [A] national Literature, so far as it can deserve that name, is not only the noblest achievement of the nation, but also the most characteristic; the truest emblem of the national spirit and manner of existence; out of which, indeed, it directly springs, as a purified essence, and disembodied celestial, [sic] likeness, and into which again, in strong influences, it continually descends. Nowhere does the mind and life of a nation, in all its specialties, and deep-laid yet light and almost evanescencent [sic] individualities, so faithfully shadow itself, as in the mirror of its Art and Literature . . . (*HGL* 6–7)

Carlyle emphasises that literature is closely bound up with national identity and of crucial importance to how it becomes externally perceived. This conceptual ambiguity echoes the circular logic behind the Herderian notion of literary nationality, which Rebecca Walkowitz has poignantly summarised as 'a feedback loop': 'nationhood owes its identity to authorship, but there is no authorship without nationhood since expressivity belongs to unique individuals who in turn belong to unique groups' (2009: 573).

The same premise resurfaces in another one of Carlyle's large-scale literary historical projects that coheres around the idea of distinct literary nationalities. The 1838 *Lectures on the History of Literature* add a comparative element to his formerly German-centred accounts, but this ends up reinforcing the idea of national difference rather than replacing it with a model of international universality. The structure of Carlyle's lecture course closely resembles de Staël's *De la littérature* and Schlegel's Vienna lectures in moving from the Greco-Roman origins of Western literature through the Middle Ages to the birth of modern European national literatures (Italian, French, Spanish, English, German) in the context of the Renaissance and the Reformation – a narrative model that, by the 1830s, had become an established template for the genre of the comparative literary historical survey.[5] That Carlyle decided to follow this historical trajectory suggests that he was hardly a primevalist when it came to explaining the origin of nations. He thinks of a gradual emergence of nationality and its accompanying forms of literary expression rather than of the nation as a natural phenomenon always already in existence. The medium in which national distinctions manifest themselves most directly – and here Carlyle comes especially close to Herder's thought – is language, a 'peculiar product' that unmistakably 'characterises each nation' (*LHL* 79).

In an essay on his fellow Scot Robert Burns, published ten years before the London lectures on European literary history, Carlyle had already hinted at the historical mutability of nationality and placed an even stronger emphasis on contingency. The fate of national literature here appeared as subject to an ebb-and-flow cycle that had not come to a close in the wake of the medieval watershed moment that, in the later lecture course, Carlyle would identify as the foundation of modern European nations. Reflecting on the fate of literary nationality during Burns's lifetime, Carlyle sketches a pre-Herderian moment at which literatures had not yet become nationally distinct. 'Among the great changes which British, particularly Scottish literature, has undergone since that period', Carlyle argued, 'one of the greatest will be found to consist in its remarkable increase of nationality':

> Even the English writers most popular in Burns's time, were little distinguished for their literary patriotism. . . . A certain attenuated cosmopolitanism had, in good measure, taken place of the old insular home-feeling; literature was, as it were, without any local environment; was not nourished by the affections which spring from a native soil. (*WTC* 5: 51)

An atavistic 'home-feeling' had existed at some point, Carlyle suggests, but it had in turn become supplanted by an eighteenth-century universalism that had turned 'our culture' into something 'almost exclusively French' (ibid., 52). If Carlyle retrospectively criticises eighteenth-century cultural cosmopolitanism, the 'remarkable increase of nationality' that he describes as the key transformation in British writing between Burns's lifetime and his own nineteenth-century present provides the narrative with a redeeming sense of closure. Burns's vernacular poetry managed to recover a Scottish literary voice that once more organically testified to its indelible attachment to the 'local environment'.

That literature, as Schlegel had noted, was 'of late ... becoming more national' (1818, 1: 7) was a phenomenon remarked upon not just in Europe but also across the Atlantic. The emergence of the Herderian paradigm of national culture coincided with the birth of the United States as an independent political entity and American writers pursued the project of defining a distinctive national literature with special intensity.[6] If, in Herder's German or Carlyle's Scottish context, the quest for national uniqueness mainly revolved around distinguishing oneself from eighteenth-century France, the creation of cultural difference in the American case first and foremost implied emphasising one's difference from England. Writing about American literary nationality in the first half of the nineteenth century almost invariably entailed a contrastive reference to British culture, taste and tradition. This was often complicated by the large ethnic and linguistic overlap between the United States and the former coloniser. Herder's idea of national culture as residing in the people and its language made it hard for post-revolutionary American writers to advance simple claims for transatlantic alterity. Commentators on the nation's literature were nevertheless often firmly moving within a Herderian framework.

Herder's writings were available in the United States early on, either in their German original or in the form of British print products such as Churchill's translation of the *Ideen* or partial translations in English periodicals. Among the earliest American proponents of Herderianism was George Bancroft, who, as a young Harvard graduate, had completed his education at the universities of Heidelberg, Göttingen and Berlin. Bancroft presented himself as a faithful disciple of Herder in an essay on the 'Life and Genius of Goethe', published in the *North American Review* in 1824. Bancroft here declared, somewhat tautologically, that '[t]he literature of each nation is national' (1824: 305). Distinctness was the chief quality at which a national tradition should aim: 'The literature of a people, if it be good, will be peculiar', he argued, and 'contain a description ... of sensations which have not been aroused or indulged by others' (ibid., 304). The logic of literary nationality was also attractive for an older generation of the New England intellectual establishment. William Ellery Channing, influential Unitarian preacher and a mentor figure for many of the Transcendentalists, in 1830 published an essay on 'National Literature' that is full of Herderian echoes. An important contribution to the American debate about cultural nationhood frequently cited by his contemporaries, Channing's text defined 'national literature' as 'the expression of a nation's mind in writing' (1830: 269). Like Herder and Bancroft, Channing emphasised the dissimilarity between different national cultures, but he went further in essentially foreclosing the possibility of intercultural comprehensibility as well as in rejecting the idea that literary otherness could be bridged through acts of cultural translation. Faced with the *de facto* absence of a home-grown literature and the reliance of American readers on books written elsewhere, Channing set out to demonstrate the need for a specifically American literature capable of displacing such imports.[7]

Later American versions of Herderianism make Bancroft's and Channing's arguments look moderate by comparison. Over the course of the 1830s and 1840s, as westward expansion and the exceptionalist ideology that underwrote it became dominant topics in the political sphere, American writing on literary nationality assumed an increasingly violent cast, developing into a fully fledged modern cultural nationalism (an intensity that English literary debates never quite reached). A previous emphasis on difference gradually turned into a claim to superiority, a comparison with the foreign into its negation. An 1847 essay on 'Nationality in Literature', published in the *Democratic Review*, the mouthpiece of the Young America movement and the venue in which John L. O'Sullivan, two years before, had coined the phrase 'manifest destiny', is characteristic of the period in its outspoken championing of a 'lofty assertion of national superiority' (Anon. 1847a: 271). Explicitly relying on de Staël's *De la littérature* and Schlegel's *Geschichte* to argue for 'the necessity of nationality' (ibid., 267) in literary and cultural matters, the author of the piece considered American literature to be superior rather than equal to other literary traditions. American geography and its literary equivalent, the *Democratic Review* suggested, 'present elements of growth, of strength, and of greatness, which give assurance of the most splendid career to be traced in the annals of the human race' (ibid., 264).

Emerson was familiar with this nativist radicalisation of cultural relativism, but his texts are often considerably less straightforward than those of his contemporaries. To be sure, towards the end of the 1837 'American Scholar' oration he famously declared that Americans had 'listened too long to the courtly muses of Europe' and should instead pursue their own path to cultural self-authorisation ('We will walk on our own feet; we will work with our own hands; we will speak our own minds') (*CW* 1: 69–70). But while this clearly sounds like Young America rhetoric, the address as a whole can just as well be read as illustrating an overall 'refusal to wave the flag' (Buell 2003: 45). The text's final sentence, after all, leaves Emerson's audience to ponder the idea of a nation composed of individuals rather than the idea of a coherent national collective: 'A nation of men will for the first time exist', he foretells, 'because each believes himself inspired by the Divine Soul which also inspires all men' (*CW* 1: 70). Imagining a 'nation of men' rather than a nation of Americans (and a literature by individual rather than national writers), Emerson here essentially denies that the nation and its distinctive literature turn individuals into a collective whole. In so doing, he argues against one of the key tenets of the discourse of literary nationalism.

A similar reservation about excessive nation-centredness also informs the essay 'The Poet' (1844), towards the end of which Emerson laments the absence of a true American literature. 'I look in vain for the poet whom I describe', he writes, admitting that '[w]e have yet had no genius in America' (CW 3: 21). Although he goes on to declare more assertively that 'America is a poem in our eyes; its ample geography dazzles the imagination, and it will not wait long for metres,' after a paragraph break Emerson ultimately deflates nationalist pathos when he remarks laconically: 'I am not wise enough for a national criticism, and must use the old largeness a little longer' (ibid., 22). Indeed, the earlier parts of the essay concern questions of a more general nature, reflections in which Emerson unfolds an idealist poetics dominated by the conceptual 'largeness' of metaphysical–religious ideas about language, representation and ontological unity rather than by more particularist political considerations rooted in the concrete literary and cultural atmosphere of his time.

Emerson's unease with 'national criticism' comes to the fore once again in his editorial introduction to the inaugural issue of the *Massachusetts Quarterly Review*, published in December 1847, when the Mexican–American War was drawing to a close and Emerson was touring northern England and Scotland as a lecturer. Here as well, he wonders about the absence of domestic 'works of the Imagination, – the surest test of a national genius' (CW 10: 342), repeating his sceptical assessment of American cultural achievement and raising doubts about the value of patriotic sentiment:

> We hesitate to employ a word so much abused as patriotism, whose true sense is almost the reverse of its popular sense. We have no sympathy with that boyish egotism hoarse with cheering for our side, for our State, for our town; the right patriotism consists in the delight which springs from contributing our peculiar and legitimate advantages to the benefit of humanity. (ibid., 343)

Emerson rejects the 'boyish egotism' of cultural nationalism while, at the same time, maintaining the individualist value of the nation ('every family of men . . . has its distinguishing virtues') (ibid.). In its combination of national allegiance and a commitment to the progress of 'humanity' at large this argument is genuinely Herderian. A similar synthesis had emerged towards the end of Carlyle's essay on Burns, published two decades earlier. While Carlyle celebrated the Romantic rebirth of literary nationality and disapproved of the 'attenuated cosmopolitanism' of eighteenth-century Francophile universalism, his tone became more conciliatory when he turned to sketching an alternative form of cosmopolitanism that was patriotic in outlook:

We hope, there is a patriotism founded on something better than prejudice; that our country may be dear to us, without injury to our philosophy; that in loving and justly prizing all other lands, we may prize justly, and yet love before all others our own stern Motherland. (*WTC* 5: 52)

Carlyle is more emphatic than Emerson in his defence of national pride, but his sentiment points in the same direction. Instead of championing a more conventional contemporary literary nationalism, the two texts contain a hybrid argument that comes close to what Kwame Anthony Appiah has described as forms of 'rooted cosmopolitanism' or 'cosmopolitan patriotism' (1997: 618).[8]

WORLD LITERATURE BETWEEN NATION AND COSMOS

If Herder provided a way of thinking of culture as nationally specific, Carlyle's and Emerson's ideas about patriotism reflect a simultaneous interest in a more capacious vocabulary. For Carlyle, in particular, Johann Wolfgang Goethe's notion of world literature offered a useful conceptual framework to combine the notion of national culture with an impulse 'to value what is foreign' (Eckermann 1839: 204).[9] Goethe's reflections on the topic were, in fact, mainly occasioned by Carlyle himself, who had been sending specimens of his literary efforts to Weimar from the mid-1820s onwards (his translation of *Wilhelm Meisters Lehrjahre* [1824] and his *Life of Schiller* [1825], as well as the four-volume anthology *German Romance* [1827], which included the translation of the second *Wilhelm Meister* novel). Confronted with the fact that a young Scottish writer seemed to have a better grasp of German literature than most Germans, Goethe noted in conversation with his confidant Johann Peter Eckermann that Carlyle's writing illustrated the 'use of a world-literature' for fostering knowledge of different national cultures (ibid., 230). Goethe reviewed *German Romance* for his journal *Über Kunst und Altertum* and quoted from the forthcoming piece in his correspondence with Carlyle in July 1827 before its eventual publication the following year. '[T]he special characteristics of a nation', he argued,

> are like its language and its currency: they facilitate intercourse, nay they first make it completely possible. . . . A genuine, universal tolerance is most surely attained, if we do not quarrel with the peculiar characteristics of individual men and races, but only hold fast the conviction, that what is truly excellent is distinguished by its belonging to all mankind. (Goethe and Carlyle 1887: 25)

Such cosmopolitan impartiality, to Goethe, was grounded in an ethics of 'intercourse and mutual recognition' (ibid.). This, in turn, was made possible through the work of literary translation, which Goethe here describes as a form of 'spiritual commerce' (ibid., 26). He himself made Carlyle's work available for a non-English readership through his support of a German translation of the *Life of Schiller*, to which he contributed an extensive introduction that reads Carlyle as a prime example of world literature in action.

Without explicitly using the term *world literature*, Carlyle was summarising the spirit of the idea in print as early as 1827. The essay 'State of German Literature', published in the *Edinburgh Review* in October of that year, features a Goethean rhetoric of intellectual exchange and celebrates intellectual openness to the foreign. Carlyle here notes that 'the commerce in material things has paved roads for commerce in things spiritual' and suggests that 'a nation that ... isolates itself from foreign influence' is like 'a man who mistakes his own contracted individuality for the type of human nature' (*CE* 26: 30). Just as Goethe, Carlyle used the idea of world literature to reflect on the networked realities of nineteenth-century life. In the second chapter of the 1830 *History of German Literature*, for example, he starts out by admiring the racial purity of the Germans, but then begins to wonder whether mixture is not, in fact, more desirable, before ultimately coming to realise that national autonomy is merely a fiction:

> [B]e our birth what it may, there is not[,] neither can there be[,] any such thing as independent, self-regulated growth and culture for a nation; least of all, in this ever-fluctuating, all-combining, all-dividing Europe, where, at this day, to say nothing of our Eastern Coffees and Cottons, such has been our frank intercourse and brotherhood, we write with Italian, perhaps Phœnician Letters, compute with Arabic or Hindoo Numerals, worship with Hebrew Books. (*HGL* 14)

Carlyle is here questioning the very idea of distinct national cultures on which his own historical project is itself, after all, predicated, and he does so by drawing attention to international commercial activity (the importation of 'Eastern Coffees and Cottons', a result of European colonialist efforts abroad) and to the distinctly textual–material dimension of transnational cultural hybridity (the foreign 'Letters' and 'Books' that have come to shape nineteenth-century European identity). Carlyle grants that nations may originally have existed in isolation, but he implies that in an 'ever-fluctuating' modern world they can no longer be seen as closed entities. In a July 1828 essay on Goethe for the *Foreign Review*, he had already argued that thinking solely along national lines had ceased to be a viable option: '[W]riting for England alone ... is no longer possible', he suggested, because '[t]raffic, with its swift ships, is uniting all nations into one' and 'Europe at large is becoming more and more one public' (*CE* 26: 207). As with the later account in the *History*, Carlyle here goes beyond Goethe in thinking of an outright dissolution of national boundaries.

For Goethe, 'world literature' was likewise coupled to what Carlyle in the late 1820s described as transnational movements of goods and people as well as print and ideas. When Goethe spoke about world literature, he often did so in order to highlight that the modern world was growing ever more closely together in both spiritual and material terms. In an early letter to Carlyle, for example, he marvels at the fact that '[b]y mail-coaches and steam-packets, as well as by daily, weekly and monthly periodicals, the nations are drawing nearer to one another' (Goethe and Carlyle 1887: 114). Emphasising the importance of interlocking revolutions in transportation and communication, Goethe here and elsewhere explicitly draws attention to the crucial role that print and its circulation played in such literary exchange. Like Carlyle, he proceeds from the material to the intellectual, suggesting that an international market for the exchange of goods provides the political, economic and logistical framework for a corresponding 'spiritual commerce'. Intellectual and material exchange are closely intertwined here: transnational literary contact depends on material networks of production and circulation that spread texts in the embodied form of books and periodicals, which in turn are both material objects and cultural containers for the 'spiritual' content they carry across national and cultural borders. Among Goethe's and Carlyle's contemporaries, this awareness of the relationship between texts and their physical identity as printed matter led to an interest in international reprinting and the intertextual nature of the periodical format. *Über Kunst und Altertum* regularly featured literary intelligence from the Paris *Globe* and the *Edinburgh Review*, and Goethe hoped that British papers such as the *Foreign Quarterly Review* would, in turn, run material from his own periodical. More than a mere discourse, world literature in this sense described a specific, materially mediated form of cultural exchange. For Goethe – as much as for Carlyle – the idea of world literature crystallised in a print internationalism that freely acknowledged, and indeed celebrated, the dependence of intellectual exchange on material forms of production and dissemination. Perhaps the most far-reaching element latent in the concept was the notion of a transnational republic of letters connecting an otherwise fractured modernity.

It is hence hardly surprising that when Emerson diagnosed the complexity of modern life in terms similar to Carlyle's, it was in the context of a discussion of Goethe. In the seventh and final lecture of the 1850 *Representative Men*, entitled 'Goethe, or the Writer', Emerson envisions a modernity marked by diversity and multiplicity. The historical moment at which Goethe 'appears' on the literary scene to Emerson was 'a time, when a general culture has spread itself, and has smoothed down all sharp individual traits' (*CW* 4: 156) – an effacement of particularity through global networking that applies to political and cultural manifestations of nationality in equal measure. The simile that Emerson uses to illustrate this modern 'miscellany' (ibid.) is drawn from the same language of commerce that Goethe had employed two decades earlier when speaking about world literature as a form of intellectual exchange akin to the transnational circulation of goods. Emerson suggests that '[t]he world extends itself like American trade' (ibid.), pointing to an increasing commercial and cultural convergence of the domestic and the global. It was precisely Goethe, in that respect the representative man of his age, who, for Emerson, became 'the philosopher of this multiplicity' (ibid.). While he is an eminently national writer ('the head and body of the German nation'), Goethe also, and more importantly for Emerson, contains global multitudes ('there is no trace of provincial limitation in his muse') (ibid., 163, 156).

Although Emerson never explicitly adopted Goethe's and Carlyle's rhetoric of world literature in his published writings, he was nevertheless well aware of its existence. In a review of Carlyle's *The French Revolution* (1837) that remained unpublished during his lifetime, he quotes from (and translates) the final three paragraphs of Goethe's commentary on *German Romance*.[10] Citing Goethe's notion of a contemporary 'spiritual commerce', Emerson here describes Carlyle's role as a transnational cultural broker and implicitly conceives of himself as one. The text opens up a triple framework of cross-cultural mediation: Carlyle, in *German Romance*, had introduced Goethe and other contemporary German writers to an English-speaking readership; through his review of *German Romance* in *Über Kunst und Altertum*, Goethe, on his part, had publicised this effort to a German audience and thus retranslated it; and Emerson, finally, triangulated such collaboration through reviewing Carlyle's *French Revolution* for American readers by way of translating from Goethe's introduction to Carlyle. While he may not himself have written about world literature explicitly, Emerson was here putting the idea of global networks of cultural mediation into practice.

Emerson's sympathy for cultural translation in the Carlyle review and elsewhere is in line with what I have described above as his scepticism about cultural nationalism. Indeed, his broad knowledge of – and sustained engagement with – classical, early modern, biblical and Eastern writing (from Plutarch and Montaigne to Confucius and the Bhagavad Gita) documents his genuinely world literary interests.[11] It would be problematic to see only this aspect, however. Like Goethe, and like Carlyle, Emerson squared a voracious appetite for reading and thinking across linguistic and cultural boundaries with the challenge of meeting the demands of a more particularist cultural politics closer to home.[12] His dialectical wavering between nationalism and cosmopolitanism surfaces at several points throughout his career, perhaps most notably in the 1844 address 'The Young American'. The text is, in many ways, Emerson's most strident nationalist statement, culminating as it does in generic slogans ('America is the country of the Future' [CW 1: 230]). Yet a contrary tendency also makes itself felt in the text. Reflecting on the 'heterogenous population' of immigrants that make up the demographic fabric of the mid-century United States, Emerson concludes that 'it cannot be doubted that the legislation of this country should become more catholic and cosmopolitan than that of any other' (ibid., 229, 230). It is a striking illustration of his equidistance from the nation and the globe that just as Emerson rehearses the nationalist idiom, he ends up pioneering the use of the word *cosmopolitan* as an adjective.[13] Since the late 1990s, theorists of the so-called 'new cosmopolitanism' have been suggesting that these two vocabularies do not necessarily contradict one another. Bruce Robbins, for example, proposes a way of reconciling seemingly exclusive commitments when he notes that 'cosmopolitanism sometimes works together with nationalism rather than in opposition to it' (1998: 2) – an approach that helpfully qualifies Appiah's strict distinction between patriotism and nationalism (and his argument that cosmopolitanism can blend with the former but never with the latter) (1997: 619). Robbins's account is nevertheless limited in that he assumes that such a hybrid cosmopolitanism is a distinct product of the late twentieth century, a mindset that he sees as departing from earlier versions of cosmopolitanism marked by a 'detachment from the bonds, commitments, and affiliations that constrain ordinary nation-bound lives' (1998: 1). What both Emerson's and Carlyle's writings suggest is that the intertwinement of cosmopolitanism and nationalism that Robbins considers a contemporary phenomenon was a discursive reality already in the first half of the nineteenth century.

Seen from such a perspective, world literature emerges as an internationalist rather than a transnationalist programme. Like many nineteenth-century authors who wrote on the relation between literature and nationhood, Goethe struggled to reconcile the reality of an increasingly internationalised literary field with a residual demand for allegiance to a particular national tradition. As Kate McInturff has pointed out, he 'emphasizes the productive possibilities of an international community of writers and readers' but 'does so with the understanding that national identifications are still powerful' (2003: 225). Goethe's championing of world literature was not, John Pizer similarly suggests, 'an announcement of the demise of discrete national literatures' (2000: 215) – not a deconstruction but a celebration of national difference (a position that calls to mind what Michael Forster has described as Herder's '*pluralist* cosmopolitanism' [2010: 212]). If the cosmopolitan mindset behind world literature was geared towards intellectual and material contact between national spheres, it did not ultimately seek to deny a plurality of national literatures fundamentally distinct from one another. Both Goethean world literature and Herderian relativism, in other words, operated within a comparative framework that was meaningful only in the presence of difference.

This coexistence of overlapping orientations was suited especially well to the alignment of the national and the global that figured crucially in mid-century transatlanticism. To British and American writers of Carlyle and Emerson's generation, an Anglo-American mindset functioned as an intermediary position that, situated between the nation and the globe, allowed them to negotiate the respective locations of English and American literature on a global literary map. The vision of an Anglo-American literary identity provided a way of imagining transnational relationships without having to dissolve particularity into universalism. The workings of this logic are fully on display in the final part of Goethe's introduction to Carlyle's *Life of Schiller*. Teeming with invocations of world literary contact and exchange, the text ends on a more particularist note, with Goethe formulating his belief that German literature could not only bring about a cultural and affective rapprochement between contemporary Germany and Britain but also serve as a means of uniting a divided England, Wales and Scotland. He feels 'convinced', Goethe writes,

> that, as the German ethic and æsthetic Literature spreads through the[se] Three Kingdoms, there will, at the same time, arise a quiet community of Philo-Germans, the members of which, in their affection for a Fourth, nearly-related Nation, will feel themselves united, nay blended together. (1887: 323)

The kind of international solidarity that Goethe here describes was one grounded in a feeling of racial consanguinity. His idea of a community of like-minded Teutons was, in fact, anticipated by Carlyle, who had advanced a racially inflected argument for Anglo-German literary contact in the conclusion of his introduction to *German Romance*, where he writes of a 'brotherhood' between both peoples, 'thirty millions of men, speaking in the same old Saxon tongue, and thinking in the same old Saxon spirit with ourselves' (*CE* 21: 6). This argument assumes a global character when Carlyle reports to Goethe in a December 1829 letter that

> a knowledge and appreciation of Foreign, especially of German Literature is spreading with increased rapidity over all the domain of the English Tongue; so that almost at the Antipodes, in New Holland itself, the Wise of your country are by this time preaching their wisdom. (*CL* 5: 49)

This language is the same that Carlyle uses elsewhere to imagine a global Anglo-Saxonism, only that literature is here more explicitly seen as the primary medium for the expression of such a sense of racial unity. What such passages, taken together, demonstrate is that the type of globalism implied in world literature discourse sat well both with the nation and with mid-level formations like the ethnically defined community between Englishmen and Americans.

The Rhetoric of Anglo-American (Dis-)Continuity

If this chapter has so far focused on how nineteenth-century writers conceptualised literature as an expression of nationality, I now turn more specifically to the genre of literary history, a crucial site for contemporary definitions of cultural nationhood. As Stefan Collini reminds us, the English literary past had worked as a 'vehicle for establishing and negotiating . . . national identity' 'since at least the late eighteenth century' (1991: 347). The key image Romantic writers used to convey the impression of a national literature's natural ontology was that of the nation as an organic whole, a figure of thought that Pheng Cheah has described as 'the organismic metaphor of the social and political body' (2003: 19). If literature could be seen as a living entity, natural rhythms of growth and decline provided a template for describing its complex temporalities, as M. H. Abrams explains in a classic definition of this view:

> By transplanting the seed-idea from the mind of the poet to the collective mind of a nation or era, theorists were enabled to apply organic categories to the phylogeny, or the ontogeny or art: an artistic genre or a national literature, seen as a *Gesamtorganismus*, was conceived to grow in time as a single work grows in the imagination of the individual artist.
>
> The life-cycle of an organism – birth, maturity, decay, death – had, of course, been one of the most ancient paradigms on which to model the conception of history. In a full-fledged organology, which exploits the detailed possibilities of living and growing things, any human product or institution is envisioned as germinating, without anyone's deliberate plan or intent, and as fulfilling its destiny through an inner urgency . . . (1971: 218)

There were several ways in which nineteenth-century authors could approach literary history as unfolding in a process of organic growth along the lines of this model. Among the most important of these were a teleological account of linear historical progress and a cyclical notion of growth and decline. The latter was more closely in tune with an organicist understanding of national literature, but it was obviously also, to some extent, informed by the idea of linear development (insofar as origin and maturation are forms of linear progression as well). The upwardly ascending linear view seemed to offer itself more readily to a self-congratulatory account of the emergence of national excellence than the cyclical model, which always already coupled the vision of cultural efflorescence to that of declining vigour. In practice, however, these two templates were modified in ways that complicate such a simple juxtaposition. In the Anglo-American context, one would tend to assume that British writers used the linear model to celebrate their tradition and argue for its unwavering excellence, whereas Americans had an interest in depicting

English literature as having entered the declining phase of its life cycle in order to make a case for the emergence of their own literary nationality. But in fact there was conceptual blending almost everywhere, especially in narratives that considered English and American literary history to be so close as to be virtually identical and that hence claimed that 'English' literature in such a more comprehensive sense was still on the rise (a redeeming vision for British writers who acknowledged that, compared to earlier achievements, eighteenth- and nineteenth-century English literary production had been a disappointment). For American writers, a simple model of cyclicality, on the other hand, raised the spectre of rootlessness (to the extent that, in the nineteenth-century discourse of literary nationality, having no past was ultimately just as problematic as having too much of it).

What radically future-oriented American versions of national literary history tended to neglect was the argumentative power of a cultural past. Read with Max Weber's idea of 'traditional authority' in mind, a nation's ability to claim its own value, achieve recognition and function as a model for others depended on making appeals to the value of its own norms of excellence. Carlyle, for example, in his *History of German Literature*, speaks of precisely this importance of history to the national project when he points out that a 'nation that has no treasure in the Past cannot be wealthy, save perhaps in money, which for nations as for individuals is the plainest, but the most transient and intrinsically the poorest sort of wealth' (*HGL* 14). Carlyle's is a typically Romantic metaphorics of value, one in which economic capital is considered the least stable and hence the least desirable type of currency. The true 'treasure' of which a nation can boast lies not in the strength of its economy but 'in the Past', by which Carlyle clearly means its more specifically literary and cultural heritage. Such reasoning anticipates Pascale Casanova's observation that the 'age of a national literature testifies to its "wealth"', that it is disputes about their relative 'antiquity' that inform the way in which 'nations seek to establish themselves as legitimate contestants in international competition' (2004: 14, 240, 240) – an idea to which I will return below.

By conventional nineteenth-century standards of measurement, the United States was, of course, a 'poor' nation in terms of the kind of capital-p 'Past' of which Carlyle is thinking in the above passage. Moving within a framework that valorised the authority of cultural tradition, American writers could resort to a compensatory strategy and imagine themselves as part of a larger English narrative, thus engaging in a transatlantic transfer of literary capital. Paul Giles has noted how, after the Revolution, Americans could find a remedy for their self-proclaimed aboriginality in turning back to a transatlantic sense of cultural belonging. 'Representatives of the new United States', Giles writes, 'frequently tried to compensate for the catastrophic disorientation of suddenly finding themselves without a history by reintegrating the English past as their own' (2011: 71). That this strategy was not confined to the immediate aftermath of independence can be gauged from a cultural artefact such as Royal Robbins's American edition of Robert Chambers's *History of the English Language and Literature*, which appeared the same year that Emerson delivered his 'American Scholar' address. Together with his brother, Chambers ran an Edinburgh printing business that supplied a growing number of lower-middle and working-class readers with affordable reading matter. Tailored to the pedagogical needs of the 'Useful Knowledge' movement, his *History* (1835) popularised the idea of a distinct English literary canon. In concise and readily palatable form, the book summarised the historical trajectory of English literature and offered 'specimens' of its 'progressive' development in the form of the lives and works of its chief protagonists (1837: v). To Robbins, however, Chambers had dealt with his subject not nearly exhaustively enough, to the extent that he had only 'made a slight reference to American contributions to the [English] language and its literature' (Chambers and Robbins 1837: iii). Robbins argued that a narrative account of English literary history needed to 'admit the notice of American productions of genius and taste', 'ornaments of the English language' and 'a valuable portion of the literature which that language contains' (ibid.). 'English literature' was written in the United States as well, in other words, if 'the intellectual efforts of the Anglo-American people' were seen as contributing to a shared transatlantic tradition (ibid., iv). To set the historical record straight, Robbins interlaced his own American additions with Chambers's originally Anglocentric account, producing his *History of the English Language and Literature: To Which Is Added a History of American Contributions to the English Language and Literature* (1837). Rather than providing an appendix to Chambers's British account (American literature as another 'chapter' in the history of English literature), the book intersperses addenda on American writers from John Winthrop to William Ellery Channing in their chronological place within Chambers's text. Quite literally an American self-inscription into the English canon, Robbins's revisions are perhaps the most graphic illustration of a larger tendency in American writing of the first half of the century to attempt to establish a link between domestic literary production and the authority of the English tradition.[14] In keeping with a Herderian identification of language and national culture, 'English literature', to Robbins, referred to writing in the English language rather than to literature written in England. It was this broad definition that allowed him to provide American literature with a transatlantic cultural pedigree. That 'American literature' itself was not a meaningful category to Robbins – that he instead preferred to speak of 'American contributions' to a larger transatlantic tradition – implies that nationalist invocations of a distinctively American way of writing were not as pervasive as their centrality in twentieth-century literary historical accounts suggests.

The argument for Anglo-American literary proximity could be made on linguistic but also on racial or political grounds. Before I turn to a combination of these factors in my discussion of Emerson's literary historical narratives in the final part of this chapter, I first want to focus on Carlyle's thought on national literature and its history, in particular on his conceptualisation of the historical emergence and global future of English writing. Given the Romantic nationalisation of literary discourse and the surge in the kind of patriotic attachment by which it was often accompanied, it is striking that Carlyle – with the exception of scattered discussions and the lecture on 'The English' in the 1838 course on the history of literature – never provided an extensive account of English literary history, just as Emerson never put together a coherent history of American literature (apart from the 'New England' lectures of the early 1840s or, by an even longer stretch, the posthumously published 'Historic Notes of Life and Letters in New England'). The most detailed account of the history of an individual national literature that Carlyle provided was not one of English but one of German writing (the 1830 *History*), and Emerson's most extensive coverage of a single tradition concerned English rather than American literature (the 1835–6 lecture course on 'English Literature'). In a larger sense, however, both were, after all, dealing with their 'own' traditions, at least insofar as German literature to Carlyle and English literature to Emerson were not in any simple way foreign. To the extent that he believed in an ethnic and cultural continuity between the two traditions, writing about German authors for Carlyle was merely another way of writing about English texts. To Emerson, there was likewise no clear-cut difference between English and American literary history because, for him, the two had to be read in conjunction with one another.

Carlyle, Literary History and the 'Spiritual Form of the Nation'

'Earlier than anyone else in England', René Wellek has pointed out, 'Carlyle had understood the German historical and organological view' of national literature, and more radically and consistently than most of his contemporaries he 'imported . . . the concept of literary evolution, and the whole ideal of narrative consecutive literary history' (1965: 97, 91–2). Carlyle's early writings emphasise the importance of literature for the nation and of literary history for 'unit[ing]' its 'scattered Present into one whole' (*HGL* 5). In the *History of German Literature*, he theorises the role of literary history (and that of the literary historian) in the process of bringing to light the otherwise opaque forces at work in the formation of national character:

> [A]ny History of a National Literature . . . might prove the most instructive of all the Histories. History is written that we may understand how men, in time past, have lived and had their being; what they have done, and, which is still more important, what they have been. (ibid., 6)

Intellectual history of such a kind can hence be more instructive than an external history of political or economic facts:

> The Historian who should picture for us, in any measure, the true significance of a national Literature, would bring the essential life of the nation far nearer us than he who treated merely of its material operations whether in War or Industry, nay even of its Laws and Polity. (ibid., 7)

The task of the literary historian here becomes 'to decipher and pourtray [*sic*] the spiritual form of the nation at each successive period', to illuminate 'the hidden inward structure of that nation' (ibid., 8, 9). Making sense of literary history to Carlyle is thus a transcendental activity, an effort of probing 'mysterious' relationships and 'invisible regions' (ibid., 10). The same exalted rhetoric also surfaces in the 1830 essay 'On History', which, originally drafted as an introduction to the *History*, addresses the problem of historiographical complexity in more general terms. Writing history, Carlyle here suggests, means to come to terms with a potential infinity of data and with the general messiness of historical processes. When the essay turns to a more positive vision of hermeneutical insight, Carlyle tellingly resorts to a scriptural metaphor. History, he implies, is like a piece of writing from which the paleographically and philologically competent reader may salvage meaning – a 'complex Manuscript, covered over with formless inextricably entangled, unknown characters', 'a *Palimpsest*' with 'once prophetic writing, still dimly legible' (*WTC* 3: 8). An especially 'prophetic' kind of 'Manuscript', literary history is here again seen as being of paramount, quasi-sacred importance ('He who should write a proper History of Poetry, would depict for us the successive Revelations which man had obtained of the Spirit of Nature') (ibid., 12).

Given this lofty notion of literature and literary history, it hardly comes as a surprise that Carlyle does not find a single successful model to emulate. The history of literary historiography, to him, has been one of failures and stalled attempts. The sheer difficulty of the task once again surfaces as a key topic of concern in his review of William Taylor's *Historic Survey of German Poetry* (1830), written at a time at which he was himself engaged in providing an account of German literary development. Carlyle here offers another, but hardly less daunting, description of national literature and the analytical skills required to render it intelligible:

> [T]he History of a nation's Poetry is the essence of its History, political, economic, scientific, religious. With all these the complete Historian of a national Poetry will be familiar; the national physiognomy, in its finest traits, and through its successive stages of growth, will be clear to him. . . .

> He has to record the highest Aim of a nation, in its successive directions and developments; for by this the Poetry of the nation modulates itself; this *is* the Poetry of the nation. (CE 27: 341–2)

Wellek finds in this passage 'all the key words of German historicism': 'individuality, nationality, development, the spirit of a nation and an age, inward form and structure, continuity' (1965: 99).

If here and in other texts of the 1820s and 1830s Carlyle is preoccupied mainly with German literature, he also at the same time describes this subject as immediately relevant to his English readers. His point is quite typically one about racial similarity, his main argument being that the Germans are 'a great people, closely related to us in blood, language, [and] character' (*CE* 27: 342–3). A 'portraiture of the national mind of Germany' (ibid., 347) would thus be of interest to an English audience as well, and Carlyle here, in fact, employs the same logic that Goethe, at around the same time, was using towards the end of his introduction to the German *Life of Schiller*. Carlyle concedes that the Germans lacked a genuine national literary past, that they 'have not indeed so many classical works to exhibit as some other nations; a Shakspeare [*sic*], a Dante, has not yet been recognised among them' (ibid., 343). But if they were deficient in one form of tradition, they were in ample possession of another: 'in regard to popular Mythology, traditionary possessions and spirit, what we may call the inarticulate Poetry of a nation, . . . they will be found superior to any other modern people' (ibid.). Carlyle here echoes the argument advanced by Herder and other late-eighteenth- and early-nineteenth-century German writers in an attempt to broaden the semantics of the concept of tradition and authorise a national literature through valuing less canonical genres, forms and media. Like Herder, he locates the true spirit of German literature in its 'popular' manifestations – a strategy that follows similar lines as that adopted by nineteenth-century American writers and critics in their 'discovery' of a domestic literary past in sites as different as Native American oral poetry, Puritan pulpit oratory or modern print journalism (a strategy that, as I demonstrate below, Emerson eschewed in favour of a transatlantic appropriation of the more traditional literariness of the English canon).

Although Carlyle never wrote a history of English literature, he occasionally toyed with the idea of doing so. In a notebook entry from the late 1820s, he included 'A History of English Literature; from the times of Chaucer' as part of a list of potential future projects (*NTC* 119). Nevertheless, he ended up first writing a history of German literature and then delivering a course of comparative lectures on European literatures before turning away from literature as a subject altogether (and towards more general historical topics instead). But while the 1838 *Lectures on the History of Literature* are broadly European in scope (like the surveys of de Staël and Schlegel discussed above), Carlyle here also writes at greater length about English literary history. His lecture on 'The English' begins with the assertion that they are merely 'one particular tribe of the Teutonic race', that 'the Dutch and English tribes are the greatest of the Germans' (*LHL* 139, 141). In a fast-paced survey of their literary and cultural history from the time of Alfred the Great to that of Elizabeth, Carlyle finds the English marked by a 'silent ruggedness' and 'Saxon energy' (ibid., 146). The literary potential of these traits, he implies, found its fullest expression in the Elizabethan age, during which the national 'whole amalgamated into some distinct vital unity' (ibid.). A period of spectacular achievement, it was, at the same time, the beginning of an end: 'like the cactus tree, which blooms but once in centuries, so here appeared the blossom of poetry for once' (ibid.). Such imagery spells out the organicist premise behind the cyclical understanding of literary development that had already surfaced earlier in the lecture series. Speaking of the national character of the Romans, Carlyle here had argued that '[d]uring a healthy, sound, progressive period of national existence there is in general no literature at all', that great literature, in other words, appeared on the scene only where the nation itself was already past its prime (ibid., 48).

Against this conceptual background, the lecture dedicated to 'The English' ends on a reasonably sombre note – with Milton, whose 'sectarian' and 'polemical' attitude Carlyle reads as foreboding the rise of eighteenth-century scepticism (ibid., 158). The remainder of the lecture course deals with Enlightenment rationality and with what Carlyle depicts as its disastrous impact on imaginative writing, a trajectory that follows his declaration, early on in the series, that '[t]here is a decline in all kinds of literature when it ceases to be poetical and becomes speculative' (ibid., 33). The eighteenth century, to him, is an age of 'suicidal ruin' and spiritual barrenness, tendencies that had found expression in the 'formalism and scepticism' of the French *philosophes* and their impact on English neoclassicism (ibid., 161, 162). If Carlyle has, at this point, still not entirely given up on literature, his hope rests not on English but on recent German writing. It is in Goethe, Schiller and Jean Paul – the subjects of his final lecture – that he locates a creative energy capable of counterbalancing English and French cultural exhaustion. The largely negative narrative of contemporary and near-contemporary literature that Carlyle presents in the *Lectures* and a number of earlier essays was a crucial factor in his eventual disillusionment with literature after the 1830s.

Despite such general pessimism, however, Carlyle was not prepared to consign English literature to the dust heap of history just yet. He returned to the subject in *Past and Present* (1843), a text in which – writing under the impression of British imperial expansion and the global rise of English settler colonialism – he recalibrated his earlier account of what exactly counted as English literature. His diagnosis of the absence of genuine contemporary literary production remains the same, but unlike in the earlier lecture series, Carlyle here reads material success as a legitimate substitute for literary achievement and abandons the idea that a national literature was the supreme expression of national character (as he had consistently argued before). At the same time, however, literature continues to matter, if only in metaphorical terms. The highest praise that Carlyle can imagine to authorise the material successes of empire is to liken them to forms of literary excellence. While the nineteenth-century English of *Past and Present* are aesthetically 'a dumb people', they amply compensate for their inarticulacy in the political department: '*their* Epic Poem is written on the Earth's surface: England her Mark!' (*WTC* 4: 159). Carlyle goes on to pursue the metaphor of land as text at greater length in a fictional speech addressed to an anthropomorphised English nation:

> A grand *vis inertiæ* is in thee; how many grand qualities unknown to small men! Nature alone knows thee, acknowledges the bulk and strength of thee: thy Epic, unsung in words, is written in huge characters on the face of this Planet, – sea-moles, cotton-trades, railways, fleets and cities; Indian Empires, Americas, New-Hollands, – legible throughout the Solar System! (ibid., 162)

Carlyle then summons 'the dark powers of Material Nature' itself to ventriloquise a panegyric on the English conquest of the globe:

> 'Waste desart-shrubs [*sic*] of the tropical swamps have become cotton-trees; and here, under my furtherance, are verily woven shirts, – hanging unsold, undistributed, but capable to be distributed, capable to cover the bare backs of my children of men. Mountains, old as the Creation, I have permitted to be bored through: bituminous fuel-stores, the wreck of forests that were green a million years ago, – I have opened them from my secret rock-chambers, and they are yours, ye English. Your huge fleets, steamships do sail the sea; huge Indias do obey you; from huge New Englands and Antipodal Australias, comes profit and traffic to this Old England of mine!' (ibid., 169)

English 'literature', in the idiosyncratic sense in which Carlyle uses the term here, is a truly global phenomenon with networked connections across the Anglophone world. The 'unsung' 'Epic' of the English manifests itself in India and Australia just as it does in the United States, with the bright material future of this colonialist configuration here appearing just as inevitable as the English spiritual demise Carlyle had diagnosed in his literary lectures five years before. This optimism, however, came at the price of a radical redefinition of literature from thought to action, from word to deed. Carlyle's vision of transatlantic literary connectedness depends on an imperial worldview that transmutes the symbolic into the material and that replaces aesthetic with political metrics of achievement.

Emerson, Transatlantic Continuity, Literary *Translatio*

Carlyle's later idea of English literary history differs markedly from the Anglo-American narrative developed by Emerson, who commented extensively on English literature and its relation to American writing throughout his career. One of the most salient themes that emerge from his many statements on the subject is an emphasis on the impact of racial characteristics on literary production. I have already hinted at how persistently he championed the idea of traits common to British and American 'Anglo-Saxons'. The question at this point of my argument is both what precisely Emerson took these defining traits to be and how he understood their relationship to national literary expression. Like many of his contemporaries, he predominantly associated Anglo-Saxon identity with the concept of liberty.[15] Closely following the doctrine of national particularities developed by Herder, Cousin and others, Emerson's writing on English literature presents freedom as the distinctive idea that the English nation – understood in flexible transatlantic terms – embodies and expresses in its literature. Another one of Emerson's key motifs is the belief that the racial composition of the 'Saxons' was marked by a strong sense of material rootedness. What stands out among 'the national qualities' of the 'English stock', he suggests in the 'Character' chapter of *English Traits*, is that its members are 'of the earth, earthy' (*CW* 5: 72–3) – a claim he had already extended into a transatlantic genealogy of democratic writing elsewhere.

The lecture series on 'English Literature' that Emerson delivered in Boston in the winter of 1835–6 is his most extended early commentary on the English canon.[16] The literary historical sections of the course are framed by a recurrent emphasis on transatlantic racial continuity (as I have shown in Chapter 1). English literary history, Emerson suggested to his New England audiences, was not something remote or foreign but a subject of crucial importance to contemporary 'Saxons' on both sides of the Atlantic. Tapping into the language of cultural relativism, towards the end of the introductory lecture he details the rationale that makes the category of the nation a structuring device in an attempt to understand literary history as coherent and meaningful. What distinguishes English literature from other national traditions, Emerson argues, is its exceptionally close relationship to the people. In 'The Age of Fable', the third of the ten lectures, he explains that English writing had flourished precisely because of such roots in the common:

> The popular origin of English letters produced, or rather I should say this popular origin favored, the unfolding of the peculiar genius of its poetry and elegant prose . . . which may be already recognized in the earliest poems whose diction is completely intelligible to us. I mean its homeliness, love of plain truth and strong tendency to describe things

> as they are and without rhetorical decoration. It imports into songs and ballads the smell of the earth and the breath of cattle and like a Dutch painter seeks the household charm of low and ordinary objects. It is the reverse of the classic taste. . . . The English muse loves the field and the farmyard. (*EL* 1: 263)

Emerson's picturesque description of the English tradition as fundamentally anti-elitist is clearly indebted to the kind of primitivist poetics of common life and ordinary language that had manifested itself in projects such as Herder's collection of folk songs or Wordsworth's 'Preface' to *Lyrical Ballads*. Yet the passage also, and perhaps more importantly, highlights correspondences between racial character and literary form. If the Anglo-Saxon constitution was 'earth[y]' and robust, the literature it produced inevitably had to seem analogous to and indicative of these features – plain, mimetic and unadorned. Since Emerson's emphasis on Anglo-American ethnic continuity gave the lecture series as a whole a distinctly transatlantic orientation, his account of the 'popular origin of English letters' had implications that went beyond English writing proper. The image of the pastoral authenticity of the English tradition closely resembles the way Emerson wrote about American literature at around the same time. In the conclusion of 'The American Scholar', for example, he speaks of recent English and German literature as having 'explored and poetized' 'the near, the low, the common' (*CW* 1: 67). If Goethe, Wordsworth and others had previously shown an interest in 'the field and the farmyard', this turned them into 'auspicious signs of the coming days', into anticipations of a future American literature that would more fully and systematically 'embrace the common' (ibid.). A comparison between the 1837 address and the 1835 lecture suggests that Emerson's espousal of 'the familiar' and 'the low' represents an extension – rather than a rejection – of the English tradition (ibid.). In 'The Age of Fable', and throughout the series as a whole, he was thus emphatically 'positioning himself in a line of continuity with the tradition of English language and literature' instead of describing it as inimical to American interests (Giles 2011: 75).

The lecture explores another layer of this transatlantic heritage when it mixes aesthetics and politics in linking the 'plain style' of English writing to what Emerson describes as its 'popular origin' and quintessentially democratic nature. This allows him not only to establish English literature as a precursor to an American tradition, but also to rebut European claims about the supposedly inferior value of democratic art (a type of criticism that surfaces, for example, in Alexis de Tocqueville's remark that in egalitarian societies 'productions of artists are more numerous, but the merit of each production is diminished' [1840, 1: 101]). Read against the background of mainstream antebellum commentary on the character of English writing, Emerson's account emerges as thoroughly unconventional. It was more common among his contemporaries to frame the British canon as politically dubious. To his Transcendentalist friend Orestes Brownson, for example, English literature was 'with some noble exceptions, aristocratic' (1838: 436), and in Walt Whitman the English tradition similarly figures as 'poisonous to the idea of the pride and dignity of the common people' (1982: 955). Reading English literature as hopelessly feudalist provided a contrastive foil to imagine, as George Bancroft did, the future 'brilliant career' of American arts and letters as an embodiment of 'the triumphs of democracy' (1838: 398). Implied in this conception was the assumption that the 'natural association of men of letters with ... democracy' (ibid., 389) was a unique New World phenomenon that differentiated American popular from European high culture. Emerson was deconstructing this dichotomy through highlighting the distinctly democratic character of English literature. Where writers like Brownson, Whitman and Bancroft tended to think of democracy in Cousinian terms as the specific national idea American literature was destined to realise, Emerson's conflation of nation and race radically levelled transatlantic difference – English literary feudalism versus the American democratic muse – into a characterological continuum. Exonerating the English tradition from the charge of anti-egalitarianism, such a strategy opened up the possibility of its transatlantic appropriation. It in turn enabled Emerson to deflect European criticism of the supposed coarseness of American writing by arguing that 'earthy expression' and 'plain style' were not signs of an American cultural impoverishment but in fact the hallmarks of English literature itself (CW 5: 131).

Rather than negating the authority of the English literary past, Emerson thus acknowledged it as a powerful source of transatlantic legitimation. The kind of distinction that underwrites such national claims to cultural authority, Pascale Casanova has demonstrated, manifests itself most tangibly in the form of a well-established and widely recognised body of works. 'Age is one of the chief aspects of literary capital', in that it certifies a literature's 'presumed or asserted priority in relation to other national traditions' (Casanova 2004: 14). Where age translates into cultural authority, emphasising transatlantic connections and inscribing American literature into the larger narrative framework of English literary history offered a potentially more effective way of arguing for the value of a comparatively 'poor' – that is, recent and relatively uncredentialled – national tradition than an outright 'fantasy of the disappearance of authority' (Sennett 1993: 28). 'A stock of national literary resources', Casanova suggests, 'can be created only through the diversion and appropriation of available assets' (2004: 232). Her prime example for such a transfer of literary capital is the late-eighteenth- and early-nineteenth-century German appropriation of the literature of Greco-Roman antiquity, which furnished an otherwise fragmentary modern national literary history with an authorised point of origin and thus provided a 'wa[y] of making up for lost time' in the campaign against the hegemony of French culture (ibid., 240).

Instead of reinventing the logic of literary history from scratch, Emerson's writing on English literature engaged in a similar repurposing of literary capital, defying Casanova's categorical claim – mainly derived from a reading of Whitman – that 'American writers needed to contest the temporal law instituted by Europe' in order to 'have any chance of being noticed and accepted' (ibid., 243). English literary history could be imagined not only as an oppressive other, but also as a retrospective projection of American literature into a transatlantic 'usable past'.[17]

Casanova's analysis is nevertheless valid to the extent that Emerson eventually came to separate the past from the present. At the same time that he appropriated the authority of English writers from Alfred to Wordsworth, he tended to locate the future of 'Saxon' literary expression in the United States rather than in Britain. This, however, is not the same as arguing that his concept of literary history dismantled the idea of a 'temporal law' or the notion of the value of tradition altogether.[18] Emerson's writing on the relevance of the English literary past for the American literary present provides a counterpoint to what has often been read as his ahistorical stance. Dating from before and after the more canonical essays and addresses of the late 1830s and early 1840s, texts such as the 'English Literature' series and the later *English Traits* raise doubts about the idea that American writers prized difference over continuity and sought to distance themselves from an overpowering English past. Emerson's consistent emphasis on the transatlantic continuity of Anglo-Saxon traits and his analysis of Anglo-American demotic literary commonalities point in the opposite direction.

If, as Robert Weisbuch has suggested, the absence of a distinctive national history plunged antebellum writers into a 'crisis of authority', the idea that authority 'might be founded anew, away from the past' was only one among many possible responses (1986: 165). Emerson was hardly alone in emphasising transatlantic continuity and in regarding English literary history as a shared possession. James Fenimore Cooper, for instance, in his *Notions of the Americans* (1828), asserted that '[t]he Authors previously [sic] to the revolution are common Property', that it was 'quite idle to say that the American has not just as good a right to claim Milton, and Shakspeare [sic], and all the old masters of the language, for his countrymen' (1991: 342). The same idea appears in Alexander Everett's reflections on the structure of the contemporary Anglo-American literary field. 'We glory, as Americans, in the literary glory of the land of our fathers,' he declared, noting that '[t]he names of Shakspeare [sic], Milton, Locke, Bacon and Burke are as dear and sacred to us, as they can be to any native son of the fast-anchored isle' (1834: 7). Many of Emerson's contemporaries, in fact, subscribed to the idea of an American access to the English tradition. William Ellery Channing judged that his countrymen could 'rejoice in our descent from England, and esteem our free access to her works of . . . genius, as among our high privileges' (1830: 292–3).

James Russell Lowell, satirising a high-flying domestic rhetoric of cultural nationalism, argued that English literature was, in fact, America's national literature, that nationalists oblivious to 'this ownership in common' were behaving '[a]s if we had no share in the puritan and republican Milton' (1849: 202). And even the staunchest of New York nationalists were prepared to concede that Americans 'retained' their 'mother-country['s]' 'letters, and the fame of her great writers, as their birth-right as Englishmen' (Anon. 1847a: 266). Imagining transatlantic authority in the economic terms referenced as well by Casanova's Bourdieusian metaphor of literary 'capital', this pervasive language of cultural 'ownership', 'property' and 'free access' advanced strong transatlantic claims on ethnic, linguistic, social and political grounds.

While commentators such as Weisbuch grant that nineteenth-century American writers at times espoused English literary history as a precedent, they commonly suggest that this kind of appropriation was limited to those parts of the past that were safely remote. Where 'Shakespeare and Milton belong to a heritage that could be considered, however giddily, common because it was essentially pre-colonial', 'the contemporary or near-contemporary British writer', in this line of argument, inevitably 'threatens his American counterpart' (Weisbuch 1986: 16). Yet Everett, for example, quite explicitly elided that distinction with an affirmative supplement to his declaration:

> Nor do we feel this sympathy only in the ancient glories of the common literature. The names of Scott, and Byron are household words, on the shores of the Hudson and the Mississippi, as well as on those of the Tweed and the Thames. (1834: 7)

Emerson could likewise read contemporaries such as Wordsworth and Carlyle as part of the same 'splendid' literary historical 'inheritance' that included Shakespeare and Milton without feeling oppressed by their contemporaneity (*EL* 1: 75).

If Emerson's tone indeed tended to become less enthusiastic when he looked at English literature beyond the Renaissance, this was less categorical than it may seem at first sight. His general critique of the empiricist scepticism of eighteenth-century English writing and the intellectual barrenness of the following century draws on writers like Coleridge and Carlyle as part of a potential solution instead of rejecting them as part of the problem.[19] If he criticises the English literary present, his vision for the American literary future is one of continuity with past standards of English achievement. The overall narrative scheme behind this belief was the result of a combination of organicist and cyclical models of history. The organicist notion of national literary history as a process of maturation and decay allowed Emerson to acknowledge English literature's former excellence and point towards its nineteenth-century failings, while the cyclical view of a succession of such organic life-cycles – coupled as it was in his writings to the idea of transatlantic racial continuity – enabled him to imply a future flowering of English literary expression in the United States.[20] Emerson's transatlantic vision of a broadly Anglo-American literary history combined deference to the English past with the belief in a potential transfer of authority from Europe to the United States. In his emphasis on the global reach of English language and literature, he thus found himself in agreement with Carlyle. Where the two parted ways was in offering a different outlook on the location of the centre and the periphery of the Anglophone cultural field of the future. As the following chapters demonstrate, such arguments emerged both in print and on the transatlantic lecture platform and were closely bound up with these nineteenth-century media environments.

Notes

1. Berlin's liberalist reading of Herder has more recently been challenged by Allen Patten, who identifies a more tangible 'politically nationalist strand of Herder's thought' about cultural difference (2010: 659).
2. Cousin gained a sizeable following among Anglophone readers both in the French original of his writings and in translation (an English version of the *Introduction* appeared in Boston in 1832). His detailed discussion of Herder forms part of the eleventh lecture of the *Introduction* (1832: 350–62).
3. Proceeding '[f]rom a curious observation of the characteristic traits which distinguish the contemporary writings of the Italians and the English, of the Germans and the French', de Staël goes on to argue 'that political and religious institutions had a principal share in the production of these continual diversities' (1812, 1: 32).
4. On the importance of German thought for Carlyle more generally, see the classic accounts by Charles Frederick Harrold (1934) and Rosemary Ashton (1980: 67–104).
5. See Wellek 1944: 62 on Schlegel's *Geschichte* as a model for Carlyle's 1838 series.
6. On Herder's American impact in the first half of the nineteenth century, see Mueller-Vollmer 1990. Andreas Wimmer has drawn attention to the later influence of Herder's notions of ethnicity and cultural identity on the conceptual repertoire of modern academic disciplines such as anthropology, sociology and political science (2013: 16–26, 177–80).
7. Following Herder's emphasis on the unity of humanity at large, Channing also, however, suggested that '[i]n all nations we recognise one great family' (1830: 272). Daniel Walker Howe notes that the 1830 essay illustrates a 'tension between nationalism and cosmopolitanism' characteristic of New England Unitarianism (1970: 183). Kermit Vanderbilt, writing about the link between Channing's praise of continental literature and his call for an independent national tradition, suggests that he 'encouraged an American spirit of self-formation, at once energized by, and resistant to, foreign literary influences' (1986: 46).
8. A 'rooted cosmopolitan', in Appiah's definition, is someone who feels 'attached to a home of one's own, with its own cultural particularities' but is at the same time 'taking pleasure from the presence of other, different places that are home to other,

different people' (1997: 618). On Emerson's anticipation of Appiah's concept, see Stievermann 2010: 171.
9. I discuss Goethe's, Carlyle's and Emerson's uses of the idea of world literature in some greater book historical detail in Sommer 2021.
10. For a transcription of this manuscript review and a discussion of its significance for Carlyle and Emerson's print relationship, see Sommer 2018/19.
11. On the impact of classical authors, see Van Anglen 2010; on Emerson's familiarity with Asian sources, see Versluis 1993: 51–79; on biblical writing and its authority, see Grusin 1991: 9–80.
12. There has been an extensive critical debate about the question of Emerson's relation to the nation in recent years, with an emerging consensus pointing in the direction of emphasising that, at some point in his career, he 'came . . . to reject narrow nationalism and to champion world literature' (Mott 2014: 21). Lawrence Buell has perhaps been the most vocal proponent of this kind of reading, reclaiming Emerson from traditional Americanist and New Americanist interpretations that had highlighted his national orientation (see Buell 2003). My argument here is that neither the earlier consensus that had stressed Emerson's national commitment (tangible in texts by Perry Miller, Harold Bloom, Sacvan Bercovitch and others) nor the more recent tendency to read him in global terms (in the work of Buell, Wai Chee Dimock, Branka Arsić and others) adequately captures his hovering between these two poles.
13. In the *Oxford English Dictionary*, 'The Young American' features as the earliest recorded instance of the adjectival use of the word; the *OED* defines 'cosmopolitan' in this sense as 'free from national limitations or attachments' (*OED*, s.v. 'cosmopolitan, adj.').
14. The story of Robbins's additions to Chambers would repeat itself two decades later with the American reprinting of English clergyman and critic Robert Aris Willmott's anthology *The Poets of the Nineteenth Century* (1857), which – prepared under the editorial supervision of the Young American Evert Duyckinck – emphatically included American writers as 'important extensions' to the literary historical narrative Willmott's English canon was telling (Duyckinck 1857: vi). (I am grateful to Meredith McGill for bringing this volume to my attention.)
15. In the 1852 lecture 'The Anglo-American', for example, Emerson speaks of 'the decided preference of the Saxon on the whole for civil liberty' (*LL* 1: 293). In *English Traits*, a few years later, he similarly stresses that 'the English stand for liberty' (*CW* 5: 79). The omnipresence of this theme in his writing well into the 1850s seems to me to point against Len Gougeon's argument that Emerson, after his European journey of 1847–8, grew disenchanted with contemporary England because of its political curtailment of liberties (see Gougeon 2006).
16. In a recent reading, Johannes Voelz has offered one of the most thorough and extensive discussions of these lectures now available (see 2010: 207–16). While our interest in Emerson's poetics, his nation-centred argument and his approach to literary history in many instances overlaps, my focus in the following is more specifically on the transatlantic dimension of the series – on how it compares both with Carlyle's metropolitan vision of English literature and with the perspective adopted by Emerson's American contemporaries.

17. Coined by Van Wyck Brooks in the 1910s and later taken up by historian Henry Steele Commager, the phrase 'usable past' has commonly been employed in a sense that differs from the way in which I am thinking of the term here. In his classic essay 'The Search for a Usable Past' (1965), Commager outlined three different strategies by means of which Americans coped with an absence of cultural history – through shifting attention from past to future ('looking forward instead of back'), through appropriating foreign pasts ('*all* Europe was the American past') or through historicising the colonial and revolutionary eras ('Americans . . . could use what they had') (1967: 8, 9, 13). My characterisation of Emerson's drawing from the English literary past seems to come closest to the second category, but the key difference is that, to Commager, the European past was 'usable' to Americans only because it provided a negative foil: 'It was there more for purposes of contrast than for enrichment; it pointed the moral of American superiority, and adorned the tale of American escape from contamination' (ibid., 13). While this may well describe the differentiating strategies employed by Brownson, Whitman and Bancroft, my reading of Emerson suggests that the usability of English literature to antebellum writers could just as well depend on an emphasis on continuity rather than contrast.
18. Critical accounts of Emerson's philosophy of history have often stressed the antihistorical thrust of his writing. Robert D. Richardson, for example, reads the 1841 essay 'History' as calling for an intellectually liberating historiography that 'would help and nourish the individual . . . rather than crushing or stifling him' (1982: 57). Robert Weisbuch suggests that the text is characteristic of an American reaction against 'the British taunt of no history' (1986: 153). Like Casanova, he argues that the pressure exerted by the English canon compelled American writers to devise alternative temporalities to destabilise traditional, European-centred concepts of history. In Weisbuch's taxonomy of such evasions, Emerson's approach in 'History' serves to illustrate the idea of 'vertical time' – a radical presentism aimed at the 'elimination of history' (ibid., 154, 163). The idea of using the European past – either in an affirmative way or in Commager's negative sense – was not, according to Weisbuch, an option available to writers of Emerson's generation.
19. When, in *English Traits*, for example, Emerson writes that what in mid-nineteenth-century Britain 'is called philosophy and letters is mechanical in its structure' and when he notes that '[t]he voice of [the English] modern muse has a slight hint of the steam-whistle' (*CW* 5: 141), he clearly echoes Carlyle's complaint, in 'Signs of the Times' (1829), that contemporary 'Philosophy, Science, Art, Literature, all depend on machinery' (*CE* 27: 61). Emerson was prepared to tone down his critique of the intellectual and cultural paralysis of contemporary Britain when it came to writers with positions congenial to his own: Wordsworth, Coleridge and Carlyle to him deserve praise because they belong to a minority of oppositional figures who have resisted the mechanisation of art and philosophy. In the Boston lecture on 'Modern Aspects of Letters' (1836), Emerson thus celebrates Coleridge's 'expressions of censure and contempt at the low state of philosophical and ethical studies in England' (*EL* 1: 380); in the 1843 essay 'Europe and European Books', he finds that Wordsworth's greatness lies in the 'antagonism . . . between his poetry and the spirit

of the age' (*CW* 10: 249); and it is from Carlyle's 'disgust at the pettiness and the cant' of the nineteenth-century present that, in *English Traits*, Emerson derives his authority to critique the contemporary condition of England (*CW* 5: 140).

20. See Nicoloff 1961: 224–33 for a discussion of how Emerson reads the historical development of English literature according to an organic template of growth and decay. For a wide-ranging reading of Emerson's 'organicist nationalism' as it surfaces in many of the texts covered in the final part of this chapter, see Voelz 2010: 205–43.

Part II

Authority and Authorisation in the Anglo-American Print Market

3

'TRANSATLANTIC BIBLIOPOLY': CARLYLE'S EARLY AMERICAN PRINT CAREER

In 1870, Carlyle donated a large part of his private library to Harvard University in an effort to demonstrate his 'gratitude to New England' for its encouraging reception of his writings over the previous three and a half decades (*CEC* 554). Emerson emphatically urged that Harvard, his own alma mater, would be 'the right beneficiary, as being the mother real or adoptive' of many of Carlyle's 'lovers & readers in America' (ibid., 560). The role of the intermediary in the scheme fell to Charles Eliot Norton, a fellow Harvard graduate and transatlantic man of letters, who subsequently became the first editor of the Carlyle–Emerson correspondence. As a gesture at once material and diplomatic, the gift, Norton suggested, would further consolidate a 'bond between the people of the two Englands' (qtd ibid., 557). Through this public recognition of the support of his American 'lovers & readers', Carlyle was paying back his transatlantic debt in the form of books, the same currency in which he had originally incurred it. When the volumes from his shelves arrived in Cambridge, their transoceanic migration provided the concluding chapter to a long history of material exchanges that had seen the circulation of manuscripts, proof sheets, individual copies and whole cargoes of Carlyle's and Emerson's books between Britain and the United States. This sustained Anglo-American interaction not only established a lasting 'bond' between the two writers but also contributed to the consolidation of the interconnected print market of what Norton described as 'the two Englands'.

Carlyle had reason enough to be grateful to his American readers. Until the late 1830s, he had trouble having his more extensive works published in England and it was mainly through the successful (re)printing of his books in the United States that he was able to convince publishers at home of the market potential of his writing. When the first British trade edition of *Sartor Resartus* appeared in 1838, for example, it had been preceded by two American editions that had sold quickly both in the United States and, in the form of imported copies, on the British market. Carlyle had become a transatlantically published author even before this, with his essays excerpted in American periodicals and some of his earlier work reprinted in book form without his knowledge.[1] Emerson had assured him of an audience early on, writing in his very first letter in May 1834 that, while there was 'no hope that you will find suddenly a large audience', in the long run 'all men' would become '*potentially* . . . your audience' (CEC 99). In the same letter, Emerson described his experience of reading the periodical instalments of Carlyle's *Sartor Resartus* as they were successively arriving in Boston. The book, he found, was indicative of its author's 'despair of finding a contemporary audience' (ibid., 98) – a despair that Emerson elsewhere in the correspondence describes as uncalled for, at least with respect to the United States, where '[y]oung men at all our Colleges' and beyond were devouring Carlyle's writings (ibid., 216). Carlyle himself soon realised that publishing in America could prove more financially rewarding than publishing at home. Observing in an 1835 letter to his English poet friend John Sterling that '[t]he Book-Trade seems to me *done* here' (CL 8: 138), over the course of the following years he would habitually juxtapose the business acumen of American publishers with what he caricatured as the sluggishness of their British colleagues.

That Carlyle's literary significance had first been recognised in the United States was something that contemporary American critics were especially keen to emphasise. Writing in the Transcendentalist periodical *The Western Messenger* in 1838, James Freeman Clarke, for example, noted that Carlyle 'has received more attention, and had more readers in this country, than in England' (1838: 417). Celebrating aesthetic independence, Clarke praised American audiences for their ability to 'open an attentive ear to the good and valuable, though it comes unauthenticated by the stamp of English approval', and he drew satisfaction from the fact that 'that which was not vouchsafed in the Old England occurred in the New' (ibid.). With a similar sense of national pride, publisher George Palmer Putnam pointed out that it was 'Americans' who had '*first* collected and *first* printed complete editions of the works of such English writers as Cudworth, Bolingbroke, Burke, Paley, and Dugald Stewart; and first printed in a book form the essays and reviews of Carlyle, Macaulay, [and] Jeffrey' (1845: 80). British commentators were prepared to concede as much. Novelist and social theorist Harriet Martineau observed that the transatlantic publication of *Sartor Resartus* was 'the first instance of the Americans having taken to their hearts an

English work which came to them anonymously, unsanctioned by any recommendation, and even absolutely neglected at home' (1837, 2: 311). What such remarks indicate at their most radical is the sense of a transformation of critical authority, with British aesthetic judgement perceived as no longer functioning as a transatlantically powerful prescriptive standard.

Although contemporaries like Clarke, Putnam and Martineau were taking note of an Anglophone field whose power dynamics were in transition, the 'effects' of literary 'provinciality' were still to be felt in the late 1830s (Rezek 2015: 13). If American critics and readers had become more independent in their assessments, this did not, in turn, lead to a sudden shift in the importance that British metropolitan literary culture was prepared to grant to American critical opinion. The American editions of his books could not offer Carlyle much symbolic consecration and at home he was never deliberately drawing attention to the fact that abroad his writings found the favour of periodicals like the *Western Messenger* or even the *North American Review*. It was mainly to American writers and critics that the symbolic significance of his transatlantic print career mattered, allowing them to stylise themselves as part of a literary avant-garde. What Pascale Casanova has described as the ability of a powerful cultural centre to position itself as a 'Greenwich meridian of literature' (2004: 88) in the case of Carlyle's transatlantic reception was claimed by the periphery. Not only were Americans more successful at trendspotting for new English talent, they were also, as Putnam implied, better at curating its past. Carlyle's 'discovery' in America served 'provincial' critics like Clarke well in that it enabled them both to declare their aesthetic independence from British standards of taste and to question the cultural authority of English literary institutions, which, in their failure to recognise Carlyle's intellectual potential, could be dismissed as out of touch with literary modernity.

The existence of an Anglophone literary sphere outside of Great Britain was important to Carlyle as well, of course, but his interest in transatlantic publishing, I will argue in this chapter, stemmed less from an intrinsic enthusiasm for the idea of speaking to American readers or of being feted by their critical arbiters than from the prospect of being able to secure a permanent source of income through meeting a demand for his writing in a new and growing foreign market that could be imagined as an extension of the domestic one. If Carlyle did not tend publicly to emphasise his success with transatlantic audiences, this was also because, like many writers of his generation, he subscribed to an ethics of misrecognition in the framework of which contemporary recognition, no matter where, largely counted as superficial and in which a true estimate of one's own aesthetic prescience could, almost by definition, come only from posterity.[2] In line with such thinking, Emerson, in the late 1830s, noted that although Carlyle had gained a sizeable American following, he remained authentically indifferent to his success, a 'man seeking no reward, warping his genius . . . to no dull public'. Admiring '[h]ow noble' he had been in following his writerly calling during his solitary years of creation, Emerson described Carlyle's transatlantic discovery as miraculous rather than premeditated, wondering at the fact

> that alone & unpraised he should still write for he knew not who, & find at last his readers in the valley of the Mississippi, and they should brood on the pictures he had painted & untwist the many colored meanings which he had spun & woven into so rich a web of sentences and domesticate in so many & remote heads the humor, the learning, and the philosophy which, year by year, in summer & in frost this lonely man had lived in the moors of Scotland. (*JMN* 5: 358)

Offering a sympathetic image of writerly withdrawal and financial disinterestedness, Emerson here formulates an authorial creed that has often been taken at face value, leading to the impression that, as ethereal Romantic intellectuals, he and Carlyle had no interest in – and, for that matter, no knowledge of – writing for the literary marketplace.

That the situation was more complex than such self-fashioning suggests can be seen from the fact that, at the same time that Emerson was celebrating Carlyle as a writer 'seeking no reward', he was actively engaged in securing him a tangible financial benefit from the American publication of his books. The success of this endeavour, in turn, depended on the globally connected nature of a nineteenth-century print culture in which texts could easily traverse the distance from 'the moors of Scotland' to 'the valley of the Mississippi' and provide the basis for an author's recognition abroad. What Emerson's journal entry describes as a self-sustaining process of transatlantic communication in fact required substantial efforts on his and Carlyle's part during the 1830s and 1840s – efforts that this chapter reconstructs and contextualises against the background of contemporary discourses of transatlantic cultural authority.

Looking back on this period of intense engagement in the early 1860s, Carlyle described such print-related activity as part of a larger system he called 'Transatlantic Bibliopoly' (*CEC* 531). His choice of words is significant because elsewhere he employs the term 'bibliopoly' to comment on the genesis and nature of professional literary authorship. The first use of the word in the correspondence with Emerson appears in the late 1830s in the context of a reference to Samuel Johnson, whom, in an earlier essay, Carlyle had treated as a prime example of the historical emergence of the 'trade of Author' (*WTC* 5: 171). This 'trade', in his analysis, revolved around an economic shift from aristocratic patronage to a financial reliance on the print market: professional and autonomous, a writer like Johnson, Carlyle suggested, 'no longer [needed] to supply [his] necessities by laudatory Dedications to the Great', but could do so through 'judicious Bargains with the Booksellers' (ibid., 172). If this implies an emancipatory teleology, as an author by trade Carlyle himself, by the early 1840s, had gained first-hand experience of the work that had to go into meeting the demands of the profession. As Richard Salmon has noted, Carlyle celebrated 'the newfound bourgeois autonomy of the professional writer' but was simultaneously aware that the demise of the patronage system linked the material subsistence of modern authors to 'the chance mechanisms of the literary market' (2013: 41). To reduce the contingencies inherent in that economic configuration, Carlyle and Emerson not only relied on publishers and booksellers to live off their writing but themselves assumed key roles in the process of getting their texts into print and making them yield a profit.

Where in the age of Johnson the 'trade of Author' had largely remained confined to a single national book market, for Carlyle and Emerson a century later the professional challenge of 'bibliopoly' entailed dealing with publishing houses, trade conventions and legal codes in a complex transatlantic environment. Analysing the historical background of these transactions and highlighting their larger cultural significance, this chapter and the following one shed light on a subject that has so far received only scant critical attention. For more than half a century, Joseph Slater's condensed overview of Carlyle's and Emerson's transatlantic publishing in the introduction to his edition of their correspondence has been the most substantial account available (see 1964: 16–29). Drawing extensively on previously neglected archival sources and contemporary paratexts, my discussion of the topic establishes a more detailed picture and, in so doing, contributes to a burgeoning field of research concerned with the print materiality of nineteenth-century transatlantic literary exchange. I go beyond Slater's summary treatment, as well as a handful of later thumbnail surveys that mainly rely on his,[3] through reading book historical facts and figures side by side with the textual strategies behind contemporary advertisements, prefaces and reviews, but also through approaching concrete print objects and practices as speaking to larger mid-century debates about transatlantic cultural, political, legal and economic authority. This chapter proceeds in largely chronological fashion, moving from Carlyle's early reception among American readers and reviewers in the mid to late 1830s to his and Emerson's subsequent attempts, over the following decade, to respond to transatlantic reprinting and its transformation of literary authorship.

Beginnings: The American *Sartor Resartus*, 'A New England Book'

Carlyle's first success on the American print market came with *Sartor Resartus*, a book that itself thematises the cross-cultural transfer of ideas (with the obscure German philosophy of its protagonist, Diogenes Teufelsdröckh, reworked by a fictitious English editor for a domestic readership). When the text appeared in Boston in 1836, it acquired an additional layer of cross-cultural complexity, although this time it was Carlyle himself who was being translated to a foreign audience. *Sartor Resartus* was initially something of a commercial failure in Britain. After unsuccessfully attempting to have his manuscript issued in book form in the summer of 1831, Carlyle eventually arranged to have the text printed in instalments in *Fraser's Magazine*, where it finally appeared between November 1833 and August 1834. Emerson had visited Carlyle at his Scottish country home in Craigenputtock shortly before the beginning of the printing and soon became one of the magazine's transatlantic subscribers in order to be able to read the book in its serialised form. Carlyle's publisher James Fraser subsequently reissued fifty-eight copies of the text from the original plates in 1834, but – privately 'printed for friends' – this pamphlet edition never reached the open market (see Tarr 1989: 35–6). Carlyle sent Emerson three copies of this reprint, which were then passed around among their 'greedy receivers' in New England, creating a demand for the book abroad (*CEC* 110; see also Jackson 1996). This system of private circulation proved so successful that, by March 1835, Emerson was imploring Carlyle to 'send out' another 'fifty or a hundred copies of the *Sartor*', which he was confident 'would be sold at once' (*CEC* 120).

Although the New England 'lovers of Teufelsdröckh' were potentially numerous, Emerson preferred to watch the market cautiously before setting out to reprint the book and 'reproduce' it as 'a naturalized Yankee' (ibid.). It took him another six weeks to inform Carlyle that '*Sartor* would now be sure of a sale' in America (ibid., 125). Despite the early interest Emerson took in the commercial fate of the book, it would ultimately be others who became the driving force behind the idea of launching an American edition. Transcendentalist Frederic Henry Hedge was involved at one point, but the main impetus came from LeBaron Russell, an engineering student at Harvard and a friend of Emerson who had been among the original readers of the imported pamphlet copies. The first domestic edition of the book was a collaborative endeavour in which the '[y]oung men at . . . our Colleges' whom Emerson singled out as Carlyle's most ardent transatlantic readers took the lead. Russell was busy gathering the subscriber names Boston publishers James Munroe and Company had made the condition for printing the book and it was only in mid-December 1835 that the required mark of 150 individuals had been reached. Emerson forwarded his private copy of Fraser's edition to serve as a template in the typesetting process.

These busy preparations received an unanticipated publicity boost through the appearance of a review of the London pamphlet reprint in the October issue of the *North American Review*. Alexander Everett, the author of the piece as well as the editor of the *North American*, had been among those who had been given access to one of Emerson's pamphlet copies. He was so impressed by the book that he confidently predicted Carlyle's future transatlantic career:

We have been partly led to take the notice of the work before us by the wish, which the author expresses, that a knowledge of his labors might penetrate into the Far West. We take pleasure in introducing to the American public a writer, whose name is yet in a great measure unknown among us, but who is destined, we think, to occupy a large space in the literary world. (1835: 482)

Everett whetted his readers' appetite for the book by printing generous excerpts from it. In addition to making parts of the text available to an American audience, his review effectively consecrated *Sartor Resartus* through a substantial notice in what, at the time, was one of the nation's most esteemed print institutions. Emerson was 'delighted' with the review, not least since Everett, as he wrote to Carlyle, 'represents a clique to which I am a stranger, & which I supposed might not love you' (*CEC* 139–40). Associating with Carlyle was already proving to be advantageous for Emerson in that it promised him access to the social capital and critical authority of a national intellectual elite of which he himself would only later become a part.[4]

Sartor Resartus finally appeared, complete with a short unsigned preface by Emerson, in early April 1836. Six months later, the 500 copies of the book had been sold and by the end of the year a new edition of twice the original print run was in preparation. Once more published by Munroe, this second edition was a success as well – by September 1837, almost 700 copies had found eager readers. Although Carlyle was beginning to enjoy a wide circulation abroad, however, both editions failed to yield him a financial profit. The net result remained with Munroe, who had taken on the risk of publication. The only money that Carlyle received from the sales of these two American editions of his book came, ironically enough, from English buyers. Upon returning from a tour of the United States in the summer of 1836, his London friend Harriet Martineau, more apt than he and his American friends at making a profit from *Sartor Resartus*, had brought twenty-five copies with her. After these had been sold off, at a substantially higher English retail price, she imported another twenty-five copies, eventually passing the net proceeds on to Carlyle (see Martineau 1877, 1: 383–4). That English readers of *Sartor Resartus* could access the book only in the form of an imported American edition that reprinted a previously exported text was, of course, richly ironic. But it also offered Carlyle a crucial argument in his attempt at convincing an English publisher to print the book. Despite the negligible sum that he received from the transatlantic sales of the early American editions of *Sartor Resartus*, in the long run he benefitted from their circulation of his name at home and abroad. When Emerson campaigned for the American publication of Carlyle's next book, his history of the French Revolution, the success of *Sartor Resartus* gave him a sound basis to negotiate with Boston publishing houses.

Emerson's main contribution to the first American edition of *Sartor Resartus* had been his preface – a text that hovers between open endorsement and careful distancing and that, in so doing, provided a template which Carlyle himself would later follow when introducing the London edition of Emerson's first volume of essays in 1841. The preface opens with Emerson's proactive assertion that he had 'no expectation that this little work will have a sudden and general popularity' – a caveat that, in the context of the Romantic ideal of deferred fame, was praise rather than censure (CW 10: 56). Consciously or not, Emerson was here echoing the book's own editorial persona pessimistically gauging the effect of his attempts to advance Teufelsdröckh's reputation among readers across the Channel (like Emerson, Carlyle's fictional editor in the book concluded that a 'paramount popularity in England we cannot promise him' [*WTC* 2: 22]). Emerson openly concedes the oddities of *Sartor Resartus* but at the same time suggests that, beneath the book's 'gay costume' and 'quaint and burlesque style', lay hidden 'speculations upon the gravest topics' (CW 10: 56). Perhaps the most important purpose of the preface was to keep American readers of the book from assuming that Carlyle was a foreign writer, to divert their attention from 'the German idioms with which he has sportively sprinkled his pages', and instead to emphasise his credentials as a genuinely Anglo-American voice (ibid.). Where conservative New England critics were raising doubts about Carlyle's national status (as detailed in Chapter 1 above), Emerson, on the contrary, affirmed that he was a 'sincere' British author whose Germanisms and stylistic idiosyncrasies were, if anything, evidence of a 'mastery' in his command of the English language (ibid.).

Emerson's almost Puritan praise of the moral sincerity of the book becomes even more pronounced in the conclusion of the preface, which reassures readers of the book that there was, after all, a sound moral message beneath the text's glittering stylistic surface:

> Under all his gaiety, the writer has an earnest meaning, and discovers an insight into the manifold wants and tendencies of human nature, which is very rare among our popular authors. The philanthropy and the purity of moral sentiment, which inspire the work, will find their way to the heart of every lover of virtue. (ibid., 57)

There is a striking similarity between Emerson's remarks throughout the preface and the frequent complaints of Carlyle's editor about Teufelsdröckh's 'needless obscurity', as well as his consternation caused by the latter's 'entangled, hypermetaphorical style of writing' (*WTC* 2: 138, 216). But where Carlyle's editorial figure was, to a large extent, a parody of English common sense, Emerson's text is too coherent to pass off as a corresponding parody of New England moralism. The preface sounds just as serious as it suggests Carlyle had been in writing his book. Emerson consistently domesticates the unorthodoxies of *Sartor Resartus* in an attempt to turn it into an aesthetic artefact more readily palatable for the average American reader. Nowhere does he reflect on the fact that he is providing a peritextual framing for a book that problematises the very idea of such framings. Deliberately downplaying the satirical character of the book, he reads it instead as a novel of ideas whose instructive content is more important than its extravagant form.

Emerson's text prefaced only the first and the second American editions of the book. Subsequent printings took their copy text from the English edition of 1838 and the original American preface was hence dropped. But through a peculiar critical portfolio that Carlyle had assembled for this edition, Emerson's text – aimed at American readers and critics – also found its way into the hands of English readers, who, until 1838, short of consulting the scarce original numbers of *Fraser's Magazine* or the even rarer pamphlet reprint, had had to procure an American edition in order to be able to read *Sartor Resartus*. Emerson's idea of the reprint as a 'naturalized Yankee' had raised questions about the national identity of the text that its subsequent transatlantic history would only intensify. When Carlyle quoted himself in an 1837 essay on the 'Memoirs of Mirabeau', he referred to *Sartor Resartus* as 'a New England Book', thus effacing the book's textual origins and yoking its perceived nationality to the geography of its material production (*WTC* 3: 158). This tangibly illustrates what Meredith McGill has described as the ambiguously 'transnational status of reprinted texts' (2003: 3) – artefacts distributed in different national markets and subject to multiple circuits of importation and exportation. When the first English edition of *Sartor Resartus* appeared in the summer of 1838, the new appendix that Carlyle had decided to include reprinted American commentary on the text and thus added to the book's already hybrid character as a transatlantic print object.

Supplementing the original text in the editions produced from 1838 onwards, the 'Testimonies of Authors' section introduces English and American paratextual and metatextual material into the fabric of the printed book. Most of what Carlyle chose to preserve in this critical appendix documents the perplexity of professional readers upon first encountering *Sartor Resartus*. Just as Emerson's 'Preface', the 'Testimonies' re-enact what happens on the level of the text itself. Like the book, they present a miscellaneous compilation of manuscript and print material and dramatise moments of hermeneutic failure. The 'Testimonies' include four excerpts: a publisher's letter to Carlyle summarising an external reviewer's opinion of the manuscript, part of an English notice of the book, several passages from Everett's 1835 review and the entirety of Emerson's preface. Where Americans like Clarke and Putnam were celebrating Carlyle's discovery in the United States as evidence of an emerging domestic literary authority, the image of American criticism conveyed in the 'Testimonies' is considerably less flattering. That this mainly has to do with the manner in which Carlyle selected and arranged his material can be seen especially in his handling of Everett. The excerpts reprinted in the appendix come from the beginning of his review, where, in a half-serious manner, Everett was exposing the fictional nature of the book, concluding that 'after a careful survey of the whole ground, our belief is, that . . . the whole account of the origin of the work before us, which the supposed editor relates with so much gravity, . . . is in plain English, a *hum*' (1835: 456). What Carlyle leaves out is the conclusion of the piece, which illustrates that Everett understood quite well from the start that *Sartor Resartus* was a cleverly contrived work of fiction. Citing only from Everett's own caricature of critical pedantry, Carlyle implied that the American reviewer was himself a naive philistine, a literal-minded Yankee unable to appreciate either the book's complex metafictional fabric or its deliberate use of irony. Concluding the 'Testimonies' section, the moralistic interpretation of the book advanced in Emerson's preface further reinforced the impression – carefully created by Carlyle – that American critics of *Sartor Resartus* were even more inept at handling its formal radicalism than their British colleagues. What this demonstrates, I want to suggest, is that Carlyle's faith in the authorising powers of provincial publishing and criticism, after all, remained weak. Rather than embracing American responses to his book as a potential alternative to the symbolic economy of the British book market, he ultimately kept a qualified distance from them.

THE *FRENCH REVOLUTION* BETWEEN LONDON AND BOSTON

This reluctance to believe that the American literary sphere could generate cultural authority on its own did not keep Carlyle from developing a keen interest in the financial potential of transatlantic publishing. The first book that returned him a tangible profit from the United States was *The French Revolution*, a text with whose Boston publication Emerson fully assumed the responsibilities of Carlyle's transatlantic literary agent and editor. It ushered in a new phase of their Anglo-American 'bibliopolic' collaboration, one marked by busy negotiations with publishers and deliberate choices about the positioning of books in the literary marketplace. Over the course of this process of professionalisation, Carlyle and Emerson became acquainted with the unwritten laws of the international book trade and increasingly more adventurous at exploring them. Their transatlantic partnership proved beneficial to both: while Carlyle began to receive regular payments from the American sales of his books, Emerson discovered not only that he had a talent for dealing with publishers but also that his indispensable activity as Carlyle's American spokesman strengthened his position within the friendship.[5]

Emerson played a crucial role in the American publication of the book and was involved at almost every stage, from production to reception. He negotiated with publishers, compared their offers, wrote an advertising prospectus to win subscribers, took care of its dissemination, sent out review copies of the book to editors, wrote a review himself, organised the distribution of a substantial part of the first edition, dealt with the publishers' accounts and eventually sent Carlyle the money the books had earned him. Emerson got to work upon receiving a copy of the English first edition through Carlyle. As in the case of *Sartor Resartus*, the initial plan was not an independent American edition but the importation of British copies. By late October 1837, Emerson had nevertheless resolved to embark on such a reprint project, intent on securing Carlyle the maximum financial benefit. Having published the Boston *Sartor Resartus*, James Munroe and Company thought themselves entitled to issue Carlyle's future works in the United States. To Emerson, the firm's proposal at first looked more promising than those of its competitors, but he abruptly changed his mind and decided in favour of publishers Little and Brown, mainly because Munroe was 'not so rich nor so extensively connected a house as Little's' (*CEC* 229) but also since the deal with the latter enabled him to increase Carlyle's profit margin. Through an additional clause in the agreement, Little and Brown offered to cede their profit of 20 per cent on the retail price for each copy that would be sold to subscribers (see ibid., 170).

There was hence a tangible incentive for Emerson to secure as many advance orders as possible, and he immediately drew up a prospectus for the book, six dozen copies of which were distributed across a far-flung network of friends and acquaintances. Emerson furnished the publishers with a list of thirty-one individuals to whom the prospectus should be sent – among them eminent Boston–Cambridge figures such as George Bancroft, William Ellery Channing and Henry Wadsworth Longfellow, with recipients outside of Massachusetts including the Transcendentalists Frederic Henry Hedge in Bangor, Hiram Fuller in Providence, William Henry Furness in Philadelphia and James Freeman Clarke in Louisville. This campaign established an extensive semi-private distribution system that coexisted alongside with Little and Brown's professional trade arrangements with local booksellers.[6] The most important sales argument Emerson advanced in the prospectus was that Carlyle himself directly stood to gain from the American edition:

> I have the hope of securing a private benefit to the author, to whom all the profits arising from it will be transmitted. With this view, the publishers have made with me a liberal contract, by which they relinquish to the author all profit on the sale of such copies as shall be subscribed for. (*CW* 10: 531)

Highlighting the consumer's debt to the producer and reconfiguring book buying as an intimate personal transaction, Emerson here becomes an early champion of ethical consumption, a morally inflected market behaviour aimed at the structural transformation of a given economic environment. He urged potential subscribers to show their solidarity with Carlyle not only through boycotting unauthorised reprints, but also through actively buycotting the editions he guaranteed would yield Carlyle the 'private benefit' he legitimately deserved.[7]

The American *French Revolution* was published on Christmas Day, 1837, but Emerson's involvement was only beginning to make itself felt at this point. In late December, he sent review copies of the book to his lawyer brother William in New York for further distribution among local editors, in the hope of securing favourable notices and thus creating additional demand for the book beyond the Boston market. How seriously Emerson took his role as Carlyle's 'bibliopolic' representative can be gauged from the minute record he kept in letters and notebooks about how many copies were sold through him, by whom they were bought and how much they netted. To Carlyle, the mere idea of receiving money from across the ocean demonstrated the extensive reach of Anglophone literary culture. Thanking Emerson for his 'brisk and helpful' support, he wrote in March 1838:

> It will be a very brave day when cash actually reaches me, no matter what the number of the coins, whether seven or seven hundred, out of Yankee-land; and strange enough, what is not unlikely, if it be the *first* cash I realize for that piece of work, – Angle-land continuing still *in*solvent to me! Well; it is a wide motherland we have here, or are getting to have, from Bass's Straits all round to Columbia River, already almost circling the Globe. (CEC 180)

The prospect of transatlantic book money conjured up the image of Anglo-American solidarity, but it also made Carlyle contemplate a more far-reaching rapprochement that not only revolved around a united transatlantic print landscape but also fused its inhabitants into a collective first-person plural that transcended the sectional divide between 'Angle-land' and 'Yankee-land'. Emerson's promise of transatlantic payments also gave Carlyle an opportunity to think about the difference between foreign and domestic business practices. At a time when most British authors were complaining of the immorality of American publishers, an astonished Carlyle acknowledged that, in his case, their anticipated munificence made British booksellers appear rapacious by comparison.[8]

Just as *Sartor Resartus*, *The French Revolution* proved a success on the American market. The edition of a thousand copies was sold off before the end of the year and Emerson could finally begin sending Carlyle money from his American publishing.[9] Upon receiving the first of many such payments, Carlyle again sounded the note of transatlantic amity and once more turned against the British book trade:

> From beyond the waters there is a hand held out; beyond the waters too live brothers. I would only the Book were an Epic, a *Dante* or undying thing, that New England might boast in aftertimes of this feat of hers, and put stupid poundless and penniless Old England to the blush about it! (*CEC* 193)

Whether Carlyle's achievement was epic or not, American commentators, as we have seen, had already begun to 'boast' of their discovery of his books and to postulate a migration of critical authority from 'Old England' to 'New England'.

If Carlyle – disheartened by the response of British readers, publishers and reviewers – at one point himself began to subscribe to this narrative of transition, he reverted to residual notions of transatlantic dependence when it came to deciding how to spend his first American book money. To Emerson he wrote that he would 'buy [him]self a sharp little nag with twenty of these Transatlantic Pounds, and ride him till the other thirty be eaten': 'I will call the creature "Yankee", and kind thoughts of those far away shall be with me every time I mount him' (ibid., 198–9). The image of New England as a horse carrying a British rider evokes a vision of Anglo-American domination that is in sharp contrast not only to Carlyle's celebration of transatlantic brotherhood but also to his prophecy of a future inversion of power structures. Dependent on the financial benevolence of the American buyers of his books, and thus on the dynamics of a newly configured transatlantic print market, Carlyle at the same time continued to think of Anglo-American authority in the terms of a more traditional hierarchy.

As the last remaining copies of Little and Brown's *French Revolution* were being sold in early December 1838, Carlyle wrote to enquire whether Emerson would be interested in selling a share of the second London edition of the book in the United States. Sending Carlyle another payment for the Boston volumes, Emerson replied that while the American edition had, in the meantime, sold out, Little and Brown were not yet predicting a demand sufficient to 'justify a new edition' (*CEC* 210). Importing a more manageable smaller number of copies from London was thus a reasonable proposition, not least because Emerson began to fear that the lack of available copies might entice unauthorised reprinters to step in and offer pirated versions, thus ruining the prospect of a potential second American edition that would continue to pay. The following February, Carlyle wrote that he was planning to have stereotype plates of the edition prepared so that 'the supply of both the New and the Old England might be profitably combined' for the foreseeable future (ibid., 212). By late March, he had resolved to 'print a second edition for England and America *together*', a scheme that would take the form of his London publisher James Fraser striking off 1,500 copies for the domestic market before printing a further 500 for American readers (*CL* 11: 62). Produced at a relatively low cost, these copies could be sold in the United States at a retail price significantly below the English standard, which, Carlyle hoped, would help Emerson to 'defy Piracy' (*CEC* 226).

It took until early September before Carlyle could announce that the copies – their title page listing Little and Brown jointly with Fraser as the publishers of the book – were about to be shipped to Boston. When the cargo arrived in the United States two months later, however, there were unforeseen complications. The import duties on the shipment were estimated at between $300 and $400, a considerable sum for which Emerson feared 'I & not Little & Co. am accountable to the Custom House' (*L* 2: 234). With the Boston publishers raising the retail price of the edition to offset these additional expenses,[10] Emerson expressed doubts about whether the plan would prove financially viable after all. 'The book is rather too dear for our market', he wrote to Carlyle, afraid that the two of them were 'in daily danger of a cheap edition from some rival neighbor' (*CEC* 253–4). Although Emerson's fears would eventually prove unfounded, Carlyle was similarly disinclined to pursue further an 'export and import speculation' that called for more and more complex forms of transatlantic material exchange (ibid., 258). The sale of the imported edition was, in fact, nevertheless a success. By July 1840, almost 200 copies had been sold, another 82 sets by mid-October, and a year later Emerson could write to Carlyle that only a handful of copies remained in stock.[11] Little and Brown subsequently issued another printing of *The French Revolution*, based on their first edition and this time distributed in collaboration with publishers in New York and Philadelphia. Throughout the first half of the 1840s, Carlyle received steady payments from Emerson on Little and Brown's behalf that derived from the sales of the American printings and the imported London copies of the book. While complicated through delayed communications, unforeseen expenses and the challenges of international accounting, Emerson and Carlyle's innovative transatlantic 'export and import speculation' had, after all, paid off.

As Little and Brown's first American edition of *The French Revolution* was going through the press, plans for another book project began to take shape. Emerson was in the early stages of preparing a compilation of Carlyle's scattered periodical essays and reviews, which had not yet been republished in England and were all but inaccessible to most American readers. Where the Boston *French Revolution* had merely been a reprint of an English book, what would become the *Critical and Miscellaneous Essays* was a genuinely American product, an original title that had not previously existed in Britain in collected form. Given that there was thus a genuinely transatlantic demand for the multi-volume edition, Emerson and Carlyle decided to export part of the American edition to London in order to cover the English market as well. In financial terms, the venture proved as rewarding as the American distribution of Fraser's

London *French Revolution*. As an additional side effect, the edition firmly reasserted Carlyle's authorial control over his early periodical writings and, in many cases for the first time, explicitly confirmed his authorship of previously anonymous essays. Consolidating his status as an established writer at home and abroad, the *Critical and Miscellaneous Essays* eventually became the textual kernel of the collected editions of his works that appeared from the later 1850s onwards. Not counting the money he had made from the London sales of the Boston *Essays*, by December 1841 Carlyle had received more than £300 through Emerson for the American editions of his writings. His publishing success in the United States had, moreover, paved the way for a corresponding success on the British market. The robust sales of *The French Revolution* and the transatlantic *Essays* made publishers on both sides of the Atlantic realise that a growing number of readers was interested in Carlyle's writing. With the American book money as a key component of his domestic economy, he was finally beginning to be able to sustain himself financially as a man of letters.[12]

Complications: Piracy and Copyright

As the 1840s unfolded, however, money from transatlantic publishing did not keep coming as easily as it had done before. Over the course of the decade, the American print market turned into an increasingly competitive business environment. Where Carlyle had struggled to sell *Sartor Resartus* in the early 1830s, ten years later there was, if anything, too much interest in his books among publishers – especially in the United States, where the appearance of unauthorised editions increasingly threatened to dry up an important source of income for contemporary British writers. This development not only forced Carlyle and Emerson to address new problems through innovative solutions but also compelled them to face the complex relationship between literary authorship on the one hand and cultural and legal authority on the other. Carlyle's success in the United States came at an inauspicious moment in the history of transatlantic print relations. Unauthorised reprinting was beginning to boom as a business model and the genteel Boston publishing that Emerson had preferred both for his own and for Carlyle's books came increasingly under fire from the more vibrant New York market. New strategies were needed to fend off such competition. One of these was the advance shipment of proof sheets aimed at simultaneous or near-simultaneous publication in Britain and the United States – a privilege for which American publishers from the 1820s onwards had been prepared to pay British novelists and poets.[13] By the early 1840s, Carlyle's non-fictional prose had become popular enough at home and abroad for authorised and unauthorised publishers alike to target it. Advance sheets secured a temporal advantage in the race for an American reprint of a new British book and many publishers of unauthorised reprints lost interest in a title if it had already appeared with a competitor. Firms often advertised when they were working from advance sheets to market their own edition of a foreign text as legitimate. Another way of signalling the authorised nature of an edition was the inclusion of an imprimatur note from the author or from a recognised representative – a strategy that Carlyle and Emerson also pursued. In the absence of a reliable legal framework, the contemporary culture of trade courtesy in which such forms of authentication counted as meaningful depended on an atmosphere of mutual trust between publishers.[14] By the late 1830s, however, this atmosphere had all but collapsed. Even explicit declarations from writers or the advantage of first publication now no longer kept rivalling publishers from issuing their own editions.

It was with the transatlantic publication of the 1840 lecture series *On Heroes, Hero-Worship, and the Heroic in History* that Carlyle and Emerson experienced the full complexity of the regionally diversified American reprint system for the first time. Carlyle wrote in late September 1840 that he had completed the manuscript of the book and would send Emerson the proof sheets for the preparation of an American edition. But before the last instalment of the sheets arrived in Boston, New York publisher Daniel Appleton had acquired a copy of James Fraser's London edition and was set on reprinting the book himself. Emerson's Boston publisher James Munroe wrote in late March 1841 to inform him that Appleton and Company

> advertise Carlyle's new book in press and say it will be out in a few weeks. We told them that you had spoken to us about it last January but they replied that the one who received the first copy had the right of printing and they should go on with theirs. (Houghton MS Am 1280 [2221])

The Boston and New York firms evidently disagreed over whether authorial sanction or temporal advantage counted as the more authoritative sign of 'the right of printing'. Munroe was not yet entirely discouraged, however, enquiring if, '[u]nder these circumstances', they should nonetheless 'put the book to press' – although the firm made clear that this would need to happen at Emerson's own risk (ibid.). The only real hope was to highlight that the Boston *On Heroes* would be the authorised version of the text – a form of legitimation that, in the past, had worked at least with New England buyers. Emerson, the publisher recommended, should 'write a preface to make your edition sell in this market' (ibid.). Printed and bound in a form similar to that of the authorised versions of *The French Revolution* and the *Critical and Miscellaneous Essays*, Munroe's *On Heroes* would sell – or so at least the publisher hoped – to a different readership and at 'a larger price' than Appleton's New York reprint (ibid.).

Once the unauthorised edition had been published, Emerson reported to Carlyle that an intransigent Appleton had threatened 'to print in future everything of yours that shall be printed in London[,] complaining in rude terms of the monopoly your publishers have exercised' (*CEC* 292). The tone in the publishing world was evidently getting rougher, with a rift emerging between two different spheres of the decentralised American print market. The predominantly 'local and parochial' Boston publishers were clashing with their more enterprising New York competitors, who, situated in a market with a larger trade volume, grew more and more powerful (Madison 1966: 37). Munroe and Company were clearly acknowledging this rivalry when they distinguished the Boston environment ('this market') from its New York counterpart. With its higher retail prices and smaller print runs, Boston publishing was, to some extent, closer to the London than to the New York market. Exchanging English copies of *The French Revolution* and American copies of the *Critical and Miscellaneous Essays* between the two cities had helped to create something of a uniform transatlantic print culture involving New England and what Carlyle liked to call 'Old England'. Initially excluded from such bilateral arrangements, New York publishers like Appleton by the early 1840s were set on interfering with the transatlantic 'monopoly' enjoyed by their Boston competitors.

Appleton's edition of *On Heroes* was soon no longer the only problem, however. As Emerson explained to Carlyle, 'the New York newspapers print the book in chapters & you circulate for six cents per newspaper at the corners of all streets' (*CEC* 293). Published in newspaper format and issued in instalments at the cheapest of prices, such reprints threatened even powerful New York firms like Appleton or Harper and Brothers.[15] Although such competition reduced Carlyle's prospects for future payments from his American sales even further, piracy had at least one advantage, Emerson suggested: Carlyle was 'gaining in fame' what he stood to 'lose in coin' (ibid.). While unauthorised reprinting entailed a loss of authorial control over details of production and distribution (as well as the forfeiting of a potential income), the appearance of pirated editions, after all, also signalled a writer's broad transatlantic appeal. As McGill has pointed out, 'it was the fiercely competitive reprint publishers who pioneered American book marketing techniques' and thus 'fortif[ied] the reputations' of the writers they published (2003: 17). Unauthorised editions of his writings guaranteed Carlyle a much wider circulation than the early Boston reprints. The predominantly regional distribution networks of firms like Munroe and Little and Brown meant that copies of their editions mostly found their way into the hands of New England buyers. It was only with the New York editions that Carlyle became widely read beyond New England, since the large New York houses were well connected with booksellers throughout the country.

As financial compensation nevertheless remained desirable, writers and their authorised publishers devised different strategies to keep the reprint business at bay. Trade-internal measures such as advance sheets or imprimatur notes were one option, but as the situation aggravated it became increasingly evident that a larger systemic solution was needed. Calls for the foreign copyright protection of British authors were becoming more frequent and Carlyle played his part in the transatlantic campaigning. He had kept track of the domestic legal situation and in April 1839 had submitted a petition in support of a bill to extend the duration of British copyright at home. Arguing that 'all honest labour is worthy of the chance of recompense', he entreated lawmakers to 'forbid ... extraneous persons ... to steal from him his small winnings' (CE 29: 205, 207). Despite numerous additional endorsements from figures including William Wordsworth and Robert Southey, the bill met with considerable opposition in parliament and took until 1842 to be passed in the form of a weaker compromise version. The initiative had nevertheless managed to launch a general debate about intellectual property and public access.

Its legal amendments notwithstanding, the 1842 Copyright Act did not have a noticeable effect on the precarious situation of British writers abroad. The subsequent International Copyright Act of 1844 defined conditions under which foreign writing could be protected in Britain, but in the absence of a reciprocal Anglo-American agreement, this effectively protected neither American writers in the United Kingdom nor British writers in the United States.[16] Carlyle was among many contemporary writers who campaigned for the passage of such more comprehensive transatlantic legislation. Since British law had no executive power abroad, he and his colleagues had to appeal to American authorities directly. Even before his negative experience with American piracy reached its peak in the early 1840s, Carlyle had supported a petition that his friend Martineau and her English publishers Saunders and Otley had prepared in order to drum up public support for the issue of international copyright. Together with Martineau, Southey, Maria Edgeworth and Benjamin Disraeli, he was among the fifty-six signatories of the document presented to Congress by Kentucky Senator Henry Clay in February 1837, with additional support from several American authors of note (including Washington Irving and William Cullen Bryant). Capitalising on transatlantic sentiment rather than presenting legal–economic arguments, the petition stressed that 'literature ... ought to constitute a bond of union and friendship between the United States and Great Britain' (Anon. 1837a: 311). Despite such emotionally charged appeals, however, Clay's bill was repeatedly voted down. Where in the case of the English legislation for which Carlyle had petitioned in 1839 at least a compromise was reached, the American plans eventually came to a halt.[17]

After Martineau and Saunders and Otley's failed attempt, it was Charles Dickens who took up the issue once again. He spoke out in favour of an international arrangement during his tour of the United States in the first half of 1842 and revived an interest in the topic among fellow writers at home. Finding himself increasingly in the crosshairs of unauthorised American reprint publishers, Carlyle went to greater lengths to support the new campaign, writing to Dickens, who subsequently set out to convince American newspapers and magazines to print the letter and an accompanying memorial signed by a dozen eminent British writers.[18] Like the petition submitted to Congress five years before, Carlyle's message highlighted Anglo-American amity, but it intensified the argument to such a degree that it effectively transformed the bilateral issue into a transatlantically domestic one. Speaking of 'an International Copyright between the Two Nations', Carlyle quickly corrected himself by arguing that, 'properly' speaking, the question of Anglo-American copyright concerned 'not Two Nations, but one – *indivisible* by Parliament, Congress, or any kind of Human Law or Diplomacy' (*CL* 14: 92). Where legal interpretations of intellectual property failed to align on both sides of the Atlantic, Carlyle instead emphasised a strong undercurrent of affective proximity between nations 'knit in a thousand ways by Nature and Practical Intercourse; indivisible brother elements of the same great SAXONDOM' (ibid., 93). If Anglo-American relations were, at bottom, a family affair, unauthorised reprinting became an act of self-harm more reprehensible than the mere violation of an international legal code or abstract ethical principle. Deconstructing cultural, political and juridical boundaries between Britain and the United States, Carlyle's racialised characterisation of the two countries as a single 'indivisible' entity at the same time represents an implicit attempt at expanding the British legal sphere of influence. His investment in the discourse of transatlantic fraternity, on the other hand, demonstrates that newly emergent questions of property and entitlement were redefining residual structures of authority. Since the vertical authority of English law was no longer being recognised across the Atlantic, British writers came to rely on a transatlantic language of solidarity that revolved around an egalitarian imagery of horizontal connection.

Authorisation Policies: *Past and Present*

If, for British authors, there would be no official legal way to assert their claims in the United States until the final decade of the century, in the meantime they continued to depend on such rhetoric, but also on the continued support of American publishers and friends. With unauthorised reprints of Carlyle's *On Heroes* already on sale before he had even had a chance of preparing the book for the press, Emerson eventually decided against launching a Boston edition. With *Past and Present*, Carlyle's next book, the two once again relied on trade-internal strategies. Emerson had learned his lesson and concluded that advancing proof sheets was no longer sufficient. The new policy to fight unauthorised reprinting, he intimated to Carlyle, was 'to have the Ms copied by a scrivener before you print at home & send it out to me' (*CEC* 293). Producing copies from manuscripts in London and Boston simultaneously could give an advantage to an authorised American edition that would guarantee sales for as long as the British books could be kept back. Heeding such advice, Carlyle, in the spring of 1843, provided Emerson with details about his plans for an American version of the new text. Since *Past and Present* was already partly available in type, he would send the first half of the book in sheets and the remaining half in the form of a duplicate manuscript, an arrangement that would give Emerson's publisher of choice 'a three-week start of any rival' (ibid., 337). When the parcel was despatched via the next available steamer in early April, however, Carlyle no longer seemed convinced that the scheme would work, afraid that 'Appleton the gibbetless thief at New York will beat us after all!' (ibid., 340).

Where, with *On Heroes*, two years before, Emerson had simply put up with Appleton's assertive market behaviour, he now decided to contact some of the most powerful New York reprinters in advance in order to stake his own claim to bring out the first and only legitimate edition of the new book. Since Appleton seemed beyond appeal, Emerson concentrated on Harper and Brothers and Park Benjamin 'to implore their clemency & forbearance' (*L* 3: 169). The tone of his letters was decisive enough for both immediately to agree not to reprint the book. The Harpers dutifully promised that they would 'not interfere with the arrangements . . . made by you, for Mr. Carlyle's benefit' (Houghton MS Am 1280 [1348]), while Benjamin, who represented the newspaper reprint segment of the market, made an even greater show of his intention to abstain from bringing out his own *Past and Present*. On 29 April 1843, he printed a detailed statement in his *The New World*, the same venue that, two years before, had run *On Heroes* in the form of cheap instalments without bothering about Carlyle's authorial sanction:

> In reply to a letter which we have received from Mr. R. W. Emerson, touching a new work by Mr. Carlyle, in the press and about to be published by Charles C. Little and James Brown, we have pleasure in saying thus publicly, that we shall interfere with the publication in no manner whatsoever; we shall not reprint the work, and we sincerely hope that Mr. Carlyle will receive a fair compensation from the sale of the proposed edition. We will add furthermore, that it is to be hoped that no publisher will be found *mean* enough to print the work after the making public – which we now do – of the following fact. Mr. Emerson received the work about to be issued in manuscript and proof-sheets, considerably in advance of its appearance in London, and it is to appear in Boston for the benefit of Mr. Carlyle. (1843: 509)

Benjamin's declaration reaffirmed the gift exchange logic of trade courtesy at a time when the system had come under serious pressure. The motivation behind his notice was not entirely altruistic, however. Demonstrating the impeccability of Benjamin's own business ethics, the statement simultaneously represented an instance of trade-internal 'public shaming' aimed at raising doubts about the professionalism of his competitors (Spoo 2013: 44). Piracy was, after all, a flexible charge. The rhetoric of print authority and authorial authorisation was at everyone's disposal, providing leverage to substantiate claims to legal and moral entitlement.

In addition to his imploring letters, Emerson hoped that a short word of his on the nature of the Boston edition of *Past and Present* would deter buyers from choosing potential New York reprints. His short 'American Editor's Notice' for the book illustrates the transformations the transatlantic print market had undergone since the end of the preceding decade. The emphases of Emerson's previous paratexts on Carlyle's behalf – his 1836 'Preface' to *Sartor Resartus* and his 1838 'Advertisement' for the *Critical and Miscellaneous Essays*, among several other short pieces – became superseded by a legal–economic discourse of property. Questions of authority and authorisation remain at the fore in the later 'Notice' to *Past and Present*, but there is a noticeable shift in the functions that these serve here. Where, in the late 1830s, the main purpose of Emerson's texts had been to furnish Carlyle with a sense of moral and intellectual authority (through vouching for the quality and 'sincer[ity]' of the books), now it was to argue for his ownership in the material results of his literary labours:

> This book is printed from a private copy, partly in manuscript, sent by the author to his friends in this country, and is published for his benefit. I hope this notice that the profits of the sale of this edition are secured to Mr. Carlyle, will persuade every well disposed publisher to respect his property in his own book. (*CW* 10: 238)

In an April 1838 prospectus aimed at attracting subscribers for the Boston *Critical and Miscellaneous Essays*, Emerson had appealed to potential readers through stressing the ethical implications of book buying. 'The profits of the sale' of the edition, he promised, would be directly 'transmitted to the author', 'the publishers . . . relinquish[ing] to him all profit on such copies as are subscribed for' (ibid., 532). The figure of the publisher, in other words, here still featured as a provider of – rather than as a threat to – authorial compensation. Although remnants of such diplomatic rhetoric survive in the 1843 'Notice' to *Past and Present*, a legalistic tone dominates the later paratext. With its focus on intellectual property, the 'Notice' was addressed not so much at the book's potential buyers and readers as it was at rival printers. But if, in detailing the transatlantic genesis of the edition, Emerson insisted on the established codes of trade courtesy, his invitation to 'well disposed publisher[s]' to comply with these codes demonstrates that the softer touch of the emotional plea had not entirely disappeared. This mixture of law and morality captures well an ambiguous contemporary discourse of transatlantic reprinting that hovered between assertions of legal entitlement and appeals to ethical conduct. Emerson's short text manages to combine the logic of property with that of propriety, the former entailing legal and material aspects of ownership, the latter a recourse to standards of mutual recognition.[19] The 'Notice' employs both of these rhetorics at once: Carlyle's 'own book' is his 'property', but without a firm legal framework to protect his copyright, it is only through mobilising the ethical imperative of 'respect' for ownership that Emerson can ultimately 'hope' to morally 'persuade' where he cannot legally enforce.[20]

Carlyle's and Emerson's elaborate attempts at protecting *Past and Present* eventually proved futile when William Colyer, a New York printer and a neophyte at publishing, cashed in on the large American demand for Carlyle's book. Even if, following Emerson's intercession, some of the major players had agreed not to interfere, the New York scene was too large and diverse to be kept under control effectively. As Robert Spoo has pointed out, the moral economy of trade courtesy was operative among an 'inner circle of genteel publishers', but it did not necessarily extend to small firms that had 'no incentive to accept a code that could bring few immediate, tangible benefits' (2013: 50). Despite – or more likely because of – such competition, Emerson continued to promote his own authorised edition of the book. In July 1843, he published an extensive review in *The Dial*, the periodical he himself had begun to edit the previous year. Like the 'Notice' that formed part of the book itself, the later metatext revolved around questions of ownership and legitimacy. Yet Emerson's focus of attention has shifted once again, from intellectual property to territorial domination, from the policies of the transatlantic book trade to the politics of Anglo-American power. Culminating in a passage that develops the outlines of a poetics of imperialism, the review reconfigures authorship and authority in relation to a new and different kind of materiality – no longer that of the (re-)printed book but that of geographical space and its appropriation. The epitome of cultural modernity, Carlyle's style to Emerson amounts to a civilisational achievement comparable only to Anglo-American global hegemony:

> Carlyle is the first domestication of the modern system with its infinity of details into style. We have been civilizing very fast, building London and Paris, and now planting New England and India, New Holland and Oregon, – and it has not appeared in literature, – there has been no analogous expansion and recomposition in books. Carlyle's style is the first emergence of all this wealth and labor, with which the world has gone with child so long. London and Europe tunnelled, graded, cornlawed, with trade-nobility, and east and west Indies for dependencies, and America, with the Rocky Hills in the horizon, have never before been conquered in literature. This is the first invasion and conquest. (*CW* 10: 267)

Although Emerson does not spell out the exact terms of the comparison, his link between literary expression and colonial expansion is explicit enough. Carlyle's style, to him, is the 'emergence' or superstructural manifestation of the broader cultural and historical base of 'invasion and conquest'.

While the passage seems concerned with modernity and civilisation at large, the actual referent of its 'we' is, in fact, more limited. With the exception of Paris, Emerson's is a decidedly Anglocentric genealogy of settlement that, in essence, maps the geographical outlines of the British Empire. To this he adds the American West, flattening the chronology of modernity into a comprehensive present tense in which, during an expansive colonial 'now', New England and Oregon can be imagined as becoming settled simultaneously. In all its incoherence and eccentricity, Carlyle's style is the quintessential expression of this Anglo-American modern moment. The review even goes so far as to credit him with having become the first genuine poet of the American 'continent' (ibid., 267) – an argument that runs counter to Emerson's more familiar claim in the essay 'The Poet', published a year later, that 'the northern trade, the southern planting, the western clearing, Oregon, and Texas' still remained 'unsung' (CW 3: 22). That Carlyle should have managed to give literary expression to 'America, with the Rocky Hills in the horizon' seems an astonishing claim, given that *Past and Present* is, in many ways, his most 'English' text. Yet Emerson's argument is heavily indebted to the book's own expansionist rhetoric, which Carlyle had used to construct a similar analogy between matter and spirit when he suggested that England's 'Epic' was 'written in huge characters on the face of this Planet' in the form of 'Indian Empires, Americas, [and] New-Hollands' (WTC 4: 162).[21] But where, in Carlyle, the material is metaphorised into the literary, Emerson's logic works the other way around, translating Carlyle's aesthetic achievement into the language of political authority.

What Emerson's text implies is not only that 'civilizing' and 'planting' colonial territories provides a way of claiming ownership of them, but also that literary expression forms a necessary additional stage in this acquisition process. Property and propriety here resurface once again, but in a form different from that which they had taken in Emerson's 'Notice' to the book itself. In the vision the *Dial* review articulates of the poet as the ultimate coloniser, foreign territories can be truly claimed only through linguistic and cultural forms of appropriation.[22] What sounds like an abstract argument about the relationship between art and power takes on a more concrete significance in the overall context of Carlyle's and Emerson's struggles with transatlantic reprinting. The shift of emphasis between the 'Notice' and the later review essay from one form of property-as-propriety to another – from a defensive reliance on the business ethics of the print market to an assertive claim about literature's contribution to political supremacy – allowed for compensating for the violation of authors' rights in the contemporary literary marketplace through an empowering fiction of authorship's cultural relevance.

Authorial Imprimaturs and the Ethics of Transatlantic Publishing

Although Emerson did not yet entirely resign himself to such compensatory fictions, the publication arrangements that followed *Past and Present* were ones in which he himself was no longer centrally involved. In early 1845, Philadelphia publishers Carey and Hart approached him with a plan to print a new edition of Carlyle's *Critical and Miscellaneous Essays*. Their initial suggestion was to buy up the remaining stock of the Boston edition, but since only a few complete sets of the four volumes were still unsold, the publishers proposed a new printing, promising Carlyle a flat payment of £50, independent of the sales of the book. Advertised as 'a new edition', the book was in print by the end of March, selling at a mere fifth of the retail price of the original Boston volumes. An imprimatur notice from Emerson gave Carey and Hart additional reason to believe that their edition would sell. By the mid-1840s, the market's collective 'mania for cheapness had abated' (Barnes 1974: 86) and trade courtesy codes were beginning to be observed again on a larger scale, with notes of authorisation correspondingly rising in value. Credentialling him as 'the American Editor of the First Edition' of the book, Carey and Hart introduced their edition with a short letter from Emerson that was aimed both at signalling Carlyle's approval and at emphasising the publisher's 'justice' in paying him (Emerson 1845: 3).

Now with a substantial Carlyle title in their portfolio, the Philadelphia publishers also expressed an interest in his new book, the forthcoming *Oliver Cromwell's Letters and Speeches*. Emerson, however, had already suggested Munroe to Carlyle as a potential publisher the year before. When, in November 1845, Carlyle sent him advance copies of the still unpublished two-volume *Cromwell* through his London publishers Chapman and Hall, Emerson assumed that these were intended to serve as a template for his Boston reprint. But misunderstanding Carlyle to mean that Emerson's American edition was doomed to fail, Chapman and Hall had sold another set to publishers Wiley and Putnam in order to net at least the £10 the latter were offering for the opportunity to reprint the book in New York. Declaring that they had been authorised to do so by Carlyle's English publishers, Wiley and Putnam refused to release Emerson's copies to protect their business interests. Unaware of its agreement with Chapman and Hall, Emerson believed that the New York firm was trying to defraud Carlyle of his American income. Once Chapman and Hall had confirmed Wiley and Putnam's account, however, Emerson offered a public apology and the New York publishers were soon suggesting a second edition of the Cromwell book to Carlyle's more immediate financial advantage.

Before long, George Palmer Putnam, one of the firm's two partners, proposed republishing Carlyle's earlier books as well. This ambitious plan once more involved Emerson, who was familiar with the specifics of the arrangements for the previous editions. In early April 1846, he sent Wiley and Putnam a detailed account of the bibliopolic affairs he had overseen during the previous decade. Drawing on this information, Putnam himself visited Carlyle in London a few weeks later to suggest new authorised editions of *The French Revolution*, *Sartor Resartus* and *On Heroes*.[23] Carlyle left the final decision to Emerson, who enthusiastically approved of the offer and urged him to collaborate with the publisher. In mid-June, Carlyle signed an agreement that stipulated that he would supply the firm with the material necessary for the preparation of revised editions, granting the American publisher 'his written authority' to bring out the titles 'exclusively in the United States' and pledging 'not to authorize or aid in any way in the reprinting of any other edition in the United States' (Houghton MS Am 1280.235 [215]). Wiley and Putnam, on their part, were reaffirming their intention to provide an appropriate form of compensation, which took the form of 10 per cent royalties on the retail price of all copies sold. Carlyle had thus 'signed one of the most favorable contracts to date between a British author and an American publisher' (Greenspan 2000: 126), but Wiley and Putnam similarly benefitted from an agreement that gave them the 'exclusive' American rights to almost the entirety of the Carlyle corpus. For these rights to be recognised by rivalling publishers, the New York firm needed to demonstrate that its new editions differed from the earlier American ones and came with the sanction of the author himself. Meeting the terms of the agreement, Carlyle revised the volumes before they went to press and wrote imprimatur notices that prefaced the new books.

Wiley and Putnam obviously were under no legal obligation to share their profits with Carlyle, but in a revived atmosphere of trade courtesy trust, royalty payments were a solid investment, securing a form of authorial assent that promised to dissuade unauthorised rivals from issuing competing reprints. To Carlyle himself, however, the agreement turned out to be less favourable than it had originally appeared. Upon repeated enquiries, he eventually received money for the two editions of *Cromwell* in the summer of 1847, but the older titles turned out to be slow sellers. Putnam wrote in May to explain that they 'had not been published long enough to yield profits as yet', suggesting at the same time that they might soon do (Houghton Autograph File P, 1554–2005). Accounting for the sales of the volumes became more challenging when the partnership of the firm was dissolved and Putnam took the Carlyle titles with him.[24] The books apparently continued to find few buyers, with the publisher complaining in June 1848 that they had 'been far less profitable than we could have expected' (Houghton MS Am 1280.226 [3944]).[25] Carlyle eventually began 'to regret very heartily that I ever bothered myself correcting my Books for them, or addressing Notices to their honest fellow citizens of the Union on *their* behalf', describing the publishers in his private correspondence as '*Privateers* (we must not say Pirates)' (*CL* 23: 25). So disappointing was the performance of the volumes that

Putnam decided to sell the plates to his competitors Harper and Brothers, who were obviously not bound by the terms of the 1846 agreement. This was all the more vexing to Carlyle because they proved considerably more successful at marketing their reprints than Putnam had been, selling thousands of copies of his books over the following three decades.[26]

While Carlyle was thus becoming ever more widely read in the United States, his transatlantic bibliopolic income gradually dried up. Despite their relatively small print runs, the early Boston editions of books such as *Sartor Resartus* and *The French Revolution* had, ironically enough, yielded him a more reliable profit than the more widely selling later New York and Philadelphia reprints (even those which he himself had authorised). Emerson's efforts during the decade between the 'Preface' to *Sartor Resartus* and the initially promising negotiations with Wiley and Putnam had crucially contributed to the financial success of the earlier books, which had established Carlyle's status in the Anglo-American print market and in turn paved the way for the mass market editions that appeared in Britain and the United States from the later 1840s onwards. Although the latter no longer automatically returned him steady payments, the size of their print runs at least testified to the existence of a large community of followers abroad. American reprinting, as Emerson had suggested, allowed authors like Carlyle to extend their popular base, 'gaining in fame' among a group of readers that could be imagined as at once foreign and familiar. Where the failure of contemporary British writers to curtail the unauthorised reprinting of their works in the United States produced a sense of disempowerment in the face of market forces beyond their immediate authorial control, the sheer empirics of 'transatlantic bibliopoly' – the numerical size and geographical extent of a combined Anglo-American audience – provided them with a more generous estimate of their position in a transatlantic literary sphere that offered a framework for their public recognition as cultural authorities.

Notes

1. See Vance 1936 for an early overview of Carlyle's American circulation before *Sartor Resartus*. The 1825 *Life of Schiller*, for instance, had appeared in Boston in 1833 with a preface by Charles Follen, a professor of German literature at Harvard, and was covered extensively in the *North American Review* the following year (see Anon. 1834).
2. On the origins and contours of this mindset as it developed with British Romantic writers such as Wordsworth, Coleridge and Byron, see Bennett 1999.
3. See Teichgraeber 1995: 214–17 and Myerson 2014: 216.
4. The critical opinion of the book prevalent in Emerson's own circle was articulated a year later in Nathaniel Frothingham's review of the first American edition for the Boston *Christian Examiner* (see Frothingham 1836). Emerson's friend George Ripley provided Carlyle with an explanation of the difference between the Unitarian–Transcendentalist and the *North American* intellectual networks

and the critical authority of their respective print organs: 'The Examiner has great weight in our highest circles of literature & society; more, in the vicinity, by far than the North American, though its influence is not so extensive throughout the country' (qtd in Slater 1952: 345).
5. Barbara Packer notes that the negotiation of the *French Revolution* deal allowed Emerson to become 'a benefactor rather than a mere disciple', a change of identity that indicated that '[p]ower' had to some extent 'shifted from London to Concord' (2010: 39).
6. The two surviving subscriber forms show the snowball effect that the prospectus had on incoming orders for the book: in New Bedford, whaling merchant and philanthropist Benjamin Rodman canvassed the names of twenty-two local subscribers and the form returned from New Haven featured subscriptions for another eight copies (Houghton MS Am 1280.226 [1460] and [1548]).
7. See Lewis and Potter 2011 on the logic of 'ethical consumption'. On the distinction between 'boycott' and 'buycott' and the economic rationale behind the latter, see Friedman 1999: 201–12.
8. 'American Booksellers sell at 15 percent', Carlyle explained to Richard Monckton Milnes in March 1839, whereas 'English Booksellers sell at the rate of 42 per cent ... and are generally reckoned to be knaves more or less besides' (*CL* 11: 62).
9. In his account book for 1836–40, Emerson notes a total of $1,251.92 in production costs for the edition and a profit of $1,989.54 for the copies sold (Houghton MS Am 1280H [112a]). The first payment, in the form of 'a bill of exchange for fifty pounds sterling', was sent in July 1838, at which point less than 200 copies remained in stock (*CEC* 189). Emerson despatched another bill of £100 in January 1839, after the edition had been exhausted.
10. See Little and Brown's letter to Emerson of 29 November, which features their updated calculation (Houghton MS Am 1280 [1924]).
11. For these figures, see Little and Brown's account of 23 July (Houghton MS Am 1280.235 [178]), their letter to Emerson of 13 October (Houghton MS Am 1280 [1926]) and *CEC* 309.
12. The size of the amounts sent by Emerson was considerable, compared to what Carlyle netted from other sources at the time. In a surviving overview of his financial status from the early 1840s, he estimated his total assets at £550, more than £350 of which had recently come from his American publishing (National Library of Scotland, MS.20752, fol. 81r). Adding to this the income from his London lecturing and the payments he was beginning to receive from British publishers, Carlyle had become a moderately well-off literary professional. He was financially confident enough, at any rate, to ask Emerson for advice about American investment opportunities: in December 1841, he enquired of him 'in *what* American funds it is that your funded money ... now lies', noting that an earlier purchase of Illinois stock had already turned him into 'a creditor to America' (*CEC* 314).
13. Walter Scott, for example, had received money under the terms of an advance arrangement from his Philadelphia publishers, Carey and Lea (see Rezek 2015: 40–61). Harper and Brothers of New York in the mid-1830s had entered into an agreement with novelist Edward Bulwer-Lytton that secured him a payment of £50 for the advance sheets of each of his future books (see Barnes 1974: 53).

14. On the history of – and the working logic behind – 'trade courtesy', see section three of the Introduction.
15. On mid-century newspaper reprints, see Tebbel 1972: 242–5 and Barnes 1974: 6–25. Park Benjamin and Rufus Wilmot Griswold's New York *Brother Jonathan* and *New World* – launched in 1839 and 1840, respectively – were two of the most successful incarnations of the new medium. Such additional competition resulted in a 'price war' that 'soon reached a point of absurdity' (Tebbel 1972: 244).
16. I provide a more general overview of mid-nineteenth-century transatlantic copyright legislation in the Introduction.
17. See Barnes 1974: 60–74. On Clay's bill, and Carlyle's American campaigning for it, see also Seville 2006: 165–9.
18. Ironically enough, one of the periodicals that complied with Dickens's request was *Brother Jonathan*, which followed its reprint of the letter with an outright attack on Carlyle and what it perceived to be his transatlantic condescension. Taking up his description of piracy as stealing, the New York paper argued that Anglo-American reprinting was ultimately a win-win situation, that 'an English writer . . . is robbed of nothing, and nothing is stolen from him, when a re-print is issued in this country, which . . . improves his property by endorsing his reputation' (Anon. 1842: 75).
19. I am departing here from the way in which these two terms are commonly used in legal and historical scholarship. 'Property' conventionally designates a modern notion of ownership as a type of commodity that can be accumulated and exchanged in the market, as opposed to an earlier idea of 'propriety', in which 'property is the material foundation for creating and maintaining the proper social order' (Alexander 1997: 1).
20. On the tension between these two kinds of argument, see Michael Everton's analysis of the discourse of 'moral propriety' among antebellum writers and publishers (2011: 8, 89–114).
21. Compare my discussion of this colonialist aspect of the book in Chapter 2.
22. 'Property' has historically been associated with 'governing authority', Carol M. Rose points out, demonstrating that a discourse of propriety which linked 'property and entitlement' played a crucial role in the legal justification of colonialism (1991: 233).
23. Carlyle was among several important British writers Putnam won over to his firm. His 'Library of Choice Reading' reprinted Victorian fiction (Dickens and Thackeray) as well as Romantic poetry and prose (Coleridge, Lamb and Hazlitt). More or less simultaneously with their series of English reprints, Wiley and Putnam launched a corresponding 'Library of American Books', which featured the first editions of Hawthorne's *Mosses from an Old Manse* and Melville's *Typee* the same year that the Carlyle reprints appeared.
24. See Tebbel 1972: 304. *On Heroes* remained with Wiley, who published eleven printings from the plates of the 1846 edition under his own name between 1849 and 1881 (see Tarr 1989: 95–6). After Putnam had ended his business partnership with Wiley, Emerson's English publisher John Chapman became Putnam's London agent (see Ashton 2006: 46–7). Chapman's transatlantic dealings with Emerson and Carlyle are discussed in greater detail in the following chapter.

25. It is unlikely that Carlyle received further money from either Wiley or Putnam after the 1847 bill of exchange for *Cromwell*. No other payment is recorded in the correspondence and Carlyle wrote to Emerson as late as 1856 that '[t]he account remains *zero*' (*CEC* 517).
26. Harper's *The French Revolution* was reprinted eight times between 1848 and 1873, and the firm issued a total of thirteen printings of Wiley and Putnam's 1846–7 compilation of *Past and Present*, *Chartism* and *Sartor Resartus* between 1848 and 1882 (see Tarr 1989: 61–2, 46–7).

4

'A YANKEE POCKET EDITION OF CARLYLE'? EMERSON ON THE BRITISH MARKET

In William Charvat's classic account of nineteenth-century American authorship and literary professionalism, Emerson emerges as a writer with a by and large provincial, New England-centred reputation for the first fifteen years of his publishing career; it was not 'until the second half of the century' that more widely circulating editions began to secure him a genuinely 'national audience' (1968: 286–7). A global perspective reveals a different picture, however. If, in the 1830s and 1840s, the Boston editions of his books confined Emerson to a limited readership at home, during the same period a whole series of reprints – some authorised, most of them unauthorised – gained him a sizeable following in Britain. It was ultimately this transatlantic reception that, in turn, 'contributed significantly to the furthering of Emerson's reputation as a literary figure' in the United States (Cayton 1987: 602). This disparity between domestic and foreign circulation was already acknowledged by Emerson's contemporaries, with his friend Theodore Parker, for instance, noting in 1850 that his 'audience steadily increases, . . . more rapidly in England than America' (1850: 205). A chief reason for the growth of Emerson's transatlantic audience was that his writings were easy prey for British publishers because they fell within the legal grey area that, during the mid-nineteenth century, affected the copyrighting of American literature abroad. The cheapest of the pirated British editions in the 1840s had print runs that Emerson's first American editions did not achieve until a decade later. With unauthorised reprints of Emerson's texts issued by the most enterprising of early-Victorian publisher–booksellers, his writings were widely available in the lower price segment of the market, just as Carlyle's books were on the other side of the Atlantic.[1]

Although Emerson, unlike Carlyle, initially did not take an active interest in the transatlantic (re)printing of his works, he was usually everything but indifferent about the publication of his books. His lack of commitment mainly stemmed from the fact that, in the absence of legal protection in Britain, he could not maintain the kind of authorial control over details of production and distribution that he was careful to exert with the American editions of his books. The close attention he paid to the publication of Carlyle's writings in the United States and the conservative arrangements he largely preferred for them are representative of a strategy that he also pursued for the domestic printing and marketing of his own works. As with most of the American Carlyle editions that he supervised, Emerson himself 'paid for the production costs of his own books' in order to maximise his profit margin in terms of sales and distribution (Myerson 2014: 216). Like his contemporary Henry Wadsworth Longfellow he 'habitually purchased the plates' for his titles, a policy that subordinated short-term profit to the goal of long-term profitability (Dowling 2014: 227). Drawing attention to such publication strategies and to how they were more specifically adapted to the transatlantic context, this chapter reconstructs Emerson's print career in Britain during the 1830s and 1840s. It focuses in particular on the genesis and paratextual framing of two of his authorised English editions, the original London versions of the first and second series of *Essays*, published in 1841 and 1844, respectively. The nature of Carlyle's involvement in these ventures and his public positioning vis-à-vis Emerson in his paratexts are key questions here. As in the previous chapter, however, my larger concern is with how these editions illustrate more general conflicts of transatlantic authority, in both legal–economic and cultural–symbolic terms.

Transatlantic Patronage: The London *Essays* (1841)

For several years, sending Carlyle and a few other English friends copies of his American publications remained the only initiative that Emerson showed to promote his writings in Britain. Once passed around, these American copies created a larger demand that was then quickly met by domestic reprints (as had been the case with Boston publisher James Munroe's *Sartor Resartus*, which emerged out of Emerson's lending scheme for Carlyle's London pamphlet version). With ties to figures such as Harriet Martineau, John Stuart Mill, Richard Monckton Milnes and John Sterling, Carlyle was the node of a Victorian literary network that privately circulated Emerson's writings in mid-century Britain. When Emerson sent him a copy of the first edition of *Nature* in September 1836, for example, Carlyle 'lent it about to all [his] acquaintance' until eventually it had been 'thumbed to pieces' (*CEC* 157, 195). The 1837 'American Scholar' oration was shared equally widely and even more systematically. Carlyle promised that he 'could dispose of a dozen' copies easily, and when these had arrived at his Chelsea home one of them went straight to Sterling, one to Martineau and another one to poet laureate Robert Southey, with others circulating 'at Cambridge, [and] among the Oxonians' (ibid., 174, 188). American copies of Emerson's oration on 'Literary Ethics' and the 'Method of Nature' address were distributed in a similar manner.[2] In the spring of 1839, Carlyle informed Emerson that, thanks to such forms of semi-private dissemination, he had managed to acquire 'a select public . . . on this side of the water' devoted to his books and his ideas (ibid., 223).

As with his earlier writing, the 1841 *Essays* – his most substantial title up to that point – reached its first English readers through the private circulation of copies of the American edition that Emerson had sent Carlyle. The book created a stir in Britain almost immediately. Sterling found it 'far ahead in compass and brilliancy of almost everything England has of late years . . . produced', and Carlyle himself noted that he had '[n]ot for a long time . . . read anything with more *profit*' (*CL* 13: 122, 132). Alexis-François Rio, a French art critic and writer residing in London at the time, discovered the book through Milnes in June 1841 and went on 'to "read it *four* times"', borrowing the copy Emerson had sent to Carlyle's wife (*CEC* 302). Desperate to own the book himself, Rio asked Carlyle whether it could 'be had any where in London' (qtd in *CL* 13: 159). Sterling immersed himself in the book with similar zeal, stating to a friend that it was well worth 'to devote three months entirely to the study of this one little volume' (Fox 1882: 128). The responses of the book's small initial British audience were thus comparable to the 'reverential and intensive readings' that marked the early reception of *Sartor Resartus* in the United States (Jackson 1999: 162). As with Carlyle's book, private circulation and word-of-mouth advertising quickly spread knowledge of the text and created a demand that was then met by a domestic edition.

By the end of June 1841, Carlyle himself was engaged in 'reprinting the Book, with a little Preface, for our English market', his private copy of the first American edition serving as a template for the printer (*CL* 13: 159). The idea for the reprint, he clarified to Emerson, had come from his own English publisher, James Fraser:

> the risk is all his, the origin of it was with him: I advised him to have it reviewed, as being a really noteworthy Book; 'write you a Preface,' said he, 'and I will reprint it'; – to which, after due delay and meditation, I consented. (*CEC* 302)

Since Carlyle was thus merely following his publisher's lead, it would be too emphatic to speak of his own 'arrangement' of the edition or suggest that he was 'instrumental' in the publication of the book (*L* 7: 24; Tarr 1989: 405).[3]

Given that Fraser was his own publisher and commonly described as excessively cautious, however, it seems reasonable to assume that Carlyle encouraged him to pursue the Emerson project. Although the actual arrangements for the production and distribution of the edition were in Fraser's hands, Carlyle contributed a substantial preface and proofread the sheets as they came from the printer. Fraser aimed at a print run of 750 copies and promised a half-profits payment. Expressing his gratitude in a playfully self-deprecating manner, Emerson showed himself glad that his 'poor little arid book' would 'be printed in London, and graced with a preface from the man of men' (*CEC* 303). He extolled 'munificent Fraser' and 'his liberal intention to divide the profits' but doubted whether the copies would find buyers in Britain (ibid., 304). Carlyle responded by affirming that the edition was sure to sell since Fraser knew 'his own trade well enough' (ibid., 306). By mid-August, the publisher had already gathered advance orders for the book, which at that point was in the process of appearing in London.

'Graced' with Carlyle's preface, *Essays* was published at the end of the month, figuring as a mere 'reprint' of the American first edition (there were no major textual changes apart from the added paratext). The book's retail price of 10s. was in line with contemporary convention – three-decker novels being commonly sold for 31s.6d. – but the title was still 'out of the price range of average middle-class readers', let alone working-class ones (Koch 2012: 23).[4] The print run of 750 copies, half of what Munroe had printed for the American market, was half-way between the first American editions of Carlyle's *Sartor Resartus* and *The French Revolution* and an average figure for a British book at the time.[5] When Emerson received two copies of the 'very handsome' edition in October, he appreciated the opportunity the book gave him 'to speak in England', and to do so with the added authority of Carlyle's sanction ('fortified by the good word of one whose word is fame') (*CEC* 308). Carlyle responded by reporting that the book had caused an 'appropriate "sensation" here', was getting reviewed and extracted across the national press and proved to be selling 'very steadily', giving Emerson 'henceforth . . . a real Public in Old England as well as New' (ibid., 312).

Unfortunately for Emerson, his audience in 'Old England' continued to be 'fast growing' in ways that did not promise immediate financial returns (ibid., 349). Fraser died in October 1841 and the sales of the book, taken over by his successor, George William Nickisson, were gradually slowing down. Two years later, the *Essays* were pirated by London publisher William Smith, who offered his copies for a mere fifth of what Fraser had originally charged. Carlyle promised that Nickisson would reduce the price for his remaining copies to compete with Smith's book, but the only transatlantic consolation he could offer Emerson was to point out that his own *Past and Present* was being pirated in the United States at around the same time (see Chapter 3). Smith's

Essays were issued in the form of a cheap double-column edition in August 1843, with another printing appearing early the following year. Although it ruined the market for the Fraser books, Carlyle greeted the success of Smith's edition as 'good news', if only to the extent that it testified to an exponential growth of the size of Emerson's British readership (*CEC* 352). With a smaller profit margin per copy sold, print runs of cheap unauthorised editions commonly ran significantly higher than those of the authorised ones, hence translating into thousands of buyers and readers.

Smith's pirated volume notwithstanding, Fraser's edition managed to pay for itself and yield Emerson a share in the revenues. Carlyle initially estimated a 'small £10 sterling perhaps of "Half-profits"', but what he eventually sent in early 1844 was more than twice that sum, although the final amount was still modest compared to the book money he himself had received from Emerson by that time (ibid., 302). The 500 copies that had been sold within two and a half years of publication resulted in an author's payment of around £25. The remaining third of Fraser's edition proved more difficult to dispose of to potential buyers in an atmosphere of constant pressure from cheap reprints (another edition of the *Essays* by publisher H. G. Clark appeared in 1845 and beat even Smith's low price). Emerson recorded another – the final – payment of £16.10s. for the edition as late as May 1848, which suggests that it had not become exhausted over a period of almost seven years (*JMN* 10: 418).[6] Since, by that point, he was earning regular money from his American publishing, the relatively small amounts that Emerson received through Carlyle from the sales of the English *Essays* were, at best, marginal items in his private economy.[7] The 'good news' of the venture was indeed mainly that it had contributed to securing him a transatlantic audience.

'WITH PREFACE BY THOMAS CARLYLE': PARATEXTUAL AUTHORITY AND CRITICAL RECEPTION

The material and paratextual features of Fraser's edition provided British readers with a specific image of Emerson and his intellectual and geographical identity. As Katie McGettigan has pointed out, mid-century British editions of American texts framed the latter 'as both distinctly national and as participants in a transatlantic print culture' (2017a: 129–30), and these two types of characterisation were clearly at work also in the London *Essays*. The title page of the book, for example, not only indicated Emerson's authorship of the volume but also informed British buyers that he resided in 'Concord, Massachusetts'. Highlighting the cultural significance of the apposition for his foreign readers, the inclusion of such toponymical information deliberately drew attention to Emerson's peripheral location in relation to metropolitan London, the book's place of publication and the centre of the contemporary Anglo-American print world. Emerson's Americanness is a major topic of concern also in the peritext that precedes and introduces the actual essays. Readers had already been alerted on the title page that the book came '[w]ith [a] Preface by Thomas Carlyle', whose name was printed in a type barely smaller than that used for Emerson's own. Even before opening the volume, potential buyers would have encountered the conjunction between the two names on the spine of the original binding. Carlyle's presence in the London edition also manifested itself more subtly in the material and economic contexts of the book. The *Essays* formed part of the catalogue of a publisher chiefly known for issuing Carlyle's works, in both 'type and shape' (*CEC* 306) it matched Carlyle's most recent publication, Fraser's edition of the lectures *On Heroes, Hero-Worship, and the Heroic in History*, and it was advertised as being 'uniform with . . . Carlyle's Works'.[8] Such textual and bibliographical signposting worked like 'the attaching of a label': they gave Emerson's writings a specific kind of legibility for British readers and guaranteed a 'transfer of symbolic capital' (Bourdieu 1999: 224). Paying attention to these artefactual dimensions of the first English *Essays* complements, in a decidedly non-metaphorical way, Scottish critic George Gilfillan's later claim that Emerson's British public generally thought of him as 'a "Yankee pocket edition of Carlyle"' (1848: 22). The paratextual framing of Emerson's early English editions contributed significantly to the consolidation of this image of his transatlantic intellectual apprenticeship (with Gilfillan's language of bibliographical inferiority – the posteriority, smaller format, poorer type and lower value of the pocket edition compared to the high-quality original – providing the material shorthand for a more abstract kind of Anglo-American dependency).[9]

A 'Preface by the English Editor', Carlyle's introduction to the London *Essays* obliquely echoes the textual strategies pursued by Diogenes Teufelsdröckh's 'English editor' in *Sartor Resartus* (*WTC* 2: 60). Carlyle's peritext similarly introduces a foreign Transcendentalist artefact to British readers, in a tone marked by the same kind of disinterested detachment that also characterises the novel's editorial persona. If such similarities opened up a rich potential for meta-irony and intertextual allusion, this remained as unexplored by Carlyle as it had been by Emerson in his American preface to the Boston edition of the book five years before. Both Carlyle and Emerson sound remarkably serious in their puritanical censure of each other's work, only that Carlyle voices his opinion at greater length (at almost 2,000 words, his preface to Emerson's *Essays* is more than five times as long as the latter's introduction to *Sartor Resartus*). Carlyle begins his discussion by anticipating the at best minor popularity that the book, according to his own estimate, could hope to enjoy with readers:

> To the great reading public entering Mr. Fraser's and other shops in quest of daily provender, it may be as well to state, on the very threshold, that this little Reprint of an American Book of Essays is in no wise

the thing suited for them; that not the great reading public, but only the small thinking public, and perhaps only a portion of these, have any question to ask concerning it. No Editor or Reprinter can expect such a Book ever to become popular here. But, thank Heaven, the small thinking public has now also a visible existence among us, is visibly enlarging itself.... For these, and not for any other class of persons, is this little Book reprinted and recommended. (*WTC* 5: 335)

What hardly sounds like an act of recommendation from Carlyle's point of view was likely intended as praise. That the essays were destined not for 'the great reading public' but a small elite of choice readers to Carlyle here clearly counts as one of their merits. When Emerson in the *Sartor Resartus* preface had suggested that there could be 'no expectation that this little work will have a sudden and general popularity', he had, after all, followed a similar strategy (*CW* 10: 56). Both prefaces tangibly illustrate the ethos of marginality that resulted from Carlyle's and Emerson's reservations about exposing themselves to a mass audience for which reading was a quotidian act of consumption. Carlyle is notably more ambiguous than Emerson, however, in that he leaves it to the readers of the book to 'ascertain for themselves' whether they had indeed purchased a work of genius worthy to be contemplated by 'the small thinking public' or merely a sham imitation of genuinely great writing ('whether this *is* a kind of articulate human voice speaking words, or only another of the thousand ... ventriloquisms, mimetic echoes, hysteric shrieks, hollow laughters, and mere *in*articulate mechanical babblements, the soul-confusing din of which already fills all places' [*WTC* 5: 335]).

Among the most salient features of the preface is its consistent provincialisation of Emerson and the concomitant transatlantic cultural criticism that this allows Carlyle to formulate. The image the text conveys of Emerson as a quintessentially American figure at the same time works to castigate an American tendency towards materialism. Carlyle's Americanisation of Emerson here links up with Fraser's title page and its explicit reference to Concord, which ultimately does more than merely signal Emerson's foreignness. It identifies a specific position marked as provincial in a double sense: as an American writer, Emerson is located on the margins of the Anglophone print world, but the name of the Massachusetts village implies that his position is peripheral even in the context of his own nation. In the London edition of the *Essays*, Concord thus features as provincial in both global and regional terms, just as Carlyle's cottage at Craigenputtock had figured as an outpost on the fringes of civilisation in the first German edition of the *Life of Schiller* (see Carlyle 1830). Both editions were using similar strategies of paratextual framing to convey an image of authorial remoteness, while at the same time emphasising the fact that the medium of print and its world literary circulation miraculously allowed for textual and material exchange on a global scale. What the London *Essays* achieved through its title page and preface, the Frankfurt edition of the Schiller book orchestrated through the inclusion of two engravings of Craigenputtock, the larger symbolic significance of which was then detailed in Goethe's introduction to the book – the latter's own withdrawal to provincial Weimar implicitly providing an additional example of eremitically authentic authorship. The relationship between geographical marginality and cultural centrality is negotiated in the paratexts of both editions, most notably in terms of how they imagine print as capable of bridging distances between and among peripheries and centres. Reading Carlyle's Scottish biography of Schiller in his Weimar home makes Goethe contemplate the bibliographical globalism of world literature, just as being able to pore over American essays in London signals to Carlyle that Emerson, though located 'on the other side of the Ocean', was 'not altogether parted from [him] either' (*WTC* 5: 337).[10]

Carlyle's preface assigned special importance to Concord because, to him, it was here that Emerson had sought refuge from the mid-century market revolution and the capitalist temptations to which the disinterested intellectual was exposed on the contemporary literary marketplace:

> That an educated man of good gifts and opportunities, after looking at the public arena, and even trying, not with ill success, what its tasks and its prizes might amount to, should retire for long years into rustic obscurity; and, amid the all-pervading jingle of dollars and loud chaffering of ambitions and promotions, should quietly, with cheerful deliberateness, sit down to spend *his* life not in Mammon-worship, or the hunt for reputation, influence, place or any outward advantage whatsoever: this, when we get notice of it, is a thing really worth noting. (ibid., 336)

The quasi-vegetal meandering of Carlyle's serpentine syntax here mirrors what he describes as Emerson's preference of nature over the *idola fori* of American capitalism. In an increasingly more agitated language, Carlyle goes on to detail the difference between the ways of the world and the life of the mind, shifting from third to first person and engaging in a dialogue with an imaginary philistine's emphasis on socio-economic actualities:

> 'Realities?' Yes, your dollars are real, your cotton and molasses are real; so are Presidentships, Senatorships, celebrations, reputations, and the wealth of Rothschild: but to me, on the whole, they are not the reality that will suffice. To me, without some other reality, they are mockery, and amount to *zero*, nay to a negative quantity. ETERNITIES surround this god-given Life of mine: what will all the dollars in creation do for me? (ibid.)

The preface at this point turns into something of a self-portrait, illustrating Pierre Bourdieu's more general observation that the writer who introduces a foreign text to a domestic audience invariably 'take[s] some sort of possession of it, and slant[s] it with his own point of view' (1999: 222). Carlyle is drawing on Emerson and his American background in order to showcase his own disdain for economic and social capital and thus to credential himself as a writer immune to the seductive allure of what, at the beginning of the preface, he dismisses as 'the great reading public'.

Encapsulated in this antagonism between the writer and the world, the image of Emerson that emerges from Carlyle's text is that of an intellectual haunted by the political and social reformist agendas of the antebellum United States. Implicitly seizing upon Emerson's own dismissal of these in the book itself, the essay on 'Self-Reliance' in particular, Carlyle intensifies the critical thrust of such remarks when he relates the hectic bustle of 'the public arena' (WTC 5: 336) to the larger systemic failure of Jacksonian America's democratic discourse, describing how the respective debates surrounding 'Pleasures of Virtue, Progress of the Species, Black Emancipation, New Tariff, Eclecticism, Locofocoism', together 'with many other ghosts and substances', were 'squeaking, jabbering, according to their capabilities, round this man' (ibid., 337). To Carlyle, it was Emerson alone among 'the sixteen millions' of his countrymen who proved strong enough to resist these siren calls through his retreat 'into rustic obscurity' (ibid.). If Emerson, in 'Self-Reliance', had himself labelled the abolitionist 'an angry bigot' and questioned the motives of the 'foolish philanthropist' (CW 2: 30), Carlyle extended these charges to implicate the contemporary United States as a whole.

Where the preface to *Essays* on the one hand celebrates Emerson's opposition to capitalist materialism and his rejection of reformist ideologies, on the other hand it strongly disapproves of the philosophical–religious elements of his thinking and writing. Just as Teufelsdröckh's fictional editor, Carlyle clearly distances himself from what he describes as the book's Romantic mysticism – although in conceding that the text he is introducing bristles with esotericisms he, ironically enough, echoes Emerson's own reservations about *Sartor Resartus*. Carlyle's disapproval of this aspect of the *Essays* is so pronounced, however, that it leaves little room for the kind of defence that Emerson's mention of the Germanic excesses of *Sartor Resartus* had served in the earlier Boston preface. 'In a very enigmatic way', Carlyle notes,

> we hear much of the 'universal soul,' of the &c. &c.: flickering like bright bodiless Northern Streamers, notions and half-notions of a metaphysic, theosophic, theologic kind are seldom long wanting in these *Essays*. I do not advise the British Public to trouble itself much with all that; still less, to take offence at it. (*WTC* 5: 337)

Emerson had similarly argued that *Sartor Resartus*'s flights of fancy had nothing to do with the actual substance of the book, but Carlyle's critique was of a more fundamental nature, not least because – unlike his own book – the *Essays* did not come with an in-built fictional framing that could justify the occasional mysticist opacity of its content.

Carlyle returns to his earlier emphasis on the link between literature and geography in the conclusion of the preface, only that this time the text's Americanisation of Emerson assumes a more positive character. Where before, his eremitic withdrawal to rural Concord had functioned as an emblem of the distance between the nature of his writings and the political and economic context from which they had emerged, Emerson's book now becomes a more abstract metonymy for the United States at large:

> A breath as of the green country, – all the welcomer that it is *New*-England country, not second-hand but first-hand country, – meets us wholesomely everywhere in these *Essays:* the authentic green Earth is there, with her mountains, rivers, with her mills and farms. Sharp gleams of insight arrest us by their pure intellectuality; here and there, in heroic rusticism, a tone of modest manfulness, of mild invincibility, low-voiced but lion-strong, makes us too thrill with a noble pride. (ibid., 338)

That Emerson hails from '*New*-England country' at this point in the preface is no longer an embarrassing marker of his provinciality (his distance from the consecrating power of 'old' England's cultural avant-garde) but instead becomes the key to his promise of spiritual rejuvenation. Carlyle's preface thus closes with a primitivist vision of an alternative America, one whose emphasis on Arcadian splendour ('the authentic green Earth') and atavistic energy ('heroic rusticism') closely resembles the assertive image of the continent that features in much mid-century American nationalist writing. The pastoral scenery that the conclusion conjures up provides an idyllic, Craigenputtock-esque counterpart to the dystopian vision of capitalist America that surfaces earlier in the preface. The juxtaposition of these two geographical settings forms an analogy to Carlyle's image of the symbolic geography of the polarised structure of the contemporary Anglo-American literary field, a configuration in which writing either caters to the vulgar desires of 'the great reading public' or speaks to the more serious concerns of 'the small thinking public'. The threat of a potential intrusion of the former on the writer addressing himself to the latter is an anxiety that tacitly informs much of Carlyle's description of Emerson's '*New*-England' rusticity. The 'all-pervading jingle of dollars and loud chaffering of ambitions' that the preface associates with American capitalism also, after all, characterised the transatlantic print market into whose orbit Carlyle had himself been drawn by the Boston edition of *Sartor Resartus* and the London edition of Emerson's *Essays*.

Describing his preface as a compilation of 'questionable parables and intimations', Carlyle in his conclusion had freely confessed to the duplicitous tone of the text (*WTC* 5: 339). Merely thanking Carlyle for his 'good word', Emerson seems to have remained oddly indifferent about the less flattering aspects of the preface (*CEC* 308). There would have been reason enough for him to worry about the effects that Carlyle's framing had on the impression the book was making on British readers. The preface certainly delivered on Fraser's promise to secure Emerson visibility with British reviewers, but in most cases it turned out to have a negative impact on the way critics responded to the book. In one of the first reviews, published in the London *Literary Gazette* in late September 1841, the reviewer's dismissal of the book was drawn almost entirely from Carlyle's text, which is quoted at length and with palpable relish. 'Mr. Carlyle approves of this book', the critical notice begins, 'and no wonder, for it out-Carlyles Carlyle himself, exaggerates all his peculiarities and faults, and possesses very slight glimpses of his excellences' (Anon. 1992a: 95). Emerson here merely figures as his 'editor's follower and *protégé*', with all the negative associations that this role entailed in the eyes of detractors of Carlyle's own writing ('[a]s the master, so the pupil; as the recommender, so the recommended') (ibid., 95, 96). To the *Literary Gazette*, no amount of paratextual emphasis on Emerson's foreignness could hide the fact that his writing was mere 'Massachusetts Carlylery' rather than genuinely American or truly original (ibid., 96). The review that appeared in the October issue of the *Monthly Review* was more nuanced in its assessment of *Essays*, but drew similarly extensive attention to the fact that the book came with Carlyle's explicit sanction. 'The mere act of godfathership, by reprinting the work in this country, and heralding it by a laudatory preface, proves that it is a book after Carlyle's own heart,' the commentator pointed out (Anon. 1992b: 97). When the *Monthly* admitted that one of the more benevolent passages of the preface constituted 'high praise from a high quarter', this concession was followed by the suspicion that Carlyle was simply praising what was Carlylean about the book (ibid., 97). Carlyle's depiction of Emerson's resistance to the allures of the market nevertheless did not fail to hit a nerve. Following an astonishing volte-face, the conclusion of the *Monthly* piece used the biographical details provided in Carlyle's preface to highlight Emerson's merits as a writer indifferent to the allure of prosperity and public recognition:

> Mr. Emerson is . . . no ordinary thinker, no every day sort of teacher. What we learn of his history from the editor might convince any one of his singularity and independence. It appears that he has relinquished the paths of business; and, even when having before him the omens of success, has withdrawn into retired walks, to 'sit down to spend his life not in Mammon worship, or the hunt for reputation, influence, place, or any outward advantage whatsoever.' (ibid., 98)

Drawing attention to the material background that had shaped Emerson's writing, Carlyle's preface thus actively influenced the way readers imagined Emerson as a literary figure beyond the essays themselves.

The *London and Westminster Review*, which, the year before, had printed Richard Monckton Milnes's celebratory account of Emerson's writings (discussed in the Introduction), was expectably well-disposed towards his first authorised English book. Its review consisted of just one sentence, followed by a reprint of favourable selections from Carlyle's preface – which, as far as the *Westminster* was concerned, provided '[t]he best account' of the book (Anon. 1841d: 491). The notice of *Essays* that had appeared in the Scottish *Fife Herald* in mid-September 1841, even before the response of the *Literary Gazette*, was one of the few reviews of the book that did not quote from Carlyle's preface. Where most metropolitan critics tended to use Carlyle's endorsement as an opportunity to dismiss Emerson's *Essays*, the northern reviewer – writing for a newspaper published on the margin of the British literary field, from a position that was provincial in both geographical and symbolic terms – argued the opposite, suggesting that Carlyle's 'recommendation' was 'sufficient in itself' to give Emerson 'a warm-hearted . . . reception from a wide and always widening circle of devoted admirers' in Britain (Anon. 1841c: 4). Explicitly affiliating with this group, the reviewer tactfully ignored that the preface with which Carlyle had introduced his 'American brother' was, after all, ambiguous rather than 'warm-hearted' (ibid.). Yet this elision ultimately enabled a larger declaration of solidarity between the Scottish newspaper critic and the Concord essayist, two marginal writers that occupied a comparable position within the gravitational field of mid-century transatlantic literary culture.

John Chapman, 'Importer of American Books'

Fraser's edition of the *Essays* and the unauthorised reprints of the book that soon appeared in its wake allowed Emerson to gain a foothold in the British market, but it had, by and large, been a disappointment both financially (because it took a long time to yield a relatively small profit) and symbolically (because its paratextual framing mostly managed to deepen rather than dispel the suspicion of transatlantic epigonality). Where, in the case of Carlyle's authorised American editions, the perceived proximity between editor and publisher had contributed to the networked distribution and the commercial success of the books, for Emerson the close association between Fraser and Carlyle ultimately proved disadvantageous. With *Essays: Second Series*, three years later, a publishing opportunity presented itself that offered a potential way of circumventing Carlyle's influence and of placing the book in a section of the English market that differed from that dominated by books like *Sartor Resartus*, *The French Revolution* or *Past and Present*. In order to be perceived by British readers as something more than his 'editor', Emerson needed to make sure that his English editions would no longer simply be placed on 'a shelf in the case assigned' to Carlyle (Anon. 1992b: 97). The first English edition of the second volume of Emerson's essays appeared with John Chapman, a young London publisher who, unknown to Carlyle at the time, was aiming for a different audience than Fraser. Although some of the outward circumstances had changed, however, Carlyle did eventually become involved in the arrangements, and despite Chapman's strenuous efforts to secure the book protection under British law, the financial outcome of the edition was even less satisfying than that of the 1841 *Essays*.[11]

Chapman had initiated a correspondence with Emerson in August 1844, backed by a recommendation from Henry G. Wright, a friend of Amos Bronson Alcott's who vouched for the publisher's credentials and confirmed that he was 'bowing reverently at' the author's 'shrine' (Houghton MS Am 1280 [3557]).[12] As Emerson learned at around the same time through Theodore Parker, Chapman, the 'transcendental bookseller', was the successor of London publisher John Green, 'the Unitarian & Transcendental Bibliopole for all England hitherto' (qtd in *L* 3: 287). Only in his early twenties at the time, Chapman had recently taken over Green's shop as well as his stock. Like his predecessor, he 'made a speciality of Americana', which he both imported and reprinted himself (Barnes 1974: 154).[13] *Essays: Second Series* became one of the first books he added to Green's list. In the years that followed, Chapman published a range of American philosophical, religious and social writing – with Andrews Norton, William Ellery Channing and Parker among his authors. He achieved notoriety in Victorian Britain through the publication of unorthodox continental writing in translation – books by Auguste Comte, but perhaps more importantly, David Friedrich Strauß's *Das Leben Jesu* (1835–6/1846) and Ludwig Feuerbach's *Das Wesen des Christentums* (1841/1854), both translated by the young George Eliot, who began editorial work for the *Westminster Review* after Chapman had acquired it in 1851. Much of the British writing the firm published was of a controversial nature as well (including books by James Anthony Froude, Herbert Spencer and Thomas Henry Huxley). Publishing with Chapman thus aligned Emerson's writing with a set of convictions that markedly differed from the largely conservative intellectual context the Fraser volume had supplied. Though radical in his own way, Carlyle was not a nonconformist in the more specific early-Victorian sense of the term; nor were his books specifically targeted at this kind of readership. On the contrary, he had long become a strident critic of the religious, social and aesthetic styles of thinking and writing to which Chapman was providing a forum.[14] Much more than a minor business detail, Emerson's change of publisher was thus an act of bibliopolic repositioning away from Carlylean associations and towards a more distinctly philosophical and religious print environment.

In his August 1844 message, Chapman had offered to print in London whatever new and still unpublished manuscripts Emerson had on his hands.

The proposition came at an auspicious moment, since Emerson was in the midst of publishing two books with James Munroe in Boston: the second series of essays and his recent address, 'On the Anniversary of the Emancipation of the Negroes in the British West Indies'. Glad to have an opportunity to correct 'important errors now irrevocable' in the Munroe edition, Emerson offered Chapman the volume of essays and announced that he would send advance sheets of the book with the next steamer (L 3: 259). By now well familiar with the strategies of unauthorised reprinters through his work on the American editions of Carlyle's writings, he promised to 'hold the publication of the book back a few days' to protect Chapman 'against any accidental competition' on the British market (L 7: 610). Although not taking an interest in production details had had negative consequences in the case of the Fraser edition, Emerson once again left it to the publisher to determine the material and textual framing of the book.[15] He decided to let Chapman print the emancipation address as well, a text whose blend of Anglo-Saxonism and abolitionism could be expected to appeal to British readers.[16]

If Emerson sought to prevent Carlyle's active interference with the preparation of the edition, he was careless enough to involve him as an intermediary, sending the first instalment of the sheets to Carlyle rather than directly to Chapman. Since he was not yet on familiar terms with the young publisher, he asked Carlyle to supervise the initial steps of the process and 'give Chapman . . . counsel, . . . enjoining on him careful correction' (CEC 365). Further Boston sheets arrived in London in October 1844, by which time Carlyle had already been in touch with the publisher and summarised their first meeting to Emerson:

> I have visited your Bookseller Chapman; seen the Proofsheets lying on his table; taken order that the reprint shall be well corrected, – indeed I am to read every sheet myself, and in that way get acquainted with it, before it go into stereotype. Chapman is a tall lank youth of five-and-twenty; full of goodwill, but of what other equipment time must yet try. By a little Book of his, which I looked at some months ago, he seemed to me sunk very deep in the dust-hole of extinct Socinianism; a painful predicament for a man! (ibid., 367)

The letter was an alarming sign of Carlyle's Calvinist dislike for Chapman's nonconformism (as evidenced by his recently published 'little Book', *Human Nature: A Philosophical Exposition of the Divine Institution of Reward and Punishment*, a reply to Unitarian philosopher James Martineau), but it also indicated Carlyle's intention to contribute to the publication of *Essays: Second Series* to a larger extent than Emerson had planned.

The intimation that he would be 'saying *imprimatur* if occasion be' implied that another preface might already be in the making, a prospect about which

Emerson had reason to be apprehensive (ibid.). As though he had intuited Carlyle's interference, he withdrew his initial request for help even before he held the above letter in his hands:

> I have much regretted a sudden note ... entreating you to cumber yourself about my proofsheets sent to the London bookseller. I heartily absolve you from all such vexations. Nothing could be more inconsiderate. Mr Chapman is undoubtedly amply competent to ordinary correction ... (ibid., 368)

All back-pedalling came too late, however, as Carlyle was already busy reading proofs and negotiating further details with the publisher. Chapman sought his advice not only about textual questions but also to make sense of the legal environment in which he suddenly found himself in his new role as an American writer's authorised English publisher.

Essays: Second Series and the Legal Ambiguities of Transatlantic Copyright

Piracy was once again the main cause for concern. Between Fraser's edition of *Essays* and Chapman's *Second Series*, Emerson's writings had become available in Britain in the form of several unauthorised reprints (whose number peaked the year that Chapman issued his book, with another boost in 1847–8, when Emerson's lecture tour of England and Scotland fanned additional demand for his writing). In 1844, Emerson's texts were available as English reprints in several formats: individual orations and addresses were issued as pamphlets and sold for as little as two pence, the first series of *Essays* had been reprinted in its entirety by W. H. Smith and several volumes that combined a range of shorter pieces were on offer for as little as one shilling.[17] In April, a few months before Chapman entered the scene, Carlyle had provided Emerson with a glimpse of the imperilled status of American writing on the British market:

> Republishing for one's friend's sake, I find on consulting my Bookseller, is out here; we have Pirates waiting for any American thing of mark, as you have for every British ... It is strange that men should feel themselves so entirely at liberty to steal, simply because there is no gallows to hang them for doing it. – Your new Book will be eagerly waited for by that class of persons ... (*CEC* 360)

Unauthorised reprinting was rampant on both sides of the Atlantic and whatever new text Emerson would publish at home was sure to become pirated in London within a short period of time. Theodore Parker told Emerson in August that he had learned from a 'Scotch Bookseller' that of his 'Essays – & another volume containing Lectures, orations &c – between 5000 & 6000 had already been sold' in Britain (qtd in *L* 3: 287). This was a positive sign, at least to the extent that it indicated Emerson's ability to attract an ever-increasing number of readers abroad. As Daniel Koch writes, his 'market and readership might have remained more or less limited to a small, wealthy elite', 'had it not been for pirates' issuing cheaper editions affordable for a larger number of middle- and lower-class readers (2012: 25). But Parker also noted the material disadvantage of this vast circulation when he pointed out to Emerson that these large editions 'could not be made to give [him] money' (qtd in *L* 3: 287). Implying that he might amend this situation, Chapman, in his first letter to Emerson, explicitly asked him for a 'manuscript that had not yet been published in America' in the hope of being able to 'procure a copy-right' for it in England, on the grounds that it would be first printed there (*CEC* 364).[18] Emerson was eager to comply – the legal protection of the book, he wrote, 'would really be desirable to me' – and promised Chapman that 'we will detain the publication of the book here, a week, or more, if needful to secure your reception of the entire book a fortnight before it can go to any other person in England' (*L* 7: 612).

Chapman's knowledge of international copyright law must have been sketchy at best, however, if he assumed that prior publication in England (or even simultaneous transatlantic publication) constituted an indisputable entitlement that could be used as leverage against unauthorised competitors. The situation was, in fact, far more complex, and both Emerson and Carlyle had reason enough for wondering whether Chapman's 'friendly plan' was anything more than wishful thinking (ibid.). In the mid-1840s, the legal status of transatlantic copyright claims was, at best, ambiguous. The British Copyright Law Amendment Act of 1842, the result of MP Thomas Noon Talfourd's efforts and the support of writers like Carlyle, had significantly extended the duration of domestic copyright, but given the absence of a bilateral Anglo-American agreement, neither the 1842 Act nor the British International Copyright Act of 1844 protected the rights of American authors in Britain with any degree of certainty (with a number of contradictory verdicts in British court cases of the 1840s and early 1850s failing to clarify the legal status of American texts on the British market).[19] At certain points during that period, prior or simultaneous publication could indeed substantiate a copyright claim, but given the 'fluctuations in the interpretation of copyright law and difficulties in proving that a British publisher had published an American text prior to its appearance in the United States', such claims were often hardly sound enough to dissuade publishers like Smith, H. G. Clarke or Charles Edward Mudie from issuing their popular reprints (McGettigan 2017a: 132). Emerson had acquired a working knowledge of transatlantic publishing in his role as Carlyle's American literary agent and editor, and he wrote a cautionary letter to Chapman in mid-September 1844, pointing to the fundamental obstacle to the Anglo-American negotiations, the unwillingness of the US legislature to recognise British copyright claims (see *L* 7: 612). He nevertheless continued to despatch his American sheets to London, in the hope that Chapman's efforts on his behalf might establish some form of precedent.

In the meantime, Chapman, new to the literary market and its 'bibliopolic tables of the Law', seemed himself to have become sceptical about his original proposition (*CEC* 295). As Carlyle wrote after his first visit to his offices in September, the publisher was now no longer 'sure of saving much copyright for' Emerson, although he would 'do honestly what in that respect is doable' (ibid., 367). Faced with a legal situation that proved harder to disentangle than he had anticipated, Chapman turned to Carlyle for support. Apparently aware of his petition in favour of Talfourd's bill five years before, he asked Carlyle to put him in contact with the politician in order to obtain reliable information about the matter. Carlyle answered with some reluctance in early October that he knew Talfourd only remotely but would nevertheless 'call upon him for Emerson's sake', should the opportunity arise (*CL* 18: 229). He wrote to John Forster (who had been instrumental in engineering the 1839 petition) to enquire about Talfourd's current address, at the same time voicing his doubts about the feasibility of Chapman's scheme:

> A certain Bookseller, one Chapman in Newgate Street, is reprinting with authority from Emerson himself a new Book of Emerson's; in which operation I am of course bound to be in all ways helpful. Chapman hopes and believes that by making some kind of application to some kind of Privy Council by virtue of some kind of Act about International Copyright, he can secure the property of this British edition for Emerson and himself; – but the poor man does not know how to proceed; and the Attornies [*sic*] whom he consults shed on the operation only darkness visible. He has heard that Serg*t* Talfourd is the oracle on all such matters; and in his despair this poor Chapman wishes me to go and ask the learned Serg*t* direct. (ibid., 228–9)

Carlyle remained doubtful about Chapman's plans and Talfourd's ability to solve the problem and told the publisher as much in another letter two weeks later. In the meantime, Chapman had apparently asked him to get in touch with Thomas Babington Macaulay, who, as a member of parliament, had opposed Talfourd's bill. This time, Carlyle openly declined to comply with the request, writing to Chapman that

> [i]t does not strike me that Mr Macaulay could be likely to throw any light on this International-Copyright affair: at all events, my acquaintance with him is not of such a kind as to authorize my troubling him on such an occasion. My own private notion begins to be that there will

be no Copyright procurable. The Act of Parliament is mere darkness visible; unfit for being read except in Chaos or Bedlam. The paragraph you have marked does seem to give anybody a privilege of copyright, who will deliver the due Books into Stationers' Hall; – but then it is *anybody*; and the learned Sergeant is dim! What if you did [briefly?] deliver your Books at the said Hall; comply in some colourable way with the outer conditions of this Act (unintelligible to mere mortals); then print upon your Fly-leaf, 'Entered at St^n Hall according to the International Copyright Act'; and *sue at law* any Pirate that violated you? Probably the meaning of the Act will never be ascertained till some such occurrence do turn up. It is our way of interpreting Acts of Parliament; which in fact I am very weary of, I for one. – Your surest chance, I believe, will be to print the Book in stereotype very accurately, and to sell it cheap, in small instalments; intimating withal that it can be rendered cheaper, down almost to the cost of the paper, if needful. (qtd in Sommer 2016: 125–7)

Carlyle's Miltonic language ('darkness visible') was aimed at the inscrutability of the recent British International Copyright Act, which had come into effect less than half a year before. The letter implies that Chapman had sent Carlyle an annotated copy of the Act, which, among other things, stipulated that

> no Author of any Book . . . shall be entitled to the Benefit of this Act . . . unless . . . such Book . . . shall be entered in the Register Book of the Company of Stationers in *London*, and One printed Copy of the whole of such Book . . . shall be delivered to the Officer of the Company of Stationers at the Hall of the said Company. (Anon. 1844d: 152–3)

This is evidently the passage to which both Chapman and Carlyle were referring, with the publisher reading the obligation to register a new book as a guarantee for subsequent protection, where Carlyle was pointing out that the Act would allow a potential 'privilege' to whoever entered their edition first and that – in the context of the British case law system – such privilege would, in all likelihood, have to be confirmed in court. Carlyle's letter illustrates the profound legal uncertainty with which British publishers and American writers saw themselves confronted in the mid-1840s. If the 'unintelligible' 'meaning' of the current legislation required a good deal of 'interpreting' to divine its actual implications, there was little hope that the Copyright Act would have a noticeable effect on the thriving reprint market. Where laws could not be relied upon, the only remedy, Carlyle implied, would be to respond through the means at the publisher's own disposal, especially pricing and distribution policy (selling stereotyped books 'cheap' and issuing them piecemeal in the 'small instalments' of a number of successive printings).

When Carlyle wrote to Chapman again in late October to return a set of corrected proofs, he once more used the occasion to express his scepticism about the copyright plans. He nevertheless encouraged the publisher to pursue his scheme and work on Talfourd to determine the meaning of the Act. Protecting Emerson's book against undesired competition, Carlyle repeated, was ultimately in Chapman's own hands. What 'would deter Pirates' in addition to a potentially doubtful legal statement, he suggested, would be 'your stereotype, your cheap price, and the face you shew in the business' (*CL* 18: 254). Writing to Emerson, Carlyle concluded that there was 'no visible real vestige of a Copyright obtainable' for *Essays: Second Series* since the piece of legislation in which Chapman put his hopes was 'of so distracted inextricable a character' that 'it may mean anything and all things' (*CEC* 370). Nevertheless, the publisher's threat to take to court anyone reprinting the book might still, Carlyle felt, have some moderate effect.

Preparing the volume for publication, Chapman remained undeterred by Carlyle's scepticism. He had the book entered in the records of the Stationers' Company in early November, listing himself as the proprietor of the copyright to circumvent the vexed problem of Emerson's own legal entitlement under the 1844 act.[20] Chapman closely followed many of the suggestions Carlyle had made in his mid-October letter. The recommendation to 'print upon your Fly-leaf, "Entered at St^n Hall according to the International Copyright Act"; and sue at law any Pirate that violated you' appeared in a very similar form as a short note placed at the very beginning of the book. Like Emerson's 'Notice' to Boston publisher Little and Brown's *Past and Present* the year before, Chapman's declaration targeted print professionals rather than lay readers, only that here it was an authorised publisher speaking directly to his competitors. Apart from the actual essays and this copyright statement, the book also eventually featured the imprimatur note Carlyle had already mentioned to Emerson as a possible contribution in late September. He had declined what must have been Chapman's suggestion to write a longer preface recommending the book to the British reading public. In the mid-October letter to the publisher he had stated that he did 'not contemplate any writing at the beginning of these *Essays*; nothing but a certificate that the Edition is correct, and brought out under the Author's sanction' (qtd in Sommer 2016: 127). Implicitly referring to his preface to the Fraser volume, Carlyle judged that what he 'had to say in introducing Emerson to the English is for the present said' (ibid.). The author of *Essays: Second Series*, he acknowledged, already had 'a little Public of his own here' (ibid.) – a followership that, thanks to Chapman's support, was becoming less and less Carlyle's own audience.

Paratextual Framing, Reception, Aftermath

Carlyle's name this time featured neither on the title page nor on the binding of the book and he merely contributed a two-page 'Notice', which, like Chapman's statement, was mainly concerned with the legal and commercial aspects of the

English edition rather than with Emerson's character or the content of the essays themselves. The 'Notice' places a similar emphasis on intellectual property and moral propriety as Emerson's 'Notice' to *Past and Present*, but Carlyle's description of piracy as grand theft (recycled from his 1839 petition in support of Talfourd's bill) strikes a more pugnacious note:

> To *un*authorized reprinters, and adventurous spirits inclined to do a little in the pirate line, it may be proper to recal [*sic*] the known fact, which should be very present to us all without recalling, that *theft* in any sort is abhorrent to the mind of man; – that theft is theft, under whatever meridian of longitude, in whatever 'nation,' foreign or domestic, the man stolen from may live; and whether there be any treadmill and gallows for the thief, or no apparatus of that kind! Such suggestion may perhaps have its weight with here and there an incipient adventurous spirit meditating somewhat in the picaroon or pirate line, and contribute to direct him into better courses: who knows? For other spirits, no longer open to such suggestions, the present Publisher trusts that he has *suggestions* of a much more appropriate, intelligible, and effectual kind, in readiness if needed. (1844: v–vi)

Combining diffuse threats with the promise of concrete legal action, Carlyle denounces '*un*authorized' reprinting as a capital offence, though as one whose exact definition depends less on formalised law than on moral common sense (with reprinting without authorial sanction counting as objectionable 'whether there be any treadmill and gallows for the thief, or no apparatus of that kind'). The 'Notice' acknowledges the fundamentally transnational character of nineteenth-century print culture when Carlyle highlights the disparity between a unified space of material exchange and a traditional system of national legislation which hopelessly lags behind a globalised market environment that no longer respects the geographical and juridical boundaries of the nation-state. In the absence of international legal cooperation, the moral absolute of bibliopolic sincerity emerged as the only principle that applied 'under whatever meridian of longitude, in whatever "nation," foreign or domestic'. At the same time, however, Carlyle's fantasies of corporal punishment betray a thinly veiled yearning for the law-and-order assertion of the legal authority of contemporary writers through national executives.

Lest Emerson should get a wrong impression of his involvement with the edition, Carlyle was careful to emphasise the minor importance of the 'Notice', which the papers, he suggested, had inflated to the status of a genuine preface (see *CEC* 369–70). Writing to Concord in early November, he implied that his text merely constituted a type of imprimatur. His criticism of the book itself – which, in the case of the 1841 *Essays*, he had communicated in the published 'Preface' – this time remained confined to the correspondence. Where Carlyle, three years before, had extolled Emerson's withdrawal from the turmoil of the market, he now found fault with his detachment ('we find you . . . a *Soliloquizer* on the eternal mountain-tops only, in vast solitudes where men and their affairs lie all hushed in a very dim remoteness' [ibid., 371]). Commenting on the unorthodox character of some of the book's passages, Carlyle was also anticipating the unfavourable reception of *Essays: Second Series* among the religious mainstream of British readers, noting that 'there are . . . one or two utterances about "Jesus," "immortality," and so forth, which will produce wide-eyes here' (ibid.).

With a copy of the London edition of the book in his hands by the end of the year, Emerson decided to speak out against Carlyle's criticism and against a paratext that had again turned out to be marked by patronising rather than patronage. Chapman should have refrained from asking him for 'an advertisement', Emerson told Carlyle, although he clearly saw the young publisher's motives for doing so: 'he was glad of a chance to have business with you; and, of course, was too thankful for any *Preface*' (CEC 372). Carlyle's endorsement, Emerson complained, would stand in the way of the kind of British reception he himself desired:

> You shall not do this thing again, if I should send you any more books. A preface from you is a sort of banner or oriflamme, a little too splendid for my occasion, & misleads. I fancy my readers to be a very quiet, plain, even obscure class, – men & women of some religious culture & aspirations, young, or else mystical, & by no means including the great literary & fashionable army which no man can count, who now read your books. If you introduce me, your readers & the literary papers try to read me, & with false expectations. I had rather hav[e] fewer readers & only such as belong to me. (ibid.)

It almost seems as though Emerson were writing about the 1841 'Preface' here, to the extent that his reservations about the adverse effect of Carlyle's paratextual support are more applicable to the longer and more judgemental earlier text than to the 1844 'Notice'.

Emerson's letter breaks with the bibliopolic gift exchange economy to whose laws of reciprocity both he and Carlyle had implicitly subscribed during the preceding decade. The support of a well-known or well-connected friend was essential as far as getting published was concerned, but once this hurdle had been cleared, the intellectual proximity that public acts of patronage tended to entail could have a negative long-term effect on an emergent reputation. In his response to the 1844 'Notice', Emerson clearly distances himself from Carlyle, describing himself as belonging to an altogether different section of the British literary sphere. What, at first, sounds like a tribute to Carlyle's success with contemporary audiences on closer inspection turns out to be a backhanded compliment. That he had managed to acquire an 'army' of friends 'which no man can count' also, of course, insinuated that he had succumbed to the temptations of the marketplace and ingratiated himself with the ordinary reader. If Carlyle's mass audience predominantly consisted of 'fashionable' types, the kind of British followership Emerson envisaged for himself was a small group of discerning devotees (precisely the kind of readers that Carlyle in his 1841 preface had called 'the small thinking public'). Where Carlyle censured the 'dim remoteness' of the 1844 book's authorial persona, Emerson still openly celebrated the ethos of marginality that both of them had formerly shared.

Emerson was not alone in disapproving of the 'Notice' and of the influence Carlyle's peritexts allowed him to exert over his British reception. Upon meeting Carlyle in London two years after the *Second Series* was first published, Margaret Fuller found herself surprised by his assessment of Emerson, of whom 'he spoke worthily' and 'most unlike the tone of his prefaces' (1987: 246). One of the original British reviewers of Chapman's *Essays* disagreed more specifically with the spirit of the 'Notice', even though he was writing in the *Prospective Review*, a Unitarian journal published by none other than Chapman himself. Emerson was probably referring to this review when, in a May 1845 letter, he thanked his publisher for his 'defence of my poor book & name' (*L* 3: 288), but the text had been written not by Chapman but by Charles Wicksteed, a Unitarian minister with strong sympathies for Emerson's writing. In other respects the kind of puff piece to be expected from its publication venue, the review turns into an acerbic attack when Wicksteed writes about the mercenary character of Carlyle's introduction. '[T]he first thing that will strike the reader on opening this volume', he complained, was 'an unrivalled oddity':

> Mr. Carlyle's Preface to the former series had a half-laughing, half-patronizing air about it, not destitute of offensiveness. . . . In the present Prefatory Notice Mr. Carlyle enacts a different part – not so much that of Patron, as that of Beggar's Boy. He holds out his hat to the English Nation, and says to each reader, 'Sixpence, if you please, for Mr. Emerson!' . . . It is very proper to scour the sea of Pirates – but we would leave the part of Pompey, for the future, to the Publisher. (1845: 255–6)

Wicksteed was evidently operating on the basis of the same logic as Emerson himself when he suggested that 'high-spirited' literary authorship had an obligation to refrain from publicly acknowledging that it was working on anything other than a moral economy (ibid., 257). The argument for just transatlantic compensation, Wicksteed implied, was – if at all – to be made on ethical rather than on financial grounds. That Carlyle used his authority to defend Emerson from potential piracies to Wicksteed was in itself a valuable service, but his violation of the implicit codes of writerly propriety threatened to override whatever positive effect an endorsement might have on British readers.

In the same book that Carlyle introduced with the intrusive insistence of a 'Beggar's Boy', Emerson himself had done his best to avoid coming across as a 'high-spirited' writer ultimately only interested in his own financial advantage. Early on, in the essay 'Experience', he offered a stoic contemplation on the contemporary copyright debate:

> So many things are unsettled which it is of the first importance to settle, – and, pending their settlement, we will do as we do. Whilst the debate goes forward on the equity of commerce, and will not be closed for a century or two, New and Old England may keep shop. Law of copyright and international copyright is to be discussed, and, in the interim, we will sell our books for the most we can. Expediency of literature, reason of literature, lawfulness of writing down a thought, is questioned; much is to say on both sides, and, while the fight waxes hot, thou, dearest scholar, stick to thy foolish task, add a line every hour, and between whiles add a line. (CW 3: 37–8)

In his role as Carlyle's American agent, most recently with *Past and Present*, Emerson had obviously demonstrated a more explicit commitment to the cause of transatlantic copyright. When it came to publicly declaring his opinion on the issue, however, his concern easily morphed into an ostensible indifference to the market and its petty struggles.

Emerson had begun to develop this public stance on the 'Copyright business' in a journal entry two years before, in which he affirmed that it was '[p]lainly . . . no work for a poet to be defending his property' in the literary marketplace (*JMN* 8: 245–6). Implicitly responding to Carlyle's characterisation of piracy as intellectual theft, Emerson here asserted that if an author 'can show well that it is stealing to print his book, plainly he was no man to write a book, for the whole use of his book, is to affirm spiritual law over material & forensic law' (ibid., 246).[21] For the way he wished to be perceived by his readers, British and American alike, it was crucial for Emerson to insist on such a distinction between the 'spiritual' and the 'material' and at the same time to profess the sincerity of his economic disinterestedness. His dislike for the 1844 'Notice' was hence motivated not so much by what Carlyle had written about the book itself – which was, after all, not much – as it was by what he had implied about its author's ulterior motives. Where the 1841 preface, despite its ambiguities, had at least highlighted Emerson's alienation from the market, the frank language of the later 'Notice' threatened to sabotage his attempts at positioning himself in the symbolic geography of the transatlantic literary field.

Essays: Second Series was already on sale in Britain when Emerson received his copy of the edition and first set eyes on Carlyle's 'Notice'. The book turned out not to be the first Emerson text published by Chapman. The address on 'The Emancipation of the Negroes in the British West Indies', delivered in Concord in August 1844, had appeared in London in pamphlet form in late September or early October, while Emerson was still sending the remaining sheets for the essay volume. Chapman also issued the lecture 'The Young American' as another cheap pamphlet and had thus already established himself as Emerson's English publisher before *Essays* appeared in early November, about three weeks after Munroe's first American edition.[22] Unlike Fraser's quickly pirated edition, the *Second Series* remained exclusively available in its authorised form until the end of the decade. This probably had less to do with Chapman's legal assertions than with the relatively low price of the book, which, as Carlyle had predicted, proved an effective means of dissuading rival publishers from issuing unauthorised reprints. At 3s.6d. for the cloth edition and 3s. for copies in wrappers, the retail price made the book affordable for readers with a lower income – readers without realistic access to the authorised 1841 *Essays*, for which Fraser had originally charged three times as much.[23]

It is difficult to ascertain the exact print run of Chapman's edition. Since the plates were stereotyped, further copies could be printed at a cheap cost whenever necessary. In mid-February 1845, Carlyle wrote to Emerson that Chapman was 'fast selling' *Second Series* and just about 'striking off a new 500 from his stereotypes' (*CEC* 377). The first was followed by five further printings (three of which were issued in 1845 and one each in 1846 and 1848) (see Myerson 1982: 116–19). Assuming that each of these was of the size mentioned by Carlyle, Chapman would have printed – and sold, since otherwise he would not have had to supply more – 3,000 copies of the book between 1844 and 1848 (possibly more, since the first printing was likely larger). For the first time, an authorised English edition of Emerson's writing came close to the print runs of the unauthorised volumes. The success of Chapman's book demonstrates that Emerson's juxtaposition of Carlyle's mass and his own select readership hardly corresponded to the empirical reality of his mid-century British sales.

The critical reception of the book in the British press was less encouraging than the size of its print run. Dashing Emerson's hope that *Essays: Second Series* would finally distance him from Carlyle, reviewers continued to remark on the connection between the two writers. Parts of the 'Notice' were reprinted, with the rest summarised, in the two-paragraph mention of the book that featured in the London *Examiner* of 30 November 1844 (see Anon. 1844c: 757). The review published in the *Spectator* a week before had contained some moderate praise, but as a whole was highly critical of Chapman's publishing programme as well as more specifically of Emerson's tendency for 'sounding vagueness' – a quality the anonymous reviewer assumed would guarantee the book a following among the nonconformist readership to which Chapman was catering, as well as among the lower-class 'coteries of men who are without any established standards of authority or of taste' (Anon. 1992c: 111). The piece ended with the more matter-of-fact declaration that the book was 'published under the typographical superintendence of Mr. Carlyle', whose 'preface' featured 'forcible remarks on the law of copyright, or rather the practice of literary piracy' (ibid., 112). Chapman forwarded several of these reviews to Emerson, who received from them the impression that his transatlantic readers did not 'like this book as well as its forerunner' (*L* 3: 274). Carlyle offered a more encouraging picture, reporting that the edition was selling fast and that Emerson's 'Public in this country . . . extends pretty much . . . thro' all ranks, and is a growing one' (*CEC* 377).

Despite this expansion of his readership base, Chapman's *Essays* were, by and large, a disappointing venture for Emerson. The comparatively poor reception of the book with British critics was not the only reason for concern. One of the hopes Emerson had had for the London reprint was that it would allow him to correct errors in Munroe's Boston edition. While some of these mistakes were indeed ironed out, Chapman's volume ended up containing a series of 'new errors' (*CW* 3: lx), although Carlyle, ironically enough, had written that the sheets he had seen were so 'fairly printed' that it would be 'a sad waste of time' to bother correcting the rest (*CEC* 370). Emerson himself found much to complain of once he had the opportunity to take a closer look at the book.[24] The financial dimension of the project was another cause for disappointment. It gradually became clear that Chapman was inexperienced not only at supervising the typesetting and printing process but also at taking care of the accounting. Where, after seven years on the market, Fraser's edition had eventually netted Emerson some £36, he seems not to have received any money for the English *Second Series* at all, although Chapman sold a large number of copies of the book, on which he effectively had a monopoly for more than five years.[25] This probably did not strike the publisher as a problem, given that his main interest was, as Daniel Koch has pointed out, 'in seeing Emerson's messages distributed amongst the largest and widest reading public possible' (2012: 26). The key problem was that 'most items on [Chapman's] list were . . . unlikely to cover the costs of printing' since the kind of writing in which he specialised 'appealed' only 'to a limited . . . readership' (Ashton 2006: 20). He presumably used the profit generated by the sales of his Emerson books to cross-finance other, less popular titles, and thus to solve his 'perpetual accounting difficulties' (Barnes and Barnes 1991: 93). When Emerson travelled to England for his 1847–8 lecture tour, he vowed that he would attempt to see whether he could 'draw any income from Chapman's publishing', noting that '[n]othing has ever come thence, . . . though my books sell here quite actively' (*L* 4: 14). It seems that this resolution was not eventually crowned with success, but Emerson apparently did not mind this as much as he minded the errata – which may well suggest that, like Chapman (and like the authorial persona of the 'Experience' essay), he was interested more in being widely read than in deriving a financial advantage from it.

Relations with Chapman, in any case, remained cordial enough for Emerson to agree with him on the publication of the first English edition of his next book, the 1847 *Poems*. He also offered Chapman the first English edition of the collected *Nature, Addresses, and Lectures* (1849) and that of the expanded version of the lecture series on 'Representative Men'. Even though Emerson had still not received any money from Chapman, he continued to speak of the same 'scheme of half profits' upon which they had agreed for the 1844 *Essays* (*L* 8: 214). While Chapman eventually did not reprint the American *Nature* volume, he published the first English edition of *Representative Men*, which he advertised as being 'printed from an original MS. revised and forwarded to England for the purpose' and thus 'alone possess[ing] the sanction of the Author' (qtd in Myerson 1982: 216). But it was more difficult to protect the book than it had been in the case of *Essays: Second Series*. Even though the London *Representative Men* went through another printing in 1851, it had, by that point, already been pirated (Carlyle wrote to Emerson in July 1850 that 'you now get the Book offered you for a shilling, at all railway stations' [*CEC* 460]). Chapman was in an increasingly difficult financial situation – in the summer of 1854, Emerson noted with regret that the firm had become economically 'embarrassed' (*L* 4: 459) – and so the more reliable George Routledge took over as Emerson's new English publisher.

Despite not bringing him any money, Emerson's association with Chapman was the first in a series of fruitful collaborations with British publishing houses whose editions circulated his name in Victorian Britain and fortified his reputation as a transatlantic intellectual. As in Carlyle's case, popular – if not necessarily unanimous critical – success abroad contributed to an increasing recognition at home. Yet, if the mid-century Anglo-American print market thus on the one hand allowed writers to reach audiences on an international scale, its legal and economic volatility at the same time painfully illustrated the limitations of authorial authority. Confronted with the vagaries of print, many writers of Carlyle and Emerson's generation were hence also drawn to other ways of making themselves seen and heard in the transatlantic public sphere. The following two chapters turn to lecturing as an important one of these alternatives.

NOTES

1. Emerson's early English publishers included both well-established houses (William S. Orr, Simpkin & Marshall, William Smith) and newer firms (Aylott & Jones, H. G. Clarke, John Chapman) (for details on these and other nineteenth-century publishers, see Brown 1982 and Joseph 2019). Summarising his presence as a

published writer in Britain until the late 1840s, Daniel Koch argues that, by the end of the decade, Emerson 'was among the most widely read living authors in Britain', with 'a large reading audience' that 'was not homogeneous and elite, but broad and mixed' (2012: 23, 27, 27). Koch estimates that 'the number of volumes of Emerson's work existing in England' at that point 'was almost certainly greater than 10,000' (ibid., 27). Richard F. Teichgraeber has argued in greater detail that the fact that Emerson was a publishing phenomenon in Britain in the 1840s qualifies Charvat's depiction of his reputation as regional until a decade later (see 1995: 172, 180, 182).

2. See *CEC* 199 and *CL* 13: 321. Carlyle features as the recipient of no less than nine copies of 'Literary Ethics' in Emerson's memorandum on the distribution of the first edition of the text (see *JMN* 12: 182).

3. Carlyle himself had been more modest about his responsibilities. In early August 1841, he admitted to John Sterling that '[a]ll that' he had '"done" for poor Ralph Waldo' was to write 'a short and very crabbed Preface; and allow James Fraser to reprint the work for his own behoof and Waldo's ... with that *imprimatur* on it; which poor Fraser was most anxious to do, without further trouble of mine' (*CL* 13: 207–8).

4. On Victorian book pricing and affordability, more generally, see Weedon 2003: 103–7 and Altick 1998: 286–7.

5. The first edition sizes of many Victorian novels were between 500 and 1,500 copies per title, with successful books reaching higher runs through subsequent printings from stereotype plates (see Eliot 2012: 54, 56). In 1836, the modal print run (that of the greatest number of individual books published) was 500, and a decade later it had risen to 750 copies per title; the mean print run (which also includes figures for bestsellers) was obviously higher, around 1,600 copies in 1836 and 2,600 a decade later (see Weedon 2003: 49).

6. Rodger L. Tarr notes that, upon Nickisson's failure in early 1847, the 'binding and distributing of the remaining sheets' was taken over by John Chapman, who had, in the meantime, become Emerson's English publisher (1989: 405). Joel Myerson describes one copy of the book bound with an 1847 catalogue by Chapman, but conjectures instead that the remaining copies were sold by Nickisson's successor, Thomas Bosworth (see 1982: 47, 747–8).

7. For an account of Emerson's income from publishing (which focuses on American firms and their payments during the second half of the century), see Myerson 1996. Myerson estimates that Emerson's collaboration with publisher James Munroe between 1836 and 1849 resulted in more than 15,000 printed volumes, for which Emerson received a total of $2,165 (see ibid., 143).

8. Quoted from Nickisson's advertisement in the *Publishers' Circular* of 1 October 1842 (no. 121, vol. V, p. 285), in which Emerson's *Essays* is listed directly after an edition of *Sartor Resartus*.

9. See also the following chapter, where I return to Gilfillan and describe Emerson's British reception in the later 1840s in greater detail.

10. On Goethe's preface to the German edition of Carlyle's book on Schiller, see also Chapter 2.

11. Emerson's mid-century British publishing has only rarely been covered. Chapman's London edition of *Essays: Second Series* is mentioned in passing in Slater 1964: 24–5, Ashton 2006: 16–19 and Koch 2012: 24–5, but the following provides a significantly more detailed account.
12. After introducing Chapman, Wright in his letter assured Emerson of his success with English readers: 'I do not suppose that I shall relate any thing new to you in informing you of the gradual and not slow dissemination of your beautiful works among the people of England. Besides Mr Carlyle's issue of the Essays, two Editions if not more have been published by a London Bookseller and now both they and Nature with the Orations are brought out in the illuminated form, & are selling well. Separate orations and Essays have moreover been published both in town & country. There is therefore no doubt now of your acceptance among the thoughtful of Great Britain. Your speech has been both broad & deep enough for her thousands and the voices of their own personal hearts have been corroborated and verified by it' (Houghton MS Am 1280 [3557]).
13. On his business stationary, Chapman figured as 'Importer of American Books'. Lists of transatlantic titles regularly featured as part of the firm's promotional material. The March 1849 catalogue, for example, advertised that Chapman's 'extensively established connexions, in various parts of America, have enabled him to make arrangements to receive full supplies, by each steamer, of all new and desirable books, published in every part of the United States, immediately after publication' (Anon. 1849e: 1).
14. On Chapman's career as a publisher and on his editorial choices, more generally, see Barnes and Barnes 1991 and, in particular, Ashton 2006. The first Emerson titles that Chapman reprinted formed part of his so-called 'Catholic Series', which was pitched as bringing together 'works of a liberal and comprehensive character' united by 'a love of intellectual freedom, and a faith in human progress', ideals to which, by the mid-1840s, Carlyle was no longer inclined to subscribe (the description of the series is quoted from a two-page list of 'Works Recently Published by John Chapman' bound with a copy of *Essays: Second Series* now at Harvard's Houghton Library [call number AC85 Em345 844eb]).
15. This liberty extended as far as the title for the book, which, Emerson wrote to Chapman, could be either '"Essays: second series. By R. W. Emerson"' or, '"The Poet, and other Essays"' (*L* 7: 610). His new publisher received a comprehensive mandate: 'You shall judge of this matter & I shall very cheerfully & thankfully confide the whole presentation of me to your countrymen to your kind charge' (ibid., 611).
16. For a more detailed analysis of Emerson's argument in the 1844 address, see Chapter 2.
17. For bibliographical details on these and other mid-century English editions, see Myerson 1982 and Myerson 2005.
18. These quotations are drawn from Emerson's summary in his letter to Carlyle of 1 September 1844. Chapman had written to Emerson four weeks earlier that 'it would not be probable that after obtaining the precedence any one could successfully compete with' the authorised London edition, adding in a postscript that he had 'had some conversation with a friend and lawyer this afternoon, who is of opinion that I

could procure a "copyright" for such of your writings as were sent here in manuscript before being published in America' (Houghton MS Am 1280 [3557]).

19. See the Introduction and Chapter 3 for a more extended discussion of transatlantic copyright. On the legal status of American writing in Britain at mid-century, more specifically, see also Gohdes 1944: 16–17 and Seville 2009: 220–5; on British political and legal debates around international copyright between 1838 and 1844, see Barnes 1974: 116–37.

20. See Chapman's entry form for the book, dated 6 November 1844, National Archives of the United Kingdom, COPY 1/569 (the title is also listed in the general registry book of the Stationers' Company, National Archives, Copyright Office: Registers, Books Literary and Commercial, Vol. 2, COPY 3/3, fol. 21).

21. For Emerson's reference to 'stealing', compare the language Carlyle had used in his public letter to Dickens in 1842: 'In an ancient Book, reverenced I should hope on both sides of the ocean, it was Thousands of Years ago, written down in the most decisive and explicit manner, *"Thou Shalt not Steal"*. That thou belongest to a different "Nation" and canst steal without being certainly hanged for it, gives thee no permission to steal. Thou shalt not in anywise steal at all!' (*CL* 14: 92–3).

22. Carlyle wrote to Emerson on 3 November that his 'English Volume of Essays . . . was advertised yesterday' (*CEC* 369–70) and Chapman's copyright entry form of 6 November lists that same day as the date of the book's publication. Neither of the two shorter books was registered for copyright protection.

23. George Slater's unauthorised 1850 reprint made *Essays: Second Series* available for the even lower price of one shilling (see Myerson 1982: 119).

24. In March 1845, Emerson sent Chapman a list of errata, highlighting the 'importance of some of the errors' and suggesting that they should 'be corrected in the plates' (*L* 8: 17).

25. Despite the promised 'half profits' arrangement, no payments from Chapman for any of the three titles he published in 1844 are recorded in Emerson's letters, journals or business papers.

Part III

Performing Nationhood on the Transatlantic Lecture Circuit

5

TOURING ANGLO-AMERICA: EMERSON AS TRANSATLANTIC LECTURER

The audience gathered at Newcastle's Nelson Street Lecture Room on the evening of 9 February 1848 was eagerly awaiting a transatlantic speaker the British newspapers had recently dubbed 'the greatest living writer of America' (Anon. 1847c: 6). At the invitation of the city's Literary, Scientific and Mechanical Institution, Emerson – the recipient of the accolade – was scheduled to speak on Shakespeare, a subject with which he had gained extensive experience at the lectern both at home and during the preceding months of his British lecture tour.[1] Despite this thematic familiarity, the Newcastle performance turned out to run less smoothly than could have been expected, as a report of the event in the local press illustrates:

> On Mr Emerson appearing on the platform, accompanied by several members of the committee, he was warmly applauded. He observed that he had been announced to deliver a lecture on 'Shakspere [sic] the poet'; that lecture had been so frequently delivered and so faithfully reported in several newspapers that he thought it scarcely respectful to an audience to read it again. With their leave, therefore, he would read a lecture on the national characteristics of the inhabitants of the States of New England. After making these observations there were shouts of 'Shakspere', and a division of opinion prevailed in the meeting, the sense of which was ultimately tested by a show of hands, when it was evident that a decided majority were in favour of the lecture being given as originally announced. (Anon. 1848e: 5)

Over the preceding months, Emerson had complained several times that the use value of his lectures steadily decreased through their almost verbatim summary by British journalists. What made things worse in Newcastle was that he was directly competing with a simultaneous performance of the country's foremost Shakespearean actor, William Charles Macready, at the local Theatre Royal, within a stone's throw of the Nelson Street Lecture Room.

There was hence reason enough to replace the original lecture and offer a different topic instead. What Emerson had probably not anticipated was that his audience would assume an agency of its own and speak back – a case of decision-making by majority vote exceptional in the history of nineteenth-century transatlantic lecturing. Emerson had effectively failed to assert his performative authority over an audience that wielded its collective social power to determine what he could – and what he could not – speak about. Compelled to yield to the demands of his audience, he was at the same time forced to realise that, in their preference of Shakespeare over 'the national characteristics of the inhabitants of the States of New England', the British ultimately seemed to show a greater interest in their own literary history than in American cultural identity.

Emerson would be given an additional opportunity to address the Newcastle audience on his topic of choice the following evening, but on the present occasion he 'at once complied' with the popular verdict and proceeded to repeat his lecture on Shakespeare, which met with 'loud and general plaudits' (Anon. 1848e: 5). Forced to decide between two thematic alternatives, the majority of the Newcastle lecture-goers had opted for the more conventional topic. Yet the excitement about hearing Emerson speak on Shakespeare was, ultimately, in large part due to a desire to learn something about his distinctly American perspective on the English literary past. Throughout the tour, British commentators emphasised that, as both an insider and an outsider at the same time, Emerson was ideally suited for the task of explaining 'the greatest of our poets' to his transatlantic audiences (Anon. 1848a: 3). Since Shakespeare's 'language' was that of his 'own country', Emerson was deemed 'well qualified' to analyse his character and works, but 'as a foreigner' he was simultaneously credited with special analytical insight, being 'free from those national prejudices which might incline an Englishman to judge with undue partiality' (ibid.). It was Emerson's geographical distance from metropolitan literature, coupled to his linguistic and cultural proximity to it, that became a key prerequisite for the transatlantic recognition of his critical authority. An American lecturer and experienced European traveller, Emerson himself seized on the potential of such national hybridity, speaking on English and American topics to audiences on both sides of the Atlantic. Shedding light on this understudied aspect of his professional career, this chapter suggests that Emerson's lecturing on subjects such as Shakespeare or New England represented a sustained rhetorical balancing act, a careful argumentative negotiation between praise and censure that made his accounts of transatlantic literary and cultural history popular at home and abroad, on stage and in print.[2]

Anglo-American subjects proved especially useful in the American lecture hall. Inviting reflection on a culture at once excitingly foreign and comfortably familiar, lectures on English history and literature acquainted American audiences with what, on stage, was often described as part of their own heritage. Such lecturing fostered audiences' contrastive sense of their own national identity at the same time that it created an awareness of their participation in a discursive community that extended across as well as beyond the nation. A topic much in demand with local lyceums and their subscribers, England and its culture soon became one of the subjects with which the young Emerson engaged not only in his journals and notebooks but also on the lecture platform. Having renounced the ministry and only recently returned from an extensive European tour that had also brought him to Britain, Emerson embarked on his new career as a lecturer in 1833, devoting his professional attention to a range of subjects whose wide scope was motivated in equal part by the adaptable nature of his specialist knowledge and by a lecturing system that allowed for such fluidity due to its own structural flexibility. In an institutional environment that was only beginning to establish its own protocols, Emerson could afford to cluster his performances around what he himself acknowledged was a loosely defined set of 'extreme & fantastic things' (*L* 2: 121). Devoting himself to what Carlyle, in *Sartor Resartus*, had described as the study of 'things in general' (*WTC* 2: 14), Emerson represented a kind of professionalism that dovetailed with the expectations of a general audience accustomed to hearing an eclectic range of subjects discussed over the course of a lecturing season. If, as Lawrence Buell has pointed out, the lyceum allowed Emerson to speak 'on topics ranging as far as he wished beyond his accredited expertise' (2013: 40), the precise nature of that expertise was itself permanently in flux.

Emerson's excitement about the occupational flexibility that the 'new spiritual element' of lecturing offered to the enterprising intellectual becomes palpable in one of his early letters to Carlyle:

> The pulpit in our age certainly gives forth an obstructed and uncertain sound, and the faith of those in it, if men of genius, may differ so much from that of those under it, as to embarrass the conscience of the speaker, because so much is attributed to him from the fact of standing there. In the Lyceum, nothing is presupposed. The orator is only responsible for what his lips articulate. Then what scope it allows! You may handle every member & relation of humanity. (*CEC* 142–3)

Providing Carlyle with a lively description of contemporary New England lecture culture, Emerson was paying special attention to the thematic openness of the lyceum. The relative novelty of the genre of the modern lecture performance guaranteed that speakers did not have to face the clash between institutional regimes and individual convictions that the letter describes as detrimentally at work in contemporary religious oratory. To the extent that the New England Unitarian pulpit represented a 'routinization of charisma of which Emerson wanted no part' (Field 2001: 472), he invested in public lecturing as a less traditional but no less charismatic alternative. If, in his letter, Emerson contrasts lecturing with preaching as fundamentally different forms of public speaking, this juxtaposition obscures the fact that, in his and Carlyle's reflections about the practice, the line that separates the two spheres is hardly straight. Emerson's own lectures testify to 'the survival of homiletical techniques' (Baumgartner 1963: 477) in an environment that he himself repeatedly described as 'the new pulpit' of 'the Lecture-Room' (*CEC* 171).[3] As I have argued in the Introduction, both his and Carlyle's ideas about lecturing were, to a considerable extent, shaped by a rhetoric of prophetic energy that sought to endow the secular practice of lecturing with the sacral authority of its ministerial counterpart. Rather than being safely dismissible as routinised, religious oratory, after all, continued to be attractive as a charismatic model. At the same time, however, Emerson managed to combine a lofty view of his new profession with a solidly commercial attitude about it – a balance that is symbolised by the effortless transition, in the above letter to Carlyle, from the solemn invocation of oratorical freedom to a detailed account of his income as a lecturer.

Throughout his career as a transatlantic performing intellectual, Emerson was tackling subjects for which he could expect a steady demand among lecture-goers at home and abroad. Focusing on his Anglo-American lecturing activity from the mid-1830s to the mid-1850s, this chapter is concerned with his sustained quest for an audience that was not only receptive to his discourses about the history and future of the transatlantic relationship but also prepared to recognise in him a cultural critic equipped with the necessary degree of authority to legitimise these speculations. My key argument here will be that Emerson identified this kind of audience with the print-propelled imagined community of the transatlantic lecture hall. The first two sections of the chapter address his early lecturing in the United States, focusing more specifically on two individual lecture series – 'English Literature' (1835–6) and 'New England' (1843–4). In both of these courses, Emerson commented extensively on the relationship between culture and nationality as well as on that between Britain and the United States, gradually moving from a filiopietistic admiration of English achievement to a more confident national criticism that, in the long run, nevertheless aimed at highlighting close transatlantic ties. Turning to Emerson's British lecture tour of 1847–8, section three revisits significant individual performances and reconstructs the heavy use of national and ethnic stereotypes through which the contemporary British press was trying to make sense of his cultural origins and of his claim to the collective attention of domestic audiences. The chapter's two remaining sections shed light on the lectures on English and American subjects that Emerson delivered upon his return home, but also on how the positions he presented on these occasions resurfaced in the argument of *English Traits* (1856), the book that – growing out of the transatlantic lecture tour – saw Emerson perfecting a versatile argumentative style which mediated between two media forms (speech and print) as well as between two national audiences (British and American).

FILIOPIETISM: THE EARLY LECTURES ON 'ENGLISH LITERATURE'

When Emerson sent Carlyle his sketch of the American lyceum landscape in the spring of 1836, he had only recently finished a series of ten lectures on 'English Literature' at the Boston Masonic Temple. Following introductory remarks and more general reflections about the relation between cultural identity and its literary manifestations, the main part of the series was dedicated to lectures on exemplary writers that proceeded in roughly chronological order from Chaucer to Carlyle. Emerson's first-hand experience of England and his personal acquaintance with some of its foremost contemporary literary figures gave him enough confidence to tackle a subject with which he could expect the members of his Boston audience to have some familiarity, but he had nevertheless turned to English reference works to prepare his lectures – Thomas Warton's *History of English Poetry* (1774–81) and Sharon Turner's *History of the Anglo-Saxons* (1799–1805) chief among them. Right at the beginning of the course, Emerson candidly confessed to his lack of expert knowledge of the topic:

> I am not so presumptuous as to undertake to present in this course of lectures a complete View of English Literature. There is no History of English Literature. Perhaps few men in this country are competent to such an enterprize [*sic*]. Our discipline in books is not extensive enough and is not exact and profound enough. But who[e]ver is able, I am not. I have not read all the books that are popularly included under that name. (*EL* 1: 217)

Demonstrating his own limitations, Emerson's opening caveat establishes a sense of the complexity of the subject under discussion – an awe-inspiringly vast corpus of literary texts that could be made meaningful only with the help of an expertise derived from long-term cultivation and 'discipline'. But at the same time that he reveals his own inability to grasp English literature's hidden meanings, Emerson implies that this ignorance is of a collective rather than of an individual nature. Having to speak about English literature before an American audience to him becomes a twofold source of postcolonial embarrassment: the richness of the topic draws attention to the corresponding poverty of domestic literary production, and the younger nation's critical culture lacks the intellectual rigour and scholarly sophistication required to make sense of an established foreign tradition.

Emerson's sense of inferiority was likely alleviated by the fact that he was hardly speaking in front of an expert audience. He lectured at the request of the Boston Society for the Diffusion of Useful Knowledge, most of whose members were, unlike him, not part of Boston's university-trained cultural elite. Established in 1829 and modelled on its transatlantic counterpart of the same name, the Society was not exactly proletarian, but although it also sponsored lectures on culture and the arts, its didactic emphasis clearly remained on utility and applicability.[4] It was this particular institutional background that invited Emerson to reflect on the urgency of literature – and on the importance of the authority of the man of letters – in his introductory lecture. Acknowledging that 'the word Literature has in many ears a hollow sound', that it 'is thought to be the harmless entertainment of a few fanciful persons and not at all to be the interest of the multitude', Emerson goes on to formulate a more inclusive definition of utility (*EL* 1: 228). 'These objections', he contends, 'proceed on the very coarse supposition that nothing but what grinds corn and bakes bread is anything worth' (ibid.). But rather than radically questioning the very idea of 'useful knowledge' and arguing in a Kantian manner that the importance of art arises from its freedom from the demands of utility, Emerson opts for a more conservative strategy that ascribes to literature a use value of its own. In the series as a whole, his defence of literature's relevance relies on a link between culture and nationality. Literary history in this line of argument derives its legitimacy as a lyceum subject chiefly from its ability to make manifest the otherwise hidden 'permanent traits of the national genius' (ibid., 234). Illustrating a larger cultural identity that informs all departments of life, literature here becomes a meta-category that subsumes under itself the fragmented instrumentalist knowledge of disciplinary discourses whose utility Emerson exposes as ultimately being of a limited kind.[5] As a topic of national concern, literary history, according to this defence, was truly and immediately in 'the interest of the multitude'. What this demonstrates is that the nexus between literature and nationhood that Emerson would go on to emphasise in his lecturing and writing over the decades to come initially emerged in response to the institutional demands of the lyceum environment.

The Boston Masonic Temple was a suitable setting for the series. Built just a few years earlier in the neo-gothic style then fashionable in Britain, it had quickly established itself as a centre of Transcendentalist activity (Amos Bronson Alcott ran his controversial 'Temple School' in one of the upper storey rooms) and provided a fitting backdrop for Emerson's explorations of the English past. English literature was a subject that had proved popular with Boston audiences in the past – most recently with Harvard professor George

Ticknor, who had delivered a series of lectures on Shakespeare in the same institutional context during the 1833–4 season. The dynamics of transatlantic cultural authority behind such thematic choices relate to the intersection of what Jeffrey Alexander has described as the 'background symbols' and 'social power' that lie behind cultural performances – the question, that is, of what a public appearance can legitimately be about (2011: 28, 32). Carlyle would not have dreamed of lecturing about American literature in Victorian Britain, but it was quite natural for Emerson to do the opposite. A taste for English literature had survived both the Revolution and the War of 1812 and most Americans were familiar with a cultural and literary tradition that was firmly enshrined in their educational curricula. As Robert D. Richardson has pointed out, the figures Emerson discussed on the stage of the Masonic Temple 'meant far more to [him] and to other Americans at the time than any earlier American writers' (1995: 214–15). Lacking both cultural prestige and an agreed-upon canon of authors, American literature failed to qualify for the kind of extensive treatment a mid-century lecture course offered. While it was a safe bet for manifesto-style performances like Emerson's own 'American Scholar' address, domestic writing was hardly suitable for a genre whose hallmark was the documentation of large-scale historical developments. The conventions of the lecture system, in other words, had a major impact on the character as well as the content of Emerson's early lecturing.

In terms of the actual transatlantic statements Emerson makes over the course of the series, 'English Literature' reads over large stretches like an expression of Anglophile deference, a recognition of English literature's transatlantically extensive claim to cultural authority. At certain points, the lectures become an exercise in national self-deprecation, for instance when, in his concluding lecture, Emerson compares the cultural achievements of England to those of the United States and notes that

> [a] degree of humiliation must be felt by the American scholar when he reviews the constellation of great geniuses from Chaucer down who in England have enlarged the limits of wisdom and then returns to this country . . . and reckons how little has been here added to the stock of truth for mankind. Where are the bards [who] have sung? Where are the scholars who have collected? (*EL* 1: 381)

This mixture of deference and dejection is mitigated, however, by Emerson's core narrative that English literature counts as the transatlantic precursor and progenitor of its American counterpart. While the historical genre in which he was moving confined him to a discussion of a glorious English past, it also allowed him to assert that the true domain of American writing would be the future. This trajectory from dependence to self-valorisation is deeply ingrained already in the stadial–cyclical definition of literary history that Emerson had presented at the outset of the course. Evolution and transformation were part of the biological nature of literary life, he suggested, and a slow but inevitable transatlantic transition of creative power thus merely a matter of time. In Chapter 2, I have shown in greater detail how Emerson at this point establishes a conceptual link between literature and nationality, but it is worth recalling here how consistently he emphasises the idea that the 'inhabitants of the United States' were 'descended from the people of England and have inherited the traits of their national character' (ibid., 233).

Yet Emerson could obviously have gone much further in his nationalist claims. That more assertive passages from his lecture notebook – a statement such as 'Claims of England; very great; yet how they sink before those of this country' (*JMN* 12: 36) – did not find their way into the final version of the series illustrates the ultimately rather muted tone of the 'English Literature' course. Even in the concluding lecture, in which he turns from the past to the present and the future, Emerson refrains from exploiting the full argumentative and rhetorical potential of the empowerment narrative. What he had originally advertised as a broadly Anglophone 'lecture upon the literary character . . . of the nations speaking the English tongue' ultimately became a significantly less diasporic account dominated by British writers (*L* 7: 250). When he finally addresses the subject of American writing, Emerson quickly turns from a diagnosis of cultural inferiority to the formulation of indeterminate hopes for the future literary achievement of the Anglo-Saxon 'race' as a whole, before concluding with generalising remarks on the idea of a literature still to come (reflections that move from the level of the nation to that of the individual writer). Unlike in most of the later lectures discussed in the remainder of this chapter, in the 'English Literature' series Emerson is consistently reverential when describing English national achievement. With an audience favourably disposed towards the British literary tradition, an outright dismantling of the subject matter would, after all, have hardly been advisable. Emerson's argumentative strategy was thus one well adapted to the concrete performative context in which he was delivering his lectures and beginning to fashion himself as a literary intellectual.

Self-Authorisation: From 'New England' to 'The Young American'

Emerson was shifting argumentative ground with another lecture course a few years later, and it was a transformation in the institutional climate in which he was moving that contributed to this reorientation. In his series on 'New England', delivered in different shapes and on various occasions in 1843 and 1844, he began to explore new terrain in terms of both his subject matter and his lecturing itinerary. He was turning west with the one and south with the other – two movements that were closely connected. Emerson's stepping outside of his cultural and professional comfort zone and his increasing acquaintance with non-New England audiences went hand in hand with his exposure to the commercial and less affirmatively Anglophile climate of the urban areas which he was touring with the 'New England' course. His metropolitan experience resulted in a brief flirtation with a more assertive variety of cultural nationalism that stood in marked contrast to the attitude behind the earlier 'English Literature' lectures.

Emerson began his tour at the Baltimore Mercantile Library Association on 10 January 1843 and then travelled up north, with lectures in Philadelphia and before the Berean Society and the New York Society Library in New York City, a course that ended on 22 February; he lectured from the 'New England' manuscripts again in January 1844, in the form of a series of four lectures at the Franklin Lyceum in Providence. With these deliveries of the 'New England' course Emerson entered a new stage of his career as a lecturer. It 'launched [his] celebrity' and saw him grow into his role as 'a major American . . . public intellectual' (O'Neill 2008: 746; Simmons 2006: 53). By 1843, he had become the author of two books – *Nature* (1836) and the first volume of *Essays* (1841) – and was read on both sides of the Atlantic – a reputation that his growing success in the lecture hall solidified just as it was itself in part predicated on it. The lecturing system was undergoing a transformation in the early 1840s as well – 'extending every year to the south and west', as Emerson noted in the series itself (*LL* 1: 45). Following in its tracks, he exploited the potential that this institutional expansion offered. With his more extensive lecturing schedule came a gradual familiarity with what he called his 'new congregations' beyond Boston and Concord (*CEC* 341) – a fresh start that, Nancy Craig Simmons has argued, saw Emerson disavow his image as an inscrutable Transcendentalist and reinvent himself as more widely accessible (see 2006: 57–8). Whatever the extent of the actual shift in his public perception, the 'New England' tour brought Emerson in touch with lecture-goers of diverse regional, social and educational backgrounds. The audiences he encountered in Philadelphia or New York did not resemble the kind of assemblies gathered in New England lecture halls, but were largely made up of the predominantly young, male and commerce-oriented attendees that Mary Kupiec Cayton and Thomas Augst have described as the key addressees of Emerson's urban lecturing from the early 1840s onwards.[6]

Emerson's professionalisation as a public lecturer and his growing awareness of new audiences came hand in hand with a corresponding shift in the topics he addressed on the platform. Moving westward from English literature to New England character, he began to experiment with a lecture genre that historian Donald Scott has described as revolving around the attempt 'to explicate life in contemporary America' (1980: 804). Where the main concern of the earlier course had been what lay across the Atlantic, the 1843–4 series was, as Simmons points out, 'self-consciously "American"' (2006: 53). While the geographical focus had undoubtedly shifted, there was also an underlying sense of continuity, however. In both courses, Emerson spoke about a subject at once foreign and familiar to those who attended his lectures (England to his New England audiences, New England 'to the Southerner[s]' of New York, Pennsylvania and Maryland [*L* 3: 100]) and in both contexts he highlighted the larger relevance of his topic: England mattered to his New England 'congregations', he argued, because it had crucially shaped their own character, and New England mattered to audiences in Philadelphia or New York because an 'hourly assimilation' was 'bind[ing]' the nation as a whole 'fast into one web' (*LL* 1: 8). Transatlantic or sectional differences were thus both what Emerson relied upon and what he sought to bridge in order to create an ethnological interest in his topics.

If, in the course of drafting and delivering the 'New England' lectures, Emerson became more 'self-consciously "American"', the idea of Anglo-American racial continuity – of crucial importance in the earlier Boston series – remained a key element of his analysis. In the later lecture course, England is once again at the heart of Emerson's understanding of the United States and its national identity, a structural centrality that can be gauged from the fact that his enquiry into New England history and manners is prefaced by an introductory lecture on 'The Genius and National Character of the Anglo-Saxon Race'. The idea of transatlantic racial permanence resurfaces here in essentially unchanged form because Emerson was drawing heavily on his earlier lecture on 'Permanent Traits of the English National Genius', the second instalment of the 'English Literature' course. Contemporary lecture reports suggest that the surviving manuscript version of the first 'New England' lecture lacks an additional section on English racial origins that must have formed part of its original deliveries (see Anon. 1843c and Simmons 2006: 75). Judging from these summaries, Emerson in the early 1840s was no less celebratory of English achievement than he had been in the earlier series. As in the course on 'English Literature', in the 'New England' lectures the United States emerge as historically rooted rather than as radically autonomous. Even when shifting focus from English culture to New England life, the lecture performances of the early 1840s thus kept a steady focus on the leitmotif of transatlantic heritage.[7]

Yet Emerson had also grown more confident in playing the role of the national cultural critic – a shift that makes itself felt most immediately in his turn away from the filiopietistic sentiment that had dominated the Boston lectures of 1835–6. The transatlantic cultural 'centre of gravity', he suggested in the fourth of the 'New England' lectures, would 'soon . . . fall within the American shore', with 'the writers of the English tongue' in future addressing themselves 'to the American and not to the island public' (*LL* 1: 58). The rhetoric with which the lecture series advanced such claims for American cultural authority chiefly derived from contemporary nationalist writing. Emerson's exposure especially to New York audiences – which were used to the more confidently national tone cultivated in the local press – proved crucial to these ideological borrowings. Remaining strong with Emerson at least during the following year, this new national tone culminated in another public address, 'The Young American', read in February 1844 before the Boston Mercantile Library Association – roughly a year after the original 'New England' lecture tour and less than a month after the repetition of the course in Providence. Emerson was now taking home to his Boston audience what he had absorbed of the local atmosphere during his New York performances the year before. Just like the fourth instalment of the 'New England' series, 'The Young American' – which, in its title, alludes to the New York-based Young America movement while at the same time shifting focus from the nation to the individual – opens with a critique of American cultural dependence on England before painting a more optimistic picture of the future ('America is beginning to assert itself to the senses and to the imagination of her children, and Europe is receding in the same degree' [CW 1: 222]). With westward expansion introducing 'a new and continental element into the national mind', Emerson confidently foretells that 'we shall yet have an American genius' (ibid., 229). To be sure, this account differed from more radical forms of cultural nationalism in that Emerson gave up neither his emphasis on distinctly English origins nor his insistence on a lack of American cultural achievement – two crucial aspects that Young America writers tended to downplay in their aggressive celebration of national potential. Nevertheless, the 'New England' lectures and 'The Young American' represent a notable departure from Emerson's more common rhetoric of transatlantic conciliation.

Two political–cultural issues dominated public debate as Emerson began to experiment with a more affirmatively national voice, and both of these help to account for the shift in the tone of his performances. The first was the heated expansionist climate in the run-up to the 1844 presidential election, in which the Democratic Party's call for the annexation of Texas and the Oregon Territory gave new currency to questions of national identity.[8] Like these disputes, the second topic at the centre of public attention between late 1842 (when Emerson began to draft the 'New England' series) and early 1844 (when he delivered 'The Young American') was Anglo-American in character, revolving around the publication of Charles Dickens's *American Notes for General Circulation* (1842) and Rufus Wilmot Griswold's *The Poets and Poetry of America* (1842). Where, in the Texas and Oregon debate, transatlantic conflict centred on territorial sovereignty and political influence, relations between the United States and Britain experienced a simultaneous era of bad feelings in the literary sphere. Published soon after his American tour of 1842, Dickens's partly favourable and partly condescending account of the young nation – a bestseller on both sides of the Atlantic – raised uncomfortable questions about American social and cultural achievement. Griswold's anthology was an effort to improve the United States' standing in the international literary field by demonstrating that the country could boast a mature poetic tradition of its own. Its 'middle-of-the-road nationalism' combined an acknowledgement of cultural belatedness with a patriotic assertion of literary identity (Gordon 2020: 89). Despite this diplomatic framing, the project failed to convince important British reviewers and a fierce dismissal of American poetry in the London *Foreign Quarterly Review* in January 1844 (see Anon. 1844a) was followed by what contemporary commentators described as a 'literary war between England and the United States' (Anon. 1844b: 2). Connected with the *Foreign Quarterly* through its recently retired editor, John Forster, Dickens was quickly identified by the American press as the author of the unsigned review essay and held accountable for a more general British 'bitterness' towards American culture (ibid.). Although Emerson, unlike many other American writers, refrained from publicly intervening in the debate, he took an implicit stand with the anti-English opening salvo of 'The Young American', which he delivered at the peak of the *Foreign Quarterly* 'war'.

It was thus in an atmosphere of mounting political and cultural tensions between Britain and the United States that Emerson used the lecture hall as a forum to reflect on the cultural status of his country. Public speaking allowed him to be more daring in his commentary than the medium of print, which compelled him to take into account the expectations of a composite transatlantic readership. Where, on stage, he fantasised about a relocation of cultural and political authority, in print he was more careful to maintain a safe distance from such claims and their potential implications. In 'The Poet', the opening piece of his second collection of *Essays* (1844), what remains of Emerson's emphatic remarks about American literature is merely a lament about its deplorable status quo ('[w]e have yet had no genius in America' [CW 3: 22]). Even where, in the conclusion of the essay, he turns to express his future-tense confidence in a poetry still to be written, the prophecy comes framed in a markedly denationalised form.[9] When Emerson republished 'The Young American' as part of the collected *Nature, Addresses, and Lectures* in 1849, he dropped much of the flamboyantly nationalist opening passage, including its deprecating remarks about the 'feudal school' of English literature as an impediment to American cultural growth (CW 1: 222). Revisions such as these suggest that Emerson realised that he was addressing audiences on both sides of the Atlantic – readers whose different cultural sensibilities rendered avoiding outright sectional partialities imperative.

'Emerson Mania': The British Lecture Tour of 1847–8 and Ethnic Stereotyping

Emerson's talent for Anglo-American cultural diplomacy was once again put to the test three years after 'The Young American', when he set out to preach to the members of what Carlyle identified as his 'Transoceanic Parish' (CEC 129).

Following an initial sojourn with Carlyle in London, Emerson commenced a lecturing itinerary that, between November 1847 and February 1848, saw him perform more than sixty times in twenty-five cities and towns throughout northern England and Scotland. After another stay in London, an excursion to Oxford and a three-week exposure to revolutionary Paris, he returned to the British capital and delivered ten more lectures there in June 1848 before eventually returning to the United States.[10] The vast overseas demand for Emerson's appearances on stage had, in large part, been created by his prior success in print. Even before the transatlantic lecture tour, there had been something of an 'Emerson mania' among British readers.[11] But where the print circulation of his writings was substantial already before his arrival in England, his British performances gave an additional boost to his reputation, both in the lecture hall itself and through reports of the lectures, which – printed and reprinted in local as well as national newspapers – secured an exponential increase in his visibility. Several contemporary British commentators even suggested that Emerson at the time was more widely known in Britain than in the United States. The most elaborate version of this argument featured in Scottish critic George Gilfillan's essay 'Ralph Waldo Emerson; or, the "Coming Man"', first published in the January 1848 issue of *Tait's Edinburgh Magazine*. Emerson's achievement was accurately measured only in Britain, Gilfillan claimed, because the country could boast critics 'unprejudiced either for or against the author[s]' they chose to praise or censure (1848: 17). This was, to some extent, a version of the kind of argument that was applied to Emerson himself where, from a British perspective, his American cultural distance was described as turning him into an unbiased critic of English literature (as I have shown at the beginning of this chapter). Yet Gilfillan more fundamentally suggested that British critical authority was per se superior, that it was exclusively at the metropolitan centre that literary merit could be impartially judged against universal standards of excellence.[12]

Most British assessments of Emerson during the lecture tour came framed in a larger narrative of literary nationality that cast him as a representative American writer who formed an exception in a national tradition that remained largely devoid of literary genius. That Emerson was, as Gilfillan noted, a 'great original standing up in an imitative country' (ibid., 22) was a convenient way for British critics to acknowledge his influence while keeping more general American claims to cultural achievement at bay. The price that Emerson had to pay for such double-edged recognition was that he became increasingly reduced to his status as an American. The pervasiveness of such nationalisation is perhaps best exemplified by the epithets the contemporary British press used to characterise him. When forced to describe Emerson in a nutshell, nationality was the shorthand to which editors and reporters most frequently resorted.[13] The more extensive pieces devoted much space to the definition of American literature's national traits and to the nature of Emerson's relation to them. An earlier essay by Gilfillan formed the template on which many subsequent discussions were modelled. It presented an image of Emerson's cultural origins that was tinged with exoticism, describing him as having 'come straight from the wilderness, dripping with the dew of the aboriginal woods' (1845: 301). The literary distinction to which Emerson, according to Gilfillan, could lay claim was that of authentically voicing the raw and uncivilised. This view obviously jarred with the desire of nineteenth-century American writers like Emerson to be recognised as equal participants in the transatlantic cultural sphere not because of their primitive otherness, but because they had successfully reached the same aesthetic and intellectual standards by which British critics were measuring domestic literary productions. When Emerson lectured in England and Scotland, the image he was trying to convey of himself was not Gilfillan's idea of the savage backwoodsman but that of the public man of letters on a par with English models of eloquence and erudition.

The link between Emerson and his national identity acquired an additional dimension when British commentators were judging not his writings but his performances on stage. In the contemporary lecture reports, his appearance regularly became the subject of anatomical and linguistic othering. While already his disembodied voice on the printed page had been seen by some as exuding foreignness (displaying the 'vulgarisms of American civic phraseology' [Gilfillan 1845: 304]), his actual voice in the lecture hall struck many in his audience as even more exotic. Where his writings could be regularised into British spelling and thus at least typographically assimilated when reprinted in London, in live performances his American accent came unfiltered, with the 'tones of his voice' perceived as strangely 'nasal and American' (Anon. 1848d: 6). Some audience members, to be sure, were surprised to encounter something other than the American savage contemporary periodical coverage had primed them to expect. '[S]ave that his shirt-collars were turned down', the *Leicestershire Mercury*, for instance, found '[s]carcely anything in his appearance of the "Yankee"' (Anon. 1847j: 2). But others were in a high state of primitivist anticipation that coloured their perception of the speaker. On the occasion of Emerson's June 1848 lectures at London's Exeter Hall, the reporter for the *British Banner* noted:

> When he came on the platform, with the gentlemen who accompanied him, it was easy to single him out as the man of the evening. His air and aspect are thoroughly American; dark, sallow, hard-featured, tall, thin, and slightly stooping, with a most imperturbable air and manner, he seemed far enough from all relationship, either to the poet or the orator . . . (qtd in Scudder 1935b: 167)

Although the selection of Emerson's 'thoroughly American' features seems arbitrary enough, what they referenced was not the image of the Boston Brahmin, but that of the western frontiersman popularised by Gilfillan. As such, Emerson remained an outsider, easy to tell apart from the British 'gentlemen' in whose company he appeared on stage (Carlyle and Richard Monckton Milnes among them on this particular occasion) – a noble savage that merely posed as 'poet' and 'orator' without being able to erase the difference between his actual identity and the role he pretended to be playing. Prepared to authenticate him as the genuine voice of an 'aboriginal' American culture, British newspaper coverage at the same time tended to deny him the cultural authority of the public intellectual. Characterised as a 'dark' transatlantic other, Emerson found himself in the vicinity of African American lecturers such as Frederick Douglass, whose recent speaking tour of the British Isles would still have been fresh in the memory of many of the members of Emerson's English and Scottish audiences (Exeter Hall, in particular, was a centre of Anglo-American antislavery campaigning).[14] Commentary of the kind published in the *British Banner* shows that black abolitionist orators were not alone in being perceived by 'the English public as an exotic spectacle' (Fisch 2000: 70). Emerson was likewise seen as marked by his supposed ethnic and behavioural deviations from the British norm.

How pervasive such stereotyping was becomes clear when one turns from British perceptions of Emerson to his own observations about the British during the 1847–8 trip. Persistently depicted by the press through a recourse to the idea of national and racial particularity, Emerson himself resorted to such charged ethnography to make sense of what he witnessed during his tour. After scarcely a week in England, he noted that the 'stunted & stocky' Englishmen he was encountering everywhere around him were 'physiognomically & constitutionally distinct from the Americans' (*JMN* 10: 178). Such stereotypes occasionally failed to add up, however. In an April 1848 letter to Margaret Fuller, Emerson wrote that he had 'seen a good many persons in England of the American type, and, what is curious, not easily distinguishable from Americans in speech', adding with a sense of bewilderment that 'at Oxford at Manchester & in London I conversed as with countrymen with young men whom I think I should have met without remark in Boston or Concord' (*L* 4: 62). While, thanks to this experience of a clash between type and individual, Emerson registered the inherent limitations of national traits as a heuristics of character, the real confusion in the letter arises from his continued investment in the idea of distinct English and American national traits. It would take him several years to work through this conundrum, which – as I demonstrate in Chapter 2 – is openly addressed, though hardly resolved, only in the 'Race' chapter of the 1856 *English Traits*.

Where, in his journals and letters home, Emerson was constantly concerned with national and racial identity, in his British lectures he largely bypassed the issue. Choosing topics such as 'Swedenborg', 'Domestic Life' or 'The Humanity of Science' allowed him to avoid having either to affirm or to disavow his American difference. There were nevertheless a handful of occasions on which he spoke directly about England and America. The first of these came early on in the tour with an invitation to address an audience of several thousand fellow guests at the annual soirée of the Manchester Athenæum on 18 November 1847. The only foreigner among a group of distinguished British speakers (eminent Victorians including historian Archibald Alison, free-trade advocate Richard Cobden and artist George Cruikshank), Emerson strove in his remarks to strike a balance between praising English achievement and asserting American potential. Mid-Victorian affluence had all but overwhelmed him ('If I stay here long, I shall lose all my patriotism, & think that England has absorbed all excellences' [*JMN* 10: 244]) and the Athenæum address captures some of this initial enthusiasm. The event was widely covered by the national press and Emerson later used a revised version of his Manchester remarks as the concluding chapter of *English Traits* (which I cover more extensively in the final part of this chapter). The transcript of the speech that appeared in the London *Times* shows Emerson at his most deferential. 'Though he stood there as a stranger', the *Times* summarised, 'he could find nothing strange in such an assembly': he 'was glad of the opportunity, as an American, of sitting near such men as he had met that night on that platform, and he rejoiced that that assembly seemed willing to reciprocate with all the nations of the globe intellectual advantages' (Anon. 1847g: 8).

Emerson's celebratory tone was motivated in equal part by his favourable impressions of England in the weeks prior to the event and by the diplomatic touch that the occasion itself called for. The latter was achieved through what the *Times* described as Emerson's 'remarks upon the identity of character in the Englishman and the American' (ibid.), sentiments in which the Manchester speech followed the textual and performative precedent of the American lecture courses discussed in the first two sections of this chapter. Towards the end of his address, however, Emerson was returning to the idea of a transatlantic transition of power, as the following account from the *Manchester Times* illustrates:

> When I see . . . that in her old age [England] is not decrepit, but is still young, still believing, still daring to believe in her power of endurance and expansion, then I say, 'Hail mother of nations – mother of heroes all hail!' – (applause) – with a strong arm still equal to the time, with a spirit to entertain and swift to execute the policy which the heart and mind of mankind at this moment require, and thereby hospitable to the foreigner

and anxious only to find the truth in him, and a true home to her own generous and thoughtful children. So be it, . . . long be it so, from age to age; but if her courage fail before the momentary calamities of her commerce, I will return to Massachusetts and to my little Indian stream, and say to my American friends, 'The old race is all gone, and if hope and elasticity are to be found, they must be on the ranges of the Alleghanies, or no where'. (Loud applause.) (Anon. 1847f: 6)

As the recorded audience responses imply, Emerson's concluding flourish was understood not as an American arrogation of power but rather as a vision of the survival of Anglo-Saxon virtues across the ocean. What, in all its conditional tentativeness, the final sentence of the speech after all implied was that 'hope' for the future of civilisation rested on a 'new' cultural arena that was indelibly marked by its transatlantic racial heritage. Even if Emerson's 'well-wishing for the reassertion of English power' grew more out of 'politeness' than out of 'personal conviction', as Philip Nicoloff has argued (1961: 83), it nevertheless achieved its intended effect with his British audience.[15]

If, in the Manchester speech, Emerson offered his most extended public commentary on England during his tour, he spoke more explicitly about American questions in his February 1848 Newcastle lecture on 'The National Characteristics of the Six Northern States of America', which I have already mentioned briefly at the beginning of this chapter. Judging from the detailed summary of the event in the *Newcastle Guardian*, Emerson was here drawing from several of his older 'New England' lecture manuscripts, supplementing them with new critical remarks about the Southern states of the Union. In delivering the lectures to his countrymen a few years before, he had still been careful to make clear that sectional difference was ultimately negligible and that what was true of New England character was ultimately true of the nation as a whole. But in the meantime, the annexation of pro-slavery Texas and the ensuing Mexican–American War had brought the nascent conflict between North and South to a boil, and it seems that Emerson wanted to publicise his own views on these developments in front of an English audience. Where, during the earlier American deliveries of the 'New England' lectures, he had invoked a sense of national unity, he was now firmly 'contrast[ing] the Northern and Southern inhabitants of America' (Anon. 1848e: 5) and making a case for transatlantic solidarity between Old and New England in the face of looming sectional divisions at home. Emerson's former emphasis on America's Anglo-Saxon heritage remained strong throughout the Newcastle lecture, but it now served him to demonstrate to his audience the importance of an allegiance with the North. He would eventually see this effort fail when, a dozen years later, the animosity between North and South resulted in an armed conflict over the course of which British sympathies tended to lie with those who eagerly cultivated an Anglo-Saxonist rhetoric with which Emerson himself had by that point grown increasingly disenchanted.[16]

Anglo-American Cultural Diplomacy in the Later Lectures

When, upon his return to the United States, Emerson resumed lecturing in the winter of 1848–9, the subjects which he selected for treatment in the lecture hall for the time being remained informed by Anglo-Saxonist imagery. Backed by the success of his foreign lecture tour, he was eagerly awaited by domestic audiences that had been able to keep track of his performances abroad through domestic reprints of British lecture reports. Performing on English and Scottish stages, Emerson had, at the same time, been speaking to a virtual American audience. Newspapers and periodicals throughout the United States ran lecture summaries, offered correspondents' reports and reprinted character sketches of him, whetting their readers' appetite for his own account of his overseas adventure. Collecting material gathered during his time in Britain and arranging it for use in the American lecture hall (and later on the transatlantic print market), Emerson was thus cashing in on a large contemporary demand. From December 1848 onwards, he read four new lectures that kept him busy at the lectern over the years to come: 'England' (1848–52, 1854–6), 'London' (1849), 'The Anglo-American' (1852–5) and 'Poetry and English Poetry' (1854). In 'England' and 'London', first delivered less than half a year after his return, Emerson's memory of his experience as a transatlantic tourist is still fresh. Travel lectures were 'one of the most enduringly popular genres on the circuit' (Wright 2017: 36) and Emerson was following in the footsteps of successful colleagues. Yet where lecturers such as Bayard Taylor could boast of a first-hand acquaintance with Egypt, India or China, Emerson's subject matter was less obviously exotic – which goes some way towards explaining why he quickly abandoned the 'London' lecture, the most generic of the four, and instead focused on the other three.

He first delivered 'England' at the Concord Lyceum before taking it to Boston, New York, Cleveland and Montreal, along with other cities in the Northeast and Midwest, between December 1848 and April 1852, subsequently mining the manuscript for other lecturing engagements until 1856. Containing several subtle shifts of rhetoric that at one point situate English success at the apex of civilisational achievement and bewail its lack of spiritual energy at the next, 'England' is a profoundly ambivalent lecture that, in its structure, closely resembles the dramaturgy of both the 'Representative Men' lectures (which Emerson turned into a book while he was lecturing on English subjects) and the later *English Traits* – texts that mix praise and censure and often seem, as Tom F. Wright observes, to 'elevate only to undercut' (2017: 97). The surviving lecture manuscript begins with a dazzling assertion of English superiority that is followed by a catalogue of national advantages, from climate to natural resources to racial strength. In the climax of the first part of the lecture, Emerson refutes American nationalist celebrations of a decline of English power – an idea with which he had himself toyed in the Manchester speech – as premature and unwarranted: if anything, he suggests, 'London and England' were 'in full growth' (LL 1: 199).

This litany of praise comes to an abrupt halt after slightly more than half of the lecture, however, when Emerson begins to probe the darker aspects of British cultural and material abundance:

> It is not to be disguised that there is much in this English culture, so much prized at home, so much admired abroad, that will not bear analysis, – is by no means the best thing in the English state; is material; is built on wealth, built on trifles, and certainly has another less reputable face. (ibid., 202)

Indicating to Emerson an absence of spiritual refinement, England's global economic success in the further course of the lecture becomes its main blemish. This form of criticism opens a narrow argumentative path for Emerson to highlight the difference between Americans and Englishmen and to state his preference for the former rather than the latter. Praising American adventurousness over English inflexibility, the middle part of the lecture reconciles Emerson's domestic audiences through overriding the potentially damaging effect of his prior remarks about English excellence. While continuing strong in the economic field, contemporary Britain had become almost entirely devoid of what Emerson calls 'mental greatness', a shortcoming to which, in 'boast[ing] the grandeur of their national genius', the British seem curiously oblivious (ibid., 206).

Having himself indulged in such boasting at the beginning of the lecture, Emerson turns back to his initial eulogistic strain in a peroration that now, in turn, attempts to balance his more critical remarks. 'England' concludes with a vision strikingly similar to that formulated in the Manchester speech, which Emerson had given a year before the first delivery of the lecture. He begins by relativising American forecasts of England's imminent demise and then turns to a racially inflected image for the global diffusion of British political, legal and cultural authority:

> It is common to augur evil of England's future and to forbode her sudden or gradual decline under the load of debt, and pauperism, and the unequal competition with new nations where land is cheap. Certainly, she has enormous burthens to carry and grave difficulties to contend with. And her wisest statesmen incline to call her home from her immense

colonial system. But though she may yield to time and change, what a fate is hers! She has planted her banian roots in the ground, they have run under the sea, and the new shoots have sprung in America, in India, in Australia, and she sees the spread of her language and laws over the most part of the world made certain for as distant a future as the science of man can explore. (ibid., 209)

The idea of a survival of English strength in the United States was something that Emerson had already hinted at in the 'English Literature' series of 1835–6 and that he had spelled out with greater confidence in the course on 'New England'. What is new in the 'England' lecture is that he approaches the subject from a decidedly British colonialist vantage point, casting 'America' as just one among the Empire's many filial appendages. This hybridisation of the ideologies of American nationalism and British imperialism allowed him to resolve the lecture's argumentative inconsistencies into a Janus-faced narrative capable of appealing to audiences on both sides of the Atlantic.

The 'England' lecture occasioned a wide range of responses from different audiences in the United States (see Wright 2017: 81–112), but it also created a stir in Britain, where the early months of 1849 witnessed a series of reprintings of American summaries throughout the country. In early February, the *Nottingham Review* was the first paper to feature coverage of the lecture, picking up a report published in the *New-York Daily Tribune* a month before (which was itself a reprint of an earlier summary in the *Boston Post*). Taking their cue from the *Nottingham Review*, more than two dozen British papers published summaries of Emerson's lecture between February and April 1849.[17] Most of them were relying on the *Tribune* source text, a report that was eminently quotable in Britain to the extent that it featured little of Emerson's criticism of England while printing most of his praise. Of the original article's eleven paragraphs, only the final one intimates his reservations, with some British reprints omitting this passage altogether. Given Emerson's habit of continually reworking his lecture manuscripts, it is hard to tell whether the earlier renditions of 'England' were more uniformly positive than the version of the text printed in the critical edition of the lectures or whether newspaper reports of the 1848–9 performances actively downplayed his more openly critical remarks. Compared to the final state of the manuscript, the account of the lecture that, in early 1849, was circulating on both sides of the Atlantic reads like a bowdlerised representation of his more complex transatlantic argument, but this disambiguation of his message promised to be indeed even more effective, at least with British audiences.

In 'The Anglo-American', another one of the English-themed later lectures, Emerson himself recalibrated his position, but through amplifying rather than toning town his criticism of England. During its first deliveries on a tour of

Ohio, Missouri and Illinois in the 1852–3 season, the lecture ran under the title 'The Anglo-Saxon', but Emerson soon began to add further material about the United States. In its final manuscript state, 'The Anglo-American' is considerably less emphatic about English achievement than the earlier lecture on 'England' had been. Emerson's object of praise has changed, and he now speaks of America's (Mid)western energy with the same enthusiasm he had previously reserved for the English. While his usual language of Anglo-Saxon strength remains, he here distinguishes more categorically between Englishmen and Americans and their respective national characters, concluding with an assertion of domestic advantage that harked back to a rhetoric Emerson had last employed in 'The Young American':

> 'Tis doubtful whether London, whether Paris, whether Berlin can answer the questions which now rise in the American mind. American geography and vast population must be considered in all arrangements of commerce and politics, and we are forced, therefore, to make our own precedents. The radiation of character and manners here, the boundless America, gives opportunity as wide as the morning . . . (LL 1: 295)

Where, in 'England', the cultural centre of such 'radiation' had still been located on the other side of the ocean, in the later lecture Emerson seems to celebrate American self-isolation.

It is easy to overemphasise this shift of tone, however. Although a comparison between 'London', 'England' and 'The Anglo-American' implies a gradual turn away from an Anglophile deference induced by Emerson's recent memories of English splendour and towards a self-consciously affirmative Americanism that emerges in the early 1850s, this development was, in fact, hardly straightforward. Emerson clearly continued to differentiate between the demands of different performative contexts and to tailor his position on England and Englishness to what a given occasion required. Invited to address Montreal's St George's Society in 1852, he again mobilised the celebratory language that had marked his speech at the Manchester Athenæum and the beginning of the 'England' lecture (whose final performance in its original shape took place at the Montreal Mercantile Library Association just four days before the St George's speech). Appearing in front of an outspokenly Anglophile audience in a city in which the 1837–8 rebellion against British rule and the April 1849 burning of the local parliament had revealed a strong undercurrent of transatlantic tension, Emerson solemnly declared that 'we Americans feel our relation to England to be so strict, – we have kept our pedigree so pure, – that we praise very willingly England' (JMN 10: 507). Speaking as an Anglo-American to a congregation of Anglo-Canadians, he effortlessly returned to his earlier notion of the racial solidarity the British Empire inspired among its far-flung colonial subjects.

Speech and Audience in *English Traits*

If the 1847–8 lecture tour had provided Emerson with rich material for his North American speaking engagements in the late 1840s and early 1850s, these lectures were, in turn, only preparatory sketches for a larger project that culminated with the publication of *English Traits* in 1856. Using a range of different genres and styles, Emerson combined travel sketch, ethnographic description and cultural criticism to rework his English experience in book form. Although this commitment to print resulted in a form of textual permanence that contrasted with an earlier argumentative flexibility in the medium of public speech, orality at the same time remained an important component of the published book. Emerson concludes *English Traits* with a revised transcript of the speech he had given at Manchester close to a decade before, but he also inserts himself as a speaking subject in one of the earlier sections of the text. Resembling the Manchester speech in its reflections about the issue of transatlantic authority, the chapter in question recounts an excursion to Stonehenge that Emerson had undertaken in Carlyle's company in July 1848. This is the closest the book gets to the conventions of the travel writing genre, but interspersed with its scenic descriptions of the tour (first Stonehenge, then Salisbury and finally Winchester, with several stops in between), Emerson reports conversations with Carlyle that do not just revolve around touristic and antiquarian subjects but quickly return to the book's more general concern with national identity, 'character' and 'race' (*CW* 5: 154). The dialogical structure of the 'Stonehenge' chapter is reminiscent of Emerson's and Carlyle's transatlantic epistolary exchange, only that Emerson here has the textual authority to select and arrange the contributions. Based on journal entries composed during his stay in England, the conversations transcribed in 'Stonehenge' largely focus on the difference between Englishness and Americanness, with Emerson effectively casting himself and Carlyle as spokesmen for their respective countries. Although 'Stonehenge' is among the more personal chapters of Emerson's book – David Robinson calls it 'one of his most emotionally revealing essays' (1993: 120) – his framing of the questions at stake clearly indicates that the overall argument of the section has wider political and cultural implications.

Centring on an American's vocal defence against British accusations of inferiority, the chapter's moments of self-characterisation jar with the blatant Anglophilia of texts such as the 1852 Montreal address, but also with the more general scepticism about race and nationality that runs through much of the rest of the book itself. What I want to suggest here is that in turning *English Traits* into an argumentatively fractured multimedial text, Emerson systematically accommodated the demands of a mixed Anglo-American audience. Where, to British readers, the book's assertions of American potential could sound safely cushioned in the future tense and were accompanied by ample diplomatic praise of English achievements past and present, Emerson's eulogy of England was, in turn, ambiguous enough to be palatable to nationally minded American buyers of the book, who were being reassured of Emerson's patriotic credentials through his periodically resurfacing visions of a transatlantic transfer of power. Responding to the varied expectations of what Lawrence Buell has described as antebellum writers' 'transcontinental readership' (1992: 425), *English Traits* shows Emerson navigating the complex reception landscape of the mid-century Anglo-American literary sphere.

In the largely dialogical 'Stonehenge' chapter, his strategy revolves around counterbalancing Carlyle's critique of the United States while at the same time giving space to both sides of the argument. At the beginning of the chapter, Emerson recalls how, 'speaking of the Americans', Carlyle 'complained that they dislike the coldness and exclusiveness of the English' and fail to 'confron[t] Englishmen, and acquir[e] their culture, who really have much to teach them' (*CW* 5: 155). Disagreeing with this proposition, Emerson responds with a praise of English success that quickly morphs into a case for American leadership (an argumentative turn with which we are by now well familiar):

> I told C[arlyle] that I was . . . accustomed to concede readily all that an Englishman would ask; I saw everywhere in the country proofs of sense and spirit, and success of every sort: I like the people: they are as good as they are handsome; they have everything, and can do everything: but meantime, I surely know that, as soon as I return to Massachusetts, I shall lapse at once into the feeling, which the geography of America inevitably inspires, that we play the game with immense advantage; that there and not here is the seat and centre of the British race; and that no skill or activity can long compete with the prodigious natural advantages of that country, in the hands of the same race; and that England, an old and exhausted island, must one day be contented, like other parents, to be strong only in her children. (ibid.)

What Robinson describes as an Emersonian 'moment of prophetic speculation on the American future' (1993: 121) in fact develops a genealogical argument that works in several directions at once, assuring the British of their parental authority and the Americans of their youthful energy, ultimately comforting both parties with the idea that they are connected through family ties that allow for a sense of mutual entitlement to each other's past as well as future civilisational achievements.

Emerson plays the American nationalism card carefully enough not to hurt British feelings, but his tone is assertive nevertheless. Where he locates American leadership in the future tense ('one day . . .'), his idea that 'there [in the United States] and not here [in England] *is* the seat and centre of the British race' advances an American claim to authority that is rooted already in the present. The language of national pride that Emerson here deploys is reminiscent of the nationalist rhetoric he had used in 'The Young American' but largely abandoned afterwards. As Leslie Eckel has argued, by the mid-1850s his attitude towards the nation had become marked by a sense of sceptical distance. Reading the above passage from the 'Stonehenge' chapter, she registers a reluctance on Emerson's part to assume a nationalist point of view and suggests that speaking the language of national isolation to him was, at that point, hardly more than a 'lapse' into vestigial sentiments that had already become superseded by an enlightened cosmopolitan perspective. Since Emerson 'goes through the motions of American nationalist rhetoric' only ultimately to demonstrate its shallowness, Eckel contends, the vehemence with which he engages it in the chapter 'appears deliberately ironic' (2013: 108). Reading the same passage in much the same light, Andrew Taylor similarly finds in its tone of national confidence 'a form of reflexive ritual rather than living faith' (2004: 172). Yet in contrast to Eckel – who depicts the mature Emerson as motivated by the zeal of the cosmopolitan convert – Taylor describes *English Traits* as evidencing a more complex 'form of comparative criticism' that ultimately 'resists' argumentative 'resolution' (ibid., 171).

If the language of unconsciousness ('lapse') and compulsion ('inevitably') shows Emerson ironically distancing himself from the nation, what is notable about the passage – and *English Traits*, more generally – is not so much that it dispenses with culturalist discrimination altogether but that it exemplifies what Paul Giles has described as a 'deflection of the historical category of the nation into a more essentialized idiom of race' (2003: 68). Ultimately, however, it is neither the nation that becomes completely deconstructed nor the concept of racial identity that unambiguously takes its place. Rather than discarding the idea of the nation, Emerson mobilises different manifestations of it – with race providing a flexible signifier whose invocation allows both for a conciliatory rhetoric of transatlantic kinship and for an authorising narrative that underwrites the claim of an Anglo-American transition of power.[18] The chapter's reference to the United States as 'the seat and centre of the British race' suggests an inversion of the colonial centre/periphery dichotomy, but Emerson's vision of a westward migration of authority from English 'parents' to American 'children' ultimately hinges on a larger notion of transatlantic genealogy and inheritance.[19]

The argumentative confrontation that results from Emerson's juxtaposition of Carlyle's cross-examination of American future potential with his own defence of it is balanced by his adoption of a *longue durée* perspective upon encountering Stonehenge itself. Contemplating the Neolithic stone circle evokes in Emerson an acute sense of the vastness of the past, a feeling of historical sublimity that relativises the nineteenth-century nation-state through an awareness of what Wai Chee Dimock has theorised as cultural 'deep time' (2001) – a large-scale temporal horizon that allows for a comparative vantage point and illustrates the non-essentialist nature of modern national identity. Stonehenge, Emerson suggests, moved his and Carlyle's 'petty differences of nationality out of sight': 'To these conscious stones we two pilgrims were alike known and near. We could equally well revere their old British meaning' (CW 5: 157). In the original journal passage on which this section of the chapter is based, Emerson had described the monument's mediating function even more explicitly when he wrote that '[t]hey understood the English language these British stones of the two talkers one from America one from Scotland who came up to this old ark of the race' (JMN 10: 431).

Stonehenge makes Emerson realise the permanence of physical records of the past and it in turn reduces his and Carlyle's dispute over transatlantic authority to the status of a mere exchange between 'two talkers', a dialogue that the ephemeral nature of oral discourse ultimately renders insignificant. To the extent that, like the 'conscious stones', the concrete materiality of the printed book freezes the fluid 'language' and 'meaning' of speech into a textual solidity that remains intact across time and space, Stonehenge here becomes a metaphor for *English Traits* itself. Where, in conversation and on stage, Emerson can insist on national particularity, the petrified medium of print calls for a more capacious mindset. As Stonehenge in its material permanence has remained legible to both Emerson and Carlyle, so the book seeks to come 'near' to its readers on both sides of the Atlantic through adopting an argumentative stance that – rather than being either American or English – is 'British' in a transatlantically comprehensive sense. For this strategy to succeed, however, both the description of the monument and the orientation of the book as a whole rely on a reinvestment in a unifying discourse of race. Where Stonehenge on the one hand erases markers of national difference that are meaningful only in the context of Emerson and Carlyle's nineteenth-century present, on the other hand it leaves modern notions of ethnic or racial identity essentially intact. The chapter, if anything, reinforces a belief in the existence of distinctive biological and cultural traits through describing these as persistent across large stretches of time. The 'meaning' of the 'stones' remains recognisably 'British' rather than transculturally transparent, just as Emerson in his book addresses a specifically Anglophone rather than a genuinely global readership.

The concluding chapter of *English Traits*, a version of Emerson's November 1847 speech at Manchester, takes its readers back both to the beginning of the British lecture tour and to the genre of the public speech event. This allows Emerson to return to the idea of a transatlantic transfer of authority that he had formulated in the opening sections of the 'Stonehenge' chapter. Like the initial response to Carlyle in the earlier chapter, the final paragraph of the book combines an assertion of American future potential with a eulogy to past English achievement:

> And so, gentlemen, I feel in regard to this aged England, with the possessions, honors and trophies, and also with the infirmities of a thousand years gathering around her, irretrievably committed as she now is to many old customs which cannot be suddenly changed; pressed upon by the transitions of trade, and new and all incalculable modes, fabrics, arts, machines, and competing populations, – I see her not dispirited, not weak. . . . I see her in her old age, not decrepit, but young, and still daring to believe in her power of endurance and expansion. Seeing this, I say, All hail! mother of nations, mother of heroes, with strength still equal to the time . . . (CW 5: 177)

Readers of *English Traits* here encounter what Taylor describes as 'a public voice . . . more formal and celebratory than that of the slippery commentator of the book proper' (2004: 173). But while Emerson diplomatically concedes that it will continue to be dominant for some time to come, his litotic commendation of England as 'not dispirited' and 'not decrepit' paves the way for the book's final sentence, which spells out an American claim to the future leadership of 'the English race' (*JMN* 10: 335). Where, in the 'Stonehenge' chapter, Emerson had alerted his readers to the 'honors and trophies' of an accumulated English past, he now switches gears to move from British senescence to American 'elasticity':

> If it be not so, if the courage of England goes with the chances of a commercial crisis, I will go back to the capes of Massachusetts, and my own Indian stream, and say to my countrymen, the old race are all gone, and the elasticity and hope of mankind must henceforth remain on the Alleghany ranges, or nowhere. (CW 5: 177)

Even if conditional, the final sentence and the passage that leads up to it still strongly envisage an American inheritance of English power. To the extent that it dispenses with the idea of transatlantic racial continuity, the book's concluding statement is even more radical than the version of the same idea that features in the 'Stonehenge' chapter. Where usually, in *English Traits* and elsewhere, race is what persists even when Emerson covers larger geographical and historical ground, in the book's final chapter race and nation are welded into one (with an obsolete England virtually synonymous with 'the old race'). But where, in concluding the book on such a note, Emerson came close to permanently disambiguating his own message in favour of an affirmative Americanism, his structural decision to do so in the context of a transcribed speech at the same time opened an argumentative loophole that allowed him to soften the radicalism of his remarks through implicitly pointing back beyond the printed book to the situational mutability of oral discourse.

If print called for greater semantic 'elasticity' than lecturing, this also manifested itself in different reception environments. The specific performative backdrop of the individual public speech event tended to create a uniform reaction – the '[l]oud applause' contemporary newspapers had reported as the unanimous opinion of the original Manchester audience – where print provided for a number of different, potentially contradictory responses.[20] The numerous readers and reviewers *English Traits* found in Britain and the United States disagreed over whether Emerson had praised or denigrated the English.[21] Robert E. Burkholder notes that in Britain the book was mainly seen as an insult to Englishness whereas American readers, by and large, complained that it was too laudatory of its subject matter (1982: 166). While this seems to illustrate the apparent failure of Emerson's attempt to meet the expectations of a transatlantic audience, in fact the two lines of interpretation that Burkholder identifies were divided not so much by nation as they were along political or regional fault lines. British radical and liberal papers and magazines were mostly more generous in their reviews than the conservative press, and in the United States Northern readings were generally more favourable than Southern ones. A number of major American periodicals celebrated Emerson for putting the British in their place. *Harper's Magazine*, for example, summarised that '[t]he general impression of England' the book provided was 'favorable' but 'by no means flattering' and that, while Emerson 'regard[ed] England as the best of actual nations', he had nevertheless ultimately depicted it as 'poor and imperfect' (Anon. 1856a: 694). In Britain, the *Westminster Review* at the same time commended the book as an American's 'friendly and honest tribute' to England, a diplomatic achievement destined to create a 'cordial understanding between all sections of the Anglo-Saxon race' (Anon. 1856b: 495, 514). If such an understanding of the book as a text that consistently celebrates the English becomes plausible only through the *Westminster*'s steady refusal to read between the lines, it was, after all, an interpretation which – just like its obverse – the transatlantically versatile prose of *English Traits* itself actively invited. The book could hence be seen by a self-consciously American audience as an exposure of English flaws and simultaneously become Emerson's biggest success with nineteenth-century British readers.

Notes

1. Emerson had dedicated two of the ten lectures of his 1835–6 Boston course on 'English Literature' to Shakespeare and returned to the topic in his series on 'Representative Men', first delivered in the 1845–6 winter season. Versions of this later Shakespeare lecture appear a total of ten times on Emerson's schedule

during his British trip (see Scudder 1936 and Koch 2012: 140) (it was eventually published together with the six other instalments of the course in 1850).
2. I have discussed Emerson's complex transatlantic treatment of Shakespeare in greater detail elsewhere (see Sommer 2018). By the mid-1840s, Emerson was adept enough at anticipating the sensibilities of his composite Anglo-American audiences simply to recycle his American 'Representative Men' manuscripts on the British lecture circuit and later have textually identical versions of the texts published in Boston and London simultaneously. British transcripts of the Shakespeare lecture (see, for example, Anon. 1847d and Anon. 1847e) correspond to the text of the 1850 book almost verbatim.
3. On the continuities between Emerson's earlier career as a Unitarian preacher and his subsequent reinvention as a prophetic presence on the 'secular' lecture circuit, see the classic studies by David Robinson (1982) and Wesley T. Mott (1989).
4. Founded three years earlier, the London Society for the Diffusion of Useful Knowledge was catering more to a lower-class audience. Aiming 'to educate its members in the professional and mercantile pursuits rather than in the mechanical ones', the Boston Society was 'the most patrician' among the city's mid-century lecturing institutions (Deese and Woodall 1986: 17).
5. At the same time, however, Emerson appropriated the pragmatic and commercial orientation of the institutional framework in which he was performing to provide a markedly materialist account of literary and cultural history (on this aspect of the lectures, see Dolan 2009: 257–61).
6. See Cayton 1987 and Augst 2003: 114–57. Just as Simmons argues that Emerson detranscendentalised himself with the 'New England' series, Cayton suggests that it was through 'a bourgeois mercantile audience' that, in the 1840s and 1850s, he 'began to be seen not primarily as a religious or literary figure but as something else' (1987: 604). The implicit claim behind Cayton's argument is that Emerson's authority gradually shifted from that of a spiritual leader (either sacral–ministerial or secular–aesthetic) to that of a provider of ethical and commercial advice. From the perspective of my argument, such different sources for the ascription of his authority do not simply replace one another but become mutually sustaining. What Cayton describes as Emerson's credibility as a commentator on the capitalist 'conduct of life' crucially depended on a common knowledge of his background in the domain of literary disinterestedness, just as his emergence as a 'literary figure' in the 1830s had hinged on the continuities between religious and secular forms of public speaking.
7. Emerson's Anglo-Saxon rhetoric was also beginning to seep into the language of his popular reception. Emphasising America's cultural emergence from its mythical racial origins, he was increasingly perceived as an exemplary representative of that very heritage, with newspapers characterising him as a 'master of pure English' whose style was marked by the 'use of good, old, terse, Saxon words' (Anon. 1843a: 2; Anon. 1843b: 2). See Chapter 1 for a more extensive discussion of the larger cultural logic behind such verdicts.
8. See Haynes 1997 on American fears of British involvement in the Texas question during the first half of the 1840s. Reflecting on the problem of American territorial expansion, Emerson at times resigned himself to the racialist determinism that features prominently in the 'English Literature' and the 'New England' series. Writing

on '[t]he question of the annexation of Texas' in his journal, he remarked: 'It is very certain that the strong British race which have now overrun so much of this continent, must also overrun that tract, & Mexico & Oregon also, and it will in the course of ages be of small import by what particular occasions & methods it was done' (*JMN* 9: 74). Critical evaluations of this passage differ in their assessment of Emerson's stance on expansion. Paul Giles points to the 'irony in Emerson attributing the overthrow of the British government's interest in the Oregon Country to the advance of a "strong British race" in North America', an Emersonian phrase that 'suggests how popular typological classifications of Anglo-Saxon racial characteristics in the mid-nineteenth century could not obviate the more immediate political antagonisms within this Anglo-Saxon world' (2006: 84). Where to Giles Emerson 'chose to justify Manifest Destiny by explaining it to himself as an inevitable phenomenon' (ibid.), Johannes Voelz, drawing attention to the passage that immediately follows the above, points out that Emerson 'deems resistance' to expansionism 'indispensable nonetheless' (2010: 232). The critical debate about the extent of Emerson's endorsement of expansionism is a complex one, ranging from indictment to exculpation (for the former, see, for example, Rowe 2003; for a tendency towards the latter, see Buell 2010; see Voelz 2010: 180–9 on the debate more generally).
9. See Chapter 2 for a more detailed discussion of this aspect of 'The Poet' and Chapter 4 for an account of the English publication history of *Essays: Second Series*.
10. Townsend Scudder was among the first to emphasise the importance of the British lecture tour (see 1935a and 1935b). William Sowder's (1966) research into Emerson's British reception added further depth to the historical data compiled by Scudder. More recent work on the topic has followed more specific lines of enquiry, such as Larry Reynolds's account of how Emerson's politics changed as a result of his exposure to revolutionary radicalism in Paris and to Chartism in London (1988: 25–43), or David Robinson's (2010) interest in Emerson's experience of British natural science. The most extensive treatment of the 1847–8 tour is Daniel Koch's *Ralph Waldo Emerson in Europe* (2012), which reconstructs Emerson's lecturing activity and sheds light on its prehistory and aftermath. My own focus in the following is on the nationalised terms of Emerson's reception in Britain and on the nature of his statements about England and America during and after the tour.
11. The phrase was coined by the High Church *English Review*, which – troubled by what it described as the pernicious influence of Emerson's writings – noted that they had long been 'reproduced in every possible form, and at the most tempting prices', enjoying a 'wide circulation . . . amongst the English public' (Anon. 1849d: 139).
12. Compare also Chapter 3, where I describe in greater detail how contemporary American critics attempted to appropriate essentially the same logic, using Carlyle's success in the United States to demonstrate the sophistication of their domestic taste.
13. Sometimes he simply figured as 'Emerson, the American' (Anon. 1848c: 6), a reference occasionally more generously premodified to 'this distinguished American' (Anon. 1847i: 6). While everyone seemed to agree that Emerson was adequately defined through his Americanness, there was less unanimity when it came to specifying the nature of his professional expertise. Some journalists thought of him as chiefly a philosopher – 'the great American thinker' (Anon. 1848b: 7) or 'the philosopher

of America' (Anon. 1847h: 5) – while others presented him as a renowned published writer, 'the celebrated transatlantic essayist and poet' (Anon. 1847b: 5).

14. Douglass's transatlantic lecturing has been analysed extensively over the past decade (see, for example, Bennett 2011, Eckel 2013: 71–98, Wright 2017: 49–80 and Murray 2020: 81–122).
15. The responses that Emerson's speech elicited in the British press were, at best, moderately challenging. Rejoicing in his Saxonist rhetoric, an essay in the January 1848 issue of the *Westminster and Foreign Quarterly Review*, for example, hailed Emerson as a 'brave . . . representative of our Transatlantic race' and begged to differ from him only in emphasising that '"[t]he hope and elasticity of mankind" shall continue to exist here, even as they shall "beyond the ranges of the Alleghanies"' (Adams 1848: 417).
16. On the development of Emerson's transatlantic cultural commentary during the Civil War years, see the Epilogue. Hanlon 2013 provides a comprehensive discussion of the shifting currencies of a reliance on transatlantic sentiment among writers in the North and the South as the two sections of the country were drifting apart.
17. The *Nottingham Review* reprint was first taken up by papers across the Midlands and northern England, where Emerson had done most of his lecturing a year before and where editors were likely anticipating a large interest in his comments (further northern and Scottish papers soon followed the trend). The text finally reached the capital in mid-March, with republication in the *Examiner*, the *Times* and the *Evening Mail*. There were several further, mainly northern, reprints of the lecture report before the wave eventually subsided in mid-April. The London reprints are mentioned by Joseph Slater (see *CEC* 453–4) and by Ronald A. Bosco and Joel Myerson (see *LL* 1: 192), but neither of these brief accounts provides a sense of the full extent of the British circulation of summaries of Emerson's performance. Similarly relying on the metropolitan coverage, Wright has described the British debate about the lecture and drawn attention to the fact that this was, in turn, covered by American papers (2017: 98–9).
18. See Chapter 1 for a more extensive exploration of the ways in which *English Traits* deals with questions of race and racial identity. See also Hanlon 2013: 17–40, a reading that offers a detailed discussion of the book against the background of an antebellum 'deliberation over Anglo-American bloodlines' (21).
19. Drawing on Robert Weisbuch's description of *English Traits* as a consistent defence of 'American ascendancy' (1999: 211), Marek Paryz detects in the book a form of 'postcolonial counter-discourse' that, to him, suggests that 'the colonial legacy' was profoundly 'troubling for Emerson' (2006: 566). My reading, by contrast, understands *English Traits* not as the result of an Emersonian 'compulsion to produce . . . oppositional texts' (ibid.) but as his way of inscribing the United States into a shared narrative of transatlantic authority precisely through emphasising – rather than rejecting – legacy and history.
20. What this suggests is that the medium through which Emerson was voicing his positions had a profound impact on how they were being understood, an impact that could, at times, matter more than the actual content of his statements (the two passages from *English Traits* cited above are largely identical with the original Manchester speech as reported in the contemporary newspaper transcripts from which I quote in the third section of this chapter).

21. The book was published in Boston by Phillips and Sampson and in London by George Routledge in the late summer of 1856. The American edition went through another two printings the same year, which brought the total number of volumes in circulation to 6,000. Routledge issued four printings in 1856, each of which comprised 6,000 copies (see Myerson 1982: 241–9) – a print run that was considerable compared both to those of Emerson's earlier British publications (see Chapter 4) and to the contemporary British average of about 3,000 copies per new title (see Weedon 2003: 49).

6

(DE-)AUTHORISING ELOQUENCE: CARLYLE AND TRANSATLANTIC PUBLIC SPEECH

Carlyle's career as a lecturer was both significantly shorter and geographically more narrowly circumscribed than Emerson's. His readiness in the late 1830s to assume this new professional identity, Richard Salmon has pointed out, 'was the result of a self-conscious decision to move away from his dependence on periodical writing in the absence of a reliable method of book publication' (2013: 46). When publishing eventually became a financially viable occupation, Carlyle was quick to turn his back on lecturing. It was only during about a decade of his professional life that he seriously contemplated the genre of the lecture performance as a supplement to – or, at his most radical, as a possible substitute for – writing. A notebook entry of October 1831 is among the earliest of his reflections on oratorical self-expression:

> Serious thoughts are rising in me about the possibility of attempting a *Course of Lectures* here. The subject should be 'Things in general' (under some more dignified title): but as yet the ground is quite unknown to me; the whole process *towards* the *cathedra*, even much of the process *there* lies hidden. Let me look and study. –
> What are the uses, what is the special province of *oral* teaching at present? Wherein superior to the written or *printed* mode, and when? – For one thing, as I can see, London is fit for no higher *Art* than that of Oratory: they understand nothing of Art; scarcely one of them anything at all. – But hast *thou* any Eloquence? *Ja wohl, ein klein weniges*, were my tongue once *untacked*. *Ach, dass es so wäre!* (NTC 212–13)

In condensed form, this passage contains the key themes around which Carlyle's thought about lecturing and public speaking would revolve in the following decade and beyond. The question of disciplinary specialisation is crucial among the series of professional anxieties that surface here. The notebook passage also foreshadows Carlyle's persistent performative insecurity about his ability to speak on stage and connect to a live audience. Coupled to these doubts was a concern with occupational hierarchy that would resurface in Carlyle's later writing on eloquence and that, already in the early 1830s, shows him apprehensive about the limited prestige of 'Oratory' as opposed to the value of other, 'higher' forms of '*Art*' – 'the written or *printed* mode', in particular.

When Carlyle decided to take on the role of public speaker later in the decade, his lecturing practice differed from Emerson's in that he appeared on stage in a single city only (metropolitan London) and in that his audiences in large part hailed from the ranks of the bourgeoisie and the aristocracy. Despite the narrow social and geographical sphere within which his actual experience as a lecturer was confined, Carlyle nevertheless imagined himself as speaking to a wide transatlantic public. As I argue in the first and second sections of this chapter, the idea of lecturing in – or even emigrating to – the United States was an escapist fiction of key importance for him insofar as it allowed him to contemplate a vast potential audience eager to recognise him as a prophet but also to envision an alternative career to that of the man of letters – one that he imagined would be possible only in an environment radically different from that to which he was accustomed at home. When, in the mid-1830s, Carlyle fantasised about touring the United States as an itinerant lecturer, unlike Emerson he not only had no experience of transatlantic travel but he also had none at the lectern. This would soon change, of course. Turning to the four lecture series he gave in London between 1837 and 1840, the chapter's third section isolates differences and similarities between the modalities of Carlyle's imaginary American tour and his actual practice, while at the same time pointing to the role contemporary lecture reporting played in making his performances transatlantically legible. The two final parts of the chapter consider Carlyle's post-lecturing writings of the 1840s and 1850s and retrace the – often transatlantic – critique of public speaking that he advanced in them.

Lecturing in Virtual America

For Victorian intellectuals, travelling to and lecturing in the United States was an endeavour that promised financial compensation as well as ethnological insight into a culture at once foreign and familiar. Several of Carlyle's British friends experienced nineteenth-century America first-hand and subsequently mined their impressions through publishing accounts of them. Harriet Martineau – novelist, social theorist and political economist – had toured the United States for two years, and upon her return to England published both the quasi-Tocquevillean

Society in America (1837) and the more conversational *Retrospect of Western Travel* (1838). Dickens toured and lectured in North America in 1842 and reworked his experiences into *American Notes for General Circulation*, which appeared later the same year, causing a stir in the transatlantic literary field.[1] Trying to convince Carlyle to come to the United States, Emerson had written to him in April 1835, emphasising that '[a]t worst, if you wholly disliked us, and preferred Old England to New, . . . you might . . . pay all your expenses by printing in England a book of travels in America' (*CEC* 125). Like Martineau's and Dickens's books, Emerson's own *English Traits* two decades later would cash in on a large demand for the kind of blend between transatlantic travel writing and cultural criticism that proved popular with British and American readers in the second third of the century. A prolific writer with a gift for trenchant social commentary, Carlyle might well have thrived in the genre. Although he eventually chose not to undertake the journey that could have provided him with the ethnographic detail required in order to be able to write such a book, the idea remained almost constantly on his mind during his late thirties and early forties.

From the very beginning of their correspondence in the summer of 1834 up until the early 1840s, Carlyle and Emerson repeatedly sounded the possibility of his coming to the United States. It was lecturing that, in most instances, featured as the express purpose of these projected visits. The epistolary exchange records a permanent back and forth of invitations and rejections. Already before Emerson entered the scene, Carlyle had contemplated not just a transatlantic tour but a potential emigration to the United States as a means of escaping Scottish poverty – an idea that first appears in his letters in 1833, a few months before Emerson's visit to Craigenputtock and about a year before his first message to Carlyle. What the American's invitation added to his own thoughts about the transatlantic passage was an element of volition. From 1834 onwards, travelling to the United States for Carlyle was no longer a form of exile into which domestic misery forced him; it increasingly became a business speculation whose advantages and disadvantages he could safely calculate from a distance. Emerson was fuelling Carlyle's expectations over a period of many years. He encouraged him as early as November 1834 to '[c]ome & found a new Academy' in New England. 'If you cared to read literary lectures', he specified, 'our people have vast curiosity & the apparatus is very easy to set agoing.' Himself only a neophyte in the profession, Emerson promised Carlyle to 'send . . . any & all particulars of information with cheerfullest speed', should he be inclined to 'think of coming here' (*CEC* 110).

There were several points in the 1830s at which Carlyle seriously thought about an American lecture tour, the first half of 1835 being a key phase. Discouraged by the poor British reception of *Sartor Resartus* and struggling with the composition of *The French Revolution*, Carlyle grew increasingly disillusioned with London life and was beginning to look for alternatives. In early

February, he responded to Emerson's offer to send details about a potential American lecture tour, asking him to

> take the business into your consideration, and give me in the most rigorous sober manner you can some scheme of it: How *many* Discourses; what Towns; the probable Expenses, the probable net Income, the Time &c &c, all that you can suppose a man wholly ignorant might want to know about it. America I should like well enough to visit; much as I should another part of my native country: it is as you see distinctly possible that such a thing might be . . . (ibid., 117–18)

Emerson's promise of a 'convertible audience' was apparently not enough to convince Carlyle to cross the Atlantic (ibid., 110). He requested a tangible estimate of what kind of financial benefit could be expected from such a scheme. At the same time, however, the February 1835 letter shows him clearly eager to demonstrate his general readiness to come, framed as his request for further business details is by a declaration of transatlantic kinship and an acknowledgement of his desire to perform in the New England lecture hall. In late April, Emerson provided Carlyle with the detailed information about the American lecture system he had requested. Having himself, by that time, gained some experience as a professional speaker, he praised the intellectual cultivation of local lyceum audiences ('Boston contains some genuine taste for literature' [ibid., 122]) before offering an account of living expenses and the estimated income to be netted from a lecture tour (implicitly offering himself as Carlyle's lecturing agent even before he assumed the role of his American print representative).

A contradictory pattern emerges in Carlyle's correspondence over the months that followed. Where to Emerson he replied in a cautious and generally evasive manner, in letters to family and friends at home the transatlantic venture became something of a more concrete proposition. Writing to his mother in early June, Carlyle summarised Emerson's suggestion in sympathetic terms as 'a project chalked out for passing a winter over the water, and *lecturing* there' (*CL* 8: 129). To John Sterling he confided at around the same time that his 'continuance in London has of late days become more uncertain, the America speculation having suddenly received a more practical form' (ibid., 140). Later that month he informed Emerson that 'this winter I ought not to go', although he continued to express his interest in the idea. Once again professing a strong sense of transatlantic belonging ('New England is as much my country and home as Old England'), he envisaged himself in ministerial fashion as speaking to his imaginary New England congregation ('I could preach a very considerable quantity of things from that Boston Pulpit') (*CEC* 134–5). Less than a week after telling Emerson that he would not be travelling in the immediate future, in a letter to his brother John

Carlyle sounded almost as though his departure for America were imminent, the image of himself as pontificating from above again taking centre stage in his thoughts about the potential tour ('I really could go . . . and open my mouth in Boston to that strange audience' [*CL* 8: 172]). Although in his letters to Emerson Carlyle was at that time generally reluctant to express his commitment, the promise of a new audience at once exotically provincial ('strange') and culturally refined (equipped with a 'taste' that, according to Emerson, was 'genuine' rather than philistine) nevertheless strongly appealed to him.

It was only over the course of the months that followed that the intentions Carlyle expressed in his domestic and his transatlantic correspondence finally converged around a rejection of the scheme. Writing to George Ripley in August 1835, he once more mobilised the image of transatlantic kinship in the abstract, only to postpone an actual visit to his American 'brethren':

> [A]s Emerson may have explained to you, I entertain always the project of looking on America one day, where now year after year I hear of new friends awaiting me. It is very 'romantic' as they call it, and yet it is very just & true; brethren of the same blood, separated only by a piece of salt water (which they are learning to cross) . . . ! Let us love one another, and forward one another as we can, as it is commanded us. . . . He & I had some correspondence about my coming to Boston this very winter. I have written him, (if I remember) two letters about it; the last full of mere uncertainty, but promising another so soon as there came any clearness. Will you tell him that it seems to be as good as settled, that I shall *not* get across this winter . . . (*CL* 8: 191–2)

To Ripley Carlyle once again voiced doubts about the feasibility of an American lecture tour, but he did the same in a letter to his mother in December, clinging to the idea as a remote option yet renouncing any definite plans for the near future: 'America we will leave as the *last* shift; so long as the bowls will roll here at all in a tolerable way, I will keep on this side the water' (ibid., 278).

Confronted with mounting performative anxieties about his first London lecture series and exhausted from work on the final volume of *The French Revolution*, Carlyle in early 1837 again began to indulge in the escapist fiction – the 'mad prophetic dream' – of going to the United States (*CEC* 105). What he imagined as in store for himself this time, however, was neither a lecture tour nor the kind of transatlantic recognition of his intellectual abilities that he had previously understood such a venture to entail. Where his original hope had been that the United States would reveal itself as a section of the Anglo-American literary sphere sophisticated enough to show an interest in his writings and acknowledge him as a prophet (neither of which his British audiences were offering at the time),

Carlyle now entertained the idea of renouncing his career as a man of letters altogether. Shifting focus from genteel New England to the landscapes west of it, he envisaged an alternative America as the setting for this professional transformation. Carlyle's plans for a potential transatlantic relocation turned from business speculation into anti-intellectual frontier romance. '[W]henever I think of myself in America', he told Emerson in February, 'it is as in the Backwoods, with a rifle in my hand' (ibid., 159). Reminiscing about the late 1830s some three decades later, he reverted to the same rhetoric of savagery and empowerment. In a summary of his struggle with *The French Revolution* which forms part of the memoir of his wife that he wrote in the summer of 1866, Carlyle remembers that his 'feeling was, "I will finish this Book, throw it at your feet; buy a rifle and spade, and withdraw to the Transatlantic Wildernesses, – far from *human* beggaries and basenesses!"' (*Rem* 93).

The image of the rough American west that Carlyle conjured up in both his letters and his later recollections represents the radical antithesis of the culturally hyper-refined and economically over-developed Britain that, from the late 1820s onwards, he increasingly perceived as mindless and oppressive. The epitome of what Jonathan Arac has called Carlyle's 'mythic sense of America' (1979: 145), the idea of the 'Transatlantic Wildernesses' was a symbolic rejection both of his cultural background and of his metropolitan identity. The primitivist imagery he employed was moving within the limits of a conventional European discourse that framed the United States as a largely uncivilised sphere – the 'utopian space of naturalness' as which North American geography figured 'in the Victorian cultural imagination' (Epstein 2000: 108). Fantasising about 'Natty Leatherstocking's Lodge in the Western Wood' as a potential refuge, Carlyle was also taking his cue from literary representations of American frontier life, which a thriving transatlantic print culture had helped to circulate among British readers (*CEC* 188). The fictional world of Cooper's novels evoked an imaginary geography whose alleged lack of cultural distinction Carlyle could envisage as encouraging more authentic modes of life, as a setting whose pastoral simplicity seemed capable of counterbalancing the downsides of industrial modernity that British intellectuals of his generation were witnessing at home.

In order to become rhetorically effective, Carlyle's vision of the American 'Backwoods' thus depended on a strong contrast between a metropolitan Britain and a peripherally rural United States. This distinction between English modernity and American wilderness followed a more general pattern that also informed his juxtaposition between his London life and his previous rural seclusion in the Scottish countryside. Located 'solitary in the wilderness', his Dumfriesshire retreat often featured in his correspondence in similar terms (ibid., 104). The transatlantic parallel is spelled out in a letter to Emerson of June 1837, in which Carlyle speaks in equal terms of 'the Back-woods, of America or Craigenputtock' (ibid., 166). Triangulating transatlantic cultural spaces, Carlyle here aligned the Scottish and the American 'Wildernesses' and their premodern temporalities to contrast them with an urban modernity he cast as representatively English. The vision of the transatlantic backcountry rested on a strategy of cultural exoticisation that ran counter to Carlyle's usual emphasis on Anglo-American commonality. If both spheres were indeed so fundamentally similar as to be 'separated only by a piece of salt water', as Carlyle had written to Ripley two years before, the United States hardly qualified as a refuge from the English problems of mass poverty, working-class rioting and a crisis of political authority that Carlyle denounced with increasing vehemence from 'Signs of the Times' (1829) onwards. Where previously, he had stressed that he could not resolve to come to the United States in spite of a strong sense of transatlantic similarity, in the late 1830s he began to suggest that America's potential therapeutic effect for him hinged on its cultural difference.

The contrast that Carlyle at that period constructed between the English and the American scenes was closely tied to his professional identity as a writer and lecturer. With '[a]ll honest . . . means of *livelihood* . . . shut against [him] in the old world', emigration to the United States entailed not simply a change of place but also a process of occupational reorientation (Carlyle 1974: 86). The kind of work that Carlyle thought of as congenial to the American 'wilderness' was precisely not that of the literary intellectual. He instead imagined himself as a hunter and builder, roaming the frontier with 'rifle and spade' rather than pen or voice as his professional tools. In their most radical form, such moments of pastoral melancholia were linked to an acute scepticism about the value of mental labour. As I will show in the second half of this chapter, the terms of this early vocational crisis would continue to resonate in Carlyle's later writing on eloquence and the public sphere.

British Imperialism and the Rhetoric of Emigration

In the late 1830s, Carlyle imagined the United States as an archaic society unaffected by the relentlessness of the capitalist labour market, a utopian setting in which industry met with just remuneration ('the man that is willing to work in America is sure of fair recompense for it' [*CL* 9: 210]). This vision was obviously inspired by the western rather than the north-eastern part of the country. Altogether too similar to the contemporary Britain from which Carlyle was hoping to escape, New England seemed to him merely 'a new Commercial England', characterised by '[t]he same unquenchable, almost frightfully unresting spirit of endeavour, directed . . . to the making of money' (*CEC* 117). His symbolic rejection of Victorian England was hence also a turn away from the Anglicised American north-east. He agreed with many contemporary British commentators (and, for that matter, with many American nationalists) in suggesting that what was quintessentially American was to be found not in New England's Anglophile postcolonial mentality but in the expansive space beyond, in those parts of the continent that were removed from British influence and authority both geographically and symbolically.

While Carlyle eventually neither travelled nor relocated to the United States, the idea nevertheless remained with him over the years that followed. His younger brother Alexander, who had struggled to earn a living as a farmer in rural Scotland, left for the United States in 1843 and later settled in Canada, which strengthened Carlyle's ties with North America and gave an added literal meaning to his invocations of transatlantic brotherhood. Yet the topic of relocation was more than a matter of private concern for him in the late 1830s and early 1840s. In some of the texts written during that period – in *Chartism* (1840) and *Past and Present* (1843), in particular – Carlyle argued in more systematic terms that emigration could solve the problem of overpopulation and relieve a new kind of mass poverty that resulted from an industrialised economy increasingly less reliant on manual labour. In both texts, emigration features as a 'safety-valve' capable of pacifying a charged contemporary political climate (*CL* 6: 373). *Chartism* and *Past and Present* are firmly rooted in a larger contemporary British debate about emigration and settler colonialism, and Carlyle was hardly alone in linking these subjects to a more far-reaching vision of Anglo-Saxon expansion that merged what Stephen Fender has called 'the paradisal and the colonial branches' of transatlantic 'emigration rhetoric' (1992: 11).[2] Edward Gibbon Wakefield, one of the chief English theorists of imperialist expansion at mid-century, emphasised that, in view of a British labour surplus and an American 'excess of land', 'the Americans and the English have a common interest in understanding the art of colonization' (1833, 1: vi).

The expansionist underpinnings of such a rhetoric of 'common interest' were fully developed already in *Chartism*, which concludes with Carlyle surveying 'on the west and on the east green desert spaces never yet made white with corn' and registering that 'to the overcrowded little western nook of Europe, our Terrestrial Planet, nine-tenths of it yet vacant or tenanted by nomads, is still crying, Come and till me, come and reap me!' (*CE* 29: 203). In the slightly later *Past and Present* Carlyle campaigned for a 'free bridge for Emigrants' that would facilitate an exchange of people as well as goods and form a market for labour and commodities at once globally extensive and ethnically particularised:

> Our little Isle is grown too narrow for us; but the world is wide enough yet for another Six Thousand Years. England's sure markets will be among new Colonies of Englishmen in all quarters of the Globe. . . . [T]he Sons of England, speakers of the English language were it nothing more, will in all times have the ineradicable predisposition to trade with England. Mycale was the *Pan-Ionian*, rendezvous of all the Tribes of Ion, for old Greece: why should not London long continue the *All-Saxonhome*,

rendezvous of all the 'Children of the Harz-Rock,' arriving in select samples, from the antipodes and elsewhere, by steam and otherwise, to the 'season' here! (*WTC* 4: 262–3)

Carlyle's vision is primarily that of a mercantile empire of free trade, but one in which the 'ineradicable predisposition[s]' of cultural heritage and racial belonging function as markers of inclusion and exclusion. The Hellenic imagery that surfaces both here and in the letters that Carlyle was writing to Emerson at around the same time served him to develop the idea of an Anglo-Saxon civilisation modelled on that of ancient Greece, but it simultaneously provided a way of reclaiming the trope of *translatio imperii* from its American champions. Rather than migrating onwards to Boston or New York, the '*All-Saxonhome*' to Carlyle would safely remain in London, with British emigration promising to bring the 'little Isle' once again 'on a par with America' (ibid., 262).[3] Emerson was contemplating the transnational dynamics of a global economy as well, but rather than consolidating British metropolitan power, 'Free Trade' in his analysis would eventually lead to 'the annexation of England to America' (*JMN* 11: 452). In contrast to Carlyle, he read British emigration to the United States not as the sign of a spreading English hegemon but as a compliment the British were clandestinely paying the Americans ('what amount of English criticism in books or journals can offset the eulogy of the swarming annual emigration from the British isles into the United States', he was wondering at one point [*TN* 1: 216]). Just like Emerson's statements, Carlyle's gesture of global embrace – his integration of people 'from the antipodes and elsewhere' into a diasporic English family – was deeply informed by the logic of transatlantic competition.

America assumes a key role in Carlyle's Anglo-Saxon colonial fantasy, especially in *Chartism*, where he once again imagines the continent's unspoilt backwoods as the site of (agri)cultural amelioration ('American forests lie untilled across the ocean', 'Canadian Forests stand unfelled, boundless Plains and Prairies unbroken with the plough' [*CE* 29: 139, 203]). This celebration of transatlantic potential was, of course, ironically undercut by the fact that, in the case of North America, the 'new Colonies' Carlyle imagined as being formed through the global dispersal of Englishmen – British Canada and the United States, respectively – had, in fact, either already been colonised by, or long become independent from, Britain. In its assumptions about colonial identity, *Chartism* illustrates a more general nineteenth-century British imperialist attitude towards transatlantic migration. Although Carlyle did not fully subscribe to Wakefield's more radical view that, given the steady influx of English emigrants, the United States had never truly ceased being a British colony, he nevertheless merged both nations in the framework of a larger colonialist perspective that remained firmly Anglocentric.[4]

While Carlyle repeatedly advocated emigration to the New World in the abstract, it was only during a short period of time that he himself was attracted to the idea of giving up the identity of the man of letters and making the transatlantic passage. He returned to his American scheme at irregular intervals, but when he did so from the late 1830s onwards it was again in the capacity of the public lecturer that he saw himself as crossing the ocean. The expansionist rhetoric with whose help he had begun to think of the continent as extending beyond the Atlantic seaboard nevertheless remained with him in later years. While Carlyle no longer conceived of himself as 'in the Backwoods, with a rifle in [his] hand', he came to imagine that lecturing would bring him in touch with the nation as a whole. The way in which he describes himself in these visions amalgamates the genteel eloquence of the lecturer with the raw physicality of the frontiersman. He speaks of 'Lecturing ... "like a roaring lion" all over the Union' and at another point promises – almost threatens – Emerson that he would come to 'belecture' Americans 'from North to South' (*CL* 11: 106; *CEC* 236). Carlyle's scriptural reference established a connection between secular performance and religious charisma, but its connotations were, in fact, diabolical rather than pastoral.[5] When, in the summer of 1840, he contemplated repeating his London lecture course on heroes and hero-worship in the United States, sermonic rhetoric again gains the upper hand, with lecturing once more figuring as a more moderate form of public speech and Carlyle no longer envisioning himself as 'raging' but as 'preaching far and wide' across the United States (*CEC* 279, 275).

As his American admirers eventually came to realise, however, they would never experience their prophetic preacher in the flesh unless they travelled to London themselves. Carlyle never ultimately went to the United States because he had good excuses for not doing so. Ironically enough, the most important of these was Emerson's transatlantic patronage. Often enough depending on the existence of a prior print reputation, a career as a public speaker enhanced a writer's visibility and consolidated his or her celebrity status (which, in the long run, also increased book sales). In Emerson's case, as in that of many other nineteenth-century author–performers, lecturing and publishing were thus closely intertwined professional practices that mutually sustained one another.[6] Yet Emerson's attempt to bring Carlyle to the United States as a lecturer ultimately failed because of a financial competition between print and oratory. With Carlyle, from *The French Revolution* onwards, receiving money from the sale of his books in the United States and with this transatlantic success creating a corresponding domestic demand for his writings, there was no longer any immediate need to embark on an American tour. Carlyle's growing recognition as a published writer also largely put an end to the vocational insecurity that, in the late 1830s, had made him toy with the idea of leading the life of an American frontiersman.

The more he became lionised at home, the less pressure did he feel to perform the role of the 'roaring lion' abroad.

The London Lectures: National Culture and Transatlantic Circulation

It was in England that Carlyle finally ascended the platform, delivering a total of four lecture courses in London between 1837 and 1840. Although they were confined to a narrowly circumscribed social, institutional and geographical setting, his performances nevertheless had a virtual transatlantic dimension. As a public speaker, Carlyle was being circulated as a performing celebrity by the transatlantic press, but he was also himself explicitly concerned with the relationship between culture and nationhood and, more specifically, with questions of English and Anglo-American national identity. If not in their immediate performative contexts, Carlyle's lectures were thus transatlantic phenomena in terms both of their content and of their reception. They allowed him to fashion himself as a public intellectual of note and to increase the visibility publishing was, at around the same time, beginning to gain him in the contemporary Anglo-American literary field.

With his courses dedicated to the subjects of German literature, comparative literary history, European revolutions and hero-worship, respectively, Carlyle was moving in fields with which, in most cases, he had already been familiar before the delivery of the lectures or with which he was acquainting himself for book projects he was working on at the time. The topics he chose for treatment at the lectern were thus ones in which his audiences were prepared to acknowledge his expertise.[7] Lacking established mechanisms for the conferral of authority on those who became an active part of the system, mid-century public lecturing did not automatically grant speakers what Max Weber has termed '*charisma of office*' (1978, 1: 249). As a freelance writer rather than the incumbent of an academic chair (the '*cathedra*' about which he had been fantasising in his notebook), Carlyle could not, in other words, lay claim to the kind of 'professorial charisma' located in the institution of the modern university (with its to some extent paradoxical 'cultivation of charismatic figures within a broader sphere of rationalization') (Clark 2006: 16, 17). In a relatively new institutional environment situated half-way between instruction and entertainment, he had to create his standing as a lecturer mostly on his own. Although his knowledge of his subjects and his publication record granted him enough 'social power' (Alexander 2011: 32) to enter the domain of public speech in the first place, his volatile authority as a lecturer needed to be constantly reaffirmed and validated in the performative act itself.

If the motivation behind Carlyle's choice of topics was, to a large extent, pragmatic, it also proved an effective way to consolidate his reputation and brand him as a recognisable intellectual commodity. Part of his success as a lecturer derived from the fact that he delivered his lectures extemporaneously rather than merely reading them from his notes. Improvised speech was Carlyle's major asset, but depending on spontaneous inspiration for its immediate effect, it simultaneously became the main source of his performative anxiety. To the manuscript-reliant Emerson he wrote that 'extempore speaking, especially in the way of Lecture[,] is an *art* or craft', and Emerson, in turn, admired Carlyle's courage to take such risks on the platform ('I should love myself wonderfully better if I could arm myself to go, as you go, with the word in the heart & not in a paper') (*CEC* 236, 308). Circumventing the hybrid orality of script-based lecturing, extemporised discourse was a key component of Carlyle's conception of himself as a public speaker. What distinguished the true 'Orator' from the merely mechanic 'Rhetorician', he had argued in an 1831 essay, was an air of 'spontaneity', 'an unconsciousness' that precluded preparation and was 'the characteristic of right performance' (*CE* 28: 7). Allowing Carlyle to present himself as forming part of a tradition of prophetic visionaries imparting revelatory insight, improvisation was key to the establishment of his authority as a performer.

Carlyle's audiences – or at least the reporters who summarised his lectures – tended to perceive his performance style as highly idiosyncratic, but also as strikingly authentic. He was 'not eloquent in the sense of studied smoothness and fluency', one commentator wrote, adding that his lecturing was marked rather by 'the eloquence of thought and feeling, and of their unstudied expression' (Anon. 1837c: 3). His special kind of eloquence thus contrasted markedly with what members of Emerson's British and American audiences often described as his monotonous, anaemic delivery.[8] Carlyle's extemporising was agonised, his eloquence strained, but deliberately so. Instead of a mere unadorned Emersonian reading or, alternatively, a display of rhetorical *sprezzatura*, what his audiences witnessed were performances that, visibly and audibly dramatising the challenges of intellectual labour, were aimed at distancing the lecture format both from entertainment and from dilettantism.

The contemporary press was at a loss when it came to classifying Carlyle according to his professional status. Some felt that, with his uncompromising delivery, he 'resemble[d] . . . German professors' while others described him as 'neither divine nor lawyer by profession, but in the best sense a "learned" man' (Anon. 1837c: 3; Anon. 1837b: 5). '[N]ew to the mere technicalities of public speaking', he struck most observers as blatantly ignoring the institutional protocols of the public lecture (Anon. 1837b: 5). By all appearances more inclined to teach than to delight, he seemed to be curiously indifferent to the performative character of his delivery. As the London *Globe* explained, on the platform he did not 'waste time in rounding periods or clothing his ideas in choice phrases' but instead cut straight to the chase, dispensing with rhetorical artifice (Anon. 1837c: 3). In so doing, Carlyle cultivated a habitus that defied the conventions of oratorical performance at the same time that it satisfied the expectations of his audiences. The peculiarities of his delivery – his prophetic air of improvisation and his pronounced Scottish accent – created a public persona whose ostensible disinterestedness was eminently marketable.

Throughout his career as a lecturer – as well as beyond, as will become clear in what remains of this chapter – Carlyle was troubled by the ambivalent status of lecturing between instruction and entertainment. In retrospect, he described the practice as a '[d]etestable mixture of Prophecy and Play actorism' (*Rem* 97) and remembered Willis's Rooms, the setting for the first of his four lecture series, as a 'shew-room . . . adapted for fiddlers[,] fire eaters and playactors' (*CL* 10: 101).[9] It was only once he had moved north from St James's to Marylebone to lecture at Portman Square from the 1838 course onwards that he felt he had exchanged the sphere of fashionable diversion for that of 'a real Lecture-room' (ibid.). Judging both from Carlyle's own accounts and from those of contemporary commentators, his audiences were distinctly upper-class, even after he left St James's. If it was no longer exclusively the 'audience of Marchionesses [and] Ambassadors' that he had anticipated before entering the lecturing trade or that 'of mere quality and notabilities' about which he wrote to Johann Peter Eckermann after concluding his initial course on German literature, it remained a mostly elite one with the three series that followed (*CL* 9: 178, 223–4).

The geographical and social narrowness of his lecturing activity notwithstanding, Carlyle's performances were widely covered both by the national press and by American papers, the latter of which either reprinted summaries that had previously featured in Britain or published material supplied by their own European correspondents. Such reporting turned appearances on the lecture platform into 'a phenomenon that involved both an active body of attendees and a broader private reading public', and in Carlyle's case – as well as in Emerson's, as I have illustrated in Chapter 5 – this 'broader, unseen public' was a genuinely transatlantic one (Wright 2013: 4; Scott 1983: 288). In addition to an institutional lecture system that exchanged figures such as Emerson and Dickens or Frederick Douglass and Anthony Trollope across national borders, there was thus also, at the same time, another, virtual sphere of transatlantic lecturing that revolved not around live events but their subsequent print dissemination. Drawing on the medium of print to compensate for Carlyle's physical absence from the United States, this virtual performative space turned him into a transatlantic lecturer after all.

Carlyle's 1839 course on European revolutions is an especially instructive case of such Anglo-American circulation and the 'viral textuality' of nineteenth-century transatlantic newspaper reprinting (Cordell 2015). The *Boston Courier* and the Washington-based *Daily National Intelligencer*, for example, ran a detailed summary of the introductory lecture of the series from the London

Morning Chronicle. Only rarely framed by editorial commentary, such reprints were, in most cases, merely echoing British impressions of Carlyle without attempting to qualify them.[10] More revealing than such simple forms of republication are cases in which his performances were described by Americans who had experienced his lecturing at first hand. A striking instance of this type of reporting is a summary of the fourth lecture of the series by the London-based correspondent of Horace Greeley's *The New-Yorker*. The short notice follows the genre's conventional trajectory from the description of context to the transcription of content, but the views voiced in the text clearly depart from the British reporting of the lectures reprinted elsewhere in the American press at the time:

> Thomas Carlyle is just closing a Course of six Lectures on the Revolutions of Modern Europe, at the Marylebone Institution. I attended the fourth, a few days since. The audience about 200, and decidedly fashionable, if one could judge from the coroneted carriages and liveried footmen in waiting. Carlyle is about 38 – rather intellectual face – glossy black hair, parted on the top of his head – speaks broad Scotch, extempore – not very fluent – often ungrammatical, but occasionally animated, pithy and eloquent – opinions decidedly democratic – the 'divine right of kings' proved absurd by glances at the Courts of the Second Charles and the Cardinal-ruled Louis of France, the sway of the Nell Gwyns and Duchesses of Portsmouth being more potent than that of the King himself – Revolutions necessary sometimes, for Nature itself is identified with change. (Anon. 1839b: 189)

Carlyle's audiences at Portman Square were regularly described as 'decidedly fashionable' by English commentators as well,[11] but the American correspondent seems especially taken with 'the coroneted carriages and liveried footmen' that formed the extravagant backdrop to Carlyle's metropolitan lecturing.

Questions of social class are more clearly in the foreground here than in most of the English reports, and so is the charge of elitism. Carlyle's British high-society audience is here implicitly played off against the democratically diversified audience structure of the American lyceum (commonly idealised as an egalitarian 'town meeting of the mind' [Bode 1968]). Greeley's correspondent clearly enjoys pointing to the ironic contrast between the context and the content of Carlyle's lectures on revolutions, between the aristocratic attendees and the subversive arguments to which they were exposed in an 'ungrammatical' manner. Putting special emphasis on the discrepancy between his 'decidedly fashionable' audience and his 'decidedly democratic' message, the *New-Yorker* provided its readers with a vivid image of Carlyle as a lecturer at the same time that it used this image for transatlantic political ends, wielding its interpretive authority to represent his lecture and its delivery in its own – rather than in borrowed and reprinted – terms.

Whether in the form of mere reprints or of such self-consciously autonomous critical assessments, American accounts of Carlyle's English lecturing fuelled a domestic desire for his appearance in the United States. The more successful and widely covered he became as a lecturer at home, the more rapidly an international demand grew for him – a demand which, with a surging British reputation, it became easier for him not to fulfil. Despite his reluctance to appear in front of them live, with the help of print Carlyle managed to reach his transatlantic audiences not just as a published writer but also as a lecturer. Although what he spoke about in the lecture hall mainly revolved around European subjects, it was also eminently suitable for audiences abroad. Physically limited to the orbit of the British capital, he tapped into a more extensive repertoire of 'background symbols' to address a larger public that he imagined as broadly Anglo-Saxon in character (Alexander 2011: 28). It was to this audience that the racialist undercurrent of many of his lectures was catering. In the first instalment of the 1837 series on German literature, for example, Carlyle not only retraced 'the early history, the growth, and characteristics of the German people', he was also – as the London *Times* reported – 'following them downwards, and involving in them those of the Saxon race – the English, the North Americans, the white rulers of India, and new colonial proprietors of the vast Eastern Archipelago' (Anon. 1837b: 5). According to another transcript of the lecture published in the London *Spectator*, Carlyle went on to suggest that 'the breed has been in some cases even improved by crossing and transplanting, – as in the instances of the English and Americans' (qtd in Kaplan 1983: 242–3). Statements such as these were destined to resonate with audiences on both sides of the Atlantic, whether with those actually attending the lectures or with those reading reports of them. The same strategy reappeared again and again in Carlyle's subsequent lectures: it surfaces in the fourth part of the 1838 series on the 'History of Literature', which celebrated English cultural achievement in broad transatlantic terms (see *LHL* 139–59), and it forms one of the key elements of the 1840 lecture on 'The Hero as Poet', in which he described Shakespeare as the emissary of a global Englishness capable of reuniting a diasporic 'Saxondom' 'into virtually one nation' (*WTC* 1: 96). Thanks to the medium of print, Carlyle himself was able to address that virtual nation in his lectures.

Critiques of Performative Authority in the Later Carlyle

Although Carlyle's appearances on the London lecture stage were frequently accompanied by anxieties about his power as a performer, they nevertheless managed to secure him access to new and larger audiences. By the time he delivered what would be his final course in the spring of 1840, his status as a sage figure was beginning to be recognised on both sides of the Atlantic. While his personal statements about lecturing at the time suggest that he welcomed the opportunity to experience his own authority on stage, Carlyle was more and more troubled by the larger mid-nineteenth-century culture of eloquence of which his lecturing had made him become a part. Although in practice he savoured the impact his lecture performances had on his British – and, by extension, his American – audiences, in theory his scepticism about the uses and abuses of public speech grew increasingly more pronounced from the 1840s onwards. This development in his views was occasioned not in small part by the shifting political landscape of the period, whose transatlantic watershed moments – the European revolutions of 1848, the American Civil War, the widening of the franchise in the wake of the 1867 Reform Act – he perceived with a growing sense of alarm. As the remainder of this chapter will demonstrate, much of the late Carlyle's notorious vilification of democracy and racial equality is rooted in his criticism of the authority of oral expression.

Carlyle's most extensive discussion of eloquence appeared as part of his controversial series of *Latter-Day Pamphlets*. In 'Stump-Orator', the fifth in a collection of eight pamphlets, first published in May 1850, the nineteenth century emerges as an age of inflated rhetoric in which the mastery of verbal performance has become the sole requirement for success and influence in the public sphere. Carlyle and his contemporaries, P. David Marshall has argued, were equally fascinated and troubled by such modern forms of celebrity, which, rather than a more slowly emerging heroism, dramatically accelerated the economy of recognition. In the new kind of celebrity culture of which worship of eloquence was one key manifestation, it was a 'mass audience' that became 'central in the definitions of individual value and worth' – a 'new power of determining value' that, for Carlyle, according to Marshall, clashed with traditional 'models of distinctive and important individuals' (1997: 8). Where, ten years before *Latter-Day Pamphlets*, Carlyle himself had gladly seized the opportunity to exert influence from the secular pulpit of the lecture stage, by 1850 he had turned to diagnosing contemporary British audiences with an exaggerated veneration of speech that found expression in a pathological preference for words over deeds. Carlyle goes so far as to liken the contemporary cult of eloquence to religious heterodoxy when he complains that '[a]ll men are devoutly prostrate, worshipping the eloquent talker; and no man knows what a scandalous idol he is' (*CE* 20: 175). There was a pronounced antagonism between speech and action already in his lectures of the late 1830s, where it came coupled to a profound uncertainty about which of the two deserved precedence in an overall hierarchy of human achievement. Philip Rosenberg has written incisively about the conflict in the early Carlyle's vision of the 'committed intellectual' between the ideals of 'the man of thought' and 'the man of action' (1974: vii), but this ambivalence continued to inform his later writing.

By 1850, his position seems to have shifted to an unambiguous endorsement of action, as is implied by his acerbic description of the deification of the public speaker and of the misrecognition in store for those that work rather than talk.

Yet Carlyle's celebration of action over rhetoric was a conflicted preference to the extent that his own professional identity as a writer compelled him to work with and through the medium of language, to represent rather than himself perform exemplary deeds. Where his sympathies had come to lie with the heroic sincerity of the man of action, the role of the man of letters confined him to the function of a passive observer. As a lecturer, Carlyle had himself been the beneficiary of the very cult of powerful speech that he went on to decry in 'Stump-Orator'. What the 1850 pamphlet suggests about the pernicious appeal of public speaking amounts, in fact, to a cancellation of his own earlier claims to intellectual relevance. As Chris R. Vanden Bossche observes, in *Latter-Day Pamphlets* Carlyle's 'inflated sense of authority makes him capable of imagining himself ruling England . . . , while at other moments his doubts about the authority of literature lead him to question the entire enterprise of writing' (1991: 139). In 'Stump-Orator', the public speaker (a role Carlyle had himself played between 1837 and 1840) becomes 'not only a ridiculous but still more a highly tragical personage' because he reaches people in the largest of numbers, but of next to no symbolic significance: 'While the many listen to him, the few are used to pass rapidly with some gust of scornful laughter, some growl of impatient malediction' (*CE* 20: 176–7). In both its spoken and written forms, language aimed at the masses failed to reach the audience that mattered to the later Carlyle. Influence over this select 'few', he argued, was the sign of true centrality in the cultural field.

With *Latter-Day Pamphlets* as a whole, Carlyle's political philosophy assumes a distinctly authoritarian shape: the ideal form of power that the book propagates is one that no longer needs to legitimise itself rhetorically because the 'soldierlike obedience' it produces in those it governs rests on the natural aristocracy of those who govern (*CE* 20: 46). In contrast to a discursive and processual notion of power as something in constant need of performative validation, the version of authority championed in the 1850 pamphlets is one that bypasses language and performance through sheer coercion. Dependent on exactly these two elements, language as well as performance, Carlyle's own claim to authority was thus itself ultimately undermined by the larger argument of 'Stump-Orator'. The stock character that Carlyle here held up for censure was also a self-portrait, and a 'tragical' one to the extent that the financial necessities of his professional identity denied him the option of staying silent. No matter what, as a man of letters, he chose to write, writing itself remained the inevitable precondition for his material survival. His fifty-page invective against the contemporary economy of eloquence was paradoxically implicated in the logic of that very economy. *Latter-Day Pamphlets* to that extent dramatises

Carlyle's 'despair at being unable to effect any meaningful change' in a culture in which he ultimately realised he was himself inextricably enmeshed (Vanden Bossche 1991: 129).[12] In addition to its more general condemnation of public eloquence, *Latter-Day Pamphlets* hence also began another chapter in the history of Carlyle's increasing disillusionment with literature and the writing profession. 'Stump-Orator' accordingly culminates in an emphatic attempt at dissuading the next generation from taking up either the business of letters or that of eloquence ('Be not a Public Orator, thou brave young British man'; 'Of Literature, in all ways, be shy rather than otherwise' [CE 20: 212]).

Carlyle returned to emphasising the harmful effects of writing and speaking at several points after the publication of the 'Stump-Orator' pamphlet. The contours of the same argument appear, for example, in his recollections of a friend whom he saw as corrupted by his career choices. In *The Life of John Sterling* (1851), the book that followed *Latter-Day Pamphlets*, Carlyle depicts himself as incessantly repeating the concluding admonitions of 'Stump-Orator' to the younger Sterling, whose life in the biography emerges as fatally marked by its unfolding during an age of eloquence:

> Of all forms of public life, in the Talking Era, it was clear that only one completely suited Sterling, – the anarchic, nomadic, entirely aerial and unconditional one, called Literature. . . . This is the chaotic haven of so many frustrate activities; where all manner of good gifts go up in far-seen smoke or conflagration; and whole fleets, that might have been war-fleets to conquer kingdoms, are *consumed* (too truly, often), amid 'fame' enough, and the admiring shouts of the vulgar, which is always fond to see fire going on. The true Canaan and Mount Zion of a Talking Era must ever be Literature: the extraneous, miscellaneous, self-elected, indescribable *Parliamentum*, or Talking Apparatus . . . (CE 11: 43)

As the epitome of the 'Talking Era', literature here becomes largely synonymous with oratory. A profession that a character of Sterling's disposition ultimately had no choice but to enter at a cultural moment that offered him no worthier pursuit, it ultimately ensnared him in a 'Talking Apparatus' that did not release its hold on him until his premature death of tuberculosis in 1844 – which, in Carlyle's biography, becomes emblematic of his generation as a whole (note the *double entendre* on '*consumed*').

The book's harshest criticism, however, is reserved not for Sterling but for Samuel Taylor Coleridge, under whose tutelage Sterling had first prepared to enter the talking profession. Coleridge, whom Carlyle had himself met during one of his early trips to London in the 1820s, had a reputation for being a great talker, both as a lecturer and as a conversationalist, but to the later Carlyle his oratorical gifts were merely indicative of the vapidity of the culture that cherished them.[13] 'Nothing could be more copious than his talk', Carlyle asserted in the *Life*, remembering it as

> not flowing anywhither like a river, but spreading everywhither in inextricable currents and regurgitations like a lake or sea; terribly deficient in definite goal or aim, nay often in logical intelligibility; *what* you were to believe or do, on any earthly or heavenly thing, obstinately refusing to appear from it. So that, most times, you felt logically lost; swamped near to drowning in this tide of ingenious vocables, spreading out boundless as if to submerge the world. (ibid., 55)

Its primary functions being phatic and performative, Coleridge's diluvian verbosity, to Carlyle, failed to communicate anything of substance. Instead of encouraging his audience to take part in a conversation, Coleridge merely wanted his interlocutors '[t]o sit as a passive bucket and be pumped into' (ibid.). What was wrong with a culture that slavishly worshipped Coleridge's 'artistically expressive words', Carlyle implied, was not only that it failed to recognise it for the 'aimless, cloudcapt, cloud-based, lawlessly meandering human discourse' which, to him, it ultimately was, but also that it strengthened the authority of a sham speaker while fostering a merely passive obedience in those who were listening (ibid., 57). Carlyle thus used Coleridge and Sterling as protagonists in a cautionary tale about the dangers of a nineteenth-century fetishisation of public speech.

Where the 'Stump-Orator' pamphlet theorised that argument on a more abstract level and the *Life of Sterling* provided individual case studies, in the 'Occasional Discourse on the Negro Question' (1849) Carlyle had illustrated the hazards of rhetorical power in semi-fictional form. His indictment of public speaking in *Latter-Day Pamphlets* provides an important, though often overlooked, context for the slightly earlier text. Seen from this angle, the 'Occasional Discourse' centres on the potential dangers of reformist oratory, with its fictional speaker polemicising against the perceived ills of a 'philanthropic stump-oratory' that employs sentimentalist rhetoric to convert its listeners to the anti-slavery cause but ultimately only lives of and for its own performative power (Carlyle 1849: 675). Carlyle's critique here was also, at least implicitly, aimed at Emerson and his British audiences. The speaker of the 'Discourse' persistently associates philanthropic eloquence with Exeter Hall, a venue chiefly known in the 1830s and 1840s for hosting evangelical and abolitionist gatherings. It was here that Emerson had delivered his final English lecture course in the summer of 1848, to an audience whose views he found coincided with his own.[14] Although he had not explicitly spoken about abolition on that occasion, the invitation had come from the Early Closing Association, a reformist group philanthropic enough to be implicated in Carlyle's wholesale dismissal of 'Exeter Hall monstrosities' in the 'Occasional Discourse' the year following Emerson's appearance there (ibid., 677).

Exeter Hall was a space for the exchange of reformist ideas, but by the time Carlyle was writing it had also become notable as a forum in which African American speakers were celebrated for the eloquence of their attacks on the evils of slavery. Read against this historical background, the 'Occasional Discourse' emerges as a symptom not only of Carlyle's dislike for philanthropic rhetoric but also, more specifically, of his dismissive assessment of the success of black oratory on the Victorian lecture stage. Frederick Douglass had appeared at the venue to great acclaim in 1846 and two years later would draw the attention of his American audiences to 'the broad platform of Exeter Hall' as a model of democracy in action (1982: 142). Speaking under the impression of the 1848 revolutions, Douglass identified public debate as a powerful alternative to the anarchical violence of revolutionary upheaval. To Carlyle, on the other hand, both formed part of the same general problem of democratic participation. The white supremacist sentiments put forth in the 'Occasional Discourse' to that extent become legible as a desperate attempt both at discrediting reformist positions and at limiting their visibility in the public sphere.[15] The futility of such an endeavour could be witnessed a mere month after the original publication of the 'Occasional Discourse', when the formerly enslaved William Wells Brown lambasted Carlyle's 'absurd doctrine of . . . the inferiority of the negro race' in front of a lecture audience in Leeds (Anon. 1850a: 7).

Although racial identity moves out of the spotlight in the 'Stump-Orator' pamphlet, the later text is clearly indebted to the 'Occasional Discourse' and its larger argument that the least effective way of organising society would be one in which 'all men' were taught that 'success in stump-oratory' was 'the real symbol of wisdom' (Carlyle 1853: 20). But while the speaker of the 'Discourse' rages against the excesses of philanthropic and reformist stump-oratory, he is, after all, himself a stump-orator who uses the same means – public speech, exalted rhetoric, graphic language – which he criticises in others (a paradox that Brown was quick to identify, noting that Carlyle 'frowns upon the Reformatory speakers upon the boards of Exeter Hall, yet he is the prince of reformers' [1852: 218]). The 1849 text here becomes a fictional anticipation of Carlyle's own aporetic position in the later pamphlet, in which he essentially plays the role of a stump-orator preaching against the ills of stump-oratory. The frame narrative that, in the 'Occasional Discourse', is constructed around the actual speech highlights the latter's concrete performative context. Contained within the dramatisation of a public speech event, the opinions that Carlyle seems to be championing in the text are more than just propositional content. Denying responsibility for 'the strange doctrines and notions shadowed forth in it' (1849: 670), Carlyle's fictional editorial persona claims to be merely reproducing a transcript of the address. Especially in the revised and enlarged 1853 version of the text, this transcript includes a running commentary in the form of audience reactions to the speaker's glaring statements. Through this mirroring of its own live reception, the 'Occasional Discourse' takes on a dialogical form. A pastiche of the genre of the lecture report, the text incorporates the social dimension of its own delivery. The overall trajectory of these recorded responses – from initial disgust to eventual assent – represents an additional semantic layer that works against the racist surface of the discourse proper. While the transcript suggests that, early on, '*various persons, in an agitated manner, with an air of indignation, left the room*', Carlyle's anti-philanthropic stump-orator ultimately proves capable of selling his 'strange doctrines' to a pliable audience that is soon enough '*sitting with increased attention*', then offering its '*assent*' and finally bursting into '*[l]aughter*' (1853: 10, 2, 14, 43, 48). Carlyle's meta-performative framing thus charts the ominous success of demagoguery, of a stump-oratory that can convince a gullible audience through its tantalising powers of delivery, no matter how outrageous the beliefs it chooses to propagate. There seems to be a general agreement among interpreters of the 'Occasional Discourse' that, as Carlyle by the late 1840s had lost his belief in the power of rational argument, he was not seriously trying to convince his readers of the validity of the opinions the text advances.[16] My point here is that this was not primarily the result of a declining belief in his own power to persuade others to subscribe to his views, but rather an acute reminder to his readers that, to the skilled public speaker (Carlyle himself implicitly included), it was all too easy to sway an audience culturally primed to fall for extravagant rhetoric.

'AMERICAN STUMP-ORATORY': DEMOCRACY AND THE TRANSATLANTIC PUBLIC SPHERE

Carlyle's argument against eloquence had a strong national dimension, an element that comes to the fore in the concluding salvo of the 'Occasional Discourse', which takes its cue from his own earlier characterisation of English culture:

> A certain man has called us, 'of all peoples the wisest in action'; but he added, 'the stupidest in speech': – and it is a sore thing, in these constitutional times, times mainly of universal Parliamentary and other Eloquence, that the 'speakers' have all first to emit, in such tumultuous volumes, their human stupor, as the indispensable preliminary, and everywhere we must first see that and its results *out*, before beginning any business! (1849: 679)

Self-quoting from *Past and Present* here leads Carlyle to voice a critique of 'universal ... Eloquence' that clearly foreshadows the later 'Stump-Orator' pamphlet.[17] What the celebratory account of the British in the 1843 book suggests in this new context is that Carlyle's compatriots were constitutionally incapable of the kind of stump-oratory he exposes in the 'Occasional Discourse' and the 1850 pamphlet (the latter of which no longer paints such a uniformly positive picture of the nation's exemption from the general ills of the 'Talking Age'). That Carlyle chooses this point as a conclusion for the 'Occasional Discourse' implies that, to him, this collective immunity to the powers of rhetoric would be the Victorians' saving grace.

Elsewhere, his celebration of British silence contrasts with his diagnosis of a detrimental effect of public speaking in the United States. In *Latter-Day Pamphlets*, Carlyle, in fact, not only argues that American culture suffered from a worship of 'stump-oratory' at least as excessive as that which was raging in Britain at the same time, he also gives divisive eloquence a specifically American pedigree:

> Probably there is not in Nature a more distracted phantasm than your commonplace eloquent speaker, as he is found on platforms, in parliaments, on Kentucky stumps, at tavern-dinners, in windy, empty, insincere times like ours. The 'excellent Stump-Orator,' as our admiring Yankee friends define him, he who in any occurrent set of circumstances can start forth, mount upon his 'stump,' his rostrum, tribune, place in parliament, or other ready elevation, and pour forth from him his appropriate 'excellent speech,' his interpretation of the said circumstances, in such manner as poor windy mortals round him shall cry bravo to, – he is not an artist I can much admire, as matters go! (*CE* 20: 175–6)

Carlyle's etymological account is, to some extent, corroborated by modern lexicography (the *Oxford English Dictionary* locates the first recorded use of the term 'stump-orator' in an 1813 letter by Thomas Jefferson).[18] But as the less than favourable depiction of the United States at other points in *Latter-Day Pamphlets* suggests, Carlyle was here portraying Americans not simply as the victims of a transatlantically pervasive craze after '"excellent speech"', but as the representatives of a culture that had created that same craze in the first place. If the British were 'worshipping the eloquent talker', to Carlyle this was the result of an increasingly democratised public sphere whose participatory character had been modelled on a distinctly American form of culture in which all gate-keeping had seemingly been abolished and all manner of improvised settings qualified as 'ready elevation' from which essentially everyone could speak (ibid., 175). Carlyle was concerned that the hierarchical distance between speaker and audience was becoming dangerously levelled. The lateral thrust of an American-style democratic public discourse that he described as rampant in mid-nineteenth-century Europe threatened to pull traditional authorities, both literally and figuratively, to the ground.

To that extent, the source of Carlyle's concern in 'Stump-Orator' was not primarily public speaking per se but its roots in an increasingly egalitarian social order. Where access to the 'stump' and, by extension, to the field of intellectual practice was becoming all but universal, the once 'elevated' practice of oral performance – Carlyle leaves no doubt about his nostalgic yearning for a bygone age of socially unadulterated eloquence (see ibid., 177–9) – ran the risk of withering into a mere branch of the nineteenth-century culture industry. 'Stump-Orator' displays a profound anxiety about the future of the authority of professional speaking and writing. To be sure, Carlyle had established a similar connection between democratisation and modern media culture a decade before, in his lecture on 'The Hero as Man of Letters', when he noted that

> Printing, which comes necessarily out of Writing, ... is equivalent to Democracy: invent Writing, Democracy is inevitable. ... Whoever can speak, speaking now to the whole nation, becomes a power, a branch of government, with inalienable weight in law-making, in all acts of authority. (*WTC* 1: 141)

Over the course of the 1840s, he shifted from such largely neutral assessments to the alarmist position he would come to adopt in the 1850 pamphlets.

Inflationary eloquence was a disease that, in Carlyle's analysis, had spread across the Atlantic, via the British importation of American political culture. Looking for a suitable image of excessive growth to voice his anxiety about the ever-growing number of competitors in the literary sphere, he appropriately enough chose America's staggering birth rate as a point of comparison: 'the Republic of Letters', he quipped, 'increases in population at a faster rate than even the Republic of America' (*CE* 20: 191). From the late 1840s onwards, Carlyle associated the United States with cultural as well as political forms of participation of which he increasingly came to disapprove. Already in 'The Present Time', the first of the *Latter-Day Pamphlets*, he turned against the kind of 'universal *Democracy*' that the European revolutions of 1848, to him, had exposed as being of a fundamentally anarchical character (ibid., 8). He was still diplomatic enough, however, to concede that American democracy looked 'nearly perfect' by contrast and for three-quarters of a century had proved capable of functioning well (ibid., 19). Carlyle went even further than that, suggesting that he could not legitimately criticise the United States because '[o]f America it would ill beseem any Englishman ... to speak unkindly, to speak *unpatriotically*': 'America is a great', he acknowledged, 'and in many respects a blessed and hopeful phenomenon', its 'hardy millions of Anglo-saxon men prov[ing] themselves worthy of their genealogy' (ibid.). But although Carlyle here still retains his earlier emphasis on transatlantic racial continuity, he quickly adopts a more critical perspective. Whatever was excellent about the United States, in his view, had originated from 'the Old-Puritan English workshop' (ibid., 20). Americans had as yet achieved nothing on their own terms, not even a distinctive ethnic identity: 'the title hitherto to be a Commonwealth or Nation at all, among the ἔθνη of the world, is, strictly considered, still a thing they are but striving for, and indeed have not yet done much towards attaining' (ibid., 19–20). The larger implications of this argument become obvious only in the further course of the pamphlet, where nothing remains of Carlyle's initial reserve and the United States, devoid of cultural achievement, is reduced to the status of a reproductive machine:

> My friend, brag not yet of our American cousins! Their quantity of cotton, dollars, industry and resources, I believe to be almost unspeakable; but I can by no means worship the like of these. What great human soul, what great thought, what great noble thing that one could worship, or loyally admire, has yet been produced there? None: the American cousins have yet done none of these things. 'What they have done?' growls Smelfungus, tired of the subject: 'They have doubled their population every twenty years. They have begotten, with a rapidity beyond recorded example, Eighteen Millions of the greatest *bores* ever seen in this world before, – that hitherto is their feat in History!' (ibid., 21)

This is by far the most damning criticism of American culture that Carlyle ever published, but its general scepticism is in line with private statements that well predate *Latter-Day Pamphlets*. As is usual in his printed commentary, Carlyle's harshest censure is voiced by a fictional character ('Smelfungus', an allusion to Sterne and Smollett, also surfaces in a number of his other texts). This does little, however, to mitigate the vehemence of Carlyle's own anti-Americanism in the passage.[19]

Where in 'The Present Time' Carlyle's ultimate target was democracy in general, in 'Parliaments', the sixth pamphlet, first published in June 1850, his critique of the democratic social order was more explicitly linked to his remarks on public speaking in 'Stump-Orator'. Concerned with speech more than with action, parliamentary democracy, in Carlyle's analysis, fails to manage the political affairs of the nation effectively. If this defect had become more clearly visible in the British than in the American context, he contended, it was simply because Washington politicians had not yet been confronted with truly serious challenges:

> If indeed America should ever experience a higher call, as is likely, and begin to feel diviner wants than that of Indian corn with abundant bacon and molasses, and unlimited scope for all citizens to hunt dollars, – America too will find that caucuses, division-lists, stump-oratory and speeches to Buncombe will *not* carry men to the immortal gods; . . . and, in fine, that said sublime constitutional arrangement will require to

be (with terrible throes, and travail such as few expect yet) remodelled, abridged, extended, suppressed; torn asunder, put together again; – not without heroic labour, and effort quite other than that of the Stump-Orator and the Revival Preacher, one day! (CE 20: 227)

Democratic public debate, the passage implies, was harmless where nothing of importance needed to be decided but would prove insufficient when it came to administering more complex political and economic structures or to creating a sense of national achievement that went beyond the material. Many of Carlyle's contemporary American readers turned away from him as a result of such statements. Abolitionist Elizur Wright's *Perforations in the 'Latter-Day Pamphlets,' by One of the 'Eighteen Millions of Bores'* (1850), for example, took issue both with Carlyle's pro-slavery attitude and with his abuse of democracy. Southern critics, on the other hand, tended to approve of both elements and instead censure Carlyle's Northern opponents. The *Southern Quarterly Review* of November 1850 insisted that his 'remarks on America' were, in essence, 'considerate' and 'written in a kindly spirit' (Holmes 1850: 336, 355, 336). The 'universal tempest of petty quibbles and impotent irritation' that they had generated 'in the newspaper literature of the country', the *Southern Quarterly* suggested, ultimately only confirmed Carlyle's larger argument about the inability of democratic public debate to recognise true merit and the authority it represented (ibid., 355).

Carlyle's dismissal of a specifically American form of stump-oratory again resurfaced in the revised version of the 'Occasional Discourse', which was published as a separate pamphlet in 1853.[20] One of the major textual changes introduced at this point was the insertion of a lengthy middle section which turned from the emancipation of slaves in the British West Indies – the main subject of the 'Discourse' – to the future of the American slave system. Explicitly addressing his transatlantic readers in the North, Carlyle implied that their acceptance of the idea of racial inequality (and of the possibility – however implausible – of an 'actually fair' form of black subordination) might prove capable of averting the escalation of a sectional conflict fuelled by pro- and anti-slavery rhetoric (1853: 31). Only then, he argued, would 'American stump-oratory, with mutual exasperation fast rising to the desperate pitch' cease to exert its power over American 'men and women of the Anglo-Saxon type' (ibid., 29). Explicitly siding 'neither with the abolitionists nor the pro-slavery lobby' (although his sympathies for the latter were not, of course, difficult to detect), Carlyle accused Northern and Southern public discourse alike of contributing to the polarisation of the American public sphere (Collins 1997: 32).

If, unlike Wright and other Northern readers, Emerson chose not to comment directly on the anti-democratic and anti-American statements Carlyle's writings featured from the 1849 'Occasional Discourse' onwards, he nevertheless raised objections to his wholesale dismissal of eloquence – even though, to some extent, he shared the later Carlyle's anxieties about public speaking as a mass cultural event. This scepticism strongly surfaces in the 'Culture' chapter of *The Conduct of Life* (1860), a series of essays based on lectures delivered in the decade following the publication of *Latter-Day Pamphlets*. Echoing Carlyle's idea of true speech as grounded in 'an inward capital of culture', Emerson here suggested that 'culture must reinforce from higher influx the empirical skills of eloquence' (*CE* 20: 179; *CW* 6: 85). In fact, he had begun to think about oral performance in more general terms at around the same time that Carlyle did, expressing a similar concern about the potentially corrupting influence of oratorical power in a lecture on 'Eloquence', delivered numerous times from December 1846 onwards.[21] 'Who can wonder at the attractiveness of Parliament, or of Congress, or the Bar, for our ambitious young men', Emerson asked, 'when the highest bribes of society are at the feet of the successful orator?' (*CW* 7: 31). But where Carlyle set out to dissuade 'young men' of the Sterling type from aspiring to the office of the 'Public Orator', Emerson's reservations were less systematically opposed to what he continued to praise as the 'art' of eloquence (*CE* 20: 212; *CW* 7: 47). Although it amplified power and influence, public speech, to him, was not alone responsible for creating them, as Carlyle was arguing in 'Stump-Orator'. In the 'Eloquence' lecture, Emerson thus thinks of '[p]ersonal ascendency' as essentially autonomous from its oratorical orchestration – it could 'exist', he writes, 'with or without adequate talent for its expression' (*CW* 7: 41).

It was in his journals that Emerson took his most explicit stance against the propositions advanced in 'Stump-Orator', appropriating the term but seeking to work against its negative connotations. Immediately after the original publication of the pamphlet, he wrote that, 'though much decried by Carlyle', 'stumporatory' was ultimately 'of great worth' (*JMN* 11: 250). Where Carlyle dreaded a mass access to the platform, Emerson emphasised that among the characteristics of genuine 'stump-oratory' was its scarcity ('There have been millions & millions of men, and a good stumporator only once in an age' [ibid.]). When Emerson later returned to the subject in another lecture on 'Eloquence', first delivered in Chicago in March 1867, his rejection of Carlyle's scepticism had grown even more pronounced. Where Carlyle contended that speaking was, in essence, an effeminate pursuit inferior to action, Emerson stylised oratory as a form of heroism worthy of veneration, suspending Carlyle's word/deed dualism through likening oral performance to military prowess. Harking back to his claim in the 1844 essay 'The Poet' that '[w]ords are also actions, and actions are a kind of words' (*CW* 3: 6), Emerson here suggested that the discourse of the 'true orator' was 'not to be distinguished from action. It is the electricity of action. It is action, as the general's word of command, or chart of battle, is action' (*CW* 8: 61). Emerson agreed with Carlyle's argument that the globally pervasive nineteenth-century culture of eloquence had originated in the United States, but what in Carlyle was intended as blame in Emerson became celebration. Affirmatively associating America with public speech, he implicitly identified himself as one of the 'admiring Yankee friends' that Carlyle had chided for naively applauding the rise of a harmful cultural practice. 'If there ever was a country where eloquence was a power', Emerson asserted, 'it is . . . the United States' (ibid., 70). This was as close as he would get to a refutation of Carlyle's devastating transatlantic critique of democratic participation. His response was informed by the first-hand experience of a cultural environment which, as lecturers, both of them had begun to explore in the 1830s and to which he – unlike Carlyle – remained committed for the rest of his life.

NOTES

1. On the Anglo-American tensions that resulted from the publication of Dickens's book, see Chapter 5.
2. The British government began endorsing emigration in the 1830s and fostered it through colonial land sales. For facts and figures on British emigration to the United States during the first half of the century, see Thistlethwaite 1959: 24–33; on 'assisted emigration', see Murdoch 2004: 85–98; on British debates about the issue, see Bell 2016: 34–6.
3. On Carlyle's Greek-style Saxonism during the early 1840s, see also Chapter 1.
4. In his *View of the Art of Colonization*, Wakefield asserted that 'the United States of America, formed by emigration from this country, and still receiving a large annual increase of people by emigration from this country, are still colonies of England' (1849: 17).
5. Carlyle is alluding to 1 Peter 5: 8 ('Be sober, be vigilant; because your adversary the devil, as a roaring lion, walketh about, seeking whom he may devour').
6. On the importance of previously established reputations for the successful marketing of lecturers, see Cayton 1987: 615–18; on the reciprocally constitutive relationship between print publication and lecture performance and their joint reliance on 'the intense personalization of literary figures', see O'Neill 2008: 747.
7. The London *Times*, for example, wrote about the introductory lecture of the 1837 series on German literature that, because of 'his deep and extensive knowledge of the capacity, the tendencies, the history, and productions of the German mind', there was 'no individual in this empire more competent' to tackle the subject than Carlyle (Anon. 1837b: 5).
8. Recalling a lecture in Manchester, George Searle Phillips noted how Emerson 'mounted the rostrum in a free and careless style; took his MS. out of his pocket, and standing bolt upright, began to read in his calm, cool way, as if he were a great overgrown school-boy, saying his task', his technique merely consisting of 'downright plain reading, and nothing more' (1855: 39).
9. Willis's Rooms had been a fashionable West End venue for upper-class social gatherings since the late eighteenth century. Coleridge gave two courses of literary lectures there in 1812. As his editor R. A. Foakes notes, the Rooms reached 'the

height of their reputation . . . between about 1810 and 1830' (Coleridge 1987, 1: 416). By the time Carlyle lectured there, the setting had deteriorated into a haunt for 'Harp-players and Dancing Masters', as Carlyle's wife noted in March 1838 (*CL* 10: 35).
10. The *Courier* (see Anon. 1839c) simply reprinted the report verbatim, while the *National Intelligencer* prefaced its reprint from the *Morning Chronicle* (see Anon. 1839a) with a short reference to 'a London paper' as its source (Anon. 1839d: 2).
11. Compare, for example, the *Morning Chronicle*'s description of the 'very numerous audience' attending Carlyle's first lecture on revolutions as one 'among whom were to be recognised various distinguished and accomplished persons' (Anon. 1839a: 3), Henry Crabb Robinson's account of the same group of individuals as 'a distinguished audience' (1938, 2: 570) and Leigh Hunt's description of them as a 'select audience . . . of literature and fashion' (1839: 278).
12. The paradoxical relationship between Carlyle's call for oratorical and writerly silence, on the one hand, and his own professional commitment to spoken and written eloquence, on the other, has been noted by several commentators. Christine Persak has traced the tension between Carlyle's claim to the status of the 'social critic' reaching 'a large segment of the public' and his scepticism about the power of language (and oratory and print as its media of dissemination) to bring about such moments of contact (1991: 41). Writing about the 'Stump-Orator' pamphlet, more specifically, Jonathan Taylor has pointed towards 'Carlyle's neurotic anxiety' of turning into a stump-orator himself, concluding that 'in order to warn against popular, demagogic orators, Carlyle became himself a popular orator' (2003: 160, 164). What I emphasise here is that Carlyle felt compelled to speak not only in order to communicate his social criticism (as Persak and Taylor suggest), but also because his very identity as a literary professional – the need to secure a steady income and maintain public visibility – ruled out silence as an alternative to speech.
13. To Emerson, Carlyle was, ironically enough, similar to Coleridge in this respect. 'Thomas Carlyle is an immense talker' is the first sentence of the eulogy that James Elliot Cabot and Ellen Emerson in 1881 composed out of several of Emerson's earlier sketches on the occasion of Carlyle's death (1884: 455). In 1847 Emerson had noted, more devastatingly still, that '[i]n Carlyle . . . one is more struck with the rhetoric than with the matter' (*JMN* 10: 78). Attendees of Carlyle's London lectures were likewise struck by the similarities between his eloquence and that of Coleridge (see, for example, Anon. 1838c), a comparison that, by the early 1850s at the latest, Carlyle himself would have found less than flattering.
14. Carlyle had been horrified by Emerson's original intention to focus his British lecturing activity on speaking to what he dismissed as the 'intellectual *canaille*' of the industrial north, suggesting that 'an audience of British Aristocracy' was awaiting Emerson in the capital (qtd in Froude 1884, 1: 422; *CEC* 417). Although he eventually followed Carlyle's advice and offered a series of lectures at London's fashionable Portman Square in June 1848, Emerson found that this 'aristocratic Lecturing' threatened to 'exclude all *my public*' (*L* 4: 84). The fees for the three 'expiatory' lectures at Exeter Hall with which he decided to conclude his British tour were affordable for the kind of audience with which he felt more at home (ibid., 87).

15. On the racialist rhetoric that features in the 'Occasional Discourse', see Chapter 1.
16. Helen Small, for example, notes that the prose of the 'Occasional Discourse' 'does not aim at participation in argument', that it 'does not look to persuade' but instead gestures 'beyond itself to a higher authority' (2017: 545). Vanden Bossche similarly observes that in the 'Discourse' and in the *Latter-Day Pamphlets* Carlyle 'seeks to coerce and attack rather than persuade and convert his audience' (1991: 126).
17. For Carlyle's earlier passage, compare *WTC* 4: 161 ('[o]f all the Nations in the world at present the English are the stupidest in speech, the wisest in action'). See also my more extended discussion of this passage in Chapter 2.
18. *OED*, s.v. 'stump, n.' (meaning C1.c). The idea of the 'stump' as a speaker's platform also has an American origin (see ibid., meaning 14.a).
19. Although *Latter-Day Pamphlets* generally antagonised his audience – Michael K. Goldberg speaks of 'a major alteration in the public's view of Carlyle' that the book effected (1976: 132) – statements like the ones quoted above notably resonated with the anti-American sentiments of some of his British readers. A staunch critic of Carlyle's 'disgusting' pro-slavery attitude, Henry Crabb Robinson, for example, 'could not but enjoy' leafing through the first pamphlet and admire how 'powerfully expressed' Carlyle's 'contempt towards the Americans' was (1938, 2: 695).
20. This later version contains a number of textual emendations and substantial additions (on which see Tarr 1981). Michael K. Goldberg and Jules P. Seigel offer a critical text in Carlyle 1983: 421–70 (see ibid., 517–24 for textual notes and a collation of the two versions).
21. Emerson drew from the manuscript of this lecture for the publication of his essay of the same title in the *Atlantic Monthly* of September 1858, a text subsequently revised for inclusion in *Society and Solitude* (1870) (see *CW* 7: 30–51; on the textual genesis of the essay, see ibid., xix). *Letters and Social Aims* (1875) includes another piece on 'Eloquence' that is textually independent of the first one (see *CW* 8: 59–71) (I discuss this later essay in the following paragraph; on the complex background of the later text, see ibid., cclxiv).

EPILOGUE: FROM SECTIONAL CONFLICT TO POSTHUMOUS CONSECRATION

If Emerson, in 1867, was thinking of public speech as the equivalent of military action, it is not hard to trace this simile back to the recent armed conflict that had occasioned his last major campaign on the lecture stage, an ardent defence of the Union and its principles. Where Carlyle's exculpation of slavery in the 'Occasional Discourse' and his critique of participatory democracy in *Latter-Day Pamphlets* had taken aim at American institutions as well as at American readers, to Emerson the Civil War gave renewed urgency to transatlantic public eloquence. The war was a military conflict as much as it was a rhetorical one and it had domestic as well as international repercussions. Although its main sectional fault line ran between North and South, it also threatened to drive a wedge between the Union and Britain to the extent that it gave rise to Anglo-American tensions previously kept at bay through a traditional emphasis on common origins and characterological similarities. Among the British aristocracy, the Anglican clergy and the Tory elite, there was much sympathy with the South and what was perceived by many members of these groups as the moral and constitutional legitimacy of secession. While liberals like Carlyle's former friend John Stuart Mill sided with the Union, the response of what seemed to American observers the overwhelming majority of British literary and cultural figures (Dickens, Tennyson, Arnold and Ruskin, among many others) took the form either of indifference or of outright admiration for the South. Although, in political terms, Britain remained neutral, to many in the North it appeared as though the British were betraying their earlier commitment to abolitionism.[1]

Even if Carlyle, as Brent Kinser observes, 'contributed no major work directly to the public discussion about the war' (2011: 13), his American readers had reason enough to assume that his general pro-slavery and anti-democracy outlook – as expressed in texts that predated the beginning of the conflict by more than a decade – made him favourably disposed towards the South. The only explicit commentary that Carlyle published on the Civil War while it was raging was a short piece in *Macmillan's Magazine* in August 1863, entitled 'Ilias (Americana) in Nuce'. Its brevity notwithstanding, the text seemed to confirm readers' suspicions about his political preferences. After two years of bloodshed, Carlyle depicted the conflict as one abetted by a democratic form of social organisation that allowed mass hysteria to determine politics. The war, he was suggesting, had ultimately been the result of Northern aggression:

> ILIAS (AMERICANA) IN NUCE.
> PETER *of the North* (*to* PAUL *of the South*). 'Paul, you unaccountable scoundrel, I find you hire your servants for life, not by the month or year as I do! You are going straight to Hell, you – !'
> PAUL. 'Good words, Peter! The risk is my own; I am willing to take the risk. Hire you your servants by the month or the day, and get straight to Heaven; leave me to my own method.'
> PETER. 'No, I won't. I will beat your brains out first!' (*And is trying dreadfully ever since, but cannot yet manage it.*)
> MAY, 1863.   T. C.
> (Carlyle 1863: 301)

Even if the vignette explicitly 'asserted next to nothing' (Waller 1965: 17), at a more fundamental level the equation of slavery and industrial wage labour – along with the caricature of a belligerent North – quite obviously indicated Carlyle's views on the conflict. The general drift of the text squares with what he expressed in his correspondence during the first half of the 1860s and it matches the kind of reception the soon notorious 'Ilias (Americana)' received on the other side of the Atlantic, where – like his books – it was widely reprinted.

It was easy enough to dismiss the text as the 'absurdest of Carlylian nonsense' (Anon. 1863b: 2), but there were also more extended arguments, often coming from former American devotees. One of them, David A. Wasson, a Unitarian minister and abolitionist, published an open letter to Carlyle in the *Atlantic Monthly* in October 1863, charging his former hero with 'narrowness and pettiness of understanding with regard to America' (1863: 497). Speaking for a whole generation of Northern readers who had taken Victorian sage writing seriously to heart, Wasson wrote to Carlyle of his regret '[t]o have lost, in the hour of our trial, the fellowship of yourself, and of others in England whom we most delighted to honor' (ibid., 503). Transatlantic disenchantment with Carlyle was also palpable in an essay Emerson's Transcendentalist friend James Freeman Clarke wrote for the September 1864 *Christian Examiner*. Like Wasson, he distinguished between 'two Carlyles', the former a moral and intellectual authority, the current one a merciless apologist of authoritarianism. One of the earliest subscribers of the American editions of his books, Clarke too was a former admirer of Carlyle and had ardently defended him against criticism in the 1830s.[2] Three decades later, he was charting Carlyle's decline from 'enthusiast' to 'hard cynic', reading 'Ilias (Americana)' as an explicit endorsement of the South (1864: 231, 218).

From Emerson, on the other hand, there was nothing that approached such outright criticism. In a journal entry jotted down in late 1863, he even finds praise for Carlyle's having 'best of all men in England kept the manly attitude in his time', his 'errors of opinion' appearing 'as nothing in comparison with this merit' (*JMN* 15: 367). It was on the lecture stage that Emerson, at around the same time, was advancing a more general critique of British attitudes about the war, arguing like Wasson that the British failure to support the North had jeopardised its role as a moral authority. In 'Fortune of the Republic', a lecture delivered fourteen times to New England and New York audiences between December 1863 and February 1864, Emerson openly used a nationalist vocabulary to declare that Americans would no longer recognise British claims to leadership:

> We shall not again give you any advantage of honor. We shall be compelled to look at the stern facts. And, we cannot count you great. Your inches are conspicuous, and we cannot count your inches against our miles, and leagues, and parallels of latitude. We are forced to analyse your greatness. We who saw you in a halo of honor which our affection made, now we must measure your means; your true dimensions; your population; we must compare the future of this country with that in a time when every prosperity of ours knocks away the stones from your foundation. (*LL* 2: 327)

Emerson here seeks to 'measure' English 'greatness' in historical and metaphorical as well as in more concretely demographic and geographical terms. This rhetoric is hardly new, of course, but whereas texts such as *English Traits* had similarly contrasted English achievement with American potential, English past with American future, Emerson now dispenses with an acknowledgement of the former in favour of a celebration of the latter – with a bluntness that is in stark contrast to the carefully crafted ambiguity that had marked his earlier statements. In 'Fortune of the Republic', Emerson is no longer addressing himself to a composite Anglo-American readership, as he had done with the 1856 book, but instead speaks from a distinctly cisatlantic point of view.

Emerson was disappointed not only with British foreign policy but also more specifically with the reaction of British intellectuals. That the Civil War created not only a transatlantic diplomatic crisis but also a series of seismic ruptures in Anglo-American literary culture can be gauged from a letter Emerson had received, a few months prior to the first delivery of the 'Fortune' lecture, from Cyrus Augustus Bartol, another one of Carlyle's early (and by now former) New England champions. The war, Bartol wrote, was a conflict fought 'with arms' as well as 'with words' (qtd in *L* 9: 112). Given that 'English scholarship' had excelled itself in exhibiting its 'unfriendliness . . . to our cause', what was urgently needed was 'an address of the literary men of this country to their Order across the sea, on the ground which learning, philosophy & poetry should take in the premises which touch them as well as legislation & politics' (qtd in Gougeon 1989: 412). In his capacity as the spokesman of the American section of the transatlantic literary field, Emerson himself should issue such a public statement, Bartol argued, 'whether it be an article simply, or a manifesto signed . . . by literary & no sort of professional men' (qtd ibid., 413). Bartol's letter implied that the moral economy of the transatlantic relationship was in the hands of otherwise independent literary figures and that conflicts of the scale and magnitude of the Civil War called for an outspoken *littérature engagée* from writers who understood themselves not just as poets, essayists or critics, but as publicly committed intellectuals. The exact opposite of that argument had only recently been advanced on the other side of the Atlantic, in an April 1863 essay on 'American Literature and the Civil War' published in the pro-Southern *Fraser's Magazine* (which had provided the original print forum for the signature texts of both of the 'two Carlyles', *Sartor Resartus* and the 'Occasional Discourse on the Negro Question'). What Bartol presented as the moral imperative of writers to participate in public debate to *Fraser's* appeared as the 'fanatical' interventions of literary authors oblivious to the limits of their own professional expertise (Anon. 1863a: 520). Where Bartol believed that activist interventions in the transatlantic republic of letters could help to overcome diplomatic gridlock, the English periodical – making a case for the autonomy of literature from the concerns of everyday politics – contended that the incendiary writing of Northern authors such as Whittier, Longfellow and Stowe had only managed to exacerbate the situation.

While Emerson did not eventually deliver the 'manifesto' Bartol was hoping for, 'Fortune of the Republic' contained at least some moderate rebuke for contemporary British intellectuals, even though it generally tended to exempt literary writers from a larger critique of British public opinion about the war. The members of a 'truly cultivated class' that extended across Europe and the Atlantic and did not 'stop at frontiers or languages', they were free, Emerson suggested, not only 'from the arrogance and mendacity of the English press' but also more generally from parochial national sentiments (*LL* 2: 333). Yet the political disinterestedness of this transnational 'cultivated class' at the same time foreclosed the kind of outspoken national commitment that Bartol imagined – and that, with 'Fortune of the Republic', Emerson himself to some extent put into performative action. Prepared to take sides in the military conflict, he seemed unwilling to enter a transatlantic war of words. What is remarkable about Emerson's commentary on the British intelligentsia in 'Fortune of the Republic' is thus mainly his reluctance to indict or pass judgement. He was evidently disappointed, but gave unfiltered expression to the sentiment only in his private writing. In an August 1864 journal entry, he complained that the high ideal of the transnationally impartial scholar championed in the lecture did not, in fact, apply to Britain's 'wise men', who, after all, persisted in seeing the American conflict 'through the diminishing lens of a petty interest':

> Could we have believed that England should have disappointed us thus? ... Edinburg [sic], Quarterly, Saturday Review, Gladstone, Russell, Palmerston, Brougham, nay Tennyson; Carlyle, I blush to say it; Arnold. Every one forgot his history, his poetry, his religion, & looked only at his shoptill, whether his salary, whether his small investment in the funds, would not be less: whether the stability of English order might not be in some degree endangered. (*JMN* 15: 433)

Given that, in private, Emerson shared his Northern contemporaries' anger with the attitude of British men of letters, it seems surprising that this response did not manifest itself in a public statement like the 'Fortune' lecture, which, at a more general level, did not flinch from questioning the coordinates of the Anglo-American relationship. Behind this self-imposed diplomatic restraint was, at least in part, the fact that Emerson never ultimately lost hope that British intellectuals could still be won over to the cause of the Union. In a letter to Carlyle written a month after the above journal entry (the first communication between the two after a silence of almost two years), he acknowledged the importance of English public opinion for the outcome of the war. 'How gladly I would enlist you with your thunderbolt, on our part', he confessed, '[h]ow gladly enlist the wise, thoughtful, efficient pens & voices of England!' (*CEC* 541). Like Bartol acknowledging the importance of the rhetorical dimension of the war, Emerson here tries to convert Carlyle to what the *Fraser's* essay dismissed as 'the literature of conscience' (Anon. 1863a: 517).

Although Carlyle did not eventually become a champion of the North, Emerson remained unwavering in his lenience. In late 1865, half a year after the end of the war, he noted with regret that Carlyle's 'violent anti-Americanism' had not abated but still conceded that his 'overpowering' abilities as a writer protected him from stricter censure (*JMN* 15: 82). This tolerance was once again put to the test when, two years later, Carlyle issued another contentious statement on the war. First published as an essay in *Macmillan's* in August 1867 and soon reprinted in the United States, 'Shooting Niagara: And After?' was Carlyle's final reckoning with democracy and abolition. Mainly triggered by the Second Reform Act and its extension of the British franchise, the text also contained a fair amount of vitriolic commentary on American affairs. In Carlyle's analysis, the Civil War had been caused by 'frantic "Abolitionists"', and the origins of the conflict to that extent were decidedly transatlantic, given the moral precedent provided by the British abolition of slavery in the West Indies and the steady stream of English philanthropical oratory and writing that had poured into the Unites States prior to and during the war (1867: 322).

Most American commentators saw 'Shooting Niagara' as a further sign of 'the deterioration of intellect and the decline of influence' which Carlyle had been suffering for the past fifteen years (Bayne 1867: 1). Some, however, were less critical. '[A]t first roused to much anger' by Carlyle's caustic attacks on democracy and racial equality, Walt Whitman, in *Democratic Vistas* (1871), described the text in largely commendatory terms as 'a conscientious declamatory cry . . . from an eminent and venerable person abroad' (1982: 943). Emerson, on his part, once again refrained from commenting in public. Writing to Carlyle in 1870, he suggested, in a characteristically placable manner, that '[e]very reading person in America holds you in exceptional regard', that the American public had, in fact, 'forgotten' about his 'scarlet sins before or during the war' (*CEC* 575). Whitman made the same argument when, on the occasion of Carlyle's death, ten years after *Democratic Vistas*, he rhetorically wondered, 'Who cares that he wrote . . . "Shooting Niagara" – and "the Nigger Question," – and didn't at all admire our United States?' (1982: 888). What this American readiness to 'forgive Carlyle' (Tamarkin 2016) suggests is that the Civil War did not lead to a lasting fragmentation of the Anglo-American literary sphere. If Carlyle's and Emerson's post-Civil War reconciliation represented a 'personification of the awkward nineteenth-century Anglo-American relationship' (Campbell 2007: 57), it also illustrated the healing powers that lodged within that transatlantic formation. Where the conflict had put pressure on transatlantic networks and individual friendships, it had not ultimately managed to disrupt the larger material and institutional frameworks in which these were embedded.

While Carlyle, for example, had alienated many of his American readers, they still continued to be attracted to and fascinated by him. As Whitman noted in 1882, 'not only the interest in his books, but every personal bit regarding the famous Scotchman . . . is probably wider and livelier to-day in this country than in his own land' (1982: 890). On both sides of the Atlantic, the 1880s and 1890s witnessed a boom in biography and literary editing which not only canonised Carlyle and Emerson but also turned them into icons of transatlantic contact and cooperation. A late-Victorian and Gilded Age culture of life-writing gave rise to a Carlyle–Emerson 'industry' that began to flourish almost immediately after their deaths (which occurred within fourteen months of each other, in February 1881 and April 1882, respectively).[3] There was a surge both in secondary writing (biographies, reminiscences, literary historical accounts) and in the publication of primary material. Carlyle himself had been pursuing the project of a complete edition of his writings for decades before his death and collections appeared in various formats from the late 1850s onwards, in London as well as in Boston and New York. The major posthumous edition of his writings was the thirty-volume 'Centenary Edition', which appeared between 1896 and 1899 under the supervision of English journalist Henry Duff Traill. Emerson's works were collected and republished by his friend James Elliot Cabot in the comprehensive 'Riverside Edition' between 1883 and 1893, a project that also included three volumes of mostly unpublished lectures, addresses, essays and other occasional pieces. Much writing previously available only in manuscript was first printed in the quarter-century after Carlyle's and Emerson's deaths. Carlyle's *Reminiscences* were published by his literary executor James Anthony Froude in 1881, and the book was followed by the transcript of the 1838 *Lectures on the History of Literature* (1892) and Charles Eliot Norton's 1898 edition of Carlyle's early notebooks. Emerson's journals appeared as a ten-volume set between 1909 and 1914, prepared by his son Edward Waldo.

As both Carlyle and Emerson had been prolific letter writers, correspondence made up much of the newly published material. The most important of these transatlantic ventures was Norton's edition of the correspondence between Carlyle and Emerson themselves. One of their chief posthumous canonisers, Norton was, ironically enough, the son of one of Carlyle's and Emerson's harshest early critics, the Unitarian divine Andrews Norton.[4] Neither Carlyle nor Emerson held a grudge against Norton junior for his ancestry, however, and he amply made up for his father's attacks through his editorial efforts on their behalf. Norton formed part of a group of New England intellectuals that Leslie Butler has described as marked by 'exceptionally extensive ties to the transatlantic world of Victorian letters' (2007: 1). Galvanised by the Civil War, their generation sought to foster Anglo-American intellectual contact and witnessed the formation of a late-nineteenth-century 'transatlantic liberal community' (ibid., 5) that included Norton along with James Russell Lowell, Thomas Wentworth Higginson, Leslie Stephen, John Morley and others. After the war, the members of this circle strove 'to mitigate hostilities between the two countries' (ibid., 13) – an agenda for which, according to Butler, Carlyle and Emerson were an explicit and vital inspiration. In Norton's case, their influence made itself felt not simply in terms of an abstract indebtedness but also more tangibly in the form of a series of editorial projects – of which the edition of the correspondence was just one example. Carlyle and Emerson had carefully preserved their letters to each other and, anticipating a posthumous transatlantic interest in them, had themselves agreed to their publication while they were still alive. Drawing on the available manuscripts, Norton, in 1883, published *The Correspondence of Thomas Carlyle and Ralph Waldo Emerson, 1834–1872*, a two-volume collection that, issued simultaneously in Boston and London, gathered more than 170 letters (the second and third editions of

1886 and 1899, respectively, would include several more items).[5] The depth of Carlyle's and Emerson's Anglo-American commitments was now, for the first time, on full public display, and this source material provided the basis for many of the biographical and literary historical accounts that appeared over the course of the next two decades.

Like Carlyle's and Emerson's books, the *Correspondence* was widely read and reviewed in Britain and the United States. The persistent image that emerges from the contemporary critical commentary on the edition is that of a fundamental difference between Emerson, the indefatigable optimist, 'ethereal in his ideality', and Carlyle, the incorrigible pessimist, 'glowing ... with the heat of a dark realism' (Woodberry 1883: 562). What is perhaps more significant than these diagnoses of a 'moral gulf' between them is that almost every reviewer noted that both had nevertheless managed to make their transatlantic friendship work (Hedge 1883: 164). Two decades after the Civil War, such an emphasis on Anglo-American amity allowed for reading Carlyle and Emerson as representatives of their two countries. The area in which the transatlantic cooperation between the two writers was most frequently located was print culture (an aspect of the relationship I have detailed at length in Chapters 3 and 4). The reviewer of the *Nation*, for example, highlighted that Emerson had 'spared no pains to introduce [Carlyle] to the notice of readers on this side of the Atlantic' and that Carlyle, in turn, 'helped Emerson in England as Emerson helped him in America' (Anon. 1883: 324). Henry James's review of Norton's edition for the New York *Century Magazine* likewise dwelled on the mid-century Anglo-American print market:

> Emerson took upon himself to present 'Sartor Resartus' and some of its successors to the American public, and he constantly reports to the author upon the progress of this enterprise. He transmits a great many booksellers' accounts as well as a considerable number of bills of exchange, and among the American publishers is a most faithful and zealous representative of his friend. Some of these details, which are very numerous, are tedious; but they are interesting at the same time, and Mr. Norton has done well to print them all. In the light of the present relations of British authors to the American public, they are curious reading. There appears to have been a fortunate moment (it was not of long duration) when it was possible for the British author to reap something of a harvest here. (1883: 267)

James's backward glance at the golden days of trade courtesy cast a harsh light on the contemporary state of Anglo-American copyright, but his remarks about transatlantic publishing testify to the continued vibrancy of the transatlantic print market in which Carlyle's and Emerson's books, half a century before, had begun to succeed.

Unlike James, Matthew Arnold voiced his opinion of the correspondence on the lecture circuit, another transatlantic institutional framework that Carlyle and Emerson had themselves explored. In his 'Emerson' lecture, delivered several times during his American speaking tour in late 1883, Arnold eschewed the eulogising tone of many of the reviews of the *Correspondence* and instead emphasised the shortcomings of both writers. While Emerson could not ultimately be placed 'among the great writers', Carlyle, in Arnold's view, was destined to fade away completely, were it not for his letters to Emerson:

> I should not wonder if really Carlyle lived, in the long run, by such an invaluable record as that correspondence between him and Emerson ... – by this and not by his works, as Johnson lives in Boswell, not by his works. (1885: 159, 167)

Ultimately, however, adulatory late-Victorian life-writing was precisely what consolidated both Carlyle's and Emerson's transatlantic reputations and what kept fuelling a demand for their work. As could be expected, there were many English books on Carlyle and many American books on Emerson – the former including Richard Herne Shepherd's *Memoirs of the Life and Writings of Thomas Carlyle* (1881), Froude's *Thomas Carlyle: A History of the First Forty Years of His Life, 1795–1835* (1882) and *Thomas Carlyle: A History of His Life in London, 1834–1881* (1884), and Charles Gavan Duffy's *Conversations with Carlyle* (1892), the latter comprising books such as Moncure Daniel Conway's *Emerson at Home and Abroad* (1882), Oliver Wendell Holmes's *Ralph Waldo Emerson* (1885) or Cabot's *Memoir of Ralph Waldo Emerson* (1887). But there were also transatlantic projects, such as Alfred H. Guernsey's American biography-cum-anthology *Thomas Carlyle: His Life – His Books – His Theories* (1881) and Conway's *Thomas Carlyle* (1881), as well as the biographical volumes assembled by Emerson's Manchester friend Alexander Ireland.

Catering to the interests of an Anglo-American audience that had bought, read and debated Carlyle's and Emerson's own books on both sides of the Atlantic, Conway's and Ireland's biographies, in particular, paid special attention to the transatlantic dimension of the lives of their subjects. A Virginia-born minister, preacher and man of letters, Conway was an outspoken abolitionist who had first moved to New England – where he had come under the influence of Emerson – and then, at the height of the Civil War, relocated to London in an effort to convince British intellectuals to support the Union. Emerson recommended him to Ireland as a man committed to 'the correcting of opinion in England', and Conway, appropriately enough, began his task with Carlyle, whom he first met in May 1863 (thanks to another letter of introduction from Emerson) (*L* 5: 323). 'It was impossible not to love this man', Conway later wrote about his first encounter, 'however much I might deplore his opinions about slavery' (1904, 1: 396). This kind of admiration remained, and it turned Conway's later biographical writing on Carlyle into an apology of his opinions. Although the 1867 'Shooting Niagara' had demonstrated that Carlyle had changed none of his ideas about the war or the United States more generally, Conway constructed a narrative of transatlantic reconciliation and harmony which revolved around the claim that Carlyle had, at bottom, always been 'admiring the Northern people for their determination to maintain their Union', that he had eventually 'awakened from his dream' of the South as an agrarian utopia (1880: 908). The 1882 *Emerson at Home and Abroad*, Conway's extensive tribute to Emerson, was in many ways the companion piece to the Carlyle book he had published the year before. Conway here again conjured up an image of Anglo-American unity symbolised by the 'personal love between Carlyle and Emerson' (1882: 79). Delivering on its title, the book included a thirty-page chapter that recounted Emerson's British lecture tour of 1847–8, along with his first and final visits to England in 1833 and 1872–3.

Ireland had been acquainted with Emerson since his first English trip and had been instrumental in bringing him across the Atlantic for his lecture tour fifteen years later. The editor of the *Manchester Examiner*, he collaborated with Conway on Emersonian print projects in England. Thanks to their extended intellectual networks, each of them became, as Robert D. Habich notes, an 'important player in the rapidly expanding arena of Anglo-American literary relations' (2011: 46). Just days after Emerson's death, Ireland published a memoir of him in the *Examiner*, which, shortly afterwards, was enlarged and reprinted in book form as *In Memoriam Ralph Waldo Emerson: Recollections of His Visits to England in 1833, 1847–8, 1872–3, and Extracts from Unpublished Letters* – which was, in turn, expanded and republished as *Ralph Waldo Emerson: His Life, Genius, and Writings: A Biographical Sketch* half a year later. Just like Conway, Ireland eulogised Emerson by drawing attention to the authority he wielded over British readers and his fellow-writers (see 1882: 48, 152–3). Emerson's transatlantic journeys and his British lecture tour take centre stage in Ireland's account of his intellectual biography and the global history of his contemporary reception.

Like Norton, Conway and Ireland, many of the late-nineteenth-century biographers, editors and commentators that contributed to the Carlyle–Emerson industry were themselves deeply involved with the dynamics of the Anglo-American literary sphere. Most of them wanted to see their writing published and sold on both sides of the Atlantic, some were transatlantically mobile figures themselves and often their concerns resonated with the transatlantic aspects of Carlyle's and Emerson's lives and writings that I have retraced throughout this book. Conway's migrations between Boston and London, James's richly transatlantic writerly existence and the American lecturing of a figure such as Arnold illustrate such overlaps. In some cases, historiographical and biographical policies were even more directly related to Anglo-American politics. Froude, for example, not only lectured in America (a decade before Arnold crossed the Atlantic); he had also inherited Carlyle's idea of global Englishness, which he subsequently developed into a fully fledged colonialist vision that included the United States in the framework of the late-nineteenth-century ideology of 'Greater Britain'.[6] Representatives of a global Anglophone literary culture, Carlyle and Emerson offered themselves as the ideal figureheads for this kind of agenda.

Emphasising Emerson's actual and Carlyle's virtual transatlantic voyages and highlighting their international print market cooperation, biographers, commentators and reviewers by and large tended to portray the Carlyle–Emerson relationship as a collaborative transatlantic endeavour. Both writers thus became posthumous cultural emissaries that could be invoked to smooth over the transatlantic tensions that had become manifest during the Civil War and in its aftermath. Such late-Victorian commemoration sat well with what historians describe as an Anglo-American 'rapprochement' around the turn of the century – a period during which Britain and the United States were committed to forming a global strategic alliance (see Perkins 1968 and Anderson 1981). This larger sentiment was encapsulated in what, in a July 1898 essay for the *Atlantic Monthly*, James Bryce, liberal historian and later British ambassador in Washington, described as 'the essential unity of Britain and America', two nations 'closely bound by the ties of blood and literature and historical tradition' (1898: 22). Crucial elements in the rhetoric of 'Greater Britain', as well as in that of transatlantic political collaboration, the discourses of empire and race revived the Anglo-Saxonist vocabulary that Carlyle and Emerson had themselves popularised in their writings from the 1830s onwards.[7] As Duncan Bell has pointed out, such '*fin de siècle* Anglo-world discourse' culminated in the vision of a political union between Britain and the United States (2016: 182). Rhetorical precedents for this idea were conveniently at hand in the correspondence between Carlyle and Emerson, who had repeatedly emphasised that the two nation-states were ultimately only 'two *parishes* of one country' (*CEC* 102).

The uses of Carlyle and Emerson for the authorisation of late-Victorian Anglo-American cultural diplomacy were illustrated by individual biographical accounts, but they also came into play in another genre to which, like biography, the two had themselves contributed extensively. By the early 1900s, literary historiography was beginning to take stock of the transatlantic nineteenth century. In his *Literary History of America* (1900), Barrett Wendell – a former Harvard student of Carlyle and Emerson's editor Norton – firmly linked the American literary tradition to the English cultural context, using a rhetoric that sounds strikingly similar to the rapprochement argument diplomats such as Bryce were advancing at around the same time. Englishmen and Americans, to Wendell, formed part of a united 'English-speaking race' that not even American independence or the Civil War had managed to pull apart:

> [T]o careless eyes the two countries have long seemed parted by a chasm wider even than the turbulent and foggy Atlantic. Wide it has surely been, but never so vague as to interpose between them the shoreless gulf of sundered principle. The differences which have kept England and America so long distinct have arisen from no more fatal cause than unwitting and temporary conflicts of their common law. (1900: 521–2)

If the nineteenth century had seen mounting transatlantic tensions, to Wendell this was merely because 'England and America have believed themselves mutually foreign' in spite of being united as part of a larger 'community of language and of ideals', a shared identity that manifested itself most tangibly in the realm of literary expression (ibid., 525). American art and culture were thus fundamentally shaped by a transatlantically persistent English 'spirit':

> The literary history of America is the story, under new conditions, of those ideals which a common language has compelled America, almost unawares, to share with England. Elusive though they be, ideals are the souls of the nations which cherish them, – the living spirits which waken nationality into being, and which often preserve its memory long after its life has ebbed away. (ibid., 521)

Readers of Carlyle and Emerson would, of course, have been well familiar with Wendell's argument that literary production was inevitably determined by national character, as well as with his idea of a transatlantic racial and intellectual bond between the United States and Britain. Where the first chapter of this book has traced the Carlylean and Emersonian prehistory of a reviving *fin de siècle* Anglo-American Anglo-Saxonism, the main premises behind Wendell's expressivist narrative template were foreshadowed by what, in Chapter 2, I have discussed as the ways in which debates about race and national identity shaped mid-century notions of literary history and Anglo-American continuity. The closing decades of the nineteenth century thus gave voice to concerns that had already been circulating well before, just as they witnessed the expansion of pre-existing transatlantic institutional formations and cultural dispositions. By the beginning of the twentieth century, Carlyle's and Emerson's transatlantic lives and writings had become firmly canonised as key points of reference in an Anglo-American literary sphere they themselves had helped to create.

NOTES

1. On transatlantic diplomatic and cultural relations during the Civil War years, see Crawford 1983 and Campbell 2007: 142–70; on British attitudes about the conflict, see Blackett 2001 and Campbell 2003.
2. For discussions of Clarke's early writing on Carlyle, see Chapters 1 and 3.
3. Lawrence Buell in 1984 took stock of what he described as the 'Emerson industry' of the 1980s, noting that 'Emerson lends himself . . . readily to the gospel of the Present' (by which Buell meant deconstructionist, feminist and other then novel kinds of reading) (1984: 135). In speaking of something like a *fin de siècle* 'Carlyle–Emerson industry', I am arguing here that, a century before, both writers were drawn upon to advance the transatlantic agendas of the period.
4. On the older Norton's criticisms of Carlyle and Emerson during the 1830s, see the Introduction and Chapter 1.
5. In the introduction to his later critical edition of the correspondence, Joseph Slater provides a useful overview of the genesis, the editorial principles and the reception of Norton's edition (1964: 64–72). On the latter aspect, see also Sowder 1966: 202–11 and Harris 1978: 162–4.
6. In *Oceana, or England and Her Colonies* (1886), published two years after the final two volumes of his Carlyle biography, Froude described the stability of American federalism as a model for the organisation of a global British empire, which he envisioned as 'united as closely as the United States are united' (1886: 91). Expressing Froude's nostalgic longing for transatlantic unity, the title and structure of his book – which recounts travels to South Africa, Australia and New Zealand along with a trip to the United States – fantasised about an even closer Anglo-American relationship. On Froude and global Englishness, see Young 2008: 215–25; on the role of the United States in late-Victorian 'Greater Britain' discourse – from 'model' (235) to 'challenger to British supremacy' (234) – see Bell 2007: 231–59. The label originated with Charles Wentworth Dilke's influential manifesto, *Greater Britain* (1868), which programmatically argued that, '[i]f two small islands are by courtesy styled "Great", America, Australia, India, must form a Greater Britain' (1868, 1: viii).
7. Compare Chapter 1. See Anderson 1981 and Kramer 2002 for more general discussions of the role of racialist thinking – Anglo-Saxonism, in particular – in late-nineteenth- and early-twentieth-century Anglo-American foreign policy and imperialist ideology.

BIBLIOGRAPHY

Abrams, M. H. (1971 [1953]). *The Mirror and the Lamp: Romantic Theory and the Critical Tradition*. New York: Oxford University Press.

Adams, Amanda (2014). *Performing Authorship in the Nineteenth-Century Transatlantic Lecture Tour*. Farnham: Ashgate.

Adams, William Bridges (1848). 'Economy of Railway Traction'. *Westminster and Foreign Quarterly Review* 48.2 (January): 416–26.

Alexander, Gregory S. (1997). *Commodity and Propriety: Competing Visions of Property in American Legal Thought, 1776–1970*. Chicago: University of Chicago Press.

Alexander, Jeffrey C. (2011). *Performance and Power*. Cambridge: Polity Press.

Almeida, Joselyn M. (2011). *Reimagining the Transatlantic, 1780–1890*. Farnham: Ashgate.

Altick, Richard D. (1998 [1957]). *The English Common Reader: A Social History of the Mass Reading Public, 1800–1900*. 2nd edn. Columbus: Ohio State University Press.

Anderson, Benedict (2006 [1983]). *Imagined Communities: Reflections on the Origin and Spread of Nationalism*. Rev. edn. London: Verso.

Anderson, Charles (1850). *An Address on Anglo Saxon Destiny: Delivered before the Philomathesian Societies of Kenyon College, Ohio, August 8th, 1849 and Repeated before the New England Society of Cincinnati, December 20th, 1849*. Cincinnati: John D. Thorpe.

Anderson, Stuart (1981). *Race and Rapprochement: Anglo-Saxonism and Anglo-American Relations, 1895–1904*. Rutherford, NJ: Fairleigh Dickinson University Press.
Anon. (1834). 'Life of Schiller'. *North American Review* 39.84 (July): 1–30.
— (1837a). 'Rights of Foreign Authors'. *American Monthly Magazine* 9 (March): 311–12.
— (1837b). 'Lecture on German Literature'. *Times* (2 May): 5.
— (1837c). 'Mr. Carlyle's Lectures'. *Globe* (27 May): 3.
— (1838a). 'Innovations in Style'. *Southern Literary Messenger* 4.5 (May): 322–7.
— (1838b). 'Mr. Carlyle's Lectures'. *Evening Mail* (1 May): 4.
— (1838c). '[Carlyle's Lectures]'. *Sheffield Independent* (2 June): 3.
— (1839a). 'Mr. Carlyle's Lectures on the Revolutions of Modern Europe'. *Morning Chronicle* (8 May): 3.
— (1839b). '[Carlyle on the Revolutions of Modern Europe]'. *New-Yorker* 7.12 (8 June): 189.
— (1839c). 'Mr. Carlyle's Lectures on the Revolutions of Modern Europe'. *Boston Courier* (27 June): 4.
— (1839d). 'On Modern Revolutions'. *Daily National Intelligencer* (28 August): 2.
— (1841a). 'Traits and Tendencies of German Literature'. *Blackwood's Edinburgh Magazine* 50.310 (August): 143–60.
— (1841b). 'Literature – English and German'. *New York Evangelist* (4 September): 4.
— (1841c). '[Review of Emerson's *Essays*]'. *Fife Herald* 1019 (16 September): 4.
— (1841d). '[Review of Emerson's *Essays*]'. *London and Westminster Review* 36.2 (October): 491–3.
— (1841e). '[Review of Emerson's *Essays*]'. *Athenæum* 730 (23 October): 803–4.
— (1842). 'The International Copy-Right Law'. *Brother Jonathan* 2.3 (14 May): 74–5.
— (1843a). 'Mr. Emerson's Lectures'. *North American and Daily Advertiser* (24 January): 2.
— (1843b). 'Mercantile Library Lectures'. *North American and Daily Advertiser* (3 February): 2.
— (1843c). 'Mr. Emerson's Lecture'. *New-York Daily Tribune* (8 February): 2.
— (1843d). 'English and German Literature'. *Christian Observer* 22.32 (11 August): 4.
— (1844a). 'American Poetry'. *Foreign Quarterly Review* 32.64 (January): 291–324.
— (1844b). 'The Literary War between England and the United States – Another Broadside'. *New York Herald* (29 January): 2.

— (1844c). '[Review of Emerson's] *Essays. Second Series*'. *Examiner* (30 November): 757.
— (1844d). *A Collection of the Public General Statutes, Passed in the Seventh and Eighth Year of the Reign of Her Majesty Queen Victoria*. London: Eyre and Spottiswoode.
— (1846). '[Review of Emerson's *Essays: Second Series*]'. *Southern Quarterly Review* 9.18 (April): 538–9.
— (1847a). 'Nationality in Literature'. *United States Magazine and Democratic Review* 20.105 (March): 264–72.
— (1847b). 'Leeds Mechanics' Institution'. *Leeds Times* (18 September): 5.
— (1847c). 'Mr. Emerson's Lecture, at Manchester'. *Hull Packet and East Riding Times* (5 November): 6.
— (1847d). 'The American Lecturer: Shakspere [sic], the Poet'. *London Express* (15 November): 3.
— (1847e). 'Fourth Lecture of Ralph Waldo Emerson, Esq.' *Liverpool Mercury* (19 November): 3.
— (1847f). 'The Fifth Annual Soirée of the Manchester Athenæum'. *Manchester Times and Gazette* (20 November): 6–7.
— (1847g). 'Manchester Athenæum Soirée'. *Times* (20 November): 8.
— (1847h). 'Huddersfield Mechanics' Institution'. *Leeds Times* (24 December): 5.
— (1847i). 'Ralph Waldo Emerson'. *Birmingham Journal and Commercial Advertiser* (25 December): 6.
— (1847j). 'Mr. Emerson in Leicester'. *Leicestershire Mercury* (25 December): 2.
— (1848a). 'Emerson's Lectures'. *Leeds Times* (1 January): 3.
— (1848b). 'Ralph Waldo Emerson's Lectures'. *Leeds Times* (8 January): 7–8.
— (1848c). 'Ralph Waldo Emerson'. *Sheffield and Rotherham Independent* (8 January): 6.
— (1848d). 'Ralph Waldo Emerson'. *Leeds Times* (15 January): 6.
— (1848e). 'Lectures by Emerson'. *Newcastle Guardian* (12 February): 5.
— (1848f). 'Carlyle's Works'. *Southern Quarterly Review* 14.27 (July): 77–101.
— (1849a). 'An Address to Anglo-Saxons'. *Anglo-Saxon* 1.1 (January): 3–8.
— (1849b). 'Thomas Carlyle'. *Methodist Quarterly Review* 31 (January/April): 119–37, 217–40.
— (1849c). 'Who Are the Anglo-Saxons?' *Anglo-Saxon* 1.3 (July): 5–16.
— (1849d). 'The Emerson Mania'. *English Review* 12.23 (September): 139–52.
— (1849e). *A Catalogue of American Books, Imported by John Chapman, 142, Strand, London*. London: John Chapman.
— (1850a). 'Slavery in America'. *Leeds Mercury* (19 January): 7.
— (1850b). 'Histories and Historians of Oliver Cromwell'. *United States Magazine and Democratic Review* 26.136 (January): 17–43.
— (1851). 'The Anglo-Saxon Race'. *North American Review* 73.152 (July): 34–71.

— (1856a). 'Literary Notices'. *Harper's New Monthly Magazine* 13.77 (October): 694–6.
— (1856b). 'Emerson's English Traits'. *Westminster Review* 66.130 (October): 494–514.
— (1863a). 'American Literature and the Civil War'. *Fraser's Magazine* 67.400 (April): 517–27.
— (1863b). 'Thomas Carlyle'. *Boston Recorder* 48.36 (4 September): 2.
— (1883). 'The Carlyle-Emerson Correspondence'. *Nation* 36.928 (12 April): 324.
— (1992a [1841]). '[Review of Emerson's *Essays*]'. *Literary Gazette* 1288 (25 September): 620–61. Repr. in Myerson 1992: 95–6.
— (1992b [1841]). 'Emerson's Essays'. *Monthly Review* 3 (October): 274–9. Repr. in Myerson 1992: 97–9.
— (1992c [1844]). '[Review of Emerson's *Essays: Second Series*]'. *Spectator* 17 (24 November): 1122–23. Repr. in Myerson 1992: 111–12.
Appiah, Kwame Anthony (1995). 'Race'. *Critical Terms for Literary Study*. Ed. Frank Lentricchia and Thomas McLaughlin. Chicago: University of Chicago Press. 274–87.
— (1997). 'Cosmopolitan Patriots'. *Critical Inquiry* 23.3 (Spring): 617–39.
Arac, Jonathan (1979). *Commissioned Spirits: The Shaping of Social Motion in Dickens, Carlyle, Melville, and Hawthorne*. New Brunswick, NJ: Rutgers University Press.
Arbour, Robert (2013). 'Mr. Emerson's Playful Lyceum: Polyvocal Promotion on the Lecture Circuit'. *The Cosmopolitan Lyceum: Lecture Culture and the Globe in Nineteenth-Century America*. Ed. Tom F. Wright. Amherst: University of Massachusetts Press. 93–112.
Arendt, Hannah (1961). 'What Is Authority?' *Between Past and Future: Six Exercises in Political Thought*. New York: Viking. 91–141.
Armitage, David (2002). 'Three Concepts of Atlantic History'. *The British Atlantic World, 1500–1800*. Ed. David Armitage and Michael J. Braddick. Basingstoke and New York: Palgrave Macmillan. 11–27.
Armstrong, Nancy (1987). *Desire and Domestic Fiction: A Political History of the Novel*. New York: Oxford University Press.
Arnold, Matthew (1885 [1883]). 'Emerson'. *Discourses in America*. London: Macmillan. 138–207.
Arnold, Thomas (1843). *Introductory Lectures on Modern History, Delivered in Lent Term, MDCCCXLII: With the Inaugural Lecture Delivered in December, MDCCCXLI*. 2nd edn. London: B. Fellowes.
Ashton, Rosemary (1980). *The German Idea: Four English Writers and the Reception of German Thought, 1800–1860*. Cambridge: Cambridge University Press.
— (2006). *142 Strand: A Radical Address in Victorian London*. London: Chatto and Windus.

Augst, Thomas (2003). *The Clerk's Tale: Young Men and Moral Life in Nineteenth-Century America*. Chicago: University of Chicago Press.

Baldwin, Peter (2014). *The Copyright Wars: Three Centuries of Trans-Atlantic Battle*. Princeton: Princeton University Press.

Bancroft, George (1824). 'Life and Genius of Goethe'. *North American Review* 19.45 (October): 303–25.

— (1838). 'On the Progress of Civilization, or Reasons Why the Natural Association of Men of Letters Is with the Democracy'. *Boston Quarterly Review* 1.4 (October): 389–407.

Barnes, James J. (1974). *Authors, Publishers and Politicians: The Quest for an Anglo-American Copyright Agreement 1815–1854*. London: Routledge and Kegan Paul.

—, and Patience P. Barnes (1991). 'John Chapman'. *British Literary Publishing Houses, 1820–1880*. Ed. Patricia J. Anderson and Jonathan Rose. Detroit: Gale. 92–4.

Baucom, Ian (1999). *Out of Place: Englishness, Empire, and the Locations of Identity*. Princeton: Princeton University Press.

Baumgartner, A. M. (1963). '"The Lyceum Is My Pulpit": Homiletics in Emerson's Early Lectures'. *American Literature* 34.4 (January): 477–86.

Bayne, Peter (1867). 'Thomas Carlyle on America and England'. *Watchman and Reflector* 48 (29 August): 1.

Bell, Duncan (2007). *The Idea of Greater Britain: Empire and the Future of World Order, 1860–1900*. Princeton: Princeton University Press.

— (2016). *Reordering the World: Essays on Liberalism and Empire*. Princeton: Princeton University Press.

Benjamin, Park (1843). 'Mr. Carlyle's New Work'. *The New World* 6.17 (29 April): 509.

Bennett, Andrew (1999). *Romantic Poets and the Culture of Posterity*. Cambridge: Cambridge University Press.

Bennett, Bridget (2011). 'Frederick Douglass and Transatlantic Echoes of "The Color Line"'. *Transatlantic Literary Exchanges, 1790–1870: Gender, Race, and Nation*. Ed. Kevin Hutchings and Julia M. Wright. Farnham: Ashgate. 101–13.

Berlin, Isaiah (1976). *Vico and Herder: Two Studies in the History of Ideas*. London: Hogarth Press.

Blackett, R. J. M. (2001). *Divided Hearts: Britain and the American Civil War*. Baton Rouge: Louisiana State University Press.

Bloom, Harold (1973). *The Anxiety of Influence: A Theory of Poetry*. New York: Oxford University Press.

Bode, Carl (1968 [1956]). *The American Lyceum: Town Meeting of the Mind*. Carbondale: Southern Illinois University Press.

Bolt, Christine (1971). *Victorian Attitudes to Race*. London: Routledge and Kegan Paul.
Bourdieu, Pierre (1993). *The Field of Cultural Production: Essays on Art and Literature*. Ed. Randal Johnson. Cambridge: Polity Press.
— (1996). *The Rules of Art: Genesis and Structure of the Literary Field*. Trans. Susan Emanuel. Stanford: Stanford University Press.
— (1999). 'The Social Conditions of the International Circulation of Ideas'. *Bourdieu: A Critical Reader*. Ed. Richard Shusterman. Oxford and Malden, MA: Blackwell. 220–8.
Bowen, Francis (1837). 'Transcendentalism'. *Christian Examiner* 21.3 (January): 371–85.
Brickhouse, Anna (2004). *Transamerican Literary Relations and the Nineteenth-Century Public Sphere*. Cambridge: Cambridge University Press.
Brown, Philip A. H. (1982). *London Publishers and Printers, c. 1800–1870*. London: British Library.
Brown, William Wells (1852). *Three Years in Europe: Or, Places I Have Seen and People I Have Met*. London: Charles Gilpin / Edinburgh: Oliver and Boyd.
Brownson, Orestes A. (1838). 'Specimens of Foreign Literature'. *Boston Quarterly Review* 1.4 (October): 433–44.
Bryce, James (1898). 'The Essential Unity of Britain and America'. *Atlantic Monthly* 82.489 (July): 22–9.
Buell, Lawrence (1984). 'The Emerson Industry in the 1980's: A Survey of Trends and Achievements'. *ESQ* 30.2: 117–36.
— (1992). 'American Literary Emergence as a Postcolonial Phenomenon'. *American Literary History* 4.3 (Autumn): 411–42.
— (2003). *Emerson*. Cambridge, MA: Belknap Press of Harvard University Press.
— (2010). 'Manifest Destiny and the Question of the Moral Absolute'. *The Oxford Handbook of Transcendentalism*. Ed. Joel Myerson, Sandra Harbert Petrulionis and Laura Dassow Walls. New York: Oxford University Press. 183–97.
— (2013). 'Inventing the Public Intellectual: Conflicting Models'. *Intellectual Authority and Literary Culture in the US, 1790–1900*. Ed. Günter Leypoldt. Heidelberg: Winter. 27–44.
Burkholder, Robert E. (1982). 'The Contemporary Reception of *English Traits*'. *Emerson Centenary Essays*. Ed. Joel Myerson. Carbondale: Southern Illinois University Press. 156–72.
Burnham, Michelle (2019). *Transoceanic America: Risk, Writing, and Revolution in the Global Pacific*. New York: Oxford University Press.
Butler, Leslie (2007). *Critical Americans: Victorian Intellectuals and Transatlantic Liberal Reform*. Chapel Hill: University of North Carolina Press.

Campbell, Duncan Andrew (2003). *English Public Opinion and the American Civil War*. Rochester, NY: Boydell and Brewer.
— (2007). *Unlikely Allies: Britain, America and the Victorian Origins of the Special Relationship*. London: Hambledon Continuum.
Campbell, Ian (1971). 'Carlyle and the Negro Question Again'. *Criticism* 13.3 (Summer): 279–90.
— (1997). 'The Scottishness of Carlyle'. *Carlyle Studies Annual* 17: 73–82.
Carlyle, Thomas (1830). *Leben Schillers*. Frankfurt am Main: Heinrich Wilmans.
— (1844). 'Notice'. In: Ralph Waldo Emerson, *Essays: Second Series*. London: John Chapman. v–vi.
— (1849). 'Occasional Discourse on the Negro Question'. *Fraser's Magazine* 40.240 (December): 670–9.
— (1850a). 'Occasional Discourse on the Negro Question'. *Littell's Living Age* 24.299 (9 February): 248–54.
— (1850b). 'Carlyle on West India Emancipation'. *DeBow's Review* 8.6 (June): 527–38.
— (1853). *Occasional Discourse on the Nigger Question: Communicated by T. Carlyle*. London: Thomas Bosworth.
— (1863). 'Ilias (Americana) in Nuce'. *Macmillan's Magazine* 8.46 (August): 301.
— (1867). 'Shooting Niagara: And After?' *Macmillan's Magazine* 16.94 (August): 319–36.
— (1892). *Lectures on the History of Literature, Delivered by Thomas Carlyle, April to July 1838*. Ed. J. Reay Greene. London: Ellis and Elvey.
— (1896–9). *The Works of Thomas Carlyle*. Ed. Henry Duff Traill. 30 vols. London: Chapman and Hall.
— (1898). *Two Note Books of Thomas Carlyle*. Ed. Charles Eliot Norton. New York: Grolier Club.
— (1951). *Carlyle's Unfinished History of German Literature*. Ed. Hill Shine. Lexington: University of Kentucky Press.
— (1974). *Two Reminiscences*. Ed. John Clubbe. Durham, NC: Duke University Press.
— (1983). *Latter-Day Pamphlets*. Ed. Michael K. Goldberg and Jules P. Seigel. Ottawa: Canadian Federation for the Humanities.
— (1993–). *The Norman and Charlotte Strouse Edition of the Writings of Thomas Carlyle*. Ed. Mark Engel et al. 5 vols to date. Berkeley: University of California Press.
— (1997). *Reminiscences*. Ed. Kenneth J. Fielding and Ian Campbell. Oxford: Oxford University Press.
—, and Jane Welsh Carlyle (1970–). *The Collected Letters of Thomas and Jane Welsh Carlyle*. Ed. Charles Richard Sanders et al. 47 vols to date. Durham, NC: Duke University Press.

Casanova, Pascale (2004 [1999]). *The World Republic of Letters*. Trans. M. B. DeBevoise. Cambridge, MA: Harvard University Press.
— (2005). 'Literature as a World'. *New Left Review* 31 (January/February): 71–90.
Cayton, Mary Kupiec (1987). 'The Making of an American Prophet: Emerson, His Audiences, and the Rise of the Culture Industry in Nineteenth-Century America'. *American Historical Review* 92: 597–620.
Chai, Leon (1987). *The Romantic Foundations of the American Renaissance*. Ithaca: Cornell University Press.
Chambers, Robert (1837 [1835]). *History of the English Language and Literature*. Edinburgh: William and Robert Chambers.
—, and Royal Robbins (1837). *History of the English Language and Literature: To Which Is Added a History of American Contributions to the English Language and Literature*. Hartford, CT: Edward Hopkins.
Channing, William Ellery (1830). 'National Literature'. *Christian Examiner* 7.3 (January): 269–95.
Charvat, William (1968). *The Profession of Authorship in America, 1800–1870: The Papers of William Charvat*. Ed. Matthew J. Bruccoli. Columbus: Ohio State University Press.
Chasles, Philarète (1844). 'Des tendances littéraires en Angleterre et en Amérique'. *Revue des deux mondes* 7 (August): 497–545.
Cheah, Pheng (2003). *Spectral Nationality: Passages of Freedom from Kant to Postcolonial Literatures of Liberation*. New York: Columbia University Press.
Clark, Lewis Gaylord (1840). '"Carlyle-ism"'. *Knickerbocker* 15.6 (June): 525–8.
Clark, William (2006). *Academic Charisma and the Origins of the Research University*. Chicago: University of Chicago Press.
Clarke, James Freeman (1838). 'Thomas Carlyle: The German Scholar'. *Western Messenger* 4.6 (February): 417–23.
— (1864). 'The Two Carlyles, or Carlyle Past and Present'. *Christian Examiner* 77.2 (September): 206–31.
Claybaugh, Amanda (2007). *The Novel of Purpose: Literature and Social Reform in the Anglo-American World*. Ithaca: Cornell University Press.
Clayton, Jay, and Eric Rothstein (1991). 'Figures in the Corpus: Theories of Influence and Intertextuality'. *Influence and Intertextuality in Literary History*. Ed. Jay Clayton and Eric Rothstein. Madison: University of Wisconsin Press. 3–36.
Coleridge, Samuel Taylor (1987). *Lectures 1808–1819: On Literature*. Ed. R. A. Foakes. 2 vols. London: Routledge and Kegan Paul / Princeton: Princeton University Press.
Collini, Stefan (1991). *Public Moralists: Political Thought and Intellectual Life in Britain, 1850–1930*. Oxford: Clarendon Press.

Collins, Carol (1997). 'Anti-Dogmatism and the "Metaphorical Quashee": Thomas Carlyle's "An Occasional Discourse on the Negro Question"'. *Carlyle Studies Annual* 17: 23–40.

Commager, Henry Steele (1967 [1965]). 'The Search for a Usable Past'. *The Search for a Usable Past and Other Essays in Historiography*. New York: Knopf. 3–27.

Connor, Walker (1994). *Ethnonationalism: The Quest for Understanding*. Princeton: Princeton University Press.

Conway, Moncure Daniel (1880). 'Thomas Carlyle'. *Harper's New Monthly Magazine* 62.372 (December): 888–912.

— (1882). *Emerson at Home and Abroad*. Boston: James R. Osgood.

— (1904). *Autobiography: Memories and Experiences*. 2 vols. Boston and New York: Houghton, Mifflin and Company.

Cooper, James Fenimore (1991 [1828]). *Notions of the Americans: Picked up by a Travelling Bachelor*. Ed. Gary Williams. Albany: State University of New York Press.

Cordell, Ryan (2015). 'Viral Textuality in Nineteenth-Century US Newspaper Exchanges'. *Virtual Victorians: Networks, Connections, Technologies*. Ed. Veronica Alfano and Andrew Stauffer. New York: Palgrave Macmillan. 29–56.

Cousin, Victor (1832 [1828]). *Introduction to the History of Philosophy*. Trans. Henning Gotfried Linberg. Boston: Hilliard, Gray, Little, and Wilkins.

Crawford, Martin (1983). 'The Anglo-American Crisis of the Early 1860s: A Framework for Revision'. *South Atlantic Quarterly* 82.4 (Autumn): 406–23.

Cumming, Mark (2004). 'Lectures of Thomas Carlyle'. *The Carlyle Encyclopedia*. Ed. Mark Cumming. Madison, NJ: Fairleigh Dickinson University Press. 275–9.

Dallal, Jenine Abboushi (2001). 'American Imperialism UnManifest: Emerson's "Inquest" and Cultural Regeneration'. *American Literature* 73.1 (March): 47–83.

Deese, Helen R., and Guy R. Woodall (1986). 'A Calendar of Lectures Presented by the Boston Society for the Diffusion of Useful Knowledge (1829–1847)'. *Studies in the American Renaissance* 17–67.

DeSpain, Jessica (2014). *Nineteenth-Century Transatlantic Reprinting and the Embodied Book*. Farnham: Ashgate.

Dickerson, Vanessa D. (2008). *Dark Victorians*. Urbana and Chicago: University of Illinois Press.

Dilke, Charles Wentworth (1868). *Greater Britain: A Record of Travel in English-Speaking Countries during 1866 and 1867*. 2 vols. London: Macmillan and Co.

Dimock, Wai Chee (2001). 'Deep Time: American Literature and World History'. *American Literary History* 13.4 (Winter): 755–75.
— (2006). 'Scales of Aggregation: Prenational, Subnational, Transnational'. *American Literary History* 18.2 (Summer): 219–28.
Dolan, Neal (2009). *Emerson's Liberalism*. Madison: University of Wisconsin Press.
Donovan, Stephen, Danuta Fjellestad and Rolf Lundén (2008). 'Introduction: Author, Authorship, Authority, and Other Matters'. *Authority Matters: Rethinking the Theory and Practice of Authorship*. Ed. Stephen Donovan, Danuta Fjellestad and Rolf Lundén. Amsterdam and New York: Rodopi. 1–19.
Douglass, Frederick (1982 [1848]). 'A Day, a Deed, an Event, Glorious in the Annals of Philanthropy: An Address Delivered in Rochester, New York, on 1 August 1848'. *The Frederick Douglass Papers. Series One: Speeches, Debates, and Interviews. Volume 2: 1847–54*. Ed. John W. Blassingame, Richard G. Carlson, Clarence L. Mohr, Julie S. Jones, John R. McKivigan, David R. Roediger and Jason H. Silverman. New Haven: Yale University Press. 132–47.
— (2018 [1869]). 'Our Composite Nationality'. *The Speeches of Frederick Douglass: A Critical Edition*. Ed. John R. McKivigan, Julie Husband and Heather L. Kaufman. New Haven: Yale University Press. 278–303.
Dowling, David (2014). 'Publishers'. *Ralph Waldo Emerson in Context*. Ed. Wesley T. Mott. Cambridge: Cambridge University Press. 221–9.
Doyle, Laura (2008). *Freedom's Empire: Race and the Rise of the Novel in Atlantic Modernity, 1640–1940*. Durham, NC: Duke University Press.
Duyckinck, Evert Augustus (1857). 'American Preface'. In: Robert Aris Willmott, *The Poets of the Nineteenth Century*. Ed. Evert Augustus Duyckinck. New York: Harper and Brothers. vi.
Easley, Alexis (2011). *Literary Celebrity, Gender, and Victorian Authorship, 1850–1914*. Newark: University of Delaware Press.
Eckel, Leslie Elizabeth (2013). *Atlantic Citizens: Nineteenth-Century American Writers at Work in the World*. Edinburgh: Edinburgh University Press.
Eckermann, Johann Peter (1839 [1836]). *Conversations with Goethe in the Last Years of His Life*. Trans. Margaret Fuller. Boston: Hilliard, Gray, and Company.
Edwards, Owen Dudley (2013). '"The Tone of the Preacher": Carlyle as Public Lecturer in *On Heroes, Hero-Worship, and the Heroic in History*'. *On Heroes, Hero-Worship, and the Heroic in History*. Ed. David R. Sorensen and Brent E. Kinser. New Haven: Yale University Press. 199–208.
Eliot, George (1992 [1855]). 'Thomas Carlyle'. *Selected Critical Writings*. Ed. Rosemary Ashton. Oxford: Oxford University Press. 187–92.

Eliot, Simon (2012). 'The Business of Victorian Publishing'. *The Cambridge Companion to the Victorian Novel.* Ed. Deirdre David. Cambridge: Cambridge University Press. 36–61.

Emerson, Ralph Waldo (1845). 'Advertisement'. In: Thomas Carlyle, *Critical and Miscellaneous Essays.* Philadelphia: Carey and Hart. 3.

— (1884). 'Carlyle'. *Lectures and Biographical Sketches.* Ed. James Elliot Cabot. Boston: Houghton Mifflin. 453–63.

— (1939, 1990–5). *The Letters of Ralph Waldo Emerson.* Ed. Ralph L. Rusk and Eleanor M. Tilton. 10 vols. New York: Columbia University Press.

— (1959–72). *The Early Lectures of Ralph Waldo Emerson.* Ed. Stephen E. Whicher, Robert E. Spiller and Wallace E. Williams. 3 vols. Cambridge, MA: Belknap Press of Harvard University Press.

— (1960–82). *The Journals and Miscellaneous Notebooks of Ralph Waldo Emerson.* Ed. William H. Gilman et al. 16 vols. Cambridge, MA: Belknap Press of Harvard University Press.

— (1971–2013). *The Collected Works of Ralph Waldo Emerson.* Ed. Alfred R. Ferguson et al. 10 vols. Cambridge, MA: Belknap Press of Harvard University Press.

— (1990–4). *The Topical Notebooks of Ralph Waldo Emerson.* Ed. Ralph H. Orth et al. 3 vols. Columbia: University of Missouri Press.

— (1995). *Emerson's Antislavery Writings.* Ed. Len Gougeon and Joel Myerson. New Haven: Yale University Press.

— (2001). *The Later Lectures of Ralph Waldo Emerson: 1843–1871.* Ed. Ronald A. Bosco and Joel Myerson. 2 vols. Athens: University of Georgia Press.

—, and Thomas Carlyle (1964). *The Correspondence of Emerson and Carlyle.* Ed. Joseph Slater. New York: Columbia University Press.

Epstein, James (2000). '"America" in the Victorian Cultural Imagination'. *Anglo-American Attitudes: From Revolution to Partnership.* Ed. Fred M. Leventhal and Roland Quinault. Aldershot and Burlington, VT: Ashgate. 107–23.

Espagne, Michel, and Michael Werner, eds (1994). *Philologiques III: Qu'est-ce qu'une littérature nationale? Approches pour une théorie interculturelle du champ littéraire.* Paris: Editions de la Maison des sciences de l'homme.

Everett, Alexander Hill (1834). *An Address to the Phi Beta Kappa Society of Bowdoin College, on the Present State of Polite Learning in England and America.* Boston: Charles Bowen.

— (1835). 'Thomas Carlyle'. *North American Review* 41.89 (October): 454–82.

Everton, Michael J. (2011). *The Grand Chorus of Complaint: Authors and the Business Ethics of American Publishing.* New York: Oxford University Press.

Fender, Stephen (1992). *Sea Changes: British Emigration and American Literature.* Cambridge: Cambridge University Press.

Field, Peter S. (2001). '"The Transformation of Genius into Practical Power": Ralph Waldo Emerson and the Public Lecture'. *Journal of the Early Republic* 21.3 (Autumn): 467–93.

Fisch, Audrey A. (2000). *American Slaves in Victorian England: Abolitionist Politics in Popular Literature and Culture*. Cambridge: Cambridge University Press.

Forster, Michael N. (2010). *After Herder: Philosophy of Language in the German Tradition*. Oxford: Oxford University Press.

Fox, Caroline (1882). *Memories of Old Friends, Being Extracts from the Journals and Letters of Caroline Fox*. Ed. Horace N. Pym. London: Smith, Elder, and Company.

Freese, Peter (1996). '"Westward the Course of Empire Takes Its Way": The *translatio*-Concept in Popular American Writing and Painting'. *Amerikastudien* 41.2: 265–95.

Friedman, Monroe (1999). *Consumer Boycotts: Effecting Change Through the Marketplace and the Media*. New York and London: Routledge.

Frothingham, Nathaniel Langdon (1836). 'Sartor Resartus'. *Christian Examiner* 21 (September): 74–84.

Froude, James Anthony (1884). *Thomas Carlyle: A History of His Life in London, 1834–1881*. 2 vols. London: Longmans, Green, and Company.

— (1886). *Oceana, or England and Her Colonies*. London: Longmans, Green, and Company.

Fuller, Margaret (1987). *The Letters of Margaret Fuller*. Vol. 4: *1845–47*. Ed. Robert N. Hudspeth. Ithaca: Cornell University Press.

Furedi, Frank (2013). *Authority: A Sociological History*. Cambridge: Cambridge University Press.

Gikandi, Simon (1996). *Maps of Englishness: Writing Identity in the Culture of Colonialism*. New York: Columbia University Press.

Giles, Paul (2001). *Transatlantic Insurrections: British Culture and the Formation of American Literature, 1730–1860*. Philadelphia: University of Pennsylvania Press.

— (2003). 'Transnationalism and Classic American Literature'. *PMLA* 118.1 (January): 62–77.

— (2006). *Atlantic Republic: The American Tradition in English Literature*. Oxford: Oxford University Press.

— (2011). *The Global Remapping of American Literature*. Princeton: Princeton University Press.

— (2016). 'Introduction: The New Atlantic Literary Studies'. *The Edinburgh Companion to Atlantic Literary Studies*. Ed. Leslie Elizabeth Eckel and Clare Frances Elliott. Edinburgh: Edinburgh University Press. 1–14.

Gilfillan, George (1845). 'Ralph Waldo Emerson'. *A Gallery of Literary Portraits*. Edinburgh: William Tait. 288–306.

— (1848). 'Ralph Waldo Emerson; or, the "Coming Man"'. *Tait's Edinburgh Magazine* 15 (January): 17–23.
Goethe, Johann Wolfgang (1887 [1830]). 'Dedication and Introduction . . . to the Translation of Carlyle's *Life of Schiller*'. *Correspondence between Goethe and Carlyle*. Trans. and ed. Charles Eliot Norton. London and New York: Macmillan. 299–323.
—, and Thomas Carlyle (1887). *Correspondence between Goethe and Carlyle*. Trans. and ed. Charles Eliot Norton. London and New York: Macmillan.
Gohdes, Clarence (1944). *American Literature in Nineteenth-Century England*. Carbondale: Southern Illinois University Press.
Goldberg, Michael (1976). 'A Universal "Howl of Execration": Carlyle's *Latter-Day Pamphlets* and Their Critical Reception'. *Carlyle and His Contemporaries: Essays in Honor of Charles Richard Sanders*. Ed. John Clubbe. Durham, NC: Duke University Press. 129–47.
Gordon, Adam (2020). *Prophets, Publicists, and Parasites: Antebellum Print Culture and the Rise of the Critic*. Amherst: University of Massachusetts Press.
Gougeon, Len (1989). 'Emerson, Carlyle, and the Civil War'. *New England Quarterly* 62.3 (September): 403–23.
— (2006). 'Emerson and the British: Challenging the Limits of Liberty'. *REAL: Yearbook of Research in English and American Literature* 22: 179–213.
Greenham, David (2012). *Emerson's Transatlantic Romanticism*. New York: Palgrave Macmillan.
Greenspan, Ezra (2000). *George Palmer Putnam: Representative American Publisher*. University Park: Pennsylvania State University Press.
Grusin, Richard A. (1991). *Transcendentalist Hermeneutics: Institutional Authority and the Higher Criticism of the Bible*. Durham, NC: Duke University Press.
Guillory, John (1993). *Cultural Capital: The Problem of Literary Canon Formation*. Chicago: University of Chicago Press.
Guinn, Matthew (1999). 'Emerson's Southern Critics, 1838–1862'. *Resources for American Literary Study* 25.2: 174–91.
Habich, Robert D. (2011). *Building Their Own Waldos: Emerson's First Biographers and the Politics of Life-Writing in the Gilded Age*. Iowa City: University of Iowa Press.
Hanlon, Christopher (2013). *America's England: Antebellum Literature and Atlantic Sectionalism*. New York: Oxford University Press.
— (2016). 'Emerson's Atlantic States'. *The Edinburgh Companion to Atlantic Literary Studies*. Ed. Leslie Elizabeth Eckel and Clare Frances Elliott. Edinburgh: Edinburgh University Press. 59–72.
Harris, Kenneth Marc (1978). *Carlyle and Emerson: Their Long Debate*. Cambridge, MA: Harvard University Press.

Harrold, Charles Frederick (1934). *Carlyle and German Thought: 1819–1834*. New Haven: Yale University Press.
Harvey, Samantha (2013). *Transatlantic Transcendentalism: Coleridge, Emerson, and Nature*. Edinburgh: Edinburgh University Press.
Haynes, Sam W. (1997). 'Anglophobia and the Annexation of Texas: The Quest for National Security'. *Manifest Destiny and Empire: American Antebellum Expansionism*. Ed. Sam W. Haynes and Christopher Morris. College Station: Texas A&M University Press. 115–45.
Hedge, Frederic Henry (1883). 'The Correspondence of Carlyle and Emerson'. *Christian Register* 62.11 (15 March): 164.
Herder, Johann Gottfried (1800 [1784–91]). *Outlines of a Philosophy of the History of Man*. Trans. T. Churchill. London: J. Johnson.
Hewitt, Martin (2002). 'Aspects of Platform Culture in Nineteenth-Century Britain'. *Nineteenth-Century Prose* 29.1 (Spring): 1–32.
Higginson, Thomas Wentworth (1868). 'The American Lecture-System'. *Macmillan's Magazine* 18.103 (May): 48–56.
Hobsbawm, Eric (1990). *Nations and Nationalism Since 1780: Programme, Myth, Reality*. Cambridge: Cambridge University Press.
Holmes, George Frederick (1850). 'Latter-Day Pamphlets'. *Southern Quarterly Review* 18.36 (November): 313–56.
Horsman, Reginald (1981). *Race and Manifest Destiny: The Origins of American Racial Anglo-Saxonism*. Cambridge, MA: Harvard University Press.
Howe, Daniel Walker (1970). *The Unitarian Conscience: Harvard Moral Philosophy, 1805–1861*. Cambridge, MA: Harvard University Press.
Hudson, Nicholas (1996). 'From "Nation" to "Race": The Origin of Racial Classification in Eighteenth-Century Thought'. *Eighteenth-Century Studies* 29.3 (Spring): 247–64.
Hunt, Leigh (1839). 'Mr Carlyle's Lectures on the Revolutions of Modern Europe'. *Examiner* (5 May): 278.
Ireland, Alexander (1882). *Ralph Waldo Emerson: His Life, Genius, and Writings: A Biographical Sketch*. London: Simpkin, Marshall, and Company.
Jackson, Leon (1996). 'The Social Construction of Thomas Carlyle's New England Reputation, 1834–36'. *Proceedings of the American Antiquarian Society* 106.1: 165–89.
— (1999). 'The Reader Retailored: Thomas Carlyle, His American Audiences, and the Politics of Evidence'. *Book History* 2: 146–72.
— (2008). *The Business of Letters: Authorial Economies in Antebellum America*. Stanford: Stanford University Press.
James, Henry (1883). 'The Correspondence of Carlyle and Emerson'. *Century Magazine* 26.2 (June): 265–72.
— (1987). *The Complete Notebooks of Henry James*. Ed. Leon Edel and Lyall H. Powers. New York: Oxford University Press.

Joseph, Marrisa (2019). *Victorian Literary Businesses: The Management and Practices of the British Publishing Industry*. Cham, Switzerland: Palgrave Macmillan.

Jurt, Joseph (2009). 'Le champ littéraire entre le national et le transnational'. *L'espace intellectuel en Europe: De la formation des États-nations à la mondialisation, XIXe–XXIe siècle*. Ed. Gisèle Sapiro. Paris: La Découverte. 201–32.

Kaplan, Fred (1983). *Thomas Carlyle: A Biography*. Ithaca: Cornell University Press.

Kaufman, Will, and Heidi Slettedahl Macpherson (2000). 'Introduction: Transatlantic Studies: A New Paradigm'. *Transatlantic Studies*. Ed. Will Kaufman and Heidi Slettedahl Macpherson. Lanham, MD: University Press of America. xvii–xxiii.

Kinser, Brent E. (2011). *The American Civil War in the Shaping of British Democracy*. Farnham and Burlington, VT: Ashgate.

Klancher, Jon (2000). 'The Vocation of Criticism and the Crisis of the Republic of Letters'. *The Cambridge History of Literary Criticism*. Vol. 5: *Romanticism*. Ed. Marshall Brown. Cambridge: Cambridge University Press. 269–320.

— (2013). *Transfiguring the Arts and Sciences: Knowledge and Cultural Institutions in the Romantic Age*. New York: Cambridge University Press.

Klipstein, Louis F. (1849). 'Introductory Ethnological Essay'. *Analecta Anglo-Saxonica: Selections, in Prose and Verse, from the Anglo-Saxon Literature, with an Introductory Ethnological Essay, and Notes, Critical and Explanatory*. 2 vols. New York: George P. Putnam. 1: 9–98.

Knox, Robert (1850). *The Races of Men: A Fragment*. Philadelphia: Lea and Blanchard.

Koch, Daniel R. (2012). *Ralph Waldo Emerson in Europe: Class, Race, and Revolution in the Making of an American Thinker*. London and New York: I. B. Tauris.

Kramer, Paul A. (2002). 'Empires, Exceptions and Anglo-Saxons: Race and Rule between the British and United States Empires, 1880–1920'. *Journal of American History* 88.4 (March): 1315–53.

Kumar, Krishan (2003). *The Making of English National Identity*. Cambridge: Cambridge University Press.

Lease, Benjamin (1981). *Anglo-American Encounters: England and the Rise of American Literature*. Cambridge: Cambridge University Press.

Lee, Yoon Sun (2004). *Nationalism and Irony: Burke, Scott, Carlyle*. New York: Oxford University Press.

Leverenz, David (1989). *Manhood and the American Renaissance*. Ithaca: Cornell University Press.

Levine, Caroline (2013). 'From Nation to Network'. *Victorian Studies* 55.4 (Summer): 647–66.

Lewis, Tania, and Emily Potter, eds (2011). *Ethical Consumption: A Critical Introduction*. London and New York: Routledge.
Leypoldt, Günter (2009). *Cultural Authority in the Age of Whitman: A Transatlantic Perspective*. Edinburgh: Edinburgh University Press.
Longfellow, Henry Wadsworth (1838). 'Anglo-Saxon Literature'. *North American Review* 47.100 (July): 90–134.
Lorimer, Douglas A. (1978). *Colour, Class and the Victorians: English Attitudes to the Negro in the Mid-Nineteenth Century*. Leicester: University of Leicester Press.
Lowell, James Russell (1849). 'Nationality in Literature'. *North American Review* 69.144 (July): 196–215.
MacDougall, Hugh A. (1982). *Racial Myth in English History: Trojans, Teutons, and Anglo-Saxons*. Hanover, NH: University Press of New England.
McGettigan, Katie (2017a). '"Across the Waters of This Disputed Ocean": The Material Production of American Literature in Nineteenth-Century Britain'. *Interventions: Rethinking the Nineteenth Century*. Ed. Andrew Smith and Anna Barton. Manchester: Manchester University Press. 129–48.
— (2017b). 'Henry Wadsworth Longfellow and the Transatlantic Materials of American Literature'. *American Literature* 89.4 (December): 727–59.
McGill, Meredith L. (2003). *American Literature and the Culture of Reprinting, 1834–1853*. Philadelphia: University of Pennsylvania Press.
McInturff, Kate (2003). 'The Uses and Abuses of World Literature'. *Journal of American Culture* 26.2 (June): 224–36.
McVey, Sheila (1975). 'Nineteenth-Century America: Publishing in a Developing Country'. *Annals of the American Academy of Political and Social Science* 421 (September): 67–80.
Madison, Charles A. (1966). *Book Publishing in America*. New York: McGraw-Hill.
Manning, Susan (2005). '"Grounds for Comparison": The Place of Style in Transatlantic Romanticism'. *Wordsworth in American Literary Culture*. Ed. Joel Pace and Matthew Scott. Basingstoke and New York: Palgrave Macmillan. 19–42.
— (2013). *Poetics of Character: Transatlantic Encounters, 1700–1900*. Cambridge: Cambridge University Press.
—, and Andrew Taylor (2007). 'Introduction: What Is Transatlantic Literary Studies?' *Transatlantic Literary Studies: A Reader*. Ed. Susan Manning and Andrew Taylor. Edinburgh: Edinburgh University Press. 1–13.
Marshall, P. David (1997). *Celebrity and Power: Fame in Contemporary Culture*. Minneapolis: University of Minnesota Press.
Marshall, Peter J. (2012). *Remaking the British Atlantic: The United States and the British Empire after American Independence*. Oxford: Oxford University Press.

Martineau, Harriet (1837). *Society in America*. 2 vols. New York and London: Saunders and Otley.
— (1877). *Harriet Martineau's Autobiography*. Ed. Maria Weston Chapman. 3 vols. London: Smith, Elder, and Company.
Mazzeo, Tilar J. (2007). *Plagiarism and Literary Property in the Romantic Period*. Philadelphia: University of Pennsylvania Press.
Mendilow, Jonathan (1993). 'Waiting for the Axe to Fall: Carlyle's Place in the Study of Crises of Authority'. *Political Research Quarterly* 46.3 (September): 601–18.
Merivale, Herman (1840). 'Carlyle on the French Revolution'. *Edinburgh Review* 71.144 (July): 411–45.
Mill, John Stuart (1850). 'The Negro Question'. *Fraser's Magazine* 41.241 (January): 25–31.
Miller, Perry (1964). 'New England's Transcendentalism: Native or Imported?' *Literary Views: Critical and Historical Essays*. Ed. Carroll Camden. Chicago: University of Chicago Press. 115–29.
Milnes, Richard Monckton (1840). 'American Philosophy – Emerson's Works'. *London and Westminster Review* 33.65 (March): 186–201.
Mott, Wesley T. (1989). *'The Strains of Eloquence': Emerson and His Sermons*. University Park: Pennsylvania State University Press.
— (2014). 'Britain'. *Ralph Waldo Emerson in Context*. Ed. Wesley T. Mott. Cambridge: Cambridge University Press. 21–30.
Mueller-Vollmer, Kurt (1990). 'Herder and the Formation of an American National Consciousness during the Early Republic'. *Herder Today*. Ed. Kurt Mueller-Vollmer. Berlin and New York: de Gruyter. 415–30.
Murdoch, Alexander (2004). *British Emigration, 1603–1914*. Basingstoke: Palgrave Macmillan.
Murray, Hannah-Rose (2020). *Advocates of Freedom: African American Transatlantic Abolitionism in the British Isles*. New York: Cambridge University Press.
Myerson, Joel (1982). *Ralph Waldo Emerson: A Descriptive Bibliography*. Pittsburgh: University of Pittsburgh Press.
—, ed. (1992). *Emerson and Thoreau: The Contemporary Reviews*. Cambridge: Cambridge University Press.
— (1996). 'Ralph Waldo Emerson's Income from His Books'. *The Professions of Authorship: Essays in Honor of Matthew J. Bruccoli*. Ed. Richard Layman and Joel Myerson. Columbia: University of South Carolina Press. 135–49.
— (2005). *Supplement to Ralph Waldo Emerson: A Descriptive Bibliography*. Pittsburgh: University of Pittsburgh Press.
— (2014). 'Money'. *Ralph Waldo Emerson in Context*. Ed. Wesley T. Mott. Cambridge: Cambridge University Press. 213–20.

Newfield, Christopher (1996). *The Emerson Effect: Individualism and Submission in America*. Chicago: University of Chicago Press.

Nicoloff, Philip L. (1961). *Emerson on Race and History: An Examination of English Traits*. New York: Columbia University Press.

Niles, John D. (2015). *The Idea of Anglo-Saxon England, 1066–1901: Remembering, Forgetting, Deciphering, and Renewing the Past*. Chichester: Wiley-Blackwell.

Nixon, Jude V. (1996). 'Racialism and the Politics of Emancipation in Carlyle's "Occasional Discourse on the Nigger Question"'. *Carlyle Studies Annual* 16: 89–108.

Norton, Andrews (1833). 'Recent Publications Concerning Goethe'. *Select Journal of Foreign Periodical Literature* 1.2 (April): 250–93.

— (1992 [1838]). 'The New School in Literature and Religion'. *Boston Daily Advertiser* 43 (27 August): 2. Repr. in Myerson 1992: 33–5.

O'Neill, Bonnie Carr (2008). '"The Best of Me Is There": Emerson as Lecturer and Celebrity'. *American Literature* 80.4 (December): 739–67.

Orr, Mary (2003). *Intertextuality: Debates and Contexts*. Cambridge: Polity Press.

Owenson, Sydney (1971 [1837]). '[Review of Carlyle's *The French Revolution*]'. *Athenæum* (20 May): 353–55. Repr. in Seigel 1971: 46–51.

Packer, Barbara L. (1995). 'The Transcendentalists'. *The Cambridge History of American Literature*. Vol. 2: *1820–1865*. Ed. Sacvan Bercovitch. New York: Cambridge University Press. 329–604.

— (2010). 'Forgiving the Giver: Emerson, Carlyle, Thoreau'. *Emerson and Thoreau: Figures of Friendship*. Ed. John T. Lysaker and William Rossi. Bloomington: Indiana University Press. 33–50.

Painter, Nell Irvin (2010). *The History of White People*. New York: Norton.

Parker, Theodore (1850). 'The Writings of Ralph Waldo Emerson'. *Massachusetts Quarterly Review* 3.2 (March): 200–55.

Paryz, Marek (2006). 'Beyond the Traveler's Testimony: Emerson's *English Traits* and the Construction of Postcolonial Counter-Discourse'. *American Transcendental Quarterly* 20.3: 565–90.

Patten, Allen (2010). '"The Most Natural State": Herder and Nationalism'. *History of Political Thought* 31.4 (Winter): 657–80.

Pease, Donald E. (1995). 'Author'. *Critical Terms for Literary Study*. Ed. Frank Lentricchia and Thomas McLaughlin. Chicago: University of Chicago Press. 105–17.

Perkins, Bradford (1968). *The Great Rapprochement: England and the United States, 1895–1914*. New York: Atheneum.

Persak, Christine (1991). 'Rhetoric in Praise of Silence: The Ideology of Carlyle's Paradox'. *Rhetoric Society Quarterly* 21.1 (Winter): 38–52.

Peterson, Linda H. (2009). *Becoming a Woman of Letters: Myths of Authorship and Facts of the Victorian Market*. Princeton: Princeton University Press.

Phillips, George Searle (1855). *Emerson, His Life and Writings*. London: Holyoak & Co.
Pizer, John (2000). 'Goethe's "World Literature" Paradigm and Contemporary Cultural Globalization'. *Comparative Literature* 52.3 (Summer): 213–27.
Poe, Edgar Allan (1846). 'Marginalia'. *Graham's Magazine* 29.6 (December): 311–13.
Poovey, Mary (1988). *Uneven Developments: The Ideological Work of Gender in Mid-Victorian England*. Chicago: University of Chicago Press.
Putnam, George Palmer (1845). *American Facts: Notes and Statistics Relative to the Government, Resources, Engagements, Manufactures, Commerce, Religion, Education, Literature, Fine Arts, Manners and Customs of the United States of America*. London: Wiley and Putnam.
Railton, Stephen (1991). *Authorship and Audience: Literary Performance in the American Renaissance*. Princeton: Princeton University Press.
Ray, Angela G. (2005). *The Lyceum and Public Culture in the Nineteenth-Century United States*. East Lansing: Michigan State University Press.
— (2013). 'How Cosmopolitan Was the Lyceum, Anyway?' *The Cosmopolitan Lyceum: Lecture Culture and the Globe in Nineteenth-Century America*. Ed. Tom F. Wright. Amherst: University of Massachusetts Press. 23–41.
Reynolds, Larry J. (1988). *European Revolutions and the American Literary Renaissance*. New Haven: Yale University Press.
Rezek, Joseph (2014). 'What We Need from Transatlantic Studies'. *American Literary History* 26.4 (Winter): 791–803.
— (2015). *London and the Making of Provincial Literature: Aesthetics and the Transatlantic Book Trade, 1800–1850*. Philadelphia: University of Pennsylvania Press.
Richardson, Robert D. (1982). 'Emerson on History'. *Emerson: Prospect and Retrospect*. Ed. Joel Porte. Cambridge, MA: Harvard University Press. 49–64.
— (1995). *Emerson: The Mind on Fire*. Berkeley: University of California Press.
Riede, David G. (1989). 'Transgression, Authority, and the Church of Literature in Carlyle'. *Victorian Connections*. Ed. Jerome J. McGann. Charlottesville: University Press of Virginia. 88–120.
— (1991). *Oracles and Hierophants: Constructions of Romantic Authority*. Ithaca: Cornell University Press.
Robbins, Bruce (1998). 'Introduction Part I: Actually Existing Cosmopolitanism'. *Cosmopolitics: Thinking and Feeling beyond the Nation*. Ed. Pheng Cheah and Bruce Robbins. Minneapolis: University of Minnesota Press. 1–19.
Robinson, David M. (1982). *Apostle of Culture: Emerson as Preacher and Lecturer*. Philadelphia: University of Pennsylvania Press.
— (1993). *Emerson and the Conduct of Life: Pragmatism and Ethical Purpose in the Later Work*. New York: Cambridge University Press.

— (2010). 'British Science, the London Lectures, and Emerson's Philosophical Reorientation'. *Emerson for the Twenty-First Century: Global Perspectives on an American Icon*. Ed. Barry Tharaud. Newark: University of Delaware Press. 285–300.

Robinson, Henry Crabb (1938). *On Books and Their Writers*. Ed. Edith J. Morley. 3 vols. London: Dent.

Rose, Carol M. (1991). 'Property as Wealth, Property as Propriety'. *Nomos* 33: 223–47.

Rosenberg, Philip (1974). *The Seventh Hero: Thomas Carlyle and the Theory of Radical Activism*. Cambridge, MA: Harvard University Press.

Rowe, John Carlos (2003). 'Nineteenth-Century United States Literary Culture and Transnationality'. *PMLA* 118.1 (January): 78–89.

Said, Edward W. (1993). *Culture and Imperialism*. London: Chatto and Windus.

St Clair, William (2004). *The Reading Nation in the Romantic Period*. Cambridge: Cambridge University Press.

Salmon, Richard (2013). *The Formation of the Victorian Literary Profession*. Cambridge: Cambridge University Press.

Schapiro, J. Salwyn (1945). 'Thomas Carlyle, Prophet of Fascism'. *Journal of Modern History* 17.2 (June): 97–115.

Schlegel, Friedrich (1818 [1815]). *Lectures on the History of Literature, Ancient and Modern*. Trans. John Gibson Lockhart. 2 vols. Edinburgh: William Blackwood.

Scott, Donald M. (1980). 'The Popular Lecture and the Creation of a Public in Mid-Nineteenth-Century America'. *Journal of American History* 66.4 (March): 791–809.

— (1983). 'Print and the Public Lecture System, 1840–60'. *Printing and Society in Early America*. Ed. William L. Joyce, David D. Hall, Richard D. Brown and John B. Hench. Worcester, MA: American Antiquarian Society. 278–99.

Scudder, Townsend (1935a). 'Emerson's British Lecture Tour, 1847–1848, Part I: The Preparations for the Tour, and the Nature of Emerson's Audiences'. *American Literature* 7.1 (March): 15–36.

— (1935b). 'Emerson's British Lecture Tour, 1847–1848, Part II: Emerson as a Lecturer in Britain and the Reception of the Lectures'. *American Literature* 7.2 (May): 166–80.

— (1936). 'A Chronological List of Emerson's Lectures on His British Lecture Tour of 1847–1848'. *PMLA* 51.1 (March): 243–8.

Seigel, Jules Paul, ed. (1971). *Thomas Carlyle: The Critical Heritage*. London: Routledge and Kegan Paul.

Sennett, Richard (1993 [1980]). *Authority*. New York: Norton.

Seville, Catherine (2006). *The Internationalisation of Copyright Law: Books, Buccaneers and the Black Flag in the Nineteenth Century*. Cambridge: Cambridge University Press.

— (2009). 'Copyright'. *The Cambridge History of the Book in Britain*. Vol. 6: *1830–1914*. Ed. David McKitterick. Cambridge: Cambridge University Press. 214–37.

Sewell, William Henry (1840). 'Carlyle's *Works*'. *Quarterly Review* 66 (September): 446–503.

Shields, Juliet (2016). *Nation and Migration: The Making of British Atlantic Literature, 1765–1835*. New York: Oxford University Press.

Shils, Edward (1972). *The Constitution of Society*. Chicago: University of Chicago Press.

Simmons, Nancy Craig (2006). 'Emerson and His Audiences: The New England Lectures, 1843–1844'. *Emerson Bicentennial Essays*. Ed. Ronald A. Bosco and Joel Myerson. Boston: Massachusetts Historical Society. 51–85.

Slater, Joseph (1952). 'George Ripley and Thomas Carlyle'. *PMLA* 67.4 (June): 341–9.

— (1964). 'Introduction'. *The Correspondence of Emerson and Carlyle*. Ed. Joseph Slater. New York: Columbia University Press. 3–94.

Small, Helen (2017). 'Speech beyond Toleration: On Carlyle and Moral Controversialism Now'. *New Literary History* 48.3 (Summer): 531–54.

Smith, Anthony D. (1986). *The Ethnic Origins of Nations*. Malden, MA: Blackwell.

— (1991). *National Identity*. Harmondsworth: Penguin.

— (2001). *Nationalism: Theory, Ideology, History*. Cambridge: Polity Press.

Smith, Sydney (1820). 'America'. *Edinburgh Review* 33 (January): 69–80.

Sommer, Tim (2016). '"If It Were in My Power to Help You": Victorian Literary Patronage in Four Unpublished Thomas Carlyle Letters'. *Harvard Library Bulletin* 27.3 (Fall): 120–40.

— (2018). 'Shakespearean Negotiations: Carlyle, Emerson, and the Ambiguities of Transatlantic Influence'. *Thomas Carlyle and the Idea of Influence*. Ed. Paul E. Kerry, Albert D. Pionke and Megan Dent. Madison, NJ: Fairleigh Dickinson University Press. 129–43.

— (2018/19). 'Transatlantic Endorsement, Metatextual Patronage: Ralph Waldo Emerson's Review(s) of Thomas Carlyle's *The French Revolution*'. *Carlyle Studies Annual* 33: 107–23.

— (2021). 'Material Exchange, Symbolic Recognition: *Weltliteratur* as Discourse and Practice in Goethe, Carlyle, and Emerson'. *Publications of the English Goethe Society* 90.1: 53–71.

Sowder, William J. (1966). *Emerson's Impact on the British Isles and Canada*. Charlottesville: University Press of Virginia.

Spencer, Benjamin T. (1957). *The Quest for Nationality: An American Literary Campaign*. Syracuse, NY: Syracuse University Press.

Spenser, Edmund (2007 [1590/6]). *The Faerie Qveene*. Ed. A. C. Hamilton. London and New York: Routledge.

Spoo, Robert (2013). *Without Copyrights: Piracy, Publishing, and the Public Domain*. New York: Oxford University Press.
Staël, Germaine de (1812 [1800]). *The Influence of Literature upon Society*. 2 vols. London: Henry Colburn.
— (1813). *Germany*. 3 vols. London: John Murray.
Stievermann, Jan (2007). *Der Sündenfall der Nachahmung: Zum Problem der Mittelbarkeit im Werk Ralph Waldo Emersons*. Paderborn, Germany: Schöningh.
— (2010). '"We Want Men . . . Who Can Open Their Eyes Wider than to a Nationality": Ralph Waldo Emerson's Vision of an American World Literature'. *Emerson for the Twenty-First Century: Global Perspectives on an American Icon*. Ed. Barry Tharaud. Newark: University of Delaware Press. 165–215.
Sussman, Herbert (1995). *Victorian Masculinities: Manhood and Masculine Poetics in Early Victorian Literature and Art*. Cambridge: Cambridge University Press.
Tamarkin, Elisa (2008). *Anglophilia: Deference, Devotion, and Antebellum America*. Chicago: University of Chicago Press.
— (2016). 'Why Forgive Carlyle?' *Representations* 134 (Spring): 64–92.
Tarr, Rodger L. (1981). 'Emendation as Challenge: Carlyle's "Negro Question" from Journal to Pamphlet'. *Papers of the Bibliographical Society of America* 75.3: 341–5.
— (1989). *Thomas Carlyle: A Descriptive Bibliography*. Oxford: Clarendon Press.
Taylor, Andrew (2004). '"Mixture is a Secret of the English Island": Transatlantic Emerson and the Location of the Intellectual'. *Atlantic Studies* 1.2: 158–77.
Taylor, Jonathan (2003). *Mastery and Slavery in Victorian Writing*. Basingstoke: Palgrave Macmillan.
Tebbel, John (1972). *A History of Book Publishing in the United States*. Vol. 1: *The Creation of an Industry 1630–1865*. New York and London: R. R. Bowker.
Teichgraeber, Richard F. (1995). *Sublime Thoughts/Penny Wisdom: Situating Emerson and Thoreau in the American Market*. Baltimore: Johns Hopkins University Press.
Tennenhouse, Leonard (2007). *The Importance of Feeling English: American Literature and the British Diaspora, 1750–1850*. Princeton: Princeton University Press.
Thackeray, William Makepeace (1971 [1837]). '[Review of Carlyle's *The French Revolution*]'. *Times* (3 August): 6. Repr. in Seigel 1971: 69–75.
Thistlethwaite, Frank (1959). *The Anglo-American Connection in the Early Nineteenth Century*. Philadelphia: University of Pennsylvania Press.

Thompson, Frank T. (1927). 'Emerson and Carlyle'. *Studies in Philology* 24.3 (July): 438–53.

Thoreau, Henry David (1975 [1847]). 'Thomas Carlyle and His Works'. *Early Essays and Miscellanies*. Ed. Joseph J. Moldenhauer and Edwin Moser with Alexander C. Kern. Princeton: Princeton University Press. 219–67.

Tocqueville, Alexis de (1840). *Democracy in America: Part the Second*. Trans. Henry Reeve. 2 vols. London: Saunders and Otley.

Van Anglen, K. P. (2010). 'Greek and Roman Classics'. *The Oxford Handbook of Transcendentalism*. Ed. Joel Myerson, Sandra Harbert Petrulionis and Laura Dassow Walls. New York: Oxford University Press. 3–8.

Vance, William Silas (1936). 'Carlyle in America before *Sartor Resartus*'. *American Literature* 7.4 (January): 363–75.

Vanden Bossche, Chris R. (1991). *Carlyle and the Search for Authority*. Columbus: Ohio State University Press.

Vanderbilt, Kermit (1986). *American Literature and the Academy: The Roots, Growth, and Maturity of a Profession*. Philadelphia: University of Pennsylvania Press.

Vardy, Alan D. (2010). *Constructing Coleridge: The Posthumous Life of the Author*. Basingstoke: Palgrave Macmillan.

Versluis, Arthur (1993). *American Transcendentalism and Asian Religions*. New York: Oxford University Press.

Voelz, Johannes (2010). *Transcendental Resistance: The New Americanists and Emerson's Challenge*. Hanover, NH: University Press of New England.

Wakefield, Edward Gibbon (1833). *England and America: A Comparison of the Social and Political State of Both Nations*. 2 vols. London: Richard Bentley.

— (1849). *A View of the Art of Colonization*. London: John W. Parker.

Walkowitz, Rebecca L. (2009). 'Comparison Literature'. *New Literary History* 40.3 (Summer): 567–82.

Waller, John O. (1965). 'Thomas Carlyle and His Nutshell Iliad'. *Bulletin of the New York Public Library* 69.1 (January): 17–30.

Walls, Laura Dassow (2003). *Emerson's Life in Science: The Culture of Truth*. Ithaca: Cornell University Press.

Warren, James Perrin (1999). *Culture of Eloquence: Oratory and Reform in Antebellum America*. University Park: Pennsylvania State University Press.

Wasson, David A. (1863). 'A Letter to Thomas Carlyle'. *Atlantic Monthly* 12.72 (October): 497–504.

Weber, Max (1978 [1921/2]). *Economy and Society: An Outline of Interpretive Sociology*. Trans. Ephraim Fischoff et al. Ed. Guenther Roth and Claus Wittich. 2 vols. Berkeley: University of California Press.

Weedon, Alexis (2003). *Victorian Publishing: The Economics of Book Production for a Mass Market, 1836–1916*. Aldershot and Burlington, VT: Ashgate.

Weisbuch, Robert (1986). *Atlantic Double-Cross: American Literature and British Influence in the Age of Emerson*. Chicago: University of Chicago Press.
— (1999). 'Post-Colonial Emerson and the Erasure of Europe'. *The Cambridge Companion to Ralph Waldo Emerson*. Ed. Joel Porte and Saundra Morris. Cambridge: Cambridge University Press. 192–217.
Wellek, René (1943). 'Emerson and German Philosophy'. *New England Quarterly* 16.1 (March): 41–62.
— (1944). 'Carlyle and the Philosophy of History'. *Philological Quarterly* 23.1 (January): 55–76.
— (1965). *A History of Modern Criticism: 1750–1950*. Vol. 3: *The Age of Transition*. New Haven: Yale University Press.
— (1970). *Discriminations: Further Concepts of Criticism*. New Haven: Yale University Press.
Wendell, Barrett (1900). *A Literary History of America*. New York: Charles Scribner's Sons.
West, Cornel (1989). *The American Evasion of Philosophy: A Genealogy of Pragmatism*. Madison: University of Wisconsin Press.
Whitman, Walt (1982). *Complete Poetry and Collected Prose*. Ed. Justin Kaplan. New York: Library of America.
Whittier, John Greenleaf (1854). 'Thomas Carlyle on the Slave Question'. *Literary Recreations and Miscellanies*. Boston: Ticknor and Fields. 34–46.
Wicksteed, Charles (1845). 'Emerson's Essays'. *Prospective Review* 1.2: 252–63.
Wider, Sarah Ann (2000). *The Critical Reception of Emerson: Unsettling All Things*. Rochester, NY: Camden House.
Williams, Daniel G. (2006). *Ethnicity and Cultural Authority: From Arnold to Du Bois*. Edinburgh: Edinburgh University Press.
Williams, Raymond (1977). *Marxism and Literature*. Oxford: Oxford University Press.
Wilson, R. Jackson (1999). 'Emerson as Lecturer: Man Thinking, Man Saying'. *The Cambridge Companion to Ralph Waldo Emerson*. Ed. Joel Porte and Saundra Morris. Cambridge: Cambridge University Press. 76–96.
Wimmer, Andreas (2013). *Ethnic Boundary Making: Institutions, Power, Networks*. New York: Oxford University Press.
Winship, Michael (1999). 'The Transatlantic Book Trade and Anglo-American Literary Culture in the Nineteenth Century'. *Reciprocal Influences: Literary Production, Distribution, and Consumption in America*. Ed. Steven Fink and Susan S. Williams. Columbus: Ohio State University Press. 98–122.
— (2007). '"In the Four Quarters of the Globe, Who Reads an American Book?"' *Literary Cultures and the Material Book*. Ed. Simon Eliot, Andrew Nash and Ian Willison. London: British Library. 367–78.
Woodberry, George Edward (1883). 'Carlyle and Emerson'. *Atlantic Monthly* 51.306 (April): 560–4.

Workman, Gillian (1974). 'Thomas Carlyle and the Governor Eyre Controversy: An Account with Some New Material'. *Victorian Studies* 18.1 (September): 77–102.

Wright, Elizur (1850). *Perforations in the 'Latter-Day Pamphlets,' by One of the 'Eighteen Millions of Bores'*. Boston: Phillips, Sampson, and Company.

Wright, Tom F. (2013). 'Introduction'. *The Cosmopolitan Lyceum: Lecture Culture and the Globe in Nineteenth-Century America*. Ed. Tom F. Wright. Amherst: University of Massachusetts Press. 1–19.

— (2017). *Lecturing the Atlantic: Speech, Print and an Anglo-American Commons 1830–1870*. New York: Oxford University Press.

— (2020). 'Carlyle, Emerson, and the Voiced Essay'. *On Essays: Montaigne to the Present*. Ed. Thomas Karshan and Kathryn Murphy. Oxford: Oxford University Press. 206–22.

Young, Robert J. C. (2008). *The Idea of English Ethnicity*. Malden, MA: Blackwell.

Zimmerman, Sarah (2019). *The Romantic Literary Lecture in Britain*. Oxford: Oxford University Press.

INDEX

abolitionism
   African American, 25, 64, 177
   British, 212, 223, 228
   Emerson and, 63–4, 140, 145
   see also slavery; Slavery Abolition Act (1833)
Abrams, M. H., 83
Adams, Amanda, 4, 23, 34n
Addison, Joseph, 42, 44, 49
   'Addisonian English', 42, 44
advance sheets (publication), 19, 117–18, 121, 126, 129n, 145
Alcott, Amos Bronson, 144, 168
Alexander, Jeffrey, 24–5, 169, 204, 208
Alighieri, Dante, 88, 115
Alison, Archibald, 178
Altick, Richard D., 34n, 158n
ameliorationism, 52, 54, 56
American Monthly Magazine, 48
Anderson, Benedict, 67n, 235n
Anderson, Charles, 54–5
Anglophilia, 33n, 64, 66n, 184
Anglophobia, 33n, 43
Anglo-Saxon, The (London periodical), 52–4
Anglo-Saxonism
   and abolitionism, 63–4
   Anglo-American, 5, 49–55
   and authorial self-fashioning, 15, 40, 56, 61

Black Anglo-Saxonism, 63–4
   Carlyle and Emerson on, 55–66, 233
   and colonialism, 58, 201–2
   language, 42, 47–8, 51–2, 67n
   liberalism, 63, 89
   literature, 82, 92, 94
   racial, 3, 49–51, 67n, 235n
   transnationalism, 53
   see also race
Appiah, Kwame Anthony, 70, 77, 81, 96–7n
Appleton, Daniel, 118, 119, 122
Arac, Jonathan, 199
Arendt, Hannah, 9
Armitage, David, 32–3n
Arnold, Matthew, 8, 33n, 223, 227, 231, 233
Arnold, Thomas, 57
Arsić, Branka, 97n
Ashton, Rosemary, 96n, 159n
Athenæum, 41, 44
Atlantic Monthly, 222n, 224, 233
Augst, Thomas, 26, 171, 190n
authority
   charismatic, 10, 11, 26, 27, 30, 31, 166, 204
   critical, 5, 18, 20, 105, 115, 128–9n, 164, 175
   cultural, 3, 8–9, 10, 18, 24, 35n, 41, 43, 93, 105, 169, 172, 181

authority (*cont.*)
  'disappearance of authority' (Sennett), 10, 17, 93
  gender and, 14–15, 33–4n
  and legitimacy, 9, 12, 24, 43, 166, 169
  literary, 8, 18, 27, 35n, 93, 111
  metropolitan, 43, 52, 56, 60, 66, 105, 175
  oratorical, 23, 27
  paratextual, 135, 136–43
  performative, 22–7, 30–1, 164, 204–5, 208–14
  political, 10, 125, 174, 200
  and power, 9
  and print, 15–22, 29, 62, 122–3, 127
  prophetic, 7–8, 20, 26–7, 30, 35n, 166, 190n, 205
  religious, 8, 27, 30, 166, 190n, 203
  of/and tradition, 10, 28, 69–99, 215
  transatlantic, 7–13, 18, 29, 30, 33n, 106, 115, 133, 184, 186–7, 192n
  Weber on, 9–10
authorship
  and authority, 11–12, 21–2, 23, 30, 33n, 124, 151, 157, 168, 216
  copyright, 19, 29–30, 120, 150
  female, 14–15, 33–4n

Bacon, Francis, 14, 17, 94
Bancroft, George, 74, 75, 93, 98n, 113
Barnes, James J., 34n, 130n, 160n
Bartol, Cyrus Augustus, 226, 227
Baucom, Ian, 59, 67n
Bell, Duncan, 220n, 233, 235n
Benjamin, Park, 122–3, 130n
Bercovitch, Savan, 97n
Berlin, Isaiah, 71, 96n
Blackwood's Edinburgh Magazine, 47, 67n
Bloom, Harold, 32n, 33n, 97n
Blumenbach, Johann Friedrich, 51
book history, 3, 15–16, 21, 107
book trade, transatlantic, 21, 104, 112, 124
Boswell, James, 8, 231
Bosworth, Thomas, 158n
boundary making, 13–15, 40, 43, 67n; see also inclusion/exclusion; language; literary field
Bourdieu, Pierre
  on boundary making, 13, 43
  capital metaphor, 95, 137
  literary field, 11–12, 13, 33n, 140
Bowen, Francis, 43–4
Brooks, Van Wyck, 98n
Brother Jonathan, 130n

Brown, James, 122
Brown, William Wells, 25, 213
Brownson, Orestes A., 10, 93, 98n
Bryant, William Cullen, 120
Bryce, James, 233, 234
Buell, Lawrence, 33n, 56, 57, 75, 97n, 165, 185, 235n
Bulwer-Lytton, Edward, 129n
Burke, Edmund, 94, 104
Burkholder, Robert E., 189
Burns, Robert, 8, 73–4, 76
Butler, Leslie, 229
Byron, George Gordon, 95, 128n

Cabot, James Elliot, 221n, 229, 231
Campbell, Ian, 68n
Carey and Hart (publishers), 126
Carey and Lea (publishers), 129n
Carlyle, Alexander, 201
Carlyle, Jane Welsh, 2, 134, 199, 221n
Carlyle, John, 197
Carlyle, Thomas
  on abolition, 61, 212, 227–8
  abolitionist responses to, 62–3, 218, 224
  on America, 8, 33n, 223–4, 227–8
  American lecture tour (planned), 26, 30, 196–200
  copyright campaigning, 29, 120–1
  and democracy, 7, 8, 31, 140, 209, 213, 214–18, 223–4, 227, 228
  and editorial fiction, 1, 21, 46–7, 61–2, 107, 110, 213–14, 217
  as Emerson's English editor, 68n, 137–42, 143–4
  in Emerson's *English Traits*, 184–5
  on emigration, 196, 200–3
  on German literature, 34n, 42, 46, 56, 72, 82, 86, 208
  as lecturer, 26–7, 30–1, 34n, 35n, 56, 68n, 88, 129, 204–8, 220n
  lecturing style, 34n, 204–6, 207
  on literary history, 72–4, 86–90
  on London as colonial centre, 9, 59, 201–2
  and public speaking, 30–1, 194–5, 208–20, 221n
  reception, 7–8, 46, 104–5, 224, 228
  as sage figure, 8, 13, 63, 208–9, 224
  Scottish identity, 15, 40, 55–6, 67n, 73, 199–200, 206
  as translator, 2, 46, 77
  WRITINGS
  'Boswell's Life of Johnson', 8, 106

'Burns', 8, 73–4, 76
Chartism, 47, 58, 60, 131n, 201–2
copyright petition (1839), 120–1, 148, 151
Critical and Miscellaneous Essays, 16, 116, 117, 118, 119, 123, 126
'Death of Goethe', 39
The French Revolution: A History, 41–2, 49, 80, 109, 112–17, 118, 119, 127, 128, 129n, 131n, 135, 143, 196, 198, 199, 203
German Romance, 77, 80, 82
'Goethe's Works', 39
On Heroes, Hero-Worship, and the Heroic in History, 2, 25, 34n, 59, 118, 119, 121, 122, 127, 130n, 137, 203
History of German Literature, 48, 56, 72, 78, 84, 86–7
'Ilias (Americana) in Nuce', 224, 225
Latter-Day Pamphlets, 31, 209–12, 215–17, 219, 222n, 223
lectures on 'German Literature' (1837), 34n, 72, 204, 206, 208, 220n
lectures on 'Revolutions of Modern Europe' (1839), 34n, 204, 206–7, 221n
Lectures on the History of Literature, 28, 34n, 56, 59, 73, 86, 88–9, 208, 229
Life of Friedrich Schiller, 77, 78, 82, 88, 128n, 138, 139, 158n
The Life of John Sterling, 211–12
'Memoirs of Mirabeau', 111
'Notice' to Emerson's *Essays* (1844), 150–2, 153–4, 155
'Occasional Discourse on the Negro Question', 7, 31, 60, 61–3, 68n, 212–15, 218, 219, 222n, 223, 226
Oliver Cromwell's Letters and Speeches, 29, 47, 126, 127, 131n
Past and Present, 47, 89–90, 121–5, 126, 131n, 135, 143, 150, 151, 154, 201, 214
'Preface' to Emerson's *Essays* (1841), 134, 135, 136–43, 150, 152, 153, 154, 158n
'The Present Time', 216, 217
Reminiscences, 229
Sartor Resartus, 1, 2, 5, 20, 21, 26, 29, 42, 45, 46–7, 104–5, 107–12, 113, 114, 117, 123, 127, 128, 131n, 133, 134, 137, 138, 140–1, 143, 158n, 165, 196, 226, 230
'Shooting Niagara: And After?', 7, 227–8, 232
'Sir Walter Scott', 8
'State of German Literature', 67n, 78
'Stump-Orator', 209–11, 213, 214, 215, 216, 217, 219, 221n

Casanova, Pascale, 12–13, 24, 84, 93–4, 95, 98n
  'Greenwich meridian of literature', 60, 105
  'national' vs. 'international' writers, 13, 24
Cayton, Mary Kupiec, 171, 190n, 220n
centralisation (of print market), 21–2, 118–19
Chace Act *see* International Copyright Act (1891)
Chambers, Robert, 85, 97n
Channing, William Ellery, 74, 75, 85, 94, 96n, 113, 144
Chapman, John, 30, 68n, 130n, 143–50, 152, 153, 155–7, 158n, 159n, 160n
Chapman and Hall (publishers), 126
character, national, 42, 44, 48, 50–1, 57, 58, 65, 68n, 69, 71–2, 77, 86, 90, 170, 172, 179, 183, 184, 234
charisma
  'charisma of office' (Weber), 204
  'charismatic authority', 10, 26, 27, 30–1, 35n, 166
  routinisation, 166
Charvat, William, 132, 158n
Chasles, Philarète, 55
Chaucer, Geoffrey, 44, 49, 66n, 88, 167, 169
Cheah, Pheng, 70, 83
Christian Examiner, 43, 46, 128–9n, 224
Churchill, Thomas, 71, 72, 74
Civil War (American), 31, 192n, 209, 223–31, 233, 234, 235n
Clark, Lewis Gaylord, 42
Clarke, H. G. (publisher), 136, 147, 157n
Clarke, James Freeman, 46, 47, 104, 105, 111, 113, 224–5, 235n
Clay, Henry, 120, 130n
Claybaugh, Amanda, 3, 13, 18
climate, 1, 54, 181
Cobden, Richard, 178
Coleridge, Samuel Taylor, 3, 22, 31n, 32n, 33n, 95, 98n, 128n, 130n, 211–12, 220–1n, 221n
Collini, Stefan, 83
Collins, Carol, 62, 218
Colyer, William, 124
Commager, Henry Steele, 98n
comparative literature, 3, 4, 32n
Comte, Auguste, 144
Concord, Massachusetts, 63, 64, 129n, 136, 138–9, 141, 151, 155, 171
Confucius, 80
Connor, Walker, 67n

Conway, Moncure Daniel, 231–2
Cooper, James Fenimore, 12, 16, 56, 94, 199
copyright
   Anglo-American, 17, 18–19, 34n, 132–3, 146–50, 156, 230
   international, 120–1, 154, 160n
   see also authorship; piracy; property; reprinting; trade courtesy
Copyright Act (1790), 19
Copyright Amendment Act (1842), 19, 120
cosmopolitanism, 6, 7, 28, 73–4, 77, 81, 97n, 186
   'cosmopolitan patriotism', 76–7, 96–7n
   and nationalism, 23–4, 70, 80, 96n
   see also Appiah, Kwame Anthony; Robbins, Bruce
Cousin, Victor, 28, 70, 72, 91, 93, 96n
   Introduction à l'histoire de la philosophie, 72, 96n
Craigenputtock, 108, 138, 139, 141, 196, 199–200
Cromwell, Oliver, 47, 49, 126
Cruikshank, George, 178
cultural nationalism *see* nationalism

De Quincey, Thomas, 31n
de Staël, Germaine *see* Staël, Germaine de
DeBow's Review, 62–3
democracy
   and literature, 91, 92–3
   and public speech, 207, 214–18
Democratic Review, 47, 48, 75
DeSpain, Jessica, 4, 16, 22, 34n
Dial, 124, 125
Dickens, Charles, 8, 16, 22, 130n, 160n, 173–4, 196, 206, 223
   American Notes for General Circulation, 173, 196, 220n
   copyright campaigning, 120–1, 130n
Dilke, Charles Wentworth, 235n
Dimock, Wai Chee, 6, 33n, 97n, 187
Disraeli, Benjamin, 120
Dolan, Neal, 66, 190n
Douglass, Frederick, 7, 8, 15, 22, 25, 177, 192n, 206, 213
Doyle, Laura, 67n
Duffy, Charles Gavan, 231
Duyckinck, Evert Augustus, 97n

Eckel, Leslie, 186, 192n
Eckermann, Johann Peter, 77, 206
Edgeworth, Maria, 120

Edinburgh Review, 17, 42, 78, 79
Eliot, George, 15, 32n, 144
eloquence, 194, 200, 205, 209, 210–11, 212, 214, 216, 219–20, 221n;
   see also oratory
Emerson, Edward Waldo, 229
Emerson, Ellen, 221n
Emerson, Ralph Waldo
   abolitionism, 63–4, 140, 145, 212
   account books, 129n
   Anglo-Saxonism, 55, 58, 63–4, 66, 145
   British lecture tour (1847–8), 30, 76, 146, 156, 163–4, 174–80, 184, 187, 191n, 232
   as Carlyle's American editor, 29, 43, 109–17, 123–4, 126, 147
   and Civil War, 192n, 223, 225–7
   and copyright, 146–50, 154, 156
   and cosmopolitanism, 6, 7, 76–7, 80, 81, 97n
   and cultural nationalism, 10, 78–7, 58, 91, 97n, 99n, 170–1, 172–3, 182, 185–7, 225
   filiopietism, 166, 172
   on literary history, 14, 91, 93–4, 97n, 168–70
   as lecturer, 6, 23, 30–1, 35n, 163–83, 225–6
   lectures in London, 26, 175–6, 221n
   lectures on English subjects, 91–3, 167–70, 180–3
   lecturing style, 205, 220n
   as minister, 25, 26, 165, 190n
   publishing strategies, 121, 132–3, 145
   on race, 57–8, 60, 63–6, 93, 170, 184–8, 191n
   reception in American South, 44, 47, 66n, 189
   reception in Great Britain, 5, 28, 35n, 40, 132, 143, 152–3, 155–6, 158n, 185, 191n
   as reviewer of Carlyle, 20, 80, 97n, 113, 124–5
   transatlantic audiences, 11, 12, 30, 91, 128, 132, 167, 174, 182, 184, 189, 190n, 231
   on world literature, 80, 97n
   WRITINGS
   'An Address on the Emancipation of the Negroes in the British West Indies', 63–4, 68n, 145, 155, 159n
   'The Age of Fable', 91–3

'American Editor's Notice' to Carlyle's
    Past and Present, 123–4, 125, 150, 151
'The American Scholar', 75, 85, 92,
    133–4, 169
'The Anglo-American', 97n, 180, 182–3
'Carlyle', 221n
The Conduct of Life, 219
'Divinity School Address', 40
'Eloquence' (1846 lecture), 219, 222n
'Eloquence' (1867 lecture), 219–20, 222n
'England', 180–2, 183
'English Literature' (1835–6 lecture series),
    30, 57, 58, 60, 86, 91–3, 94, 97n, 98n,
    167–70, 171, 172, 182, 189n, 190n
English Traits, 9, 12, 28, 30, 64, 65, 66,
    91, 94, 97n, 98–9n, 167, 177, 178, 180,
    184–9, 192n, 196, 225
Essays: First Series, 20, 29, 44, 133–43,
    144, 158n, 171
Essays: Second Series, 20, 133, 144, 146–57,
    159n, 160n, 174, 191n
'Fortune of the Republic', 225–7
'Historic Notes of Life and Letters in New
    England', 86
'History', 98n
'Literary Ethics', 134, 158n
'London', 180, 183
Manchester Athenæum Speech, 178–9,
    181, 183, 184, 187, 189, 192n
'The Method of Nature', 134
'The National Characteristics of the Six
    Northern States of America', 163–4, 179
Nature, 2, 26, 43, 44, 133, 159n, 171
Nature, Addresses, and Lectures, 157,
    174
'New England' (1843–4 lecture series), 30,
    60, 86, 166, 170–3, 179, 182, 190n
'On the Best Mode of Inspiring a Correct
    Taste in English Literature', 17
Poems, 157
'The Poet', 76, 125, 174, 191n, 219
'Preface' to Carlyle's *Sartor Resartus*,
    45–6, 109, 110–11, 112, 123, 128,
    137, 138, 140
prospectus for Carlyle's *Critical and
    Miscellaneous Essays*, 123
prospectus for Carlyle's *The French
    Revolution*, 112–13, 129n
Representative Men, 2, 25, 79, 157
'Representative Men' (lecture series), 157,
    180, 189n, 190n
'Shakspeare', 163–5, 189–90n, 190n

'Stonehenge', 184–8
'The Young American', 21, 80, 97n, 155,
    173–4, 183, 186
Emerson, William, 114
empire, 90, 202, 233
    British Empire, 33n, 52, 59–60, 69, 125,
        183, 235n
    imperialism, 33, 59, 66, 89
    and nation, 67n
Englishness, 45, 49, 55–6, 59, 61, 69, 184,
    208, 235n
Everett, Alexander Hill, 5, 9, 94, 95, 108–9,
    111–12
Everton, Michael, 130n
Examiner (London), 155, 192n
Exeter Hall, 176, 177, 212–13, 221n
expansionism, 58–9, 69, 75, 125, 173, 190–1n,
    201; *see also* 'Manifest Destiny'

Fender, Stephen, 201
Feuerbach, Ludwig, 144
Follen, Charles, 128n
Foreign Quarterly Review, 79, 174
Forster, John, 148, 174
Forster, Michael, 81
Fox, Caroline, 134
Fraser, James, 29, 108, 115, 116, 134–5, 136,
    137, 142, 143, 144, 155, 158n
Fraser's Magazine, 61, 62, 63, 108, 111, 226,
    227
Frothingham, Nathaniel Langdon, 46, 47,
    128n
Froude, James Anthony, 144, 229, 231,
    233, 235n
Fuller, Hiram, 113
Fuller, Margaret, 15, 153, 177
Furedi, Frank, 10, 11
Furness, William Henry, 113

Gall, Franz Joseph, 51
Gellner, Ernest, 67n
Genette, Gérard, 32n
German
    Carlyle as 'hyper-Germanized', 2, 5, 15,
        40, 43, 45
    contrasted with English, 42, 44, 48
    see also language; literature
Gibbon, Edward, 14
Giles, Paul, 3, 84–5, 92, 186, 191n
Gilfillan, George, 29, 137, 158n, 175–6,
    177
Globe (London), 79, 205

265

Goethe, Johann Wolfgang, 2, 39, 74, 81, 82, 89, 92
   Carlyle on, 39, 78, 89
   Elective Affinities, 39
   Emerson on, 79–80, 92
   'Introduction' to Carlyle's *Life of Schiller*, 82, 88, 139, 158n
   The Sorrows of Young Werther, 39
   Wilhelm Meister, 77
   'world literature', 24, 70, 77–9, 81, 97n
Gohdes, Clarence, 160n
Gougeon, Len, 97n
'Greater Britain', 233, 235n
Greeley, Horace, 207
Green, John, 144
Greenham, David, 32n
Griswold, Rufus Wilmot, 130n, 173–4
Guernsey, Alfred H., 231

Habich, Robert D., 232
Hanlon, Christopher, 3, 6, 33n, 68n, 192n
Harper and Brothers (publishers), 119, 122, 128, 129n, 131n
Harper's Magazine, 189
Harris, Kenneth Marc, 4, 32n, 235n
Harrold, Charles Frederick, 96n
Harvard University, 40, 43, 103, 108, 128n, 233
Harvey, Samantha, 32n
Hawthorne, Nathaniel, 12, 130n
Hazlitt, William, 22, 130n
Hedge, Frederic Henry, 108, 113, 230
Herder, Johann Gottfried, 28, 69, 70, 81, 88, 91, 92
   cosmopolitanism, 81
   and cultural nationhood, 44–5, 71–4, 85
   'Herderian Revolution' (Casanova), 44
   Ideen zur Philosophie der Geschichte der Menschheit, 71, 74
   reception beyond Germany, 71–2, 74–5, 96n
Higginson, Thomas Wentworth, 27, 229
history, 9, 28, 51, 86–7, 94, 98n, 165, 234; *see also* literary history
Hobsbawm, Eric, 41, 50, 67n
Holmes, Oliver Wendell, 231
Horsman, Reginald, 49–50, 51, 57, 61, 67n
Howe, Daniel Walker, 66n, 96n
Hunt, Leigh, 221n
Huxley, Thomas Henry, 144

idealism, 3, 32n, 46, 48, 57, 65
imperialism *see* empire

inclusion/exclusion, 15, 41, 43, 45, 48, 202
influence, 2–3, 5, 31n, 32n, 96
International Copyright Act (1838), 19
International Copyright Act (1844), 120, 147–50
International Copyright Act (1891), 19
intertextuality, 32n, 137
Ireland, Alexander, 231, 232
Irving, Washington, 16, 56, 120

Jackson, Leon, 20
James, Henry, 33n, 230, 231
Jean Paul *see* Richter, Jean Paul Friedrich
Jefferson, Thomas, 51, 215
Jeffrey, Francis, 104
Johnson, Samuel, 8, 46, 106–7, 231

Kant, Immanuel, 3, 48, 168
Kemble, John Mitchell, 51
Kinser, Brent, 223
Klipstein, Louis, 53–4, 55
Knox, John, 14
Knox, Robert, 53–4, 55
Koch, Daniel, 64, 147, 156, 157–8n, 191n
Kristeva, Julia, 32n

Lamb, Charles, 130n
language
   and Anglo-Saxonism, 51–2, 54, 57, 67n, 187, 234
   and boundary making, 15, 40–1, 86, 176
   'linguistic nationalism', 41–2
   and national identity, 41–4, 47–8, 66n, 71, 73, 74, 85, 92, 164
   and performance, 210, 221n
Lavater, Johann Kaspar, 51
Lease, Benjamin, 32n
lecturing, 22–7
   African American, 25, 64
   American lyceum, 22, 23, 24, 34n, 165–6, 168, 207
   British, 22, 34n
   and nationhood, 23–4
   and print, 13, 15–16, 22–3, 25, 27, 35n, 166, 174, 187, 203, 220n
Levine, Caroline, 6
Leypoldt, Günter, 12, 33n
Linnaeus, Carl, 51
literary field, 15, 21, 40, 143, 210
   Bourdieu on, 11–12, 13
   national vs. international, 12, 13, 33n, 81, 173–4

transatlantic, 13, 18, 40–1, 43–5, 94, 141, 154, 196, 204, 226
  see also boundary making; Bourdieu, Pierre; inclusion/exclusion; provinciality
Literary Gazette, 142, 143
literary history, 28, 70, 83
  American, 84, 86, 93
  and authority of the past, 94
  English, 70, 85, 93, 94–5
  as genre, 83, 95
  late-nineteenth-century, 233–4
literature
  American, 12, 17–18, 75, 85, 92–4, 169
  development of modern concept of, 13–14, 33n
  English, 12, 17, 28, 83–5, 88–95, 98n, 99n, 167–74
  German, 46–7, 77, 82, 86, 88, 204, 206
  see also literary history; nationalism
Littell's Living Age, 63
Little and Brown (publishers), 113, 115–16, 119, 122, 129n, 150
Locke, John, 94
Lockhart, John Gibson, 71
London
  Carlyle and, 55–6
  as publishing centre, 5, 13, 18, 119, 136, 139
London and Westminster Review see Westminster Review
Longfellow, Henry Wadsworth, 51–2, 113, 133, 226
Lorimer, Douglas, 61
Lowell, James Russell, 95, 229
lyceum *see* lecturing

Macaulay, Thomas Babington, 104, 148
McGettigan, Katie, 16, 21, 136
McGill, Meredith L., 4, 16, 17, 22, 111, 119
McInturff, Kate, 81
Mackintosh, James, 14
Macmillan's Magazine, 27, 224, 227
Macready, William Charles, 164
Manchester Athenæum, 178, 183
Manchester Examiner, 232
'Manifest Destiny', 69, 75, 190–1n; *see also* expansionism; nationalism
Manning, Susan, 3, 32n, 72
Marshall, P. David, 209
Marshall, Peter J., 33n
Martineau, Harriet, 15, 104–5, 109, 120, 133, 134, 195–6

Martineau, James, 145
Masonic Temple (Boston), 167, 168, 169
Massachusetts Quarterly Review, 76
Melville, Herman, 130n
Mexican–American War, 76, 179, 191n
Mill, John Stuart, 8, 62–3, 133, 223
Miller, Perry, 33n, 97n
Milnes, Richard Monckton, 1–2, 4, 5, 7, 32n, 129n, 133, 134, 143, 177
Milton, John, 17, 44, 49, 58, 89, 94, 95, 149
Montaigne, Michel de, 80
Monthly Review, 142
Morley, John, 229
Mott, Wesley T., 97n, 190n
Mudie, Charles Edward, 147
Munroe, James, 109, 118, 126, 133, 135, 145, 155, 156, 158n
Munroe and Company (publishers), 113, 119
Murray, Hannah-Rose, 25, 64, 192n
Myerson, Joel, 133, 155, 158n, 192n

nation
  as analytical category, 32–3n, 186
  definitions, 50, 67n, 83
  literary nationality, 40, 41–3, 45, 47, 84
  'modernist' and 'primordialist' explanations of genesis of, 50, 67n
  and race, 24, 45, 49–50, 56, 70, 93, 184, 188
national character *see* character, national
national identity, 15, 28, 42–3, 45, 59, 165, 176, 204, 234; *see also* language; nationalism
nationalism, 50, 66n, 70
  and cosmopolitanism, 23, 28, 96n
  cultural, 28, 45, 70–7, 80, 81, 95
  ethnic, 24, 40, 60, 67n
  'philological', 41
  see also cosmopolitanism; nation
national literature, 72–3, 81, 83, 86–8
Newcastle, 163–4, 179
Newfield, Christopher, 57
'New School' label, 2, 39, 41, 43, 48–9
New World, 122, 130n
Nickisson, George William, 135, 158n
Nicoloff, Philip L., 57, 99n, 179
North American Review, 43, 52, 54, 74, 105, 108, 128–9n
Norton, Andrews, 2, 4, 5, 7, 20, 39–40, 41–2, 43, 46, 48, 66n, 144, 235n
Norton, Charles Eliot, 103, 229, 230, 232, 233, 235n
Novalis (Friedrich von Hardenberg), 48

267

O'Neill, Bonnie Carr, 35n, 220n
oratory
   and print, 27, 88, 203, 221n
   religious and secular, 24, 35n, 166
   see also eloquence; lecturing
organicism, 32n, 51, 71, 83, 89, 95, 99n
O'Sullivan, John L., 75
Owenson, Sydney (Lady Morgan), 41–2, 44

Packer, Barbara L., 32n, 129n
Painter, Nell Irvin, 57, 66
Parker, Theodore, 132, 144, 146–7
Paryz, Marek, 192n
patriotism, 54
   Carlyle on, 73–4, 75–6, 216
   'cosmopolitan patriotism' (Appiah), 77, 81
   Emerson on, 76, 178
   see also nationalism
Persak, Christine, 221n
Petheram, John, 51
philanthropy, 63, 140, 212–13, 228
Phillips, George Searle, 220n
phrenology, 51
piracy, 116, 119, 120
   publishers described as pirates, 127, 146, 149, 150–1, 153
   rhetoric of, 122–3
   as stealing, 130, 151, 154
   see also copyright; reprinting
Pizer, John, 81
Plutarch, 80
Poe, Edgar Allan, 2
Poovey, Mary, 14
postcolonial
   American writers as, 33n, 167–8, 192n, 200
   postcolonial studies, 5
print
   and orality, 15–16, 22–3, 25, 27, 35n, 166, 174, 187, 203
   print culture, 4, 18, 25, 106, 136, 199, 230
   transatlantic print market, 3, 8, 16, 18, 103, 115, 123, 141, 157, 230
   see also reprinting
profession
   authorship as, 106–7, 132, 199–200, 210, 221n, 226
   lecturing as, 4, 25, 30, 31, 35n, 165, 194–5, 211
   professionalisation, 112, 171

property
   intellectual property, 19–20, 120–1, 151
   as opposed to 'propriety', 123–4, 125, 130n
   see also copyright; piracy
provinciality, 13, 55–6, 105, 138–9, 141; *see also* Rezek, Joseph
Putnam, George Palmer, 18, 34n, 104, 105, 111, 126, 127, 130n; *see also* Wiley and Putnam (publishers)

Quarterly Review, 42, 227

race, 28, 40–1, 45, 49–66, 233–4
   Carlyle on, 28, 49, 55–7, 58–9, 60–3, 68n, 89, 208
   Emerson on, 57–8, 60, 63–6, 93, 170, 184–8, 191n
   and nationalism, 50–1, 70
   racism, 57, 61, 63
   'scientific' racialism, 51
   white supremacism, 15, 48, 53, 57, 60–1, 213
   see also Anglo-Saxonism; inclusion/exclusion; nation; nationalism
Ray, Angela, 23–4, 34n
relativism
   cultural relativism, 70, 71, 75, 91
   and world literature, 81
reprinting, 16–19, 121, 151
   and authorship, 21–2, 107
   scholarship on, 16, 33–4n
   and transatlantic authority, 29
   see also copyright; piracy
revolution
   American Revolution, 9, 10, 33n, 74, 84, 94, 98n, 169
   Carlyle on, 34n, 109, 206–7, 221n
   European revolutions of 1848, 64, 175, 191n, 209, 213, 216
   French Revolution, 49, 109
   market revolution, 139
Rezek, Joseph, 4, 13, 16, 33n, 34n, 55, 56, 105
Richardson, Robert D., 98n, 169
Richter, Jean Paul Friedrich, 89
Riede, David G., 8, 33n, 35n
Rio, Alexis-François, 134
Ripley, George, 128–9n, 198, 200
Robbins, Bruce, 81
Robbins, Royal, 85
Robinson, David, 184, 185, 190n, 191n
Robinson, Henry Crabb, 3, 221n, 222n
Rodman, Benjamin, 129n

INDEX

Romanticism, 31n, 32n, 48, 69, 70–1, 86
   American, 6
   British, 3, 33n, 128n, 130n
   German, 3, 46
   and nation, 70–1, 76, 83, 86
   see also idealism; Victorian
Roper, Moses, 25
Rosenberg, Philip, 209
Ruskin, John, 223
Russell, LeBaron, 108

sage writing, 8, 11, 13, 63, 208–9, 224
Said, Edward, 61–2
St Clair, William, 34n
Salmon, Richard, 35n, 107, 194
Saunders and Otley (publishers), 120
Saxonism *see* Anglo-Saxonism
Schelling, Friedrich Wilhelm Joseph, 3, 31n
Schiller, Friedrich, 89, 139, 158n
Schlegel, Friedrich, 28, 70, 71–2, 73, 74, 75, 88
   Geschichte der alten und neuen Literatur, 71, 73, 75, 88, 96n
Scott, Donald, 24, 34n, 171, 206
Scott, Walter, 8, 16, 69, 95, 129n
Scudder, Townsend, 191n
Sennett, Richard, 10, 11, 17, 93
Sewell, William Henry, 42, 44, 66n
Shakespeare, William, 14, 17, 44, 58, 71, 88, 94, 95, 163–4, 169, 189n, 190n, 208
Shepherd, Richard Herne, 231
Shils, Edward, 35n
Simmons, Nancy Craig, 171, 172, 190n
Slater, George, 160n
Slater, Joseph, 107, 159n, 192n, 235n
slavery, 62, 64, 213, 222n, 223–4
   American, 62, 63–4
   in British West Indies, 61–2, 218, 228
   see also abolitionism
Slavery Abolition Act (1833), 64
Small, Helen, 7, 61, 68n, 222n
Smith, Anthony, 45, 67n
Smith, Sydney, 17, 18, 34n
Smith, William, 135–6, 157n
Smollett, Tobias, 217
Southern Literary Messenger, 42
Southern Quarterly Review, 44, 47, 48, 49, 218
Southey, Robert, 120, 134
Sowder, William, 191n, 235n
Spectator, 155, 208
Spencer, Herbert, 144

Spenser, Edmund, 42, 44, 47, 49, 66n
Spoo, Robert, 34n, 124
Staël, Germaine de, 28, 70, 72, 73, 75, 88, 96n
   De la littérature considérée dans ses rapports avec les institutions sociales, 72, 73, 75, 96n
   De l'Allemagne, 72
Stephen, Leslie, 229
Sterling, John, 46, 104, 133, 134, 158n, 197, 211–12, 219
Sterne, Laurence, 14, 217
Stewart, Dugald, 14, 104
Stievermann, Jan, 32n, 97n
Stowe, Harriet Beecher, 22, 34n, 226
Strauß, David Friedrich, 144

Talfourd, Thomas Noon, 147, 148, 150
Tamarkin, Elisa, 3, 7, 9, 33n, 43, 59, 64
Tarr, Rodger L., 158
Taylor, Andrew, 3, 186, 188
Taylor, Bayard, 180
Taylor, Jonathan, 221n
Taylor, William, 87
   Historic Survey of German Poetry, 87
Teichgraeber, Richard F., 128n, 158n
Tennyson, Alfred, 223, 227
Teutonism, 48, 56–7, 58, 67n, 82, 89
Texas annexation, 173, 179, 190–1n
Thackeray, William Makepeace, 42, 130n
Thompson, Frank T., 32n
Thoreau, Henry David, 45, 48–9
Thorpe, Benjamin, 51, 53
Ticknor, George, 168–9
Times (London), 42, 68n, 178, 192n, 208, 220n
Tocqueville, Alexis de, 92, 195
trade courtesy, 19–20, 34n, 118, 122–4, 126, 127, 230; *see also* copyright
Traill, Henry Duff, 229
transatlantic studies, 3–4, 5–6, 27–8, 32n, 50–1
Transcendentalism, 3, 8, 32n, 39, 45, 46, 48–9, 74, 128–9n, 144, 168
translatio imperii et studii trope, 53, 60, 67n, 202
transnational
   Anglo-American transnationalism, 53, 39–40, 82
   contact and exchange, 2, 6, 69
   economic circulation, 79–80, 202
   print, 111, 151
   transnationalism paradigm, 5, 33
   see also cosmopolitanism; nation; nationalism

Trollope, Anthony, 206
Turner, Sharon, 51, 68n, 167
   History of the Anglo-Saxons, 51, 68n, 167

Über Kunst und Altertum, 77, 79, 80
Unitarianism, 2, 28, 42, 66n, 96n, 128–9n, 145, 153, 190n
universalism, 57, 73, 76, 82
Useful Knowledge
   concept, 168
   movement, 85
   Society for the Diffusion of, 168, 190n

Vanden Bossche, Chris R., 8, 33n, 210, 222n
Vanderbilt, Kermit, 96n
Victorian
   female authorship, 33–4n
   fiction, 130n, 158n
   late-Victorian reception of Emerson and Carlyle, 228–9, 231, 233–4
   literature, 5, 11, 13, 14, 18, 144
   race discourse, 61, 63
   reception of American writers, 18, 25, 157
   see also Romanticism
Voelz, Johannes, 33n, 58, 68n, 97n, 99n, 191n

Wakefield, Edward Gibbon, 201, 202, 220n
Walker, James, 43
Walkowitz, Rebecca L., 72–3
Walls, Laura Dassow, 57, 64
War of 1812, 9, 169
Warton, Thomas, 167
Wasson, David A., 224, 225
Weber, Max
   'charisma of office', 204
   on traditional authority, 28, 84
   on types of authority, 9–10, 11, 28

Weisbuch, Robert, 6, 32n, 33n, 67n, 94–5, 98n, 192n
Wellek, René, 32n, 71, 86, 88, 96n
Wendell, Barrett, 233–4
West, Cornel, 57
Western Messenger, 46, 104, 105
Westminster Review, 1, 5, 143, 144, 189, 192n
Whitefield, George, 14
Whitman, Walt, 8, 12, 33n, 93, 94, 98n, 228
Whittier, John Greenleaf, 62, 63, 226
Wicksteed, Charles, 153
Wilde, Oscar, 22
Wiley and Putnam (publishers), 126–8, 130n, 131n; *see also* Putnam, George Palmer
Williams, Raymond, 13–14
Willis's Rooms (London), 206, 220–1n
Willmott, Robert Aris, 97n
Wimmer, Andreas, 15, 96n
Winship, Michael, 17, 34n
Winthrop, John, 85
Wordsworth, William, 33n, 92, 94, 95, 98n, 120, 128n
Workman, Gillian, 68n
'world literature', 5, 24, 70, 77–82, 97n, 138–9
Wright, Elizur, 62, 218
Wright, Henry G., 144, 159n
Wright, Tom F., 4, 23–4, 25, 34n, 35n, 180, 192n

Young, Robert, 50, 52, 59, 67n
Young America, 28, 42, 43, 75, 97n, 173

Zimmerman, Sarah, 34n

EU representative:
Easy Access System Europe
Mustamäe tee 50, 10621 Tallinn, Estonia
Gpsr.requests@easproject.com